Civil Society Revisited

Studies on Civil Society

Editors: **Dieter Gosewinkel,** *Wissenschaftszentrum Berlin,*
and **Holger Nehring,** *University of Stirling*

Civil Society stands for one of the most ambitious projects and influential concepts relating to the study of modern societies. Scholars working in this field aim to secure greater equality of opportunity, democratic participation, individual freedom, and societal self-organization in the face of social deficits caused by globalizing neo-liberalism. This series deals with the multiple languages, different layers, and diverse practices of existing and emerging civil societies in Europe and elsewhere and asks how far the renewed interest in the concept can contribute to the gradual evolution of civil society in the wider world.

CIVIL SOCIETY REVISITED
LESSONS FROM POLAND

Edited by
Kerstin Jacobsson and Elżbieta Korolczuk

berghahn
NEW YORK · OXFORD
www.berghahnbooks.com

Published in 2017 by

Berghahn Books

www.berghahnbooks.com

© 2017 Kerstin Jacobsson and Elżbieta Korolczuk

Library of Congress Cataloging-in-Publication Data

Names: Jacobsson, Kerstin, editor. | Korolczuk, Elzbieta, editor.
Title: Civil society revisted : lessons from Poland / edited by Kerstin
Jacobsson and Elzbieta Korolczuk.
Description: New York : Berghahn Books, 2017. | Series: Studies on civil
society | Includes bibliographical references and index.
Identifiers: LCCN 2017010900 (print) | LCCN 2017015773 (ebook) | ISBN
9781785335525 (eBook) | ISBN 9781785335518 (hardback : alk. paper)
Subjects: LCSH: Civil society–Poland. | Poland–Politics and government.
Classification: LCC JN6766 (ebook) | LCC JN6766 .C5 2017 (print) | DDC
300.9438–dc23
LC record available at https://lccn.loc.gov/2017010900

British Library Cataloguing in Publication Data

A catalogue record for this book is available from the British Library

ISBN: 978-1-78533-551-8 hardback
ISBN: 978-1-78533-552-5 ebook

CONTENTS

LIST OF FIGURES AND TABLES

Figures

Tables

PREFACE

This volume is part of a larger research endeavor in which we have been engaged for the past seven years, trying to provide new perspectives on social movements and civic activism in Central and Eastern Europe.[1] All the grassroots initiatives that take place on the ground in this part of Europe—as reflected in social media as well as in the national press and research publications, although much less so in the international research literature—urged us to challenge the frequent narratives of the "weak civil society" in the region, questioning the empirical basis as well as the theoretical lenses behind such a characterization of the postsocialist civil societies.

In no other case is the need to rethink the nature of civil society more evident than in Poland. This volume was prepared before the 2015 election and the subsequent counter-mobilizations, but these recent developments serve to confirm the validity of our assessment of Polish civil society: the outbreak of political activism after the right-wing Law and Justice (PiS) government that came into power in October 2015 shows that contrary to prevailing opinion, civil society in Poland is neither weak nor underdeveloped, but rather there is a great potential for political engagement that erupts in times of political crisis. To give just a brief account of some of these developments: by November, when the ruling party began taking steps to centralize power, to weaken the institutions of liberal democracy such as the Constitutional Tribunal, to repoliticize the civil service, and to establish party control of public media, many Poles started to oppose the changes. The most visible and active oppositional movement is KOD (Committee for the Defense of Democracy), which started as a Facebook group in November 2015 and developed into an association with local chapters in many Polish cities, capable of organizing mass demonstrations, gathering tens of thousands of Poles in protest of the new government's efforts to erode democracy. On 7 May 2016, KOD organized a march that gathered up to 240,000 participants expressing their support for the European Union and the democratic rule of law. In addition to organizing street protests, KOD undertook other activities as well, such as publishing open letters to authorities, organizing public debates, and preparing a civic law proposal regarding the Constitutional Tribunal, which quickly gathered the required 100,000 citizen signatures.

However, the Committee for the Defense of Democracy is not the only case of a new wave of grassroots mobilizations of citizens protesting against the recent changes in the country. In the spring of 2016, for instance, the anti-choice network "STOP abortion" started to gather signatures supporting a citizens' law proposal, which included a total ban on abortion and the threat of criminal prosecution (entailing up to five years in prison) for both women undergoing the termination of pregnancy and their doctors. Polish law already strictly limits access to abortion, which is illegal unless one of the three exceptions applies: if the pregnancy is the result of criminally proven rape or incest, if the woman's life is in danger, or if the fetus is "seriously malformed," and the women's movement in Poland has been vocal on this issue over the last two decades. However, the new wave of mobilization against restricting Polish abortion law further is much larger and involves different groups and networks, including an informal grassroots network of over 100,000 women and men who joined the Facebook group Dziewuchy dziewuchom (Gals for Gals), the new left party Razem (Together), and a feminist pro-choice coalition Ratujmy Kobiety! (Save the Women!), which gathered over 200,000 signatures in support of civic law proposal liberalizing abortion law in spring and early summer 2016. These and other groups organized mass rallies in Warsaw and eighteen other cities on 3 and 9 April, gathering up to eight thousand participants in Warsaw only. Opposition to the proposal for stricter law thus led to mobilization of an unprecedented scale: on the 3 October, dubbed as "Black Monday" because protesters dressed in black to mourn the loss of reproductive rights, hundreds of thousands of Polish women went on strike and took to the streets in over 120 cities and villages. According to a recent poll by the Centre for Public Opinion Research (CBOS) 88 percent of Poles were aware of the Black Protests, while 17 percent of women dressed in black to show solidarity and 4 percent took part in the protests. In the face of this mass mobilization of Polish women, the ruling Law and Justice made a U-turn and on the 6 October its MPs voted against a proposal, which they had supported earlier. The Black Protests thus turned out to be a huge success: Polish women not only managed to stop the plans for implementing further restrictions of reproductive rights, but for the first time since the new government came to power in 2015 the street protests actually worked and brought an immediate political effect. To what extent this effect will be lasting is yet to be seen, but the Black Protests showed that the potential for mass mobilization in Polish society is significant, and it is not restricted to the older generation supporting KOD or to big cities, where most protests took place so far. While the most spectacular and numerous demonstrations during autumn 2015 and in 2016 were organized by the opponents of the new regime, its proponents were also active, both online and offline. Thus, a wide range of social groups have become mobilized, including members of the urban middle class supporting KOD and the young generation that took part in anti-abortion protests, but also conservative networks, including anti-choice activists and extreme right groups, such as the nationalist, racist, and anti-Semitic National-Radical Camp (ONR). It is clear that Polish society has become highly polarized, but also much more engaged and politically active, and the long-term effects of this trend are yet to be seen.

The anti-government protests also displayed a highly creative repertoire of contention. For instance, the protests against the law proposal banning abortions included producing and sharing content via social media (with hashtags such as #czarnyprotest which became the most popular hashtag in Polish social media in 2016, generating over 44 million interactions), wearing black and/or posting photos in black on Facebook and Instagram, sending letters to Prime Minister with details of women's menstrual cycles and packages with coat hangers, which became symbol of unsafe, back-alley abortions. Nevertheless, in addition to such eventful politics as the mass protests, our volume stresses the importance of local, low-key forms of grassroots activism, which too provides the fabric of civil society and often serve as an important background context for more ephemeral outbreaks of mass protest.

Our collective thinking about Polish civil society has benefited from several different conferences, workshops, and discussions with our team members. We wish to thank our research team, Jolanta Aidukaitė, Christian Fröhlich, Renata Hryciuk, Dominika V. Polanska, and Steven Saxonberg for their contributions to our collective research work as well as for the fun we have had together along the way. We are grateful to the participants of a conference we organized on Polish civil society at University of Warsaw for generously sharing their ideas and views, and to Sławomir Mandes for co-organizing this event with us. We also wish to thank Gabriella Elgenius, Margit Mayer, and Chris Pickvance, who joined us at a workshop in Gdynia, offering their comments and encouraging a dialogue across different disciplines and theoretical interpretations. Most importantly, our work has been enabled by a generous research grant from the Swedish Research Council on "Institutional Constraints and Creative Solutions: Civil Society in Poland in a Comparative Perspective" (Grant 421/2010/1706). In addition, the Swedish Research Council's framework program for research on civil society has provided a most fertile collegial environment for our thinking about civil society, and we wish to thank all colleagues who attended these workshops and offered comments on our work.

Gothenburg and Warsaw, December 2016
Kerstin Jacobsson and Elżbieta Korolczuk

Notes

1. Earlier publications include the edited books *Urban Grassroots Movements in Central and Eastern Europe* (edited by K. Jacobsson, Ashgate 2015), *Social Movements in Post-communist Europe and Russia* (edited by K. Jacobsson and S. Saxonberg, Routledge 2015, based on a special issue of *East European Politics*), *Beyond NGO-ization: The Development of Social Movements in Central and Eastern Europe* (edited by K. Jacobsson and S. Saxonberg, Ashgate 2013), and *Niebezpieczne związki. Macierzyństwo, ojcostwo i polityka* [Dangerous Liaisons: Motherhood, Fatherhood, and Politics] (edited by R.E. Hryciuk and E. Korolczuk, WUW 2015).

Introduction
Rethinking Polish Civil Society

Kerstin Jacobsson and Elżbieta Korolczuk

This volume provides new perspectives on civil society and social activism in contemporary Poland. It offers a much-needed update of the state of social activism in the country and suggests new ways of conceptualizing civil society that are relevant beyond the postsocialist context.

We argue that a reassessment of the postsocialist civil societies in general, and of Polish civil society in particular, is called for on both empirical and theoretical grounds. For the purpose of such rethinking, this volume critically addresses the way in which postsocialist civil society has been conceptualized, with special focus on Poland. Second, it discusses the limitations of the common indicators used to assess the strength and character of the civil societies in the region. It is argued that there are forms of collective action that have tended to escape observers' lenses for theoretical, methodological, normative, and ideological reasons. Consequently, the volume calls attention to the exclusionary practices entailed in the "making up" of civil society in the region, revealing how the concept of civil society, as commonly applied in political discourse as well as empirical research, excludes many forms of social activism.

As argued by Kubik (2005), there are two dominant strategies for applying the concept of civil society. Some scholars propose a fixed definition of this phenomenon and then look for the social arrangements that can be subsumed under the concept, while others attempt to reconstruct its content and scrutinize "the ever-changing and often tension-ridden interaction between the concept and the realities within which it emerged (the modern West) and to which it is sometimes employed (non-Western contexts)" (Kubik 2005: 1; see also Hann and Dunn 1996). While much of the existing scholarship on Polish civil society follows the former strategy, in this volume we position ourselves firmly in the latter tradition, as we are interested not only in the actual practices by which civil societies are "made" from above, but also in the political and ideological consequences of the usage and promulgation of specific notions of civil society. On the basis of up-to-date empirical studies of a range of mobilizations and cases of collective action that exist in contemporary Poland, we scrutinize how certain forms of activism and types of claims are legitimized in public discourses as representing "genuine" civil society, while others are delegitimized. In doing so, the volume critically approaches the ways in which civil society is "made from above" by the elites, by the media, by public institutions, and in academia, thus complementing and contrasting this vision with the views "from below."

Based on the case studies included in the volume, we propose a conceptualization of civil society that is less normative and more process- and practice-oriented and that includes a variety of activities ranging from low-key local informal initiatives to organized forms of action and mass social movements. These collective activities take place in what Alexander termed a "solidaristic sphere" (2006: 31), a sphere where people associate and cooperate to advance common interests and concerns; however, we argue that this sphere is not clearly separated from, but rather interconnected with, the family, state, and market.

The remaining part of this introductory chapter is structured as follows: first, we introduce in more detail our conceptualization of civil society. Next, we position our volume in relation to the wider debate on postsocialist civil societies, developing the theoretical and methodological reasons that underlie our reassessment of these societies. Then we present an overview of existing research on Polish civil society. We start by looking at existing scholarship on civil society engagement, then we point to forms of social activism that have been missed or are only recently gaining attention, explaining how specific conceptual frameworks and methodologies narrowed the view on local civil society. Finally, we provide an introduction to the individual chapters and the various ways in which they contribute to a problematization and/or rethinking of Polish civil society.[1]

Conceptualizing Civil Society

Approaching civil society as an object of study with fluid boundaries rather than as a fixed point of departure allows us to critically assess the consequences of the use of specific empirical indicators or specific definitions of civil society. Thus, we propose rethinking and challenging a number of dichotomies that form the definitions of civil society dominant in the existing literature on postsocialist civil society, including in Poland. These dichotomies concern:

- the ideological and normative level, which means that there is a strong focus on the post-1989 "civil society" as an ethical project that entails promoting tolerance, equality, and inclusion by well-established democratic means, while organizations inherited from socialist times and different forms of rebellious, radical, "uncivil," or illiberal activism tend to be marginalized or excluded;
- organizational forms, which means that most research focuses on civil society organizations (CSOs), whereas less attention has been paid to informal or semiorganized types of civic engagement;
- the functional dimension, as there is an assumption that civil society organizations and groups can act either as apolitical service providers and self-help groups *or* as claim makers, lobbyists, and protesters, but that they rarely combine these functions.

Later, we discuss how such dichotomous perspectives (new-old, civil-uncivil, formal-informal, noncontentious-contentious, apolitical-political) function in practice, preventing us from seeing the richness and diversity of the civil society that actually exists in Poland. The theoretical effort that follows is to move toward a practice-based and locally embedded understanding of what we could call "vernacular" civil societies (cf. Kennedy 2013). One of the consequences of such an approach is to focus on practices rather than predispositions and norms. Whereas civil society is a much broader term than social activism, as it encompasses individual behaviors (e.g., signing petitions) and attitudes (e.g., level of trust or pro-democratic orientation), this volume focuses mostly on social activism, which is based on recognizing oneself as part of the social fabric, oriented toward influencing the way society works, and which includes different types of engagement. Consequently, we include all forms of intentional action undertaken collectively, including low-key, local activism oriented toward practical goals as well as promoting or opposing social change. This endeavor is in line with recent efforts by Polish scholars and activists who stress the importance of local grassroots initiatives and informal activism in local urban and rural communities, and critically approach highly normative and narrow understandings of civil society (e.g., Bilewicz and Potkańska 2013; Bukowiecki et al. 2014; Erbel 2014; Herbst and Żakowska 2013; Jawłowska and Kubik 2007; Mocek 2014; Piotrowski 2009). In focusing on social activism thus conceived, we also call into question established analytical divisions between civil society research on the one hand and social movement studies on the other. Indeed, our practice-based conception of civil society is a way to bridge the two research traditions, including in terms of the methodology used. While civil society scholars rarely use conceptual and methodological tools evolving from social movement studies, we intend to overcome this division with the goal of cross-fertilization of these two types of analysis. Thus, we include studies that employ approaches and methodologies typical of social movement analyses (e.g., frame analysis, protest event analysis, qualitative case studies) along with analyses that use quantitative political participation data or analyze secondary sources to discern the extent and relative strength of existing organizations or the financial condition of nongovernmental actors. Such an approach enables us to give analytical coherence to the growing body of literature showing that there is a significant potential for robust social activism in Poland (e.g., Chimiak 2014; Ekiert and Kubik 2014; Herbst and Żakowska 2013; Krześ 2014; Mocek 2014), but representing different kinds of civic engagement than the formal organizations and volunteering that have been the dominant focus in Polish civil society research.

Moreover, we see civil societies as relational and processual phenomena, suggesting that it is fruitful to think of civil society not exclusively in terms of organizational structures but also as processes of overcoming constraints to collective action. This process-oriented approach is useful to conceptualize and analyze the relationships and fluid boundaries between the civil sphere, the family, the state, and the market. We thus conceive of these spheres not as clearly separated from each other but rather as interconnected, with the way they relate to each other changing over time. Even if it is analytically possible to distinguish between the domestic sphere (family and kinship relationships), the market sphere, the civil sphere, and political society (political parties), in reality these spheres are interpenetrated, interdependent, and in constant flux, as argued not least by feminist scholars (Hagemann et al. 2008; Okin 1998; Mulinari 2015; Scott and Keates 2004; see also Alexander 2006 and Ginsborg 2013). For instance, private resources can be used in civil society activity, identities embedded in the domestic sphere can be politicized and drawn on in collective action formation, civil society organizations can be formed by groups of friends or family members, and so on. Especially in a postsocialist context, it has been found that organizations and mobilizations tend to be based on extended private networks (Chimiak 2006; Howard 2003; Fábián and Korolczuk 2017; Jacobsson 2012, 2013; see also Jacobsson's and Korolczuk's chapters in this volume). This is, in part, a legacy of state socialism, when the domestic sphere—networks of families and friends—functioned as a locus of opposition in the absence of an autonomous public sphere. As put by Kubik, during state socialism "mobilizing for action within dissident groups is unthinkable without the support of familial, kinship, and friendship networks … In fact, civil society cannot exist without a base in domestic society" (Kubik 2000: 198). These networks were also critical for the struggles to meet day-to-day needs, and they still are for many people in capitalist Poland (Mazurek 2012). Consequently, we argue that in order to understand civil society making in postsocialist and "transitional" societies in particular, it is necessary to call into question dichotomous views of private versus public and personal versus political, and to investigate the relatedness of different societal spheres as they change over time.

Thus, our analysis of civil society making begins with what people do, from actual real-life experiences, practices, and processes of overcoming constraints to collective action and building social relationships, which are sometimes unsuccessful in the short run, but which can be fruitful in a longer perspective. Rather than measuring only the present level of engagement, a process perspective allows one to see how individual grievances may be generalized and contribute to trust building in a long-term perspective, helping citizens to overcome the fragmentation of collective action space, not uncommon in postsocialist countries (Clément 2015; Jacobsson 2015a). In addition, we advocate that more attention be paid to the development of both deliberative and collaborative processes and structures (which we see as quintessential components of civil society), instead of focusing merely on organizational development or individual acts of participation. We also aim to challenge the dichotomous tendencies (described above) by including the infralevel of resistance and activism (Scott 1990).[2] This means studying everyday practices, informal activism, participation in more fluid deliberative processes, and local grassroots initiatives around issues that transgress the public-private divide (Mocek 2014; Chimiak 2014; see also Hryciuk in this volume). It also means interpreting nonparticipation as a form of response to specific conditions (as Kiersztyn shows in her chapter; see also Greene 2014), rather than just an expression of a lack of civic spirit (cf. Charkiewicz 2012; Garapich 2014).

Finally, our aim is to theorize social activism in the Polish context by taking into consideration not only the recent historical past, but also current global trends as well as transnational and national structural, political, and social tensions. This positions the volume within a broader discussion concerning the challenges of collective action in the contemporary world (e.g., Bennett et al. 2013, Kubik and Linch 2013). Our argument is that this challenge, especially in the postsocialist region, has too often been defined in terms of individual motivations, specific types of mentality, and historical contingencies. Instead, it should also be analyzed in relation to specific local ideals and practices of activism in conjunction with discursive, political, and economic opportunity structures in a given context and transnational as well as global processes. We thus believe that while the legacy of state socialism is clearly an important factor influencing social activism in the country, we also need to account for more recent global trends. Thus, the volume attempts to analyze social activism in the Polish context, taking into account the precarization of work conditions, the retrenchment of welfare provisions, (re)privatization and rising economic inequalities, migration, and the renewal of nationalist ideologies and discourses, which clash with the liberal ideals of citizenship promulgated and promoted in the rebuilding of civil societies after 1989.

Rethinking Postsocialist Civil Societies

In this volume, we side with recent scholarship calling for a reassessment of the postsocialist civil societies on both empirical and theoretical grounds. The first and most obvious reason is that several decades have passed since the regime change and the most intense years of political and economic transformation are behind. Some recent studies have argued that we now have entered a new phase of postsocialist civil societies with a revival of grassroots activism across the region in a number of fields, maybe most notably in the field of urban activism (e.g., Ishkanian 2015; Jacobsson 2015a). This gives us reason to speak of a civil society development "beyond" NGO-ization, which was more characteristic of the first period of political and economical transformation (Jacobsson and Saxonberg 2013a; Sava 2015). Moreover, as Ekiert and Kubik argue in their chapter in this volume, the differences among the former state-socialist countries are huge and in fact growing, whereas the civil societies in Central European countries that belong to the EU are not significantly different from civil societies in some established European democracies, at least in organizational terms.

Second, as several chapters in this volume illustrate, rather than being built "from scratch," postsocialist civil societies can be better understood as "recombined" (Ekiert and Kubik 2014, and in this volume), meaning that new and old organizational forms and types of civic engagement coexist, combine, and sometimes compete within a transforming political, social and economic environment. Related to this debate is the call for a reassessment of the type of civil society that existed *during* state socialism and its relevance for civil society development after 1989. Civil society under state socialism, of course, was not autonomous in relation to the state, but took the character of what Kubik (2000) names "imperfect civil societies." Apart from the state-controlled associational life (sport clubs, youth clubs, professional associations, etc.) informal groups existed, as well as networks anchored in informal economic activities, clandestine civil society (everyday resistance, youth subcultures, religious groups, etc.) and dissident circles (anti-socialist illegal opposition, intellectuals, the Workers' Defense Committees of the 1970s and Solidarity in the

Polish context) (Kubik 2000; see also Buchowski 1996). Even the state-controlled associations were, as Buchowski put it, "political at the top and non-political at the bottom" (Buchowski 1996: 84), enabling activity and relationship-building at the local level. Thus, we agree with Ekiert and Kubik's contention that while Poland did not inherit a full-fledged civil society from the previous regime, it "inherited a comprehensive and solidly institutionalized associational sphere" (2014: 4; see also Ekiert and Kubik in this volume). The character of this "imperfect" civil society is relevant to later developments. Thus, a fair picture of postsocialist civil societies needs to pay careful attention to how older and newer forms of activism combine.

Third, it has become increasingly clear that conventional ways of measuring civic engagement fail to do justice to, or reflect in a fair way, the existing postsocialist civil societies—due to the indicators used, such as numerical strength or organizational density of NGOs, or the number and size of protest events reported by the media (Ekiert and Foa 2012; Ekiert and Kubik 2014; Herbst and Żakowska 2013; Jacobsson and Saxonberg 2013a; Jacobsson 2015a; Mocek 2014; White 2006). As developed by Ekiert and Kubik and Giza-Poleszczuk in their chapters in this volume, discrepancies exist between the findings of international surveys, such as the World Value Study and European Social Survey, and national studies. One problem with commonly used survey methods concerns translation, especially of the wording of questions. As Giza-Poleszczuk argues in her chapter, local citizens who might be helping in local schools, for instance, might not identify this with "volunteering," which for some remains a new and alien term (see also Przewlocka et al. 2013: 18). The resonance of different concepts also reflects the experiences of different generations, as younger people, on the other hand, may not identify with older concepts, such as *przodownik* (leader) or *społecznik* (social activist, person engaged in social work) in the Polish context (e.g., Bojar 2004).

Another problem in adequately capturing of the strength of civil society concerns quantitative indicators, such as organizational density. The frequent research focus on NGOs does not necessarily reflect that they are the most important civic actors in the postsocialist context, but rather that they are recorded in official registers and thus easier to count than informal forms of activism (Mocek 2014; Szustek 2008). Protest event analysis carried out in the Czech Republic, Slovakia, and Bulgaria suggests that local "self-organized" civic activism, that is, collective action mobilized without the involvement of an organization, is the most frequent kind of activism in this context (e.g., Císař 2013a; 2013b; 2013c). This form of activism is based on "many events, no organizations, and few participants" (Císař 2013c: 143). However, such very local and low-key activism easily escapes the researchers' lens when the focus is on advocacy organizations capable of lobbying policy makers or catching media attention or on traditional protest events, such as mass demonstrations.

To attend to informal activism is particularly important in a postsocialist context, where formal membership in organizations may not be the preferred form of engagement given memories of encouraged or forced membership in state-controlled organizations (e.g., Howard 2011; White 2006). Instead, informal initiatives or loose affiliations may be more attractive for citizens. This is the case in contemporary Armenia or Bulgaria, for instance, where the activists involved in recent waves of social activism often distance themselves from NGOs and subscribe to a more political understanding of civil society than was introduced in the 1990s (Ishkanian 2015; Sava 2015). The prevalence and importance of informal activism in Poland has already been confirmed in recent studies of local grassroots activism (Chimiak 2014; see also Bilewicz and Potkańska 2013; CBOS 2014; Erbel 2014; Herbst and Żakowska 2013; Mocek 2014; Polanska and Chimiak 2016).

Individual-based ways of measuring civil society strength, such as surveys of voluntary engagement, also fail to consider the more relational dimensions of civil society building and development as well as deliberative processes, which may also be important for civil society functioning. Examples of such deliberative structures developed *within* civil society in the Polish context range from the Congress of urban movements and tenants' coalitions (Polanska in this volume) to the local mobilizations around participatory budgeting and the National Council of Rural Women's Organizations (Matysiak in this volume), to be described in more detail later in this Introduction. An important reason for this civil society development is that NGO-based models have been criticized not only by scholars but also by practitioners. Moreover, short-term ad hoc mobilizations or informal, low-key types of engagement do not require as many resources as the establishment of formal organizations, and mobilization around pressing local issues tends to mobilize more people than do more abstract issues such as national reforms. Informal activism is usually based on preexisting social relationships between neighbors, parents whose children go to the same school, or people who live on the same street, making it considerably easier to overcome lack of trust. Consequently, these emerging forms of social activism can be interpreted as a response to the main challenges to collective action in the postsocialist context identified in the literature, such as general apathy, low level of trust, and lack of resources (Gawin and Gliński 2006; Gumkowska et al. 2006; cf. Jacobsson and Saxonberg 2013b), and as a step toward overcoming them.

A fourth reason for re-evaluating the nature of postsocialist civil societies is conceptual, as models developed in one part of the world (mostly the "West") might not be fit for, or do full justice to, civil society in other parts of the world. Social anthropologists researching the region were already offering this critique in the 1990s, arguing that "real" civil societies may diverge from ideal-type models provided by, for instance, political theory; the nature of civil society is seen here as reflecting diverse realities in different social contexts (Buchowski 1996; Hann and Dunn 1996; cf. Trutkowski and Mandes 2005; Gagyi 2015). Likewise, social movement scholars have argued that in expecting collective action in the postsocialist context to follow the same repertoire of action and contention as in Western Europe or North America, researchers risk missing out on important forms of engagement and collective action (e.g., Jacobsson and Saxonberg 2013a; Jacobsson 2015a). For instance, it has been argued that social movement organizations in postsocialist Europe may be less able to mobilize people into traditional forms of participatory activism; however, they have been quite effective in so-called transactional activism. This type of activism entails building productive relationships with public authorities as well as other civil society actors (e.g., Císař 2013a, 2013c; Petrova and Tarrow 2007). Thus, movements here simply display a partly different repertoire of contention (see also Flam 2001).

Moreover, dichotomous views of social actors—either as engaged in contentious action or as becoming service organizations or self-help groups—are not particularly helpful for understanding collective action in the postsocialist context. In many cases groups are in fact engaged in both types of activism in parallel, as illustrated in the analyses of tenants' organizations and mothers' and fathers' initiatives (Hryciuk; Polanska; Korolczuk, all in this volume), and even those groups that currently have a quite narrow focus, such as networks of rural women, carry a potential to undertake other types of activism (Matysiak in this volume).

A final argument calling for a reassessment of postsocialist civil societies is that there are ideological and normative reasons as to why some forms of social engagement have been privileged and others disqualified, in research as well as in public policies. Building civil society has been part and parcel of the political project of developing capitalism and democracy, and has thus functioned as a reform ideology in the transition process of state-socialist countries (e.g., Buchowski 2006; Górniak 2014; Lane 2010; Załęski 2012).[3] As such, it can be seen as a form of political coordination under capitalism; the promotion of civil society has thus become "a social component of the move to markets and polyarchy" (Lane 2010: 311). The (neo)liberal organizational models (with NGOs as the prototype) were introduced and sponsored from abroad, especially during the first two decades of political and economic transformation, but (in most countries) they were also embraced by domestic policy makers and elites. Through this process of de facto channeling of engagement, civil society in Central and Eastern European countries developed into a "third sector" that would provide auxiliary services and expert knowledge to the state (Żuk 2001: 114). Detrimental effects of this trend include the bureaucratization and depoliticization of civil society actors, which shows that promoting civic engagement from the outside often serves the political and economic interests of the promoters rather than local society. As mentioned above, the recent resurgence of grassroots activism and the search for new models of organizing across Central and Eastern Europe are in part a reaction to such "transplanting" of models and practices from abroad (Fábián and Korolczuk 2017; Jacobsson 2015b).

So far, some types of activism have been too easily interpreted as the expression of "genuine" civil society, while other groups and organizations are delegitimized. The process of delegitimization is manifest, for instance, in a highly normative language used when some organizations and groups are discussed. They are often referred to as "old," self-serving or corrupt, disruptive, "backward," as "the remnants of the state-socialist era" (see, e.g., Hryciuk and Korolczuk 2013). For example, in a widely referenced analysis of the organizational patterns of Polish NGOs, the organizational styles of most postsocialist organizations studied come under such labels as "resistant to transformation" (*odporni na transformację*), "nostalgic clientelism and nepotism" (*nostalgiczny klientelizm i kolesiostwo*), or "real enemies of democracy" (*prawdziwi wrogowie demokracji*), (Gliński 2006a: 66–73). This is not to deny that clientelism or anti-democratic attitudes exist among representatives of organizations but rather to highlight the exclusionary discourses that may prevent us from seeing the heterogeneity of existing organizations. Another example of how this exclusionary logic works is presented by the Polish Voluntary Fire Brigades (*Ochotnicza Straż Pożarna*), which were routinely excluded in the statistics of civil society organizations and civil society literature, even though they are often the most influential organizations in rural areas.[4] Even when they are included, as in Gliński's study analyzing the activities of one local brigade, they appear as an exemplary case of organizations "resistant to transformation" that do not engage in any meaningful type of action but "remain in a nostalgic slumber" (2006a: 86–88). Until recently the voluntary fire brigades were typically seen as an example of "old" civil society, which works to integrate the local community mainly in rural areas by organizing local festivities and celebrations, but is not oriented toward social change (Gawin 2004). Reasearch shows, however, that the fire brigades also fulfill other roles. For example, they are important for local political life, because their members can recommend candidates in local elections and sometimes "the number of activists recommended by fire brigades is bigger than the candidates recommended by political parties" (Bartkowski 2004: 290). They generate social capital and can be interpreted as examples of bottom-up, self-organizing civil society (Adamiak 2013). This shows that organizations can combine different functions such as service provision with exerting political influence, and therefore that dichotomous understandings of civil society organizations are not helpful if we are to understand local civil societies.

The logic of exclusion pertains also to the activism of economically disadvantaged groups or social movements making claims about welfare and socioeconomic problems (Charkiewicz 2009; Hryciuk and Korolczuk 2013; Hryciuk and Polanska in this volume). People who belong to these groups easily fall victim to the process of what Buchowski termed "internal societal orientalization" (2006: 466). They are seen not as a vital part of the process of democratization and modernization of the country (understood as "successful transition"), but rather as interest groups that are "tainted" by their postsocialist origins or type of mentality. Consequently, they become discursively and practically disqualified from being "legitimate" civil society actors that, in turn, affects the way civil society is defined and theorized in Poland (Górniak 2014).

This exclusionary process takes place not only with regard to class position but also with regard to the gender or ideological and religious orientations of the citizen groups. It affects specific social groups or organizations, such as poor mothers fighting for the restoration of the Alimony Fund (Hryciuk and Korolczuk 2013; see also Hryciuk and Polanska in this volume), labor unions protesting pension reform and precarious working conditions (Kubisa 2014), people living in communal buildings mobilizing against reprivatization plans (see Polanska in this volume), or rural women's organizations (*Koła Gospodyń Wiejskich*) (see Matysiak in this volume). Also, the activism of conservative religious organizations and groups, such as the Family of Radio Maryja, is rarely seen as an expression of civil society (see, however, Kamiński 2008; Krzemiński 2009; Rogaczewska 2008). The same is true of right-wing or nationalist mobilizations and radical groups practicing violence or other forms of illegality that stand in contrast to the "civilized" repertoire of contention exhibited by most other movements in the region (see, however, Pankowski 2010; Płatek and Płucienniczak in this volume; cf. Piotrowski 2009; Polanska and Piotrowski 2015; Wrzosek 2008). The grassroots movements arising and developing in Central and Eastern Europe encompass a wide spectrum of claims ranging from notably progressive to notably reactionary ones (from the perspective of liberal democracy) (e.g., Graff and Korolczuk 2017; Fábián and Korolczuk 2017; Kováts and Põim 2015). Thus, to better understand the dynamics of existing "vernacular" civil societies, we need to identify less normative and more inclusive conceptions of civil society and social movements, allowing an analytical openness to the variety of ways in which social engagement occurs (Kopecký and Mudde 2003b).

In this volume, we propose approaching these exclusionary practices as an object of study, thus analyzing the process of legitimization and (de)legitimization of specific groups, repertoires, and claims by the elites, the media, and academia due to class, gender, ideological standpoint, etc. We see this logic of exclusion as connected to the local trends (postsocialist transition) as well as to transnational or global processes, such as neoliberalization, globalization, and migration. Consequently, a practice-based and processual approach to civil society enables us to see how local and transnational trends, discourses, and practices interact with and contradict each other, resulting in a rich, heterogeneous, and evolving array of different types of social activism.

Making Sense of Contemporary Polish Civil Society

Poland is a particularly interesting case to focus on not only because of the legacy of Solidarity but also due to the long traditions of social activism (Bartkowski 2003 and 2004; Szustek 2008; Zagała 2014), and its fairly well-developed and diverse associational sphere during the years of state socialism (Ekiert and Kubik 2014). Some scholars propose to go even further back and study the influence of the long-term historical processes dating back to the eighteenth and nineteenth centuries, when Poland lost its independence and was divided among the three neighboring countries (Bartkowski 2003; Leś 2001). They argue that until today there have been significant differences pertaining to social capital, level of socioeconomic development, and vitality of institutions of local democracy and self-government that are rooted in the period of partitions. Social activism on the local level is significantly stronger in Galicia, Greater Poland, Pomerania, and Upper Silesia, the regions with long-term traditions of local associationism. Bartkowski concludes that until today the "local press is much more developed in these regions and there are more local and regional associations, which not only help to uphold 'civic spirit' but also serve as schools of social activism" (2004: 298). The legacy of the past is also significant when it comes to material resources, e.g., the availability of spaces where people can gather. According to Bartkowski, today 85 percent of all so-called people's houses (*dom ludowy*), which are buildings owned by local rural communities where meetings and festivities can take place, are located in the Galicia region, where traditions of associationism and local government dating back to the eighteenth and nineteenth centuries, the period of the Galician autonomy introduced by the Austro-Hungarian Empire, are the strongest (2004: 291).

Most international readers, however, would associate the country with the mass movement capable of mobilizing grassroots as well as challenging the socialist regime (Arato 1981). Founded in the Gdańsk Shipyard in 1980, the Independent Self-governing Trade Union Solidarity (*Niezależny Samorządny Związek Zawodowy Solidarność*) reached 10 million members in

1981, which at the time constituted one-third of the total adult population of Poland. Despite the introduction of martial law in 1981, and the nearly decade-long period of abeyance when thousands of activists were forced to emigrate or to go underground, the mass mobilization was an important factor in bringing regime change in 1989. In the long run, however, Solidarity's legacy remains contested, mostly due to "the inability of the Polish elites and the population at large to formulate once and for all a clear and broadly accepted interpretation of the movement's history, its heroes, and its most significant successes" (Kubik 2015: 164). This trend stems partly from the fact that even though, thanks to Solidarity, Polish workers seemed to have won the battle, it soon turned out that the newly introduced capitalist system led to growing inequalities and the economic and political marginalization of the working class. Ost (2005) argues that these developments left many workers frustrated and angry, thus enabling the right-wing nationalist groups to take over the leadership in the Solidarity union and form political opposition to liberal elites.

There is also evidence that by the wake of the transformation Polish elites did not support spontaneous grassroots activism of workers or women's groups, fearing mass protests and uncontrollable mobilization (e.g., Ekiert and Kubik 1999; Penn 2003; Załęski 2012). A well-known example of such a dynamic is the case of local citizens' committees, which emerged at the end of 1988 as semilegal organizations supporting the democratic opposition and spontaneously evolved into a nationwide movement (Borkowski and Bukowski 1993). Soon after the elections in 1989 local commitees collided with the Solidarity Union, and due to the conflicts between Solidarity's leaders they were partly centralized and dismantled within a year. This case illustrates a broader trend in that "both political options dominant at the time were deeply distrustful of the vibrant grassroots 'civil society.' First, the elites attempted to take over and use these initiatives, and when it proved to be impossible … they were extinguished and the whole issue (of bottom-up civic activism) put aside" (Gliński 2008: 16, translated by the editors).

These findings suggest that the apathy and lack of social engagement among Poles observed in the 1990s did not stem only from the economic hardships or postsocialist mentality, but resulted from the democratic state's efforts to discourage mass mobilization and channel social activism into NGOs. Gliński (2008) claims that distrust toward mass mobilization and the elitist vision of civic organizing were also common among scholars, explaining why there was relatively little interest in studying Solidarity and social activism throughout the 1990s. The renewal of interest in civil society by both scholars and practitioners in the beginning of the twenty-first century resulted from new trends emerging in the country, but it was also linked to the process of EU accession, when promotion of civil society emerged as a response to the democratic deficit of European institutions and the challenges of the integration process (Lane 2010).

Until recently, the conventional view of contemporary Polish civil society depicted it as weak, passive, and nonparticipatory in nature, still in need of "catching up" with Western Europe, and Polish civil society organizations are frequently conceived as NGO-ized, that is, donor-dependent, bureaucratic, and apolitical (e.g., CBOS 2014; Czapiński and Panek 2014; Gawin and Gliński 2006; Kościański and Misztal 2008; Przewłocka et al. 2013; Sułek 2009). Indeed, most quantitative indicators show that the number of Poles engaging in any type of social activism is low. According to recent studies, the percentage of Poles who participate in voting and volunteering, who are members of nongovernmental organizations, or who take part in demonstrations is the lowest among EU countries (BBVA International Study 2013). The Social Diagnosis Report shows that 86 percent of Poles do not belong to any organizations (Czapiński and Panek 2013: 289; cf. GUS 2013). Only 13.7 percent declared that they belong to "organizations, associations, parties, committees, councils, religious groups, or clubs," of which the most commonly mentioned are religious organizations (23 percent), sports clubs (15 percent), and hobby clubs (13 percent). Only 2.5 percent of Poles belong to more than one organization. Another popular measure of civic engagement is participation in activities for the benefit of one's community, including "commune, housing estate, town or neighborhood" in which only 15 percent of respondents took part during the last year (2013: 291). Slightly more popular was taking part in unpaid work or providing services for persons outside the family or for a social organization (19 percent) and participation in public meetings outside of the workplace (17 percent). In general, participation is said to be more popular among well-educated persons living in big cities than among other parts of the population (Czapiński and Panek 2013: 290).

To explain the lack of citizens' engagement, researchers often point to lack of social capital, especially low level of social trust (Lewenstein and Theiss 2008; Szymczak 2008), the weaknesses of civic education (Napiontek 2008; Torney-Purta et al. 2001), and a generally low level of interest in the democratic culture of participation (Sułek 2009). Apathy and notorious Polish "learned helplessness" (e.g., Gliński 2006b: 279) are highlighted in scholarship as the main obstacles to social activism and engagement in the civil sphere; instead people are resourceful in the sphere of work, informal economy, professional career, or when coping with poverty; thus civic engagement is allegedy limited to "enclaves" of engaged citizens surrounded by general passivity (e.g. Gliński 2004 and 2006b; Czapiński 2008). These anticivil attitudes are often attributed to the specific type of mentality molded by a state socialist past that combines a sense of entitlement with lack of responsibility for the common good, impeding civic spirit and social engagement (Sztompka 1991; 1998; cf. Masłyk 2013). Some researchers also point to the persistence of "sociological void," a term coined by Nowak (1979) to describe Poles' lack of identification with intermediary-level institutions and strong identification with family and the nation in the 1970s. Pawlak (2015) shows that this concept is still evoked by Polish sociologists as an obstacle to the development of civil society and democratic culture in the country today, even though most scholars have ceased to examine the extent to which Nowak's idea fits current trends.

Scholars have also stressed economic and sociopolitical factors that hamper the development of civil society understood as not-for-profit activism on behalf of the common good. The lack of financial resources and know-how are often pointed out in literature as an obvious obstacle to the development of the third sector (Gliński 2006b; Przewlocka et al. 2013), especially in the case of smaller organizations based outside of Warsaw (Korolczuk 2013).

International studies show that individuals' levels of education and income have a profound impact on participation and political activism on an individual level (Schlozman et al. 2010; see also Kiersztyn in this volume). The rapid and thorough economic transformation initiated in 1989 resulted in relatively high levels of economic inequalities in contemporary Poland.[5] Neoliberal reforms prompted many Poles to focus on the economic survival of their families rather than social activism on behalf of others. Such an interpretation, stressing the economic factors behind Poles' lack of social engagement, is partly confirmed by surveys showing that people who earn above the average income tend to engage in some sort of social activism more often than those who earn below the average; that they are more likely to accept helping others and to think that people acting together can bring about positive social change (Adamiak 2014). Nevertheless, Kiersztyn (in this volume) demonstrates that in the Polish context economic determinism may be less important as a factor explaining political and civic involvement than is assumed, even though the statistical analyses reveal a positive relationship between household income and civic activism—showing that precarious employment causes the equalization of participation rates across social groups with different levels of education by leveling down.

The (alleged) enclave-like character of Polish civil society is also interpreted as resulting from existing regulations that channel social activism into nongovernmental organizations, marginalizing other types of engagement (Jacobsson 2013; Mocek 2014; Szustek 2008). The 2003 Act on Public Benefit and Volunteer Work (with a 2010 amendment), which regulates many important issues concerning civil society's functioning, focuses mostly on formal types of activism. It sets the rules of engaging in public benefit work by NGOs, regulates their cooperation with public administration, and establishes the terms for securing public-benefit organization status as well as for state supervision over public-benefit work. In practice, this means that even though informal groups and individuals are not entirely excluded from cooperating with authorities (as we develop later), they are not eligible for certain types of public support. They are also not represented in the Public Benefit Works Council, which is an advisory and supportive body contributing to the formulation of tax provisions, expressing opinions about the government's plans, and facilitating cooperation between civil society organizations and the state (Gumkowska et al. 2006: 49).

Financial resources are channeled toward formal organizations, especially those that received the status of Public Benefit Organizations in accordance with the Act on Public Benefit and Volunteer Work. Only the entities that perform "public benefit work" are eligible for state support, and since the act defines such work as "a work performed to the benefit of the public and society by nongovernmental organizations," by definition it excludes any informal groups and networks. Only nongovernmental organizations can enter the contest for state subsidies organized by the state-funded Civic Initiatives Fund (*Fundusz Inicjatyw Obywatelskich*) and acquire public-benefit organization status, making them eligible for 1 percent of tax revenue. The so-called percentage law enabling citizens to support the third sector directly, not via the state, was introduced in 2003 to stimulate engagement, to educate citizens, and to help the organizations become less financially dependent on the state (Goliński 2004; Wygnański 2004).

The process of introducing regulations concerning the relationship between civil society actors and the state is ongoing. Adjustment to new regulations takes time, thus, there is a need for constant re-evaluation of how specific tools work. One example concerns the development of structures for relationships with public authorities, such as the social consultation bodies in place at the local level in all communes, both urban and rural, and the other local government units. The 2003 Act on Public Benefit and Volunteer Work introduced a provision that obliges local authorities to set up plans for cooperation with local NGOs every year and, according to the Ministry of Labor and Social Policy reports, most local governments prepare such plans. While implementing such regulations is not always successful, there are some indications that Poles are becoming more and more interested in such cooperation and more effective in influencing decisions on the local level (e.g., Garpiel 2014).[6]

To sum up, existing literatures on civil society in Poland show that the level of citizens' engagement reflects local institutional mechanisms, such as financial incentives and regulations aimed at stimulating social activism, but also larger processes of social, economic, and political change. In pointing to a number of important cultural, institutional, and financial factors that impede citizens' engagement, existing scholarship gives us a valuable picture of civil society activity in the post–state socialist context. However, such a view appears increasingly one-sided as new, often informal, more or less spontaneous grassroots mobilizations and types of engagement emerge in the country. Thus, there is a need to rethink the ways in which civil society is defined and analyzed. We believe that this task requires rethinking the conceptual and methodological approach to capture the various types of activism as well as bridging civil society and social movement studies.

Rethinking Polish Civil Society

Whereas most existing literature on civil society in Poland laments the weakness of civil society in the country, and most quantitative measures confirm a generally low level of social engagement, people observing the events in Warsaw in the early autumn of 2015 might have had a different impression. To give one illustrative example: in just three days between 10 and 12 September 2015, the Polish capital saw a protest against the influx of refugees, gathering five thousand participants, as well as a demonstration of two thousand people under the banner "Refugees Welcome," organized by left and liberal groups. There were also several thousand nurses mobilized by the All-Poland Trade Union of Nurses and Midwives, who took to the streets to demand better pay and working conditions, and a demonstration of a couple hundred people, mostly elderly, who marched under the banner "Jesus Christ the King of Poland." Additionally, Warsaw hosted the VII Congress of Women, organized by the Congress of Women Association, which gathered approximately four thousand women from across Poland demanding more gender equality in all areas of social and political life.

Such a scale of social mobilization is not atypical for contemporary Poland, as in recent years many groups took to the streets on a mass scale, including right-wing nationalist groups, trade unions, as well as feminists (Kubisa 2014; Regulska and Grabowska 2013) or people protesting against the Anti-Counterfeiting Trade Agreement (ACTA) (Jurczyszyn et al. 2014). These initiatives were not limited to Warsaw, as smaller demonstrations in support of helping refugees took place in other Polish cities such as Kraków and Białystok, and in 2014 alone twenty-one local Congresses of Women took place in different regions. In some cases, citizens were mobilized by existing organizations such as trade unions, football fan clubs, or associations; in other cases, there were more spontaneous grassroots initiatives, e.g., the demonstration welcoming refugees in Poland or protests of ACTA. The sheer scale of these mobilizations calls into question the validity of the view of Polish civil society as currently weak and underdeveloped.

Our claim is that some types of social activism have escaped researchers' attention, not only due to their relative novelty or the sometimes low-key nature of their action, but also because of the specific definitions of civil society that circulate in both academia and public discourse in Poland (cf. Jawłowska and Kubik 2007). As shown by Jezierska in this volume, most representatives of Polish think tanks conceptualize civil society as a provider of public services, moral blueprint, or control on power. However, such narrow understandings of civil society do not only appear characteristic of the elite group of people working for influential NGOs. As noted by Trutkowski and Mandes, studies on civil society often come down to debating which institutions fit the normative definitions of civil society and thus should be included in the analysis, and which should be excluded (Trutkowski and Mandes 2005: 30; cf. Górniak 2014; Jawłowska and Kubik 2007). Thus, the types of social activism that do not fit such a narrow understanding of ideological, organizational, and functional characteristics of civil society tend to be marginalized and/or excluded.

The example of extreme right-wing movements shows that the ideological and normative orientation of the activists is an important factor in determining whether they are seen as part of civil society. People protesting immigration with slogans such as "All Poland says 'No!' to these Islamic barbarians"[7] appear to be in direct and unequivocal opposition to the values that civil society is expected to epitomize, such as openness, responsibility, and solidarity (e.g., Gawin and Gliński 2006; Kocka 2006; Wrzosek 2008). Thus, many researchers would rather consider such movements as a reflection of uncivil society (cf. Kopecký and Mudde 2003a), which employs highly disruptive tactics to achieve its goals and/or reflects the "populism and illiberalism [that] are tearing the region apart" (Krastev 2007: 56). However, our view is that such groups are rarely as homogenous as they appear, and in any case their attitudes and activities need to be studied and interpreted rather than evaluated and disqualified.

Moreover, researchers often also exclude other groups, such as trade unions, as part of contemporary Polish civil society, interpreting their activism as a fight for the interests of a narrow group rather than for the common good (cf. Uzzell and Räthzel 2013). Even though scholars recognize the historic role of Solidarity, "which originated in 1980 as a trade union and also a citizens' movement … a 'moral avant-garde' which was struggling to free and modernize the country" (Krzywdzinski 2011: 68; Ost 2005), trade unions are seldom included in civil society studies and in statistics (see, however, GUS 2013). These exclusions influence the general picture of social activism in Poland. A few existing studies of traditional forms of organizing, such as trade unions and farmers' activism, show that these groups are able to mobilize on a mass scale and have an important impact on the political sphere and the broader society. Kubisa's (2014) study of the mobilization of nurses in Poland, for instance, shows that over the last decade the All-Poland Trade Union of Nurses and Midwives not only managed to significantly increase its membership, actively recruiting new members during protests and strikes, but also succeeded in changing public discourse on health-care reforms. Similarly, the analysis of farmers' activism over the last twenty-five years shows that there were two major waves of protests (in 1989–1993 and 1997–2001) during which the farmers mobilized on a mass scale to defend their rights, which influenced the development of agricultural policy (Foryś 2015).

A similar tendency toward "invisibilization" can be observed in the case of conservative religious activism. According to several studies, members of religious organizations and communities make up as much as 75 percent of all people who belong to Polish civil society organizations (Szymczak 2011: 64; cf. Herbst 2005), but in the public discourse they are often depicted as "backward" and representing values that are antithetical to the norms that civil society actors should promote. Also, there is still little research examining different forms of religious activism and their social consequences (see, however, Bylok and Pędziwiatr 2010; Krzemiński 2009). In our view, these as well as other types of activism included in this volume are worth scholarly attention as they attest to the ability of Polish citizens to overcome major challenges to collective action, frequently pointed out by scholars, in the Polish context, such as widespread apathy, lack of interpersonal trust, disdain for political actions, and resource constraints.

Moreover, whereas previous research often focused on organized forms of activism, mostly through NGOs, currently there is a growing recognition of the many informal initiatives that successfully mobilize Polish citizens. Recent studies indicate that these mostly grassroots, often informal mobilizations constitute an important part of Polish civil society (e.g., Mocek 2014; CBOS 2014; Domaradzka 2015; GUS 2013; Herbst and Żakowska 2013). An example of traditional deliberative structures at the local level that have been little studied so far is the village assemblies (*zebrania wiejskie*) (Matysiak 2011). In recent years, we witnessed increased collaboration and the development of new deliberative structures within civil society that take the form of the organization of forums such as the informal Congress of Urban Movements in Poland (Polanska in this volume; Kowalewski 2013; Pobłocki 2014) or the national Congress of Women (Korolczuk 2014). Other examples of organized or semiorganized forms of participatory practices include participatory budgeting, parents' activism focusing on child care or educational reforms, conservative mobilization against "gender ideology," grassroots urban movements, mobilizations around civic law proposals,[8] tenants' networks, the cooperative movement (e.g., food cooperatives), and groups promoting the sharing economy (e.g., time banks), as well as various types of online organizing, such as groups on Facebook, mailing lists, or groups gathering on specific thematic sites and blogs (Bukowiecki et al. 2014; Erbel 2014; Grzebalska 2016; Herbst and Żakowska 2013; Korolczuk 2014; Krześ 2014; Polanska 2014).

Sometimes informal organizing is just a phase in organizational development. For example, the Congress of Women that emerged in 2009 as a loose group of individuals and representatives of various organizations became an association in 2013. In many other cases, however, avoiding registration and maintaining nonhierarchical, informal relationships among participants is a preferred strategy, as in the case of Women's 8 of March Alliance, a feminist group that has existed since 2001, organizing yearly mass demonstrations in Warsaw (Regulska and Grabowska 2013). This type of activism can be termed semiformal because there is a set of rules that regulates the functioning of the group and the Alliance's members engage not only in ad hoc actions but also long-term cooperation with other groups and trade unions (Korolczuk 2014). We interpret them as functional equivalents of formal democratic structures, which can become rather effective in forging dialogue and cooperation as well as introducing specific changes in society.[9]

Some recent studies indicate that informal local activism can be an effective tool to bring about social change. More and more Poles believe that they can influence the way things work at the local level, which can be interpreted as a sign of a growing sense of agency, and as a signal of trust in the positive outcomes of collective actions. During the last decade, the percentage of people convinced that they can effect change in their local communities when acting together has grown steadily. While in 2002 only 50 percent of respondents were convinced that "people such as myself, in cooperating with others, can help the needy or solve some of the problems of the local community, my village or my city," 77 percent of respondents agreed with this statement in 2014 (CBOS 2014). There are some recent examples of how cooperation on the local level can bring social change, and how loose groups of citizens can effectively use certain tools, e.g., the possibility of entering into social consultation with authorities to change important decisions regarding urban planning or the decision-making process regarding hosting the Olympics, as was the case in Kraków (Erbel 2014; Garpiel 2014; Krześ 2014).

Informal types of organizing and social engagement are recognized by Polish law and international agreements such as the Lisbon Treaty. Even though the legal provisions tend to channel social activism into nongovernmental organizations, they also allow individuals and informal groups acting on behalf of all people to engage in the process of democratic deliberation and to cooperate with local authorities (Makowski 2014). Makowski points to the fact that such cooperation is often difficult in practice due to the lack of clear legal provisions, characteristics of Polish legal culture, and a general tendency toward engaging formal organizations in social consultations and cooperation with authorities. However, interest in such practices appears to be increasing, as the growing popularity of participatory budgeting shows. As of today, participatory budgeting has been introduced in over seventy cities in Poland (Kraszewski and Mojkowski 2014; Prykowski 2011). The participatory budgeting mechanism also exists in rural areas. It was introduced already in 2009 in the form of the village fund (*fundusz sołecki*). The Act on the Village Fund allows the communal councils to allocate funds from their budgets to finance projects, which are collectively chosen by the residents of rural subcommunes (*sołectwa*) located within their administrative areas. Even if participatory budgeting usually concerns a small share of the budget, and sometimes only a limited number of local citizens take part in the decision making,[10] the growing popularity of this and other forms of participation outside of formal organizations suggests that many Poles want to engage in informal, possibly more spontaneous and ad hoc types of social activism (Gerwin and Grabkowska 2012).

Furthermore, the view of Polish society as uniformly weak and apathetic can be contested on methodological grounds, as there are some significant discrepancies in available quantitative data. Whereas studies show low levels of engagement in formal types of activism, this is not the case concerning informal types of activism. When asked more generally whether they engaged in any "voluntary and non-profit pro-social activity" during the last year, as many as 78 percent of Poles answered "yes" (CBOS 2014; cf. GUS 2013). Most respondents declared that they devoted their time to help friends, family members (living separately), and neighbors. While one might debate whether such activities can be interpreted as activities strengthening civil society, these findings signal the existence of a sphere of social engagement that may have escaped surveys focusing exclusively on formal activism. They indicate a preference for noninstitutional types of activism and suggest that quantitative measures focusing on volunteering may show a distorted picture of actual engagement.

Such an interpretation is in line with international scholarship, which shows that traditionally applied indicators of institutionalized political and civic participation do not include the more informal activities that have emerged in many industrialized countries in recent decades (e.g., Baiocchi et al. 2014; Stolle and Hooghe 2005). Such low-key, grassroots forms of engagement can be interpreted as a response to skepticism about and distrust in politics, which has been growing in most democratic countries (e.g., Bennett et al. 2013). Analyzing these phenomena allows us to see that everyday life and political protest in many cases are mutually constitutive, and that daily practices, including service provision, "are politicized and politiciz*ing* as they unfold and develop over time and through diverse networks" (Yates 2015).

All in all, this research overview indicates that there are good reasons to update and revise our knowledge of Polish civil society, a project with implications for the debate on postsocialist civil societies more generally.

Introduction to the Volume

Our volume takes a broad view of civil society in Poland, as it covers both formal and informal forms of activism, including NGOs as well as loose networks, social movements, and other informal types of social engagement. The contributions focus in particular on initiatives and types of collective action that have not been much reflected in the international research literature thus far, such as the cases of animal welfare activism, rural women's activism, tenants' mobilizations, and mothers' groups as well as right-wing and migrant communities. In particular, our case selection reflects the ambition to call attention to forms of activism that have tended to be delegitimized as "backward," uncivil, or nonconsequential. As with all selections, this means that some very interesting types of social activism, including LGBTQ and feminist activism, religious mobilizations, and online networks, are not included.

The first section of this book challenges the common picture of, and narrative about, Polish civil society. In chapter 1, Ekiert and Kubik effectively counter three prevailing myths about postsocialist civil societies. First, they confront the myth that civil societies had to be built from scratch after 1989. They point to the associational sphere that existed, to various extents in various countries, during state socialism and argue that "recombined civil societies" is a more truthful description of the existing civil societies in the region. Second, they challenge the myth that a distinct type of postsocialist civil society developed in the region after 1989, showing the growing divergence of civil societies in the region. Third, they challenge the characterization of these civil societies as systematically weak, arguing that (irrespective of the internal diversity) the civil society sector in postsocialist Europe may function somewhat differently than in the West but that it is not necessarily weaker or less politically consequential.

In chapter 2, Giza-Poleszczuk sheds light on how to explain the contradictory findings in national and international surveys of civic engagement and how the narrative of a "weak civil society" in Poland could remain so pervasive. She shows, inter alia, that in the elite discourse on civil society in Poland, traditional notions of social activism (e.g., *czyn społeczny, ochotnik*) were replaced by "foreign" notions (e.g., volunteering—*wolontariat*), one consequence of which is that much local grassroots engagement may escape the lens of civil society surveyors as respondents often do not associate what they actually do in their local communities with these given labels. Taking into account what actually happens on the ground and in a diverse range of organizations (old *and* new), she concludes that Polish civil society has much more vitality than is commonly acknowledged.

In chapter 3, Jacobsson, too, takes issue with the characterization of Polish civil society as weak; in contrast, she finds it dynamic and entrepreneurial. Based on a case study of animal rights activism in Poland, she explores some distinct qualities of the civil society organizations developed after 1989. She argues that in civil society organizing, there tends to be a spillover of action logics from the domestic sphere, such as a tendency to personalize civic and organizational relationships, as well as spillover from the market sphere, such as a preference for individualist forms of action and thinking. She conceptualizes this as a form of "civic privatism," referring not to passivity but to civic engagement colored by logics from the private sphere, resulting in a highly dynamic but also fragmented civil society sector.

In chapter 4, Jezierska analyzes the existing discourses on civil society within Polish elite NGOs, concluding that one specific understanding of civil society—civil society as service-providing NGOs—has gained a hegemonic position. Examining how the leaders of the main Polish think tanks conceptualize civil society is of utmost importance because they have significant impacts on the shape of Polish civil society through policy influence, grant giving, and training of local civil society organizations. Consequently, the way they frame civil society plays an important role in delimiting the space of possible actions not only for think tanks themselves but also for other civil society organizations.

The second section of the book examines how specific groups struggle with the tendency toward delegitimization of their fight and their claims in the public sphere. In Chapter 5, Korolczuk examines social activism of Polish parents in contemporary Poland. She demonstrates that parental activism challenges the "field approach," which presupposes a clear separation between private/domestic and public/political spheres, as well as the "normative approach" to civil society. Parents' rights activism transgresses the public/private divide by showing that parenting does not take place only within the realm of the home, but also in the public sphere, and that people may politicize their experiences and identities related to the "domestic" sphere. Social mobilizations of mothers and fathers also attest to the difficulty in differentiating between common good and particularistic interests of individuals and families. Finally, parents' rights activism shows that civic participation is a gendered process, as are the definition of the political and the shape of the public/private divide.

In chapter 6, Hryciuk examines the case of the Single Mothers for the Alimony Fund Movement, which has so far been the most spectacular response on the part of civil society to the neoliberal dynamics of social and economic transformation in Poland. The author shows how the mobilization of economically underprivileged women was marginalized in public discourse and how the activists attempted changing the discriminatory law as mother-citizens fighting for social rights, neither using the essentialist notions of womanhood nor calling themselves feminists. Hryciuk observes that while most motherist movements in Latin America legitimize their claims by drawing upon the feminine imagery of Catholicism against the state and by evoking the image of the suffering mother and her sacrifice, the Polish Single Mothers downplayed their cultural role as mothers and called on the civil rights and the constitutional principle of the protection of family instead.

A similar dynamic is examined by Polanska in chapter 7, which focuses on the Polish tenants' movement. Representing a hybrid of transactional types of activism and self-help activism, the tenants' movement is neither donor-dependent nor depoliticized as the conventional view on Polish civil society would have it. Moreover, it mobilizes mostly impoverished people in their fifties and sixties motivated by pragmatic factors like poor housing situations and socioeconomic positions. The author examines how this economically weak group overcomes the challenges of collective action, such as lack of resources and low social capital and fights the neoliberal discourse dominant in the Polish context, which defines the poor as unable to adapt to the new economic system and as remnants from the socialist past.

Finally, in chapter 8, Kiersztyn offers an assessment of the potential impact of precarious employment on civic and political participation among Poles. Contemporary literature consistently points to the existence of a participation gap associated with socioeconomic status, age, and gender, which means that males and wealthier, better educated people have been shown to be more politically active. Kiersztyn's analysis shows that political voice is determined mostly by the educational level of respondents, while economic determinism seems far less important as a factor explaining political and civic involvement in the Polish context. At the same time, Kiersztyn concludes that in light of the results of quantitative studies on civic activism and precarious employment, it appears that current changes in the labor market may, in the long term and indirectly, turn out to be much more detrimental to civic participation than the often-debated trends like postsocialist legacy of apathy.

The final section explores civil society making "between the past and the present" and how some civil society actors struggle to preserve or redefine the past and negotiate its relevance for the present.

In chapter 9, Matysiak focuses on the rural women's organizations (*Koła Gospodyń Wiejskich*) and the role they play at local level, representing a type of civic activism that is frequently disqualified and "invisibilized" in Polish civil society research. She shows that they are often dismissed as an "old type" of civil society that does not fit the model of civil society promoted in contemporary Poland, and their actual numbers are underestimated, as some of them are informal and thus not counted in the organizational statistics. Matysiak calls for an analysis of civic activism that is attentive to the local context and the local-rootedness of civic activism in order to see how it is shaped by both gender and local traditions and needs.

In chapter 10, Elgenius discusses the increasingly active and diversified social activism of Polish migrants in the United Kingdom. The chapter considers three significant waves of Polish migration (post–Second World War, Solidarity, and post-1989, pre–EU enlargement and post–EU expansion), showing how the different national narratives and experiences are reflected in the civil society making of the different generations of migrants, thus contributing to the diversification of contemporary activism of the Polish migrant community.

In Chapter 11, Płatek and Płucienniczak analyze the types of social mobilizations that deviate from a normative vision of civil society as a sphere populated by civic-minded organizations that build social capital and trust and support democracy. They examine extreme-right groups and organizations in Poland, characterized by the use of violence and anti-state, undemocratic ideology. They follow Kopecký and Mudde (2003b) in claiming that such "uncivil movements" should be included in the study of civil society in postsocialist countries, including Poland, because the extreme right claimed its place in the very center of the public sphere and its repertoire of action changed as the movement managed to blend into the broader civil and political society. The authors conceptualize the specific field of mobilization of the Polish extreme right as a combination of political and discursive opportunities, showing that the extreme-right movement is relatively stable in its anti-systemic and anti-minority aims, but the action repertoire and targets change according to the shifts in Polish opportunity structures. As it adapts to current social and political trends, it transcends the boundaries between civil and uncivil society.

Finally, in a brief conclusion, Jacobsson and Korolczuk synthesize some general findings and theoretical lessons emerging from the volume.

Notes

1. This research has been enabled by a generous research grant from the Swedish Research Council (Grant 421/2010/1706). We are grateful to Grzegorz Ekiert, Katalin Fábián, Katarzyna Jezierska, Jan Kubik, Julia Kubisa, Sławomir Mandes,

Ilona Matysiak, Dominika Polanska, and Karolina Sztandar-Sztanderska as well as the participants of our workshop in Gdynia for commenting on earlier versions of this Introduction. Any mistakes are, of course, ours.

2. Infralevel includes everyday acts of resistance that are "quiet, dispersed, disguised or otherwise seemingly invisible" (Vinthagen and Johansson 2013: 4, drawing on Scott 1990), but that have political meaning and may lead to more visible forms of activism.

3. Apart from the inherent normativity in the concept of civil society as propagated by policy makers and foreign donors in the transition process, dissident thinkers in the region were also promulagating their versions of legitimate civil society by the 1970s and 1980s. Václav Havel, György Konrád, and Adam Michnik, for instance, saw civil society as a civilized, moral sphere standing apart from and above the sphere of party politics (e.g., Celichowski 2004; Jezierska 2015).

4. For instance, the Klon/Jawor reports, which count the number of registered foundations and associations in Poland, exclude the voluntary fire brigades (see, e.g., Przewłocka 2012).

5. The level of economic inequalities in Polish society, measured by Gini's coefficient, fell recently (from 0.301 in 2009 to 0.299 in 2013), but 5.1 percent of Polish households still live in extreme poverty and 44.7 percent live below "the prosperity level," meaning that they cannot afford to spend money on education, culture, or leisure (Czapiński and Panek 2013). Moreover, according to the Polish Central Statistical Office, the percentage of Poles living in extreme poverty rose in 2013, indicating that there is a group of people who are affected by a long-term social and economic exclusion (CBOS 2013). Another dimension of economic inequality pertains to the labor market; for example, the rate of temporary employment in Poland is around 27 percent, which is almost twice the EU average (EUROSTAT 2013).

6. Some studies suggest that many organizations do not know that such regulations exist and that the cooperation between authorities and nongovernmental organizations in Poland is not based on partnership but rather depends on the good will of civil servants (e.g., Fuszara et al 2008). This trend is related to the failures of the administrative, political, and fiscal decentralization process that was to limit the role of the central state. The decentralization process was only partially implemented, which further complicates the relationship between civil society and local authorities (Regulska 2009).

7. Available at https://www.youtube.com/watch?v=nNYp3UftdiYandfeature=youtu.be. Retrieved 15 September 2015.

8. The law in Poland allows citizens to demand that parliament discuss a law proposal if they can collect 100,000 signatures supporting the proposal. It is not ensured, however, that the proposal would be accepted.

9. This is not to deny that this informal way of organizing also has a flip side, including the formation of informal status and power hierarchies and unequal voice opportunities among participants (see Jacobsson 2013, and in this volume), a topic to be explored more deeply in future research.

10. Participatory budgeting is often perceived as a tool that helps to engage people in local affairs; promotes interpersonal trust, transparency, and communication; allows people to control the authorities; helps to create local communities; and educates people in civic activism (Gerwin and Grabkowska 2012). At the same time, existing research shows that it can be detrimental to the development of civil society as it can legitimize the privileged position of a narrow elite, transfer the duties from the

authorities to people without providing adequate resources, and narrow down public debates to issues that can be financed through such a system (Krześ 2014). The case of Sopot, which was the first Polish city to introduce participatory budgeting in 2011 in the amount of 5 million PLN (1 percent of the total city budget), shows that there are some significant discrepancies between ideals, plans, and reality. Introducing participatory budgeting in Sopot did not engage people on a mass scale: only a handful of people generally took part in informational meetings and only 7 percent of citizens took part in voting. In 2013, only 4.5 percent of local citizens participated in voting, which shows that such forms of enhancing people's participation are not always successful (Krześ 2014).

References

Adamiak, P. 2013. *Ochotnicze Straże Pożarne w Polsce. Raport z badania 2012.* [Voluntary Fire Brigades in Poland. Report from Research 2012]. Retrieved 12 May 2015 from http://www.ngo.pl/OSP_2012_raport/#/1.

———. 2014. *Zaangażowanie Społeczne Polek i Polaków. Raport z Badania* [Social Engagement of Poles: Research Raport]. Stowarzyszenie Klon/Jawor. http://civicpedia.ngo.pl/files/wiadomosci.ngo.pl/public/civicpedia/publikacje_okladki_LAST/201404 07_RAPORT_final.pdf.

Alexander, J. 2006. *The Civil Sphere.* Oxford: Oxford University Press.

Arato, A. 1981. "Civil Society vs. the State: Poland 1980-1981." *Telos* 47: 23–47.

Baiocchi, G., E. Bennett, A. Cordner, P.T. Klein, and S. Savell. 2014. *The Civic Imagination: Making a Difference in American Political Life.* Boulder, CO: Paradigm Publishers.

Bartkowski, J. 2003. *Tradycja i Polityka. Wpływ Tradycji Kulturowych Polskich Regionów na Współczesne Zachowania Społeczne i Polityczne* [Tradition and Politics: The Influence of Cultural Traditions of Polish Regions on Contemporary Social and Political Behaviour]. Warsaw: Wydanictwo Akademickie Żak.

———. 2004. "Tradycja Zaborów a Współczesne Zachowania Społeczne w Polsce" [Traditions of Partititions and Modern Social Behavior of Poles], in *Oblicza Lokalności. Tradycja i Nowoczesność* [Faces of Localities: Tradition and Modernity], ed. J. Kurczewska. Warsaw: IFiS Publishers, 267–304.

BBVA International Study. 2013. Values and Worldviews. April. http://www.fbbva.es/TLFU/dat/presentacionwordviewsandvalues.pdf.

Bennett, E.A., A. Cordner, P.T. Klein, S. Savell, and G. Baiocchi. 2013. "Disavowing Politics: Civic Engagement in an Era of Political Scepticism." *American Journal of Sociology* 119, no. 2: 518–548.

Bilewicz, A., and D. Potkańska. 2013. "Jak kiełkuje społeczeństwo obywatelskie? Kooperatywy spożywcze w Polsce jako przykład nieformalnego ruchu społecznego" [How Does Civil Society Develop? Food Coooperatives in Poland as an Example of Informal Social Movement], *Trzeci Sektor* [Third Sector] 31, no. 3: 25–44.

Bojar, H. 2004. "Liderzy lokalni wobec przeszłości" [Local Leaders about the Past], in *Oblicza Lokalności. Tradycja i Nowoczesność* [Faces of Localities: Tradition and Modernity], ed. J. Kurczewska. Warsaw: IFiS Publishers, 164–184.

Borkowski, T., and A. Bukowski, eds. 1993. *Komitety Obywatelskie Powstanie, rozwój upadek?* Kraków: Universitas.

Buchowski, M. 1996. "The Shifting Meanings of Civil and Civic Society in Poland," in *Civil Society: Challenging Western Models*, ed. C. Hann and E. Dunn. London: Routledge, 79–98.

———. 2006. "The Specter of Orientalism in Europe: From Exotic Other to Stigmatized Brother." *Anthropology Quarterly* 79, no. 3: 463–482.

Bukowiecki, Ł., Obarska, M., and X. Stańczyk, eds. 2014. *Miasto na żądanie* [City on Demand]. Warszawa: Wydawnictwo Uniwersytetu Warszawskiego.

Bylok, K., and K. Pędziwiatr. 2010. *The Family of Radio Maryja and One of Its Activists.* Kraków: Tischner European University.

CBOS. 2014. *Aktywność społeczna Polaków- poziom zaangażowania i motywacje* [Social Activity among Poles: Level of Engagement and Motivations]. Komunikat Badań BS/62/2011. Warszawa: CBOS.

Celichowski, J. 2004. "Civil Society in Eastern Europe: Growth without Engagement," in *Exploring Civil Society: Political and Cultural Contexts*, ed. M. Glasius, D. Lewis, and H. Seckinelgin. London: Routledge, 71–79.

Charkiewicz, E. 2009. "Matki do sterylizacji. Neoliberalny rasizm w Polsce" [Mothers to Be Sterilized: Neoliberal Racism in Poland]. *Biblioteka On-line Think Tanku Feministycznego.* Retrieved 15 September 2015 from http://www.ekologiasztuka.pl/pdf/f0053charkiewicz_szkic2.pdf.

———. 2012. "Partycypacja nie dla wszystkich" [Participation Not for All], in *Partycypacja. Przewodnik Krytyki Politycznej* [Participation: Political Critique Guidebook], ed. J. Erbel and P. Sadura. Warsaw: Wydawnictwo Krytyki Politycznej, 329–341.

Chimiak, G. 2006. *How Individualists Make Solidarity Work.* Warsaw: Ministerstwo Pracy i Polityki Społecznej.

———. 2014. "Nowe oblicza społecznikostwa w Polsce" [New Faces of Social Activism in Poland], in *Polska i Ukraina w dobie transformacji* [Poland and Ukraine in the Time of Transformation], ed. W.E. Draus and P. Trefler. Przemyśl: Pro Carpatia, 87–96.

Císař, O. 2013a. "The Diffusion of Public Interest Mobilisation: A Historical Sociology Perspective on Advocates without Members in the Post-communist Czech Republic." *East European Politics* 29, no. 1: 69–82.

———. 2013b. "A Typology of Extra-parliamentary Political Activism in Post-communist Settings: The Case of the Czech Republic," in *Beyond NGO-ization: The Development of Social Movements in Central and Eastern Europe*, ed. K. Jacobsson and S. Saxonberg. Farnham: Ashgate, 139–168.

———. 2013c. "Post-communism and Social Movements," in *The Wiley-Blackwell Encyclopedia of Social and Political Movements*, ed. D. Snow, D. della Porta, B. Klandermans, and D. McAdam. London: Blackwell, 994–999.

Clément, K. 2015. "From 'Local' to 'Political': The Kaliningrad Mass Protest Movement of 2009-2010 in Russia," in *Urban Grassroots Movements in Central and Eastern Europe*, ed. K. Jacobsson. Farnham: Ashgate, 163–193.

Czapiński, J. 2008. "Molekularny rozwój Polski" [The Molecular Development of Poland], in *Modernizacja Polski. Kody kulturowe i mity* [Poland's Modernization: Cultural Codes and Myths], ed. J. Szomburg. Gdańsk: IBnGR, 95–102.

Czapiński, J., and T. Panek, eds. 2013. *Social Diagnosis: Objective and Subjective Quality of Life in Poland.* Warsaw: The Council for Social Monitoring.

Domaradzka, A. 2015. "Changing the Rules of the Game: Impact of the Urban Movement on the Public Administration Practices," in *Civil Society and Innovative Public Administration*, ed. M. Freise, F. Paulsen, and A. Walter. Nomos, 218–237.

Ekiert, G., and R. Foa. 2012. "The Weakness of Post-Communist Civil Societies Reassessed." *CES Papers–Open Forum 11.* Harvard University: Center for European Studies.

Ekiert, G., and J. Kubik 1999. *Rebellious Civil Society, Popular Protest and Democratic Consolidation in Poland.* Ann Arbor: University of Michigan Press.

Ekiert, G., and J. Kubik. 2014. "Myths and Realities of Civil Society." *Journal of Democracy* 25, no. 1: 46–58.

Erbel, J. 2014. "Czego Nie Widać z Perspektywy III Sektora?" [What Remains Invisible from the Third Sector Perspective?]. *Animacja Życia Publicznego. Zeszyty Centrum Badań Społeczności i Polityk Lokalnych* 1, no. 18: 19–22.

EUROSTAT. 2013. "European Social Statistics 2013 Edition." Eurostat Pocketbooks. Luxembourg: Office for Official Publications of the European Communities.

Fábián, K., and E. Korolczuk, eds. 2017. *Rebellious Parents: Parental Movements in Central-Eastern Europe and Russia.* Indiana University Press.

Flam, H. 2001. "Introduction: In Pursuit of Fundable Causes," in *Pink, Purple, Green: Women's, Religious, Environmental and Gay/Lesbian Movements in Central Europe Today,* ed. H. Flam. Boulder: East European Monographs, 1–19.

Foryś, G. 2015. "Kulturowe Aspekty Aktywności Protestacyjnej Rolników w Polsce" [Cultural Aspects of Farmers' Protests in Poland]. *Studia Socjologiczne* 1, no. 216: 19–43.

Fuszara M., Grabowska M., Mizielińska J. and J. Regulska eds 2008. *Współpraca czy konflikt. Państwo, Unia i kobiety* [Cooperation or Conflict? The State, European Union and Women]. Warszawa: Wydawnictwa Akademickie i Profesjonalne.

Gagyi, A. 2015. "Why Don't East European Movements Address Inequalities the Way Western Movements Do? A Review Essay on the Availability of Movement-Relevant Research." *Interface* 7, no. 2, 15–26.

Garapich, M. 2014. "*Homo Sovieticus* Revisited: Anti-Institutionalism, Alcohol and Resistance Among Polish Homeless Men in London." *International Migration Special Issue: Polish Migration after the Fall of the Iron Curtain* 52, no. 1: 100–117.

Garpiel, R. 2014. *Raport z przebiegu konsultacji społecznych dotyczących koncepcji organizacji Zimowych Igrzysk Olimpijskich 2022 w Krakowie* [Report from Social Consultations Concerning Organizing Winter Olympics 2022 in Cracow]. Kraków. Retrieved 12 September 2015 from http://www.dialogspoleczny.krakow.pl/files/objects/6911/35/Raport%20ZIO2014.pdf.

Gawin, D. 2004. "Między Ideologią a Społecznikostwem. Lokalny Wymiar Polskiej Polityki" [Between Ideology and Social Work: Local Dimensions of Polish Politics], in *Oblicza Lokalności,* ed. J. Kurczewska. *Tradycja i Nowoczesność* [Faces of Localities: Tradition and Modernity]. Warsaw: IFiS Publishers, 305–326.

Gawin, D., and P. Gliński., eds. 2006. *Civil Society in the Making.* Warsaw: IFiS Publishers.

Gerwin, M., and M. Grabkowska. 2012. "Budżet obywatelski" [Participatory Budgeting], in *Partycypacja. Przewodnik Krytyki Politycznej* [Participation: Political Critique Guidebook], ed. J. Erbel and P. Sadura. Warsaw: Wydawnictwo Krytyki Politycznej, 100–111.

Ginsborg, P. 2013. "Uncharted Territories: Individuals, Families, Civil Society and the Democratic State," in *The Golden Chain: Family, Civil Society and the State,* ed. J. Nautz, P. Ginsborg, and T. Nijhuis. New York and Oxford: Berghahn Books, 17–42.

Gliński, P. 2004. "How Active Are Social Actors? Deficient Citizenship versus Day-To-Day Resourcefulness in Poland." *Polish Sociological Review* 4: 429–450.

———. 2006a. *Style działań organizacji pozarządowych w Polsce. Grupy interesu czy pożytku publicznego?* [Nongovernmental Organisations' Mode of Activities in Poland: Interest Groups or Public Benefit]. Warsaw: IFiS Publishers.

———. 2006b. "The Third Sector in Poland: Dilemmas of Development," in *Civil Society in the Making*, ed. D. Gawin and P. Gliński. Warsaw: IFiS Publishers, 265–288.

———. 2008. "Przedmowa: o miejscu problematyki społeczeństwa obywatelskiego w socjologii polskiej" [Foreword: On the Position of Research on Civil Society within Polish Sociology], in *Społeczeństwo obywatelskie. Miedzy teoria a praktyka* [Civil Society: Between Theory and Practice], ed. A. Kościański and W. Misztal. Warsaw: IFiS Publishers, 7–26.

Goliński, I. 2004. "How the 1% System Was Developed in Poland," in *Percentage Philanthropy*, ed. M. Török and D. Moss. Retrieved 10 May 2015 from http://www.oneper cent.hu/Dokumentumok/Poland_changes_in_mechanism.pdf.

Górniak, K. 2014. "Społeczeństwo obywatelskie w Polsce – spojrzenie postkolonialne" [Polish Civil Society: Postcolonial Perspective]. *Trzeci Sektor* 32: 17–29.

Graff, A., and E. Korolczuk. 2017. "'Worse than Communism and Nazism Put Together': War on Gender in Poland," in *Anti-gender Campaigns in Europe: Religious and Political Mobilizations against Equality*, ed. R. Kuhar and D. Paternotte. Lanham: Rowman and Littlefield (forthcoming).

Greene, S. 2014. *Moscow in Movement: Power and Opposition in Putin's Russia.* Stanford: Stanford University Press.

Grzebalska, Weronika. 2016. "Why the War on 'Gender Ideology' Matters—and Not Just to Feminists." *Visegrad Insight* 7 March 2016. Retrieved 15 April 2016 from http://vise gradinsight.eu/why-the-war-on-gender-ideology-matters-and-not-just-to-feminists/.

Gumkowska, M., J. Herbst, J. Szołajska, and J. Wygnański. 2006. "The Challenge of Solidarity: The CIVICUS Civil Society Index Report for Poland 2006." Retrieved 25 October 2010 from http://www.civicus.org/new/media/Poland_Country_Report.pdf.

GUS. 2013. *Jakość życia. Kapitał społeczny, ubóstwo i wykluczenie w Polsce* [Quality of Life: Social Capital, Poverty, and Exclusion in Poland]. Warszawa: GUS.

Hagemann, K., Michel S., and G. Budde, eds. 2008. *Civil Society and Gender Justice: Historical and Comparative Perspectives.* New York, Oxford: Berghahn Books.

Hann, C., and E. Dunn, eds. 1996. *Civil Society: Challenging Western Models.* London: Routledge.

Henderson, S.L. 2002. "Selling Civil Society: Western Aid and the Nongovernmental Organization Sector in Russia." *Comparative Political Studies* 35: 139–67.

Herbst, J. 2005. *Oblicza Społeczeństwa Obywatelskiego* [Faces of Civil Society]. Warszawa: Fundacja Rozwoju Społeczeństwa Obywatelskiego.

Herbst, K., and M. Żakowska. 2013. *Ruchy nieformalne a kierunek rozwoju ekonomii społecznej. Rekomendacje dla polityk publicznych* [Informal Movements and the Direction of Development of Social Economy: Recommendations for Public Policies]. Warszawa: Centrum Rozwoju Zasobów Ludzkich.

Howard, M.M. 2003. *The Weakness of Civil Society in Post-Communist Europe.* Cambridge: Cambridge University Press.

———. 2011. "Civil Society in Post-communist Europe," in *The Oxford Handbook of Civil Society*, ed. M. Edwards. Oxford: Oxford University Press, 134–145.

Hryciuk, R.E., and E. Korolczuk. 2013. "At the Intersection of Gender and Class: Social Mobilization around Mothers' Rights in Poland," in *Beyond NGO-ization: The De-*

velopment of Social Movements in Central and Eastern Europe, ed. K. Jacobsson and S. Saxonberg. Farnham: Ashgate, 49–70.

Ishkanian, A. 2015. "Self-Determined Citizens? A New Wave of Civic Activism in Armenia." *Open Democracy / ISA RC-47: Open Movements.* Retrieved 16 June 2015 from https://opendemocracy.net/armine-ishkanian/selfdetermined-citizens-new-wave-of-civic-activism-in-armenia.

Jacobsson, K. 2012. "Fragmentation of the Collective Action Space: The Animal Rights Movement in Poland." *East European Politics* 28, no. 4: 353–370.

———. 2013. "Channeling and Enrollment: The Institutional Shaping of Animal Rights Activism in Poland," in *Beyond NGO-ization: The Development of Social Movements in Central and Eastern Europe,* ed. K. Jacobsson and S. Saxonberg. Farnham: Ashgate, 27–47.

———, ed. 2015a. *Urban Grassroots Movements in Central and Eastern Europe.* Farnham: Ashgate.

———. 2015b. "Conclusion: Towards A New Research Agenda," in *Urban Grassroots Movements in Central and Eastern Europe,* ed. K. Jacobsson. Farnham: Ashgate, 273–287.

Jacobsson, K., and S. Saxonberg, eds. 2013a. *Beyond NGO-ization: The Development of Social Movements in Central and Eastern Europe.* Farnham: Ashgate.

Jacobsson, K., and S. Saxonberg. 2013b. "Introduction: The Development of Social Movements in Central and Eastern Europe," in *Beyond NGO-ization: The Development of Social Movements in Central and Eastern Europe,* ed. K. Jacobsson and S. Saxonberg. Farnham: Ashgate, 1–25.

Jawłowska, A., and J. Kubik. 2007. "Discussion on Social Activity in Contemporary Poland." *Societas/Communitas* no. 4–5: 11–40.

Jezierska, K. 2015. "Apolitical and Non-ideological? Polish Civil Society Without Identity." Unpublished manuscript.

Jurczyszyn, Ł., J. Kołtan, P. Kuczyński, and M. Rakusa-Suszczewski, eds. 2014. *Obywatele ACTA* [Citizens of ACTA]. Gdańsk: Europejskie Centrum Solidarności.

Kamiński, T. 2008. "Kościół i trzeci sektor w Polsce" [Church and the Third Sector in Poland]. *Trzeci Sektor,* 15: 7–22.

Kennedy, M.D. 2013. "Afterword: Mobilizing Justice Across Hegemonies in Place: Critical Postcommunist Vernaculars," in *Post-Communism from Within: Social Justice, Mobilization, and Hegemony,* ed. J. Kubik and A. Linch. New York: New York University Press, 385–408.

Kocka, J. 2006. "Civil Society from a Historical Perspective," in *Civil Society: Berlin Perspectives,* ed. J. Keane. New York and Oxford: Berghahn Books, 37–50.

Kopecký, P., and C. Mudde. 2003a. *Uncivil Society: Contentious Politics in Post-Communist Europe.* London: Routledge.

Kopecký, P., and C. Mudde. 2003b. "Rethinking Civil Society." *Democratization* 10, no. 3: 1–14.

Korolczuk, E. 2013. "Promoting Civil Society in Contemporary Poland: Gendered Results of Institutional Changes." *VOLUNTAS: International Journal of Voluntary and Nonprofit Organizations* 25, no. 4: 949–967.

———. 2014. "Ruchy społeczne a płeć—perspektywa intersekcjonalna. Kongres Kobiet i ruch na rzecz przywrócenia Funduszu Alimentacyjnego" [Social Movements and Gender—Intersectional Analysis: The Congress of Women and the Alimony Fund Movement]. *Kultura i społeczeństwo* 1: 97–120.

Korolczuk, E., and S. Saxonberg. 2014. "Strategies of Contentious Action: A Comparative Analysis of the Women's Movements in Poland and the Czech Republic." *European Societies* 17, no. 4: 404–422.

Kościański, A., and W. Misztal. 2008. *Społeczeństwo obywatelskie. Między ideą a praktyką* [Civil Society: Between Idea and Practice]. IFiS PAN Publishers, Warsaw.

Kováts, E., and M. Põim, eds. 2015. *Gender as Symbolic Glue: The Position and Role of Conservative and Far Right Parties in The Anti-Gender Mobilizations in Europe.* http://www.feps-europe.eu/assets/cae464d2-f4ca-468c-a93e-5d0dad365a83/feps-gender-as-symbolic-glue-wwwpdf.pdf.

Kowalewski, M. 2013. "Organizowanie miejskiego aktywizmu w Polsce: Kongres Ruchów Miejskich" [Organizing Urban Activism in Poland: Congress of Urban Movements]. *Social Space Journal.* Retrieved 10 November 2015 from http://socialspacejournal.eu.

Krastev, I. 2007. "The Strange Death of the Liberal Consensus." *Journal of Democracy* 18, no. 4: 56–63.

Kraszewski, D., and K. Mojkowski. 2014. *Budżet obywatelski w Polsce* [Participatory Budget in Poland]. Warsawa: Fundacja im. Stefana Batorego. Retrieved 12 November 2015 from http://www.maszglos.pl/wp-content/uploads/2014/03/Budzet-obywatelski-w-Polsce-D.-Kraszewski-K.-Mojkowski.pdf.

Krzemiński, I., ed. 2009. *Czego nas uczy Radio Maryja?* [What Can We Learn from Radio Maria?]. Warszawa: WAiP.

Krześ, A. 2014. "Budżet Obywatelski Jako Inicjatywa Wspierająca Postawę Społeczeństwa obywatelskiego" [Participatory Budgeting as an Initiative Supporting the Attitudes of Civil Society]. *Research Papers of the Wrocław University of Economy* 341: 93–103.

Krzywdzinski, M. 2011. "Trade Unions in Poland. Between Stagnation and Innovation." *Management Revue* 23, no. 1: 66–82.

Kubik, J. 2000. "Between the State and Networks of 'Cousins: The Role of Civil Society and Noncivil Associations in the Democratization of Poland,'" in *Civil Society Before Democracy,* ed. N. Bermeo and P. Nord. Lanham: Rowan and Littlefield Publishers, 181–207.

———. 2005. "How to Study Civil Society: The State of the Art and What to Do Next," *East European Politics and Societies* 19, no. 1: 105–120.

Kubik, J., and A. Linch, eds. 2013. *Post-Communism from Within: Social Justice, Mobilization, and Hegemony.* New York: New York University Press.

Kubik, J. 2015. "Solidarity's Afterlife: Amidst Forgetting and Bickering," in *Polish Solidarity: Social Activism, Regime Collapse, and Building a New Society,* eds A. Rychard and G. Motzkin. Frankurt am Main: Peter Lang Edition. 161–202.

Kubisa, J. 2014. *Bunt Białych Czepków: Analiza Działalności Związkowej Pielęgniarek i Położnych* [White Caps Strike: Analysis of Trade Union Actvity of Nurses and Midwives]. Warszawa: Wydawnictwo Naukowe Scholar.

Lane, D. 2010. "Civil Society in the Old and New Member States." *European Societies* 12, no. 3: 293–315.

Leś, E. 2001. *Zarys Historii Dobroczynności i Filantropii w Polsce* [History of Charity and Philantrophy in Poland]. Warszawa: Prószyński i Spółka.

Lewenstein, B., and M. Theiss. 2008. "Kapitał społeczny, lokalne społeczstwo obywatelskie, aktywizacja: zachodnie koncepcje, polskie doświadczenia" [Social Capital, Local Civil Society, Activism: Western Concepts, Polish Experiences], in *Społeczeństwo obywatelskie. Między teorią a praktyką* [Civil Society: Between Theory and Practice], ed. A. Kościański and W. Misztal. IFiS Publishers, Warsaw, 109–135.

Makowski, G. 2014. "The Main Conclusions and Recommendations," in *The Conflict of Interest in the Polish Government Administration: Legal Regulations, Practice, Attitudes of Public Officers,* ed. G. Makowski, N. Mileszyk, R. Sobiech, A. Stokowska, and G. Wiaderek. Warsaw: Batory Fundation, 11–20.

Masłyk, T. 2013. "Obywatel w Państwie. Normatywna Autonomia i Roszczeniowy Pragmatyzm" [Citizen and the State: Normative Autonomy and Restitutionary Pragmatism]. *Przeglad Socjologiczny* 62, no. 4: 67–94.

Matysiak, I. 2011. "Wiejskie społeczeństwo obywatelskie na przykładzie działalności Sołtysów i Sołtysek" [Rural Civil Society], in *Rozdroża Praktyki i Idei Społeczeństwa Obywatelskiego* [Between Practices and Ideas of Civil Society], ed. A. Kościański and W. Misztal. Warsaw: IFiS Publishers, 155–180.

Mazurek, M. 2012. "Keeping It Close to Home: Resourcefulness and Scarcity in Late Socialist Poland," in *Communism Unwrapped*, ed. P. Bren and M. Neuburger. Oxford: Oxford University Press, 298–320.

Mocek, S., ed. 2014. *Nieodkryty Wymiar III Sektora. Wprowadzenie do Badań nad Nowym Społecznikostwem* [Undiscovered Dimension of the Third Sector: Introduction to Research on New Social Activism]. Warsaw: Collegium Civitas and CAL.

Mulinari, D. 2015. "Human Rights in Argentina: Between Family Memories and Political Identities." *Journal of Civil Society* 11, no. 2: 123–136.

Napiontek, O. 2008. "Społeczeństwo obywateli – o kształceniu obywatelskim w Polsce" [Civil Society: On Civic Education in Poland], in *Społeczeństwo obywatelskie. Między teoria a praktyka* [Civil Society: Between Theory and Practice], ed. A. Kościański and W. Misztal. Warsaw: IFiS Publishers, 170–180.

Narozhna, T. 2004. "Foreign Aid for a Post-euphoric Eastern Europe: The Limitations of Western Assistance in Developing Civil Society." *Journal of International Relations and Development* 7: 243–266.

Nowak, S. 1979. "System wartości społeczeństwa polskiego," [Value system of Polish society] in *Studia Socjologiczne* [Sociological Studies] 4: 261-280.

Okin, Moller S. 1998. "Gender, The Public and the Private," in *Feminism and Politics,* ed. A. Phillips. Oxford, New York: Oxford University Press, 116–141.

Ost, D. 2005. *The Defeat of Solidarity: Anger and Politics in Postcommunist Europe.* Ithaca, N.Y.: Cornell University Press.

Pankowski, R. 2010. *The Populist Radical Right in Poland.* London: Routledge.

Pawlak, M. 2015. "From Sociological Vacuum to Horror Vacui: How Stefan Nowak's Thesis Is Used in Analyses of Polish Society." *Polish Sociological Review* 1, no. 189: 5–26.

Penn, S. 2003. *Podziemie Kobiet* [National Secret: The Women Who Brought Democracy to Poland]. Warszawa: Rosner & Wspólnicy.

Petrova, T., and S. Tarrow. 2007. "Transactional and Participatory Activism in the Emerging European Polity: The Puzzle of East-Central Europe." *Comparative Political Studies* 40, no. 1: 74–94.

Piechota, G. 2015. *Fakty i Mity o Jednym Procencie Podatku: Odpis Podatkowy w Procesie Kreowania Społeczeństwa Obywatelskiego* [Facts and Myths on One Percent: Tax Reduction as Part of the Process of Creating Civil Society]. Kraków: Universitas.

Piotrowski, G. 2009. "Civil Society, Un-Civil Society and the Social Movements." *Interface: Journal for and about Social Movements* 1: 166–189.

Pobłocki, K. 2014. Nowe miasto, nowa dekada? [New City, New Decade?], in *Miasto na żadanie* [City on Demand], ed. Ł. Bukowiecki, M. Obarska, and X. Stańczyk. Warszawa: Wydawnictwo Uniwersytetu Warszawskiego, 53–61.

Polanska, D.V. 2014. "Cognitive Dimension in Cross-Movement Alliances: The Case of Squatting and Tenants' Movements in Warsaw." *Interface: A Journal for and about Social Movements* 6, no. 2: 328–356.

Polanska, D.V., and G. Piotrowski. 2015. "The Transformative Power of Cooperation between Social Movements. Squatting and Tenants' Movements in Poland." *City* 19, no. 2–3: 274–296.

Polanska, D. V., and G. Chimiak. 2016. "Organizing without Organizations. On Informal Social Activism in Poland." *International Journal of Sociology and Social Policy* 36, no. 9–10: 662–679.

Prykowski, Ł. 2011. "Public Consultations and Participatory Budgeting in Local Policy-Making in Poland," in *Learning for Local Democracy: A Study of Local Citizen Participation in Europe,* ed. J. Forbrig. Central and Eastern European Citizens Network, 89–106. Retrieved 12 November 2015 from http://ceecn.net/storage/2011/CALLDE/complete%20study.pdf.

Przewłocka, J. 2012. *Polskie organizacje pozarzadowe 2012.* [Polish Non-governmental Organizations 2012]. Warszawa: Stowarzyszenie Klon/Jawor. Retrieved 12 November 2015 from http://civicpedia.ngo.pl/files/civicpedia.pl/public/FaktyNGO_broszura_full.pdf.

Przewłocka, J., Adamiak, P., and A. Zajac. 2013. *Życie codzienne organizacji pozarzadowych w Polsce* [Everyday Life of Non-governmental Organizations in Poland]. Warszawa: StowarzyszenieKlon/Jawor. Retrieved 12 November 2015 from http://civicpedia.ngo.pl/files/civicpedia.pl/public/2012_Klon_ZycieCodzienneNGO.pdf.

Regulska, J. 2009. "Governance or Self-Governance in Poland? Benefits and Threats 20 Years Later." *International Journal of Politics, Culture & Society* 22, no. 4: 537–556.

Regulska, J., and M. Grabowska. 2013. "Social Justice, Hegemony, and Women's Mobilizations," in *Post-Communism from Within: Social Justice, Mobilization, and Hegemony,* ed. J. Kubik and A. Linch. New York: New York University Press, 139–190.

Rogaczewska, M. 2008. "Polska parafia w obrębie społeczeństwa obywatelskiego" [Polish Parish as Part of Civil Society], *Trzeci Sektor* 15: 30–42.

Sava I. N. 2015. "Introduction: A Second Generation of Grassroots Movements in Central and Eastern Europe?" in *Social Movements in Central and Eastern Europe: A Renewal of Protests and Democracy,* ed. G. Pleyers and I. Sava. Bucharest: Editura Universitatii din Bucuresti, 7–11.

Schlozman, K.L., S. Verba, and H.E. Brady. 2010. "Weapon of the Strong? Participatory Inequality and the Internet." *Perspectives on Politics* 8, no. 2: 487–509.

Scott, J. 1990. *Domination and the Arts of Resistance: Hidden Transcripts.* New Haven and London: Yale University Press.

Scott, J.W., and D. Keates, eds. 2004. *Going Public: Feminism and the Shifting Boundaries of the Private Sphere.* Urbana and Champaign: University of Illinois Press.

Stolle, D., and M. Hooghe. 2005. "Inaccurate, Exceptional, One-sided or Irrelevant? The Debate About the Alleged Decline of Social Capital and Civic Engagement in Western Societies." *British Journal of Political Science* 35, no. 1: 149–167.

Sułek, A. 2009. "Doświadczenia i umiejętności obywatelskie Polaków" [Civic Experiences and the Competence of the Poles], in *Socjologia i Siciński* [Sociology and Siciński], ed. P. Gliński and A. Kościański. Warsaw: IFiS PAN Publishers, 13–25.

Sztompka, P. 1991. "The Intangibles and Imponderables of the Transition to Democracy." *Studies in Comparative Communism* 24, no. 3: 295–311.

———. 1998. "Mistrusting Civility: Predicament of a Post-Socialist Society," in *Real Civil Societies: Dilemmas of Institutionalization*, ed. J. Alexander. London: Sage, 191–210.

Szustek, A. 2008. *Polski sektor społeczny* [Polish Social Sector]. Oficyna Wydawnicza ASPRA-JR: Warsaw.

Szymczak, W. 2008. "Zaufanie społeczne i kondycja społeczeństwa obywatelskiego w Polsce" [Social Trust and the Condition of Civil Society in Poland], in *Civil Society: Between Theory and Practice* [Społeczeństwo obywatelskie. Między teorią a praktyką], ed. A. Kościański and W. Misztal. Warsaw: IFiS Publishers, 151–169.

———. 2011. "Pomiędzy liberalizmem a republikanizmem. W poszukiwaniu polskich idei społeczeństwa obywatelskiego" [Between Liberalism and Republicanism], in *Społeczeństwo obywatelskie. Między teorią a praktyką* [Civil Society: Between Theory and Practice], ed. A. Kościański, and W. Misztal. Warsaw: IFiS Publishers, 47–72.

Torney-Purta, J., R. Lehmann, H. Oswald, and W. Schulz. 2001. *Citizenship and Education in Twenty-Eight Countries: Civic Knowledge and Engagement at Age Fourteen.* Amsterdam. Retrieved 12 October 2015 from http://www2.hu-berlin.de/empir_bf/iea_e1.html.

Trutkowski C., and S. Mandes. 2005. *Kapitał Społeczny w Małych Miastach* [Social Capital in Small Cities]. Warsaw: Wydawnictwo Naukowe SCHOLAR.

Uzzell, D., N. Räthzel, and R. Lundström. 2013. "Are Trade Unions Part of Civil Society? Why? Why Not?" Presentation at VR Seminar, May, Stockholm.

Vinthagen, S., and A. Johansson. 2013. "'Everyday Resistance': Exploration of a Concept and its Theories." *Resistance Studies Magazine* 1: 1–46.

White, Anne. 2006. "Is Civil Society Stronger in Small Towns?," in *Russian Civil Society: A Critical Assessment*, ed. A.B. Evans, L.A. Henry, and L. McIntosh Sundstrom. New York: M.E. Sharpe, 284–304.

Wrzosek, T. 2008. "Młodzież Wszechpolska i Kościół: Uregilijnienie Polityki i Politycyzacja Religijności" [All-Poland Youth: Making Politics Religious and Politicizing Religiosity]. *Societas/Communitas* 2, no. 4: 215–230.

Wygnański, K. 2004. "The Percentage System in Central and Eastern Europe: Implications for Civil Society and Public Philanthropy," in *Percentage Philanthropy*, ed. M. Török and D. Moss. Retrieved 12 November 2015 from http://www.onepercent.hu/Dokumentumok/Poland_changes_in_mechanism.pdf.

Yates, L. 2015. "Everyday Politics, Social Practices and Movement Networks: Daily Life in Barcelona's Social Centres." *The British Journal of Sociology* 66, no. 2: 236–258.

Zagała, Z. 2008. "Miejskie społeczeństwo obywatelskie i jego przemiany" [Civil Society in the City and Its Changes], in *Civil Society: Between Theory and Practice* [Społeczeństwo obywatelskie. Między teorią a praktyką], ed. A. Kościański and W. Misztal. Warsaw: IFiS Publishers, 219–234.

Załeski, P.S. 2012. *Neoliberalizm i społeczeństwo obywatelskie* [Neoliberalism and Civil Society]. Toruń: Wydawnictwo Naukowe Uniwersytetu Mikołaja Kopernika.

Żuk, P. 2001. *Społeczeństwo w działaniu. Ekolodzy, feministki, skłotersi* [Society in the Making: Ecologists, Feminists, Squatters]. Warsaw: Wydawnictwo Naukowe Scholar.

PART I

Civil Society in Contemporary Poland: Myths and Realities

Chapter 1

CIVIL SOCIETY IN POSTCOMMUNIST EUROPE
POLAND IN A COMPARATIVE PERSPECTIVE

Grzegorz Ekiert and Jan Kubik

Introduction

The condition and role of civil society in East Central Europe after 1989 is one of the most misunderstood aspects of postcommunist transformations. The prevailing wisdom has it that decades of communist rule destroyed foundations of civic life and dramatically diminished the capacity of the civic sphere to regenerate itself, and that as a result civil society—conventionally seen as an indispensable pillar of a democratic system—has been too weak to play any significant role in shaping emerging democracy and the market economy or to prevent authoritarian reversals. Thus, the countries that managed to successfully democratize have done so through reforms from above, supported by powerful international actors, and without any significant input from civil society.

Ralf Dahrendorf formulated the most influential version of this argument when shortly after the revolutions of 1989 he famously quipped: "It takes six months to create new political institutions, to write a constitution and electoral laws. It may take six years to create a half-viable economy. It will probably take sixty years to create civil society. Autonomous institutions are the hardest to bring about" (Dahrendorf 1990: 42). Dahrendorf's claim was startlingly provocative, since the 1989 collapse of communist regimes was seen at that time as a heroic victory of civil society over the ossified and repressive party states. Communism did not disappear because of a defeat in a war, but it was smashed by citizen movements animated by liberal ideas and a longing for political and civic rights that only democracy can guarantee. And yet Dahrendorf's thesis took hold. Paradoxically, as many of the postcommunist polities have been becoming more democratic and liberal, complaints about the weakness of their civil societies have been growing louder (Howard 2003; Celichowski 2004; Sissenich 2007; Bernhard and Karakoc 2007).

Most of the early empirical comparative research on civil society in postcommunism reaffirmed the Dahrendorf thesis that has acquired the status of received wisdom applicable to all societies and countries that emerged from the communist rule. This view persisted despite the existing evidence of considerable variance in political, economic, and social outcomes across the region, including the growing disparity in the condition of civil society (see below). The systemic weakness of postcommunist civil societies has been demonstrated mostly through an analysis of several cross-national surveys of attitudes: the World Value Survey and similar cross-European surveys. This is surprising since there is a wide range of other data that are easily available and can shed light on civil society development and transformations, such as public opinion surveys on volunteering and membership in civil society organizations conducted at the national level, registers of organizations, expert assessments, protest event analysis, and case studies. Taken together, these sources make it possible to assess the state of civil society—most importantly its activities across the region—with greater precision than cross-national surveys of attitudes alone.[1] As David Kertzer (1988: 68) once noted: "socially and politically speaking, we are what we do, not what we think."

In this chapter, we will make a number of interconnected claims that challenge the prevailing wisdom according to which the state of civil society is more or less uniform in the whole region and uniformly weak.[2] This diagnosis is based on four errors: (1) it underestimates the significance of legacies of communist associationism in at least some countries of the region, (2) it minimizes the differences between the countries, (3) it does not pay enough attention to the changing nature of postcommunist civil societies over time, and (4) it relies on limited and questionable empirical evidence. There is no room here to offer full empirical support for our arguments regarding the whole region, so we will illustrate our points with selected data from Poland. Since Poland had a specific crisis-driven trajectory and powerful tradition of protest under communist rule, it is often conceived as a unique or exceptional case. In our view, however, the developments in Poland tend to reveal and magnify the phenomena and trends common to a subset of countries located in Central Europe. These countries have become even more similar to each other over the last two decades or so, following the fall of state socialism, as they have experienced massive institutional transformations and standardization as a result of accession to the European Union.[3]

This chapter is organized in three sections. First, we analyze the origin of postcommunist civil societies, emphasizing the communist legacy and focusing mostly on Poland.[4] Second, we explore differences among really existing civil societies in the region along several crucial dimensions. In the conclusion, we challenge three "myths" about civil society in postcommunism and assess the role of civil societies in democratization. We also provide answers to some pressing questions of the day concerning the role of civil society in undermining authoritarian rule and in facilitating regime change, as well as the impact of civil society on the policies of governments and the quality of democracy, particularly after regime change.

Origin of Postcommunist Civil Societies: Inheritance, Organizational Expansion, and Recombination

Postcommunist countries did not inherit from the old regime a civil society. Yet, they—particularly Poland—inherited a comprehensive and solidly institutionalized associational sphere. It included powerful trade unions and professional organizations, organized churches, and organizational representations of various groups and interests, including youth, farmers, veterans, consumers, women, and ecologists. There were also recreational, cultural, and leisure organizations, sports clubs, and many others. These organizations had large membership, massive resources, national headquarters, local branches across the country, and professional personnel with considerable organizational skills.

State-socialist countries had a distinct (politicized, bureaucratized, centralized, and comprehensive) regime of associational life that recognized and institutionalized diverse interests. In fact, the existence of such a regime was a defining element of totalitarianism (and particularly post-totalitarianism) and constituted one of the most fundamental institutional differences between the communist Eastern Europe and other regions or countries dominated by different authoritarian regimes (Riley and Fernández 2014). Since the 1960s, mass organizations controlled by the communists were less ideological and often functioned as effective "interest groups" able to lobby the party-state and extract from it various economic concessions for their members, especially in the more pragmatic and reformist countries, such as Hungary and Poland. In orthodox Czechoslovakia and East Germany or semitotalitarian Romania and Albania these organizations still served as traditional "transmission belts" and their autonomy and capacity to represent interests were seriously constrained. This diversity of inherited practices, which had evolved along a distinct trajectory in each country, despite the common "communist" institutional form, is one of the factors explaining the broad range of post-1989 real civil societies in the region.

The associational sphere in communist Poland underwent the deepest transformations in the region. It became gradually more diverse, less controlled by the communist state, and even more pluralistic, particularly after 1956 (Ekiert 1996; Ekiert and Kubik 1999). Poland also experienced a number of political crises involving significant mobilization from below by various segments of society (workers, students, intellectuals, peasants, Catholics), culminating in the emergence in 1980 of the massive Solidarity movement and its suppression in 1981. As a result, the associational landscape of Poland was not populated exclusively by centralized mass organizations. Some precommunist civil society traditions and even organizations (mostly in the realms of leisure, education, and culture) survived under communist rule, especially at the local level (Kurczewska 2004; Gąsior-Niemiec and Gliński 2007). They served as semiofficial carriers of local traditions and provided a modicum of public space somewhat sheltered from direct political interference of the Communist Party. Moreover, the powerful Polish Catholic Church secured considerable autonomy and supported various movements and organizations. Thus, by the mid 1980s, Poland had what can be described as *incomplete civil society* with a relatively numerous and a dense structure of organizations at various levels and in all functional domains. This incipient civil society was incomplete, for it did not have much autonomy and was not ensconced in a legally delineated public space, protected by enforceable rights and liberties. Several other communist countries (Hungary, Czechoslovakia, Slovenia, and the Baltic states) had smaller dissident sectors of informal/oppositional/independent political, religious, and cultural movements and organizations alongside the communist-controlled formal associations.

These organizational resources, both formal and informal, provided a foundation for the reformulation of civil society after 1989, as many associations previously controlled by the Communist Party instituted complex and, by and large, successful reforms that allowed them to adapt to new democratic conditions. They often lost a significant portion of their members and resources, frequently split into smaller organizations, and changed their names, leaders, and agendas. Yet, many of these organizations survived the transition to democracy and managed to protect most of the resources they had had before 1989.

More importantly, the collapse of communism spawned the organizational revolution within the domain of civil society, often initiated and sustained by generous international assistance. In the midst of mass political mobilization associated with regime change, scores of new movements and organizations burst onto the public stage. These newcomers appeared mostly in sectors disallowed under communism (for example, NGOs, charities, and foundations), but quite a few entered the existing sectors and began competing directly with the inherited organizations (independent trade unions and new professional associations). Many of these organizations failed to secure resources and attract members and disappeared as quickly as they emerged, especially in the sectors of civil society where they faced competition from the former communist-era organizations.

Since 1989 the number of civil society organizations has been growing rapidly across the region and it has been particularly impressive in Poland. As Figure 1.1 shows, an average of some 4,000 new NGOs and some 1,000 foundations have been registered every year.

Moreover, Polish civil society emerged as a highly diverse space representing all interests, ideological orientations, and organizational forms. Its organizational growth has been balanced across all sectors of civil society. While the most spectacular growth was observed in the NGO sector, other sectors also show clear gains. Polish civil society organizations are also well distributed geographically (only 24 percent of all organizations are based in large cities while 20 percent are active in villages), and many tend to be equally dynamic on the national and local levels. The sector of NGOs and foundations is clearly stronger in western and northern Poland, while voluntary fire brigades and religious organizations are more prevalent in the central and eastern parts of the country (Przewłocka et al. 2013: 29–31). These two types

Figure 1.1. Number of new associations (top line) and foundations (bottom line) registered every year in Poland: 1989–2012

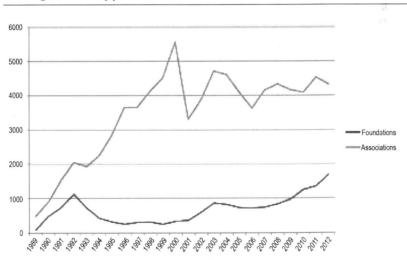

(Source of data: Przewłocka et al. 2013: 27)

of civic activity correspond, arguably, to two different forms of civicness: one more "modern" (NGOs), the other more "traditional" (voluntary fire brigades and religious organizations). It is not clear that one is "better" than other, although the literature on civil society clearly privileges the former. What we have here is not the problem of *inequality in civicness*, but rather *two different types of civic cultures* mediated by different organizational vehicles and embedded in different normative orientations. This picture of organizational effervescence is generally similar in other countries of Central Europe (Mansfeldova et al. 2004; Nagy and Sebesteny 2008; Kuti 2010).

Yet, the differences in timing, rates of emergence, and sectoral composition of civil societies across the postcommunist region have been considerable. They reflect, first, the political conditions in each country. The organizational growth was instant and most dynamic in countries that experienced early and successful transition to democracy. In the authoritarian postcommunist countries the associational revolution was either comparatively weaker or nearly absent. Today (2016), it is estimated that Russia has around 227,652 registered NGOs, while Belarus has 2,607, Uzbekistan has an "unknown" number, and Turkmenistan "slightly over 100" (NGO Law Monitor).

The revamping of the legal and regulatory foundations of civil society was crucial as well. In the 1990s, all the countries of East Central Europe began a major overhaul of legislation pertaining to rights of assembly, freedom of association, public gatherings, nonprofit status, etc., in order to create a civil society–friendly legal environment. Major legislative acts were introduced in rapid succession and were changed and amended frequently. In Poland, fundamental guaranties of freedom of assembly and association were secured in 1989 and 1990 and enshrined in the 1997 Constitution. The acts regulating civil society activities inherited from the old regime were amended and new legislation relating to charitable activities and volunteering was introduced, creating a civil society–friendly legal environment and financial incentives. Similarly, Hungary had eight major legislative acts regulating the functioning of foundations between 1987 and 2003. By 2003 there were 19,700 foundations in Hungary, but only 363 in the Czech Republic, a country of similar size and level of development (Lagerspetz and Skovajsa 2006). This difference reflects the different requirements and incentives provided by law in these two countries. In contrast to the developments in Central Europe, in the authoritarian countries the legal rules were used to restrict the public space and curtail the activities of civil society organizations. The recent Russian changes in registration procedures and restrictions on financing civil society organizations from abroad illustrate this trend well (Chebankova 2013; Greene 2014).

In organizational terms, civil society in Poland and the civil societies of other Central European countries are dense, diverse, and not significantly different from civil societies in some established European democracies.[5] Yet, differences between new member states of the EU and other postcommunist countries, particularly the post-Soviet states, are massive. In authoritarian countries such as Belarus the inherited associational sector is dominant while the emergence of new organizations is highly constrained. Similarly, the level of institutionalization of the new civil society sectors varies. In fully consolidated democracies civil societies are highly institutionalized and enjoy legal protections, but in authoritarian and hybrid regimes new civil society operates more as a "dissident" social movement network that is mobilized in response to major state violations of legal or electoral rules, or governmental efforts to change existing regulation in a more authoritarian direction. The so-called "color revolutions" that occurred in several countries and sporadic protest waves in Russia and Belarus are good examples.

In sum, the actual emergence of postcommunist civil societies has been a combination of two processes: the institutional adjustment within the inherited associational sphere and the emergence of the new organizations and sectors. These two developments, rapid and sustained in some countries, such as Poland, and rather anemic in others, resulted in *recombined civil societies*. Their features in each country are shaped by the type, speed, and outcome of democratization, but also by specific institutional incentives and historical traditions. Thus, the claim that postcommunist civil societies had to be created from scratch, in all their dimensions, is obviously incorrect. On the other hand, the conversion patterns of the inherited sector of civil society and the speed and breadth of organizational creation have varied considerably and resulted in the divergent trajectories of civil society developments across the postcommunist world.

Postcommunist Civil Society—One or Many?

Jacques Rupnik once noted that "the word 'postcommunism' lost its relevance. The fact that Hungary and Albania, or Czech Republic and Belarus, or Poland and Kazakhstan shared a communist past explains very little about the paths that they have taken since" (Rupnik 1999: 57). This observation applies to the civil society sphere as well. Civil societies in the postcommunist world differ along several dimensions and this diversity is shaped by a variety of factors (Ekiert and Foa 2012). One of these conditions is the country-specific communist inheritance in the associational sphere and uneven intensity of organizational growth that followed the collapse of communist rule discussed above. Postcommunist countries differ also due to the different historical traditions of civil society, dating back to their emergence as nation-states in the nineteenth and early twentieth centuries. Thus, differences in civil society's density among European countries must be at least partially attributed to their specific cultural traditions and legal regulations and cannot be derived solely from the characteristics of the communist regime. Finally, civil societies are shaped by increasingly divergent contemporary political conditions. Thus, postcommunism produced an entire range of civil society types, some of which are assertive and robust while others are anemic and severely constrained by their respective states.

In contrast to studies of public opinion, evaluations produced by expert panels emphasize considerable variance in civil society condition and capacity across the postcommunist region. The World Bank Governance Index shows that in the new members of the EU—particularly in Estonia, Poland, and Slovenia—civil society's organizational composition and its role in providing citizens with voice and the capacity to make their states increasingly accountable is not much worse than that in Western Europe. It is actually better than in some countries, such as Italy and Greece (World Bank 2013). The USAID 2012 report on the sustainability of civil society organizations also documents diverse and diverging paths of civil society development. The ex-communist members of European Union score 2.7 on average, with Estonia (2.0), Poland (2.2), and Czech Republic (2.6) leading the pack. The countries of Eurasia (Russia, West NIS, and Caucasus) score 4.4, and the five states of Central Asia score, on average, 5.0 (The 2012 CSO). Freedom House's experts rating the strength of civil society from 1 to 7, 1 being the strongest, confirm growing diversification in the region. The average score for new EU members in 2012 was 1.95, with *Poland achieving the strongest result of 1.50.* For the Balkans, the average score was 3.04, and for the Eurasian States it was 5.28, with Turkmenistan and Uzbekistan sharing the dubious privilege of achieving the weakest possible grade of 7 (Freedom House 2013).[6]

In short, a systematic comparison of existing postcommunist civil societies shows different patterns of transformation, diverging paths of organizational expansion, and growing intraregional disparities. A more systematic analysis shows that these civil societies differ from each other along at least four crucial dimensions:

- Constitution of public space and the access of civil society organizations to policy making
- Forms of civil society, its composition, and its organization
- Patterns of civil society's behavior
- Dominant normative orientation of civil society actors

Constitution of Public Space

The constitution of public space in a given country is determined by many factors, among which the relationship between civil society and the state is most important. The state and its agencies define the parameters of public space by issuing laws, building (or not) institutions, protecting or disregarding rights and liberties and implementing policies that can either constrain or empower civil society organizations. The health, composition, and capacity of civil society depend on these institutional strictures. They vary across the formerly communist space and thus generate different types of civil societies.

Although none of the postcommunist countries has a regime that prohibits all activity by autonomous organizations of civil society, some states, such as Belarus, Uzbekistan, and Turkmenistan, come close to such an extreme regime type. The situation of independent civic actors in these countries recalls the period of 1970s and 1980s in Central Europe when civil society was not totally suppressed, but rather severely constrained and repressed by "friendly" means. In fact, these countries have an incomplete "dissident" civil society, resembling the pre-1989 situation in Poland, Czechoslovakia, and Hungary.

A less extreme authoritarian condition exists in several other countries of the region. There, civil society organizations are allowed to exist, but their activities are subjected to arbitrary restrictions. Some organizations, especially newly created NGOs, are marginalized while others (often with ex-communist pedigrees) are rewarded with special relations with the state, including state financing. So, state corporatism—combined with arbitrary restrictions of specific civil society sectors in such areas as registration procedures, funding, types of activity allowed, and international contacts—is the norm. In Russia, for example, such restrictions have been increasingly severe even though, as several authors argue, Russian civil society is still capable of resistance, as evidenced by the persistent protest waves of the last several years (Aron 2013; Beissinger and Sasse 2013; Greene 2014; Smyth et al. 2013).

Finally, in the countries that entered the European Union, the rule of law protects civil society actors and their actions quite effectively and civil society organizations are often supported and financed by the state and external sources. In general, the situation in Central Europe is not that different from the situation in quite a few established democracies of the "Western" part of the continent. In many new member states, certainly in Poland, civil society organizations are formally incorporated into policy decision making and governance, especially at the local level. These organizations are also routinely involved in lobbying and sometimes engage in contentious actions to influence policy making both locally and nationally, although their effectiveness still does not match that of their counterparts in Western Europe (Gąsior-Niemiec 2010; Petrova 2007).

The diversity in constitution of public space in the postcommunist world is well documented. For example, according to the Bertelsmann analysts, "association/assembly rights" in 2015 were of the highest quality (scores 9–10) in all eleven ex-communist members of the EU, while all of the thirteen post-Soviet states scored only 8 or less (in the total set of 129 analyzed "transforming" countries, only 25 percent of them achieved the highest score of 9 or 10). Also, protection of civil rights under the rule of law was assessed to be much firmer in the seventeen countries of postcommunist Europe than in the whole set of countries undergoing transformations (Bertelsmann 2015).[7] In 2015, Freedom House used a 16-point scale to assess "Associational and Organizational Rights" in 195 countries and 15 territories. The mean score for the 210 political units of the world was 7.34. It was much higher for the countries of East Central Europe: 11.6. It was, however, quite dismal for the post-Soviet Eurasia: 1.8.[8]

To summarize, in several postcommunist countries—mostly in Central Europe—the formation of full-fledged public spheres was possible due to the development of solid democratic guarantees of the rule of law and creation of the civil society–friendly regulatory environment. In such countries civil society has become stronger, more diversified, incorporated into governance procedures, and politically consequential than in the authoritarian or semiauthoritarian regimes, predominant among the countries that emerged from the Soviet Union. As a result, in East Central Europe—most definitely in Poland, notwithstanding intensifying ideological polarization after 2015—civil societies are secure, organizationally diverse, relatively well funded from both domestic and external sources, and effectively connected to transnational civil society networks.

Dominant Forms of Civil Society, Its Composition, and Organization

Although the differences in the guarantees of rights and liberties and in the predictability and friendliness of the institutional environment constitute the crucial dimension of diversity across the region, forms of civil society organization and levels of institutionalization differ as well.

Countries of East Central Europe entered regime transition with an "old-fashioned" associational domain based on centralized trade unions and professional organizations embedded in state-corporatist arrangements. As noted before, the crux of the post-1989 change was the transformation of this old associational sector *combined* with the emergence of a diverse NGO sector and other social organizations prohibited by the old regime, including religious and nationalist associations. The pace and extent of this process varied significantly across the region, as the state corporatist arrangements remained influential in some countries, while in others they began to wither away.

One of the most important dimensions of civil society recasting was the waning of trade unions. Although this trend is not limited to the region, the decline of union membership in postcommunist countries has been faster than in the countries of Western Europe or the United States. This is due to three sets of factors: country-specific, system-specific, and global. The most important factor is system-specific: the changing role of trade unions in post-transformation economies. Under state socialism, union membership was essentially automatic, with density close to 100 percent as unions were charged with distributing many in-kind benefits. The high membership figures under the old regime do not indicate the ability or willingness to self-organize and engage in policy battles. It is also important to remember that the declining union membership reveals a shift from corporatist strategies of interest representation and the endorsement of a neoliberal model by many postcommunist states.

Yet, the trade union movement did not collapse entirely. While the levels of union membership in East Central Europe declined significantly over the last twenty-five years, the resultant level varies from country to country and in some postcommunist states is not drastically different from many West European countries.[9] The political influence of the unions is no longer founded on mass membership, but on their organizational strength, the tradition of union–state relations, and their relationship with the parties of the left (if they are strong) (Sil 2013a). Polish trade unions, for example, are numerically weak and divided, but they are vocal and sometimes quite effective in opposing changes in government welfare or labor policies. Again, the most significant dividing line across the postcommunist world runs between the new EU members from East Central Europe and the majority of the post-Soviet states, but in a recent study, the Russian labor sector was shown to be more effective than is usually assumed (Sil 2013b).

The relationship between the inherited associational sphere and the new, post-transition civil society sectors is not the only source of difference between postcommunist civil societies. Another is the nature of state–civil society relations. We observe here two distinct patterns: pluralist and corporatist, whose geographic distribution does not always conform to subregional divisions. In Central Europe, Poland is the example of predominantly pluralist relations while Slovenia and Hungary are largely corporatist, with other countries falling between these two poles. Countries in other subregions, especially those with authoritarian regimes, have restored state-corporatist forms. These patterns shape the rate of organizational growth, privilege certain types of organizations, and influence forms of competition and the intensity of contentiousness instigated by civil society organizations (CSOs).

Postcommunist civil societies differ from each other also in terms of the form of institutionalization and the level of centralization. Persistence and relative significance of informal groups, while common, is especially pronounced in less democratic and authoritarian countries. Social movements and sporadic popular mobilizations are the most consequential forms of civil society activity in such countries, while in postcommunist democracies formal organizations, NGOs, unions, and professional organizations dominate. What is also common to postcommunist civil societies is the fragmentation and decentralization of their organizational structures and patterns of action. This feature makes the situation in postcommunist countries different from the historical patterns observed in the West. This may be, however, a more general feature of contemporary civil societies, not a specific trait of postcommunism.

The politics of identity penetrates postcommunist civil societies unevenly. In some countries, especially those with ethnic and religious divisions, the salience of collective identity influences the matrix of civil society organizations and their activities more prominently than in others. It is reflected in a more influential role of religious or nationalistic organizations and movements and higher visibility of conflicts among organizations representing various identities. The distribution of identity-related tensions and conflicts does not conform to subregional divisions. The difference between Poland and the Czech Republic may be as significant as it is between Poland and Ukraine.

In sum, civil societies in postcommunist countries are dissimilar and diverse, across time and space. Their structures and strategies depend on many factors, the type of political regime being most decisive. The condition of civil society in authoritarian countries such as Belarus resembles the situation known from the post-totalitarian phase of communism. There is an *official sector* of state-controlled labor unions and other mass organizations and there is a *dissident civil society* engaged in the struggle against the nondemocratic regime. In the countries that entered the European Union, civil society is quite diverse and vibrant and not much different from its counterparts in many countries of the old EU. But even there, civil society has several features that may be unique for the postcommunist condition. First, many sectors of postcommunist civil societies are *not centralized* to the same degree as they are in the Western or Northern Europe. A good example of this difference is the sector of women's organizations (Regulska and Grabowska 2013). Second, many voluntary civic activities are organized in an *informal manner* via networks of neighbors, circles of friends, etc. In fact, postcommunist civil societies of East Central Europe are not passive or organizationally anemic; but they are often structured differently than in the West and their activities may easily escape the attention of some Western observers (Kubik 2013).

Patterns of Civil Society Behavior

To understand civil society's role and evaluate its "strength"—understood as a pillar of democracy—in a specific country it is imperative to examine the activities of various groups of actors. To learn about them we need to focus in particular on politically relevant forms of action such as lobbying and protest. Studies of public opinion aimed at determining membership in voluntary organizations or rates of volunteering are insufficient (see, e.g., Bernhard and Karakoc 2007); so are data from NGO registers used to determine the density of civil society. In general, instead of measuring civil society's "strength" by counting the number of organizations per capita or accepting the declaration of survey participants at face value, we need to assess the rate and form of civic engagement in political and public life and the effectiveness of linkages with other areas of the polity (Bermeo and Nord 2000).

One way to study this engagement is to focus on contentious politics. In some countries, collective actors are more prone to challenge authorities and to employ contentious forms of behavior to pursue their interests. In others, cooperation between the state and civil society is extensive, often institutionalized, and the level of political contention is lower. Such patterns are shaped not only by institutional arrangements but also by legacies of past interactions between the state and society. Accordingly, one can distinguish between *contentious* and *accommodating* civil societies. During the first decade of transformations Poland had a contentious civil society, while most other countries had significantly lower level of contention. This trend has flipped in recent years (Szelenyi and Wilk 2013). As Figure 1.2 shows, magnitude of contention in Poland measured as the number of protest days declined significantly, although the number of protest events has not showed a similar consistent decline (see also Figure 1.3). This simply means that protests in Poland in the first decade of 2000s were smaller and shorter than those at the beginning of post-1989 transformations.[10] Other countries such as Hungary or Bulgaria have become more contentious than Poland.

What explains the changes in the dominant mode of civil society's behavior? The most important factor seems to be the country's type of political regime (authoritarian, semiauthoritarian, or democratic) and its specific features, such as the structure and consolidation of the party system. In countries where the party system works well both as an aggregator of inter-

Figure 1.2. Declining magnitude of protest in Poland
(number of protest days yearly)

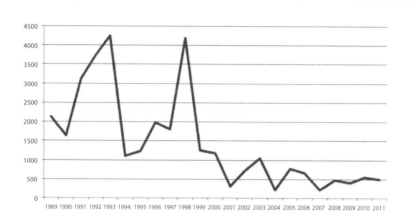

ests and the mechanism for exerting political pressure on the government, the political role of civil society is predominantly complementary. In unstable party contexts, for example in Poland, civil society tends to become supplementary. In the postcommunist world the supplementary function predominates, for two distinct reasons. One is the general decline of political parties that postcommunist Europe shares with many countries. In the postcommunist EU members, party systems are not fully consolidated and are sometimes volatile; as a result civil society actors often take on the role

Figure 1.3. Number of protest events in Poland
(number of events yearly)

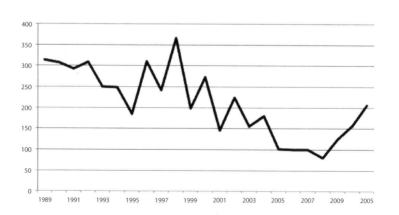

of policy-articulating protagonists in contentious disputes with the government. Second, in authoritarian and semi-authoritarian countries, periodic waves of protest and "dissident" types of activities replace the nonexistent or weak interest representation via political parties (Russia, Ukraine, and the countries of Central Asia).

Although postcommunist civil societies are no strangers to political involvement, due to the lack of clear alternatives to a market economy and democracy, civil society actors rarely engage in anti-systemic mobilization. We called this phenomenon *contentious reformism* in our study of the early years of Polish democratic consolidation (Ekiert and Kubik 1999), but it is quite common across the region. During the first fifteen or so years of postcommunist transformations, civil societies in the region have been by and large liberal-minded and moderate, both in their demands and dominant strategies of action. In authoritarian and semiauthoritarian regimes, the bulk of "dissident" civic actions have focused on securing political freedoms and expanding the public sphere in which citizens can (safely) engage their governments. In democratic countries, most organizations have been supportive of liberal democracy and market economy and have focused their actions on improving the mechanisms of representation and governance.

Dominant Normative Orientation

Several countries of the region, particularly those with autocratic or weak democratic regimes, experienced waves of popular mobilization, triggered by outrage directed at corrupt politicians, rigged democratic procedures, inept administrations, and sluggish economic growth. By far the most spectacular wave of protests came to be known as "color revolutions": Serbia's *Bulldozer Revolution* (2000), Georgia's *Rose Revolution* (2003), Ukraine's *Orange Revolution* (2004), and Kyrgyzstan's *Tulip Revolution* (Hale 2005; Beissinger 2007; Tucker 2007; Bunce and Volchik 2011). They were often organized around the principles of social justice and political rights, recently reinvigorated in Russia, where protestors challenged Putin's regime in the name of "honor, decency, dignity, and conscience" (Aron 2013: 64).

The normative and political orientations in the postcommunist world have begun to change since 2006–2008. Reformism anchored partially in a neoliberal consensus has started fading away and distinctly populist and sometimes radically right-wing parties and movements have become more visible. Growing numbers of people are turning to them for ideological explanations and organizational vehicles needed to channel their rising discontent and frustrations triggered by the worldwide economic crisis and a series of political scandals, often related to political corruption.

This turn to the right is well documented.[11] It is, however, important to remember that the acceptance of right-wing, populist ideologies is very uneven across the postcommunist region. In some countries, such as Ukraine, Bulgaria, Latvia, and Hungary, the number of potential supporters of far-right parties and movements is the highest in Europe. But in Poland, Estonia, and Slovenia it seems to be more moderate, actually lower than in Italy and Portugal (Derex Index 2010). Our own work on protest politics in Hungary and Poland provides additional evidence for significant disparities. While since 2008 in both countries there has been a noticeable increase of protest actions organized by right-wing groups and the public space has become more saturated with right-wing rhetoric, the pace of growth and the extent of popular support for these types of ideologies has been more extensive in Hungary than in Poland.

In sum, in many countries of the region there has been the rise of right-wing radicalization, coalescing around the slogans of national purification, opposition to the EU, and return to "true values." As a result civil societies have become increasingly polarized in their normative orientations. It is not clear how politically destructive this polarization will prove to be. The left leaning and centrist civil society organizations mobilized in Poland in 2016. It is, however, unknown whether such counter-mobilization will emerge in other countries of the region.

Conclusions

There are three persistent myths about post-1989 civil societies in former communist countries. We challenge them all. First, as we have shown, post-communist civil societies *were not built from scratch.* To a significant degree they were based on associational spheres inherited from the old regime and on the organizational traditions going back to the precommunist period.

Second, some comparative analyses of European civil societies suggest that a new type of civil society emerged in postcommunist countries. It is supposedly different from the continental, Anglo-Saxon, or Nordic types and its roots are in the common communist past and the specific nature of 1989–1991 revolutions (Archambault 2009). We argue the opposite. There is no convergence to a single model. To the contrary, there is a growing divergence in sectoral composition, behavior, normative orientations of civil society actors, and the dominant type of relations between them and their respective states. These differences reflect not only long-standing historical traditions of various subregions of the former Soviet bloc and contrasting outcomes of postcommunist transformations, but also new divisions of the European space generated by the EU enlargements.

Finally, we also challenge the well-established myth that postcommunist civil societies are systemically weak. While strength and weakness are not very useful categories, we have shown above that some civil societies in the region have dense and comprehensive organizational structures, operate in a relatively "friendly" institutional and legal environment, and have some capacity to influence policy making on local and national levels. In other postcommunist countries, especially those that reverted to various forms of authoritarian rule, civil societies are often organizationally weak and politically irrelevant. Civil society actors are excluded from routine consultation and governance and come together to influence politics only in extraordinary moments of rage triggered by economic downturns or gross violations of laws and constitutional provisions by their states.

To conclude, we wish to return to two questions dominating debates on civil society. Is civil society necessary to undermine authoritarian rule and to facilitate regime change? And what is the impact of civil society on the policies of governments and the quality of democracy, particularly after regime change? Experiences of postcommunist countries shed much light on these questions.

In general, we agree with Philippe Schmitter (2010) that the role of civil society in precipitating the regime change is not significant (see also Kotkin 2013). Except for Poland, there is no convincing evidence that *organized* civil society contributed to the collapse of communist regimes. In 1989, however, several countries in Eastern Europe experienced cascading cycles of mobilization that tipped the balance of power and contributed to the collapse of the old system. As a result, several countries of Eastern Europe (Poland, Czechoslovakia, Hungary, Slovenia, the Baltic states) had influential civil societies *around the time of regime transition* and a comparative study shows that the strength of civil society during that period is associated with a higher quality of liberal democracy, faster and more robust post-transitional economic recovery, and a lower level of social inequality years later (Bernhard and Kaya 2013).

The experience of postcommunism shows that civil society does play an important role in the consolidation of democracy. After twenty-five years of massive transformations, civil societies in the postcommunist region of Europe have come a long way, building their organizational capacity and ability to influence both policy making and politics. In many countries, in Poland perhaps most prominently, civil society organizations have been shaping political and economic developments through contention, voluntary activities, and assorted consultative arrangements. For example, Polish trade unions and farmer organizations were able to defeat or delay many economic and social reform projects and policies. In other countries, civil society organizations resisted authoritarian reversals and electoral fraud (color revolutions) and made rulers more accountable even in countries that have become authoritarian (Bunce and Wolchik 2011). Case studies and anecdotal evidence demonstrate the impact of civil society organizations on the design and implementation of specific policies (labor, environmental, human rights, minority rights, women's rights, etc.).

What is most striking, however, is the disparity of paths and outcomes. There are three types of situations in the postcommunist space. Under authoritarianism—in such countries as Belarus, Turkmenistan, Tajikistan, and Uzbekistan—independent civil society organizations are persecuted, numerically weak, poorly institutionalized, and often resemble the incomplete dissident civil societies of the pre-1989 era (Kendzior 2012). In semiauthoritarian regimes—Russia and Ukraine being the best examples—independent citizens' activities via NGOs have been often subjected to harassment and governmental interference (Lanskoy and Suthers 2013), but social movements have managed to make their mark on public life via waves of protest actions. Moreover, many authoritarian governments have learned to live side by side their (often truncated) civil societies and effectively manage the crucial aspects of their mutual relations (Krastev 2011; Greene 2014). It is not the end of civil society but rather the institutionalization of a situation in which civil society actors remain inconsequential in shaping most if not all policy outcomes.

The most dynamic and sustained growth of civil society has occurred in the democratic states of postcommunist Central Europe, although in terms of numbers of organizations these civil societies are not as strong as those in the older democracies of Western Europe, particularly its northern tier. There are, however, several areas, including the legal architecture of public sphere or transnational networking, in which some Central European civil societies do not differ much from their Western European counterparts and are ahead of such Southern European states as Greece, Portugal, and Italy. In some countries, people have already developed an intimate sense of closeness with civil society actors. In Poland (but also in Romania, and Hungary) people declare that they "share the values or interests" of civil society organizations and "trust them to act in the right way to influence political decision-making" more often than the average citizen of the EU (European Commission 2013). They also acknowledge that civil society organizations have a significant impact on policy making in their respective countries.

And, finally, two thoughts on the current challenges facing civil societies in the region. The political and economic crises that have engulfed the world since 2008 have clearly influenced the situation of civil societies. The relationships between the state and civil society in many countries have become tenser as the governments have become less responsive to civil society demands or more repressive. In this climate, many civil society organizations have resorted to contention and embraced right-wing populism as their political program. Years ago, Bela Greskovits marveled over the patience of Eastern European publics subjected to massive and often painful social and political transformations. Given the recent intense wave of protest that swept the postcommunist countries, one might ask: *is the end of this patience coming?* Beissinger and Sasse, who confront this question head on, answer: it depends. "In Tolstoyan fashion, those 'happy' countries that continued to experience economic growth in the midst of global crisis were all little affected by protest, while those 'unhappy' countries that experienced significant economic contractions were all 'unhappy' in their own ways, displaying quite varied protest responses to economic decline," they conclude (2013: 363–364). But recent political changes and mass protests in Poland (the country least affected by the economic crisis in Europe) may foreshadow a new cycle of popular mobilizations triggered by the reduced capacity of many European governments to satisfy their publics' expectations and thus buy social peace.

The second issue is arguably most important. *Do we observe the end of moderation in the behavior and ideological orientation of civil society actors?* The recent upsurge of political radicalization, extremism, and aggressive rhetoric is uncontestable. But these developments are unevenly distributed throughout the postcommunist world and while some countries in Eastern Europe record the highest intensity of right-wing sentiment on the continent, some others, like Poland, do not differ at all from the West, and their civil societies are far less "extreme" than those in other regions of the world (for example, the Middle East). In short, many postcommunist civil societies, including Poland, made considerable progress in building autonomous institutions and securing a role in shaping the policy decisions of their respective states. Yet, this does not mean that the gains cannot be reversed. It has already occurred in Russia and as the present Polish and Hungarian developments suggest may occur even in the democratic member state of the European Union.

Notes

1. The most recent and truly comprehensive large-N study concludes that there is no evidence that civil society in the postcommunist world is weak or underdeveloped compared with that in other regions of the world. See Bernhard et al. (2015).

2. This chapter is the expanded and revised version of the essay that was published in the *Journal of Democracy* (25, no. 1, 2014) and we wish to thank the journal for the permission to publish a new version of the article. We are grateful to a number of colleagues who worked with us over the years on various projects covering various countries and who will find many of these ideas familiar. In particular we would like to thank Michael Bernhard, Roberto Foa, George Soroka, Bela Greskovits, Jason Wittenberg, Sunhyuk Kim, and Michal Wenzel.

3. In this study, eleven former countries of the Soviet Bloc that are now members of the EU constitute East Central Europe. They include: the Czech Republic, Estonia, Hungary, Latvia, Lithuania, Poland, Slovakia, and Slovenia (2004 enlargement), Bulgaria and Romania (2007), and Croatia (2013). When we write about Central Europe we exclude from this definition Bulgaria, Croatia, and Romania. "Eastern Europe" is the largest subset we write about. This region is used in the Bertelsmann Transformation Index we occasionally cite. In addition to the eleven countries of "East Central Europe," it includes: Albania, Bosnia-Hercegovina, Kosovo, Macedonia, Montenegro, and Serbia.

4. Following Diamond, we define civil society as "the realm of organized social life that is open, voluntary, self-generating, at least partially self-supporting, autonomous from the state, and bound by a legal order or set of shared rules … it involves citizens acting collectively in a public sphere to express their interests, passions, preferences, and ideas, to exchange information, to achieve collective goals, to make demands on the state, to improve the structure and functioning of the state, and to hold state officials accountable" (Diamond 1999: 221).

5. For example, Italian civil society had some 221,000 organizations in 2005 (Mastropaolo 2008: 43). Poland, a significantly smaller country (38.2 million versus 59.3 million population in 2010), with much a shorter duration of democracy and EU membership, has more than 100,000 organizations (Przewłocka, Adamiak, and Herbst 2013: 23). The methods of collecting data and counting civil society organizations vary broadly, so the actual figures should be taken with a grain of salt. The point is, however, that relative to their total populations, the sizes of the Polish and Italian civil societies are not dramatically different.

6. For a comprehensive analysis of the state of civil society in Central Asia, see Ziegler (2015).

7. Bertelsmann Transformation Index ranks countries on the scale from 1 to 10 on various dimensions of "democracy status." In the 2014 ranking, only 10 out 129 analyzed countries (8 percent) achieved the highest score (9 or 10) on the civil rights scale (component of political participation—rule of law). Out of 17 countries of Eastern Europe, 6 achieved such a score (35 percent). None of the 13 post-Soviet Eurasian countries scored that high (Bertelsmann 2015).

8. The authors' own calculations based on the Freedom House data retrieved 1 September 2015 from https://freedomhouse.org/report/freedom-world-aggregate-and-sub category-scores#.VeW2S7xViko. On the countries included in East Central Europe in this study, see note 3. Central Asia includes: Kazakhstan, Kyrgyzstan, Tajikistan, Turkmenistan, and Uzbekistan.

9. This becomes particularly clear when the outlier Scandinavian countries are removed from the sample, and the comparison is focused on the European nations that have a legacy of authoritarian rule, such as Portugal, Germany, and Spain (Visser 2006). According to Visser (2006: 45), in 2001 the union density in Poland was 14 (not much different from that in Spain (16.1) or Switzerland (17.8)), while in Slovakia it was 36.21, in the Czech Republic 27.0, and in Hungary 19.9. See also http://www.worker-participation.eu/National-Industrial-Relations/Compare-Countries.

10. There are, however, exceptions. A comparison of Polish and Czech women's movements shows that some sectors of civil society in Poland are still more prone to participatory, contentious actions than their counterparts in other countries (Korol-

czuk and Saxonberg 2014). In addition, Płatek and Płucienniczak's study on far-right mobilizations (in this volume) shows a contentious face of Polish civil society.
11. Evidence can be found in the modest increase in the identification with the right political ideologies captured by the World Value Survey (Melzer and Serafin 2013, Inglehart and Norris 2016). For works analyzing the earlier period see Kopecky and Mudde (2003) and Ost (2005).

References

The 2012 CSO Sustainability Index for Central and Eastern Europe and Eurasia. 16th Edition. Washington, DC: US Agency for International Development.

Archambault, E. 2009. "The Third Sector in Europe: Does It Exhibit a Converging Movement?," in *Civil Society in Comparative Perspective,* ed. B. Enjolras and K.H. Sivesind. Emerald Books, 3–24, Comparative Social Research, vol. 26.

Aron, L. 2013. "The Long Struggle for Freedom." *Journal of Democracy* 2, no. 3: 62–74.

Beissinger, M. 2007. "Structure and Example in Modular Political Phenomena: The Diffusion of Bulldozer/Rose/Orange/Tulip Revolutions." *Perspectives on Politics* 5: 259–276.

Beissinger, M., and G. Sasse. 2013. "An End to Patience? The 2008 Global Financial Crisis and Political Protest in Eastern Europe," in *Mass Politics in Tough Times: Opinions, Votes and Protest in the Great Recession,* ed. L. Bartels and N. Bermeo. New York: Oxford University Press, 334–370.

Bermeo, N., and P. Nord, eds. 2000. *Civil Society Before Democracy: Lessons From 19th Century Europe.* London and Boulder, CO: Rowman and Littlefield.

Bernhard, M., and R. Kaya. 2013. "Civil Society and Regime Type in European Post-Communist Countries: The Perspective Two Decades after 1989-1991." *Taiwan Journal of Democracy* 8, no. 2: 1–13.

Bernhard, M., and E. Karakoc. 2007. "Civil Society and the Legacies of Dictatorship." *World Politics* 59 (July): 539–567.

Bernhard M., E. Tzelgov, D. Jung, M. Coppedge, and S. I. Lindberg. 2015. "The Varieties of Democracy Core Civil Society Index." Working Paper. Varieties of Democracy Project.

Bertelsmann Transformation Index 2104 (Fifth Edition). 2015. Retrieved 31 August 2015 from http://www.bti-project.org/bti-home/.

Bunce, V., and S. Wolchik. 2011. *Defeating Authoritarian Leaders in Postcommunist Countries.* Cambridge: Cambridge University Press.

Celichowski, J. 2004. "Civil Society in Eastern Europe: Growth without Engagement," in *Exploring Civil Society: Political and Cultural Contexts,* ed. M. Glasius, D. Lewis, and H. Seckinelgin. London: Routledge, 62–69.

Chebankova, E.A. 2013. *Civil Society in Putin's Russia.* London: Routledge.

Dahrendorf, R. 1990. "Has the East Joined the West?" *New Perspective Quarterly* 7, no. 2: 41–43.

Derex Index. 2010. *Back by Popular Demand: Demand for Right-Wing Extremism* (Derex) Index. Budapest: Political Capital Policy Research and Consulting Institute.

Diamond, L. 1999. *Developing Democracy: Toward Consolidation.* Baltimore: Johns Hopkins University Press.

Ekiert, G. 1996. *The State Against Society: Political Crises and Their Aftermath in East Central Europe.* Princeton: Princeton University Press.

Ekiert, G., and R. Foa. 2012. "The Weakness of Postcommunist Civil Society Reassessed." Harvard University, CES Papers–Open Forum.

Ekiert, G., and J. Kubik. 1999. *Rebellious Civil Society: Popular Protest and Democratic Consolidation in Poland.* Ann Arbor: University of Michigan Press.

European Commission. 2013. *Europeans' Engagement in Participatory Democracy: Report: Flash Eurobarometer 373.* March, 9.

Freedom House, *Nations in Transit 2013.*

Gąsior-Niemiec, A. 2010. "Lost in the System? Civil Society and Regional Development Policy in Poland." *Acta Politica* 45: 90–111.

Gąsior-Niemiec, A., and P. Gliński. 2007. "Polish Tradition of Self-organization, Social Capital and the Challenge of Europeanisation," in *Social Capital and Governance,* ed. F. Adam. Berlin: Lit Verlag, 237–266.

Greene, S.A. 2014. *Moscow in Movement: Power and Opposition in Putin's Russia.* Stanford: Stanford University Press.

Greskovits, B. 1998. *Political Economy of Protest and Patience.* Budapest: Central European University Press.

Hale, H. 2005. "Regime Cycles: Democracy, Autocracy, and Revolution in Post-Soviet Eurasia." *World Politics* 58 (October): 133–165.

Howard, M.M. 2003. *The Weakness of Civil Society in Post-Communist Europe.* Cambridge: Cambridge University Press.

Inglehart, R., and P. Norris. 2016. "Trump, Brexit, and the Rise of Populism: Economic Have-Nots and Cultural Backlash." (July 29). HKS Working Paper No. RWP16-026.

Kendzior, S. 2012. "Stop Talking about Civil Society." *Foreign Policy* (3 December 2012).

Kertzer, D. 1988. *Ritual, Politics, and Power.* New Haven: Yale University Press.

Kopecky, P., and C. Mudde. 2003. *Uncivil Society? Contentious Politics in Post-Communist Europe.* London: Routledge.

Korolczuk, E., and S. Saxonberg. 2014. "Strategies of Contentious Action: A Comparative Analysis of the Women's Movements in Poland and the Czech Republic." *European Societies* 17, no. 4: 404–422.

Kotkin, S. (with Jan Gross). 2013. *Uncivil Society: 1989 and the Implosion of the Communist Establishment.* New York: The Modern Library.

Krasnodębska, U., J. Pucek, G. Kowalczyk, and J.J. Wygnański. 1996. *Podstawowe statystyki dotyczące działań organizacji pozarządowych w Polsce.* Program PHARE-Dialog Społeczny.

Krastev, I. 2011. "Paradoxes of New Authoritarianism." *Journal of Democracy* 22, no. 2: 5–16.

Kubik, J. 2013. "What Can Political Scientists Learn about Civil Society from Anthropologists?," in *Anthropology and Political Science,* M. Aronoff and J. Kubik. New York: Berghahn, 198–239.

Kurczewska, J. 2004. "Tradycje w przestrzeni lokalnego społeczeństwa obywatelskiego," in S*amoorganizacja Społeczeństwa Polskiego: III sektor i wspólnoty lokalne w jednoczącej się Europie,* ed. P. Gliński, B. Lewenstein, and A. Siciński. Warszawa: IFiS PAN, 302–332.

Kuti, E. 2010. "Policy Initiatives Towards the Third Sector under the Conditions of Ambiguity: The Case of Hungary," in *Policy Initiatives Towards the Third Sector in an International Perspective,* ed. B. Gidron and M. Bar. Berlin: Springer, 127–158.

Lagerspetz, M., and M. Skovajsa. 2006. "Non-Profit Foundations in Four Countries of Central and Eastern Europe." *Polish Sociological Review* 2, no. 154: 187–208.

Lanskoy, M., and E. Suthers. 2013. "Outlawing the Opposition." *Journal of Democracy* 24, no. 3: 75–87.

Mansfeldova, Z., S. Nalecz, E. Priller, and A. Zimmer 2004. "Civil Society in Transition: Civic Engagement and Nonprofit Organizations in Central and Eastern Europe after 1989," in *Future of Civil Society: Making Central European Nonprofit-Organizations Work*, ed. A. Zimmer and E. Priller. Wisbaden: VS Verlag fur Sozialwissenschaften, 99–121.

Mastropaolo, A. 2008. "A Democracy Bereft of Parties: Anti-political Uses of Civil Society in Italy," in *Changing Images of Civil Society: From Protest to Governance*, ed. B. Jobert and B. Kohler-Koch. Abingdon: Routledge, 32–46.

Melzer, R., and S. Serafin, eds. 2013. *Right-Wing Extremism in Europe*. Berlin: Friedrich Ebert Foundation.

Nagy, R., and I. Sebesteny. 2008. "Methodological Practice and Practical Methodology: Fifteen Years in Non-profit Statistics." *Hungarian Statistical Review*, Special Issue No. 12.

NGO Law Monitor, The International Center For-Not-for-Profit Law, 2016. Retrieved 17 December 2016 from http://www.icnl.org/research/monitor/.

Ost, D. 2005. *The Defeat of Solidarity: Anger and Politics in Postcommunist Europe*. Ithaca: Cornell University Press.

Petrova, V. 2007. "Civil Society in Post-Communist Eastern Europe and Eurasia: A Cross-National Analysis of Micro- and Macro-Factors." *World Development* 35, no. 7: 1277–1305.

Przewłocka, J., P. Adamiak, and J. Herbst. 2013. *Podstawowe fakty o organizacjach pozarzadowych. Raport z badania 2012*. Warszawa: Stowarzyszenie Klon/Jawor.

Regulska, J., and M. Grabowska. 2013. "Social Justice, Hegemony, and Women's Mobilizations," in *Postcommunism from Within: Social Justice, Mobilization, and Hegemony*, ed. J. Kubik and A. Linch. New York: NYU Press, 139–190.

Riley D., and J.J. Fernández. 2014. "Beyond Strong and Weak: Rethinking Postdictatorship Civil Societies." *American Journal of Sociology* 120, no. 2: 432–503.

Robertson, R. 2011. *The Politics of Protest in Hybrid Regimes: Managing Dissent in Post-Communist Russia*. Cambridge University Press.

Rupnik, J. 1999. "The Postcommunist Divide." *Journal of Democracy* 10, no. 1: 57–62.

Schmitter, P. 2010. "Twenty-Five Years, Fifteen Findings." *Journal of Democracy* 21, no. 1: 17–28.

Sil, R. 2013a. "Labor and the Left in Postcommunist Europe: Pathways of Transition, the Stability of Parties, and the Inheritance of Legacy Unions in Poland and the Czech Republic," paper presented at the Annual Meeting of the American Political Science Association, Chicago, IL, 31 August 2013.

———. 2013b. "The Fluidity of Labor Politics in Postcommunist Transitions: Rethinking the Narrative of Russian Labor Quiescence," in *Political Creativity: Reconfiguring Institutional Order and Change*, ed. G. Berk, D. Galvan, and V. Hattam. Philadelphia: University of Pennsylvania Press, 188–208.

Sissenich, B. 2007. *Building States without Society: European Union Enlargement and the Transfer of EU Social Policy to Poland and Hungary*. Lanham: Lexington Books.

Smyth, R., A. Sobolev, and I. Soboleva. 2013. "Patterns of Discontent: Identifying the Participant Core in Russian Post-Election Protest," paper prepared for the conference, "Russia's Winter of Discontent: Taking Stock of Changing State-Society Relationships," Uppsala University, Sweden, 7–6 September 2013.

Szelenyi, I., and J. Wilk. 2013. "Poverty and Popular Mobilization in Postcommunist Capitalist Regimes," in *Postcommunism from Within: Social Justice, Mobilization, and Hegemony,* ed. J. Kubik and A. Linch. New York: NYU Press, 229–264.

Tucker, J. 2007. "Enough! Electoral Fraud, Collective Action Problems, and Post-Communist Colored Revolutions." *Perspectives on Politics* 5 (September): 537–553.

Visser, J. 2006. "Union Membership Statistics in 24 Countries." *Monthly Labor Review* January: 38–49.

World Bank Voice and Accountability Index 2013. Retrieved 9 October 2015 from http://info.worldbank.org/governance/wgi/index.aspx#home.

Ziegler, C.E., ed. 2015. *Civil Society and Politics in Central Asia.* Lexington: The University Press of Kentucky.

Chapter 2

(Mis)understanding Social Activism in Poland

Anna Giza-Poleszczuk

Introduction

A special report in *The Economist,* published 25 October 2001, presents Poland as a country of self-doubts and surprisingly low self-esteem. The author claims that when President George W. Bush stopped off in Warsaw in June 2001 and praised Poland's achievements, many people were surprised and thought he must have been wearing rose-tinted glasses, as today "Poles are among Central Europe's most inherently pessimistic people." As former Science Minister Andrzej Wiszniewski, quoted in the article, put it: "To admit that life is good is seen in some circles as almost indecent. The only thing we don't grumble about is our children."

Indeed, the set of auto-stereotypes shared by the majority of Poles is composed of strongly negative features: an inability to come to a consensus, unwillingness to cooperate, malevolence, etc.[1] The few positive features Poles see in themselves include "hospitality," "strong family ties," and an "attachment to religion." However, not everybody would consider those features positive. Some progressive journalists and the liberal wing of the political scene find them to be barriers to the country's modernization and believe they slow down collective advancement.[2] The issue of what the sources and consequences are of such a negative self-image is in itself worth examination (cf. Giza 2013). However, what is important for subsequent analysis is that the question of the nature of civil society lies at its very core. Looking carefully into the attributes of the Polish "soul," or what some theorists have termed specific Polish "cultural DNA," one may notice that they come together in the overall conviction that Poles form a good nation (at least they did during the war), but a poor society (see Czapiński 2005, 2007; Czapliński 2009). The question is whether such a view reflects actual practices, or rather, as will be suggested in this chapter, exposes the process of imperfect translation of concepts and terms coined in a different cultural and political context. The widespread diagnosis of the poor condition of Polish civil society is based on the assumptions, definitions, and models that do not fit Polish reality, thus distorting the way it is perceived. In this chapter, I will try to prove that Polish civil society is misunderstood, trying to identify the sources and consequences of this misconception.

The initial assumption concerns the past. In the prevailing view, the difficult history of Poland's prior statelessness and marginal democratic experience, together with fifty years of socialism, have left Poles with no tradition or tools with which to form a modern "civil society." As stated by Piotr Gliński, a leading Polish sociologist, "one of the three key aims for Poland's transformation—alongside the introduction of such institutions as a free market and democracy—was the development of a civil society" (2010: 2).

The assumption that there was no civil society in Poland prior to 1989 was also implicitly adopted by the leaders of the new third sector, most journalists, commentators, and politicians. Thus, the main challenge, as stressed by the elites, was to mobilize fellow citizens and encourage them to take an active part in civic organizing. In the early 1990s, a social campaign was aired on public TV aimed at mobilizing society with the participation of distinguished celebrities from the world of culture, including well-known poets such as Ernest Bryl and actors like Krystyna Janda. The slogan of the campaign referred to the famous challenge of President Kennedy: "We are finally at our own home. Do not stand idle, do not wait! What to do? Help!" In the public discourse, the notion of civil society was strongly linked to democracy: without the citizens' involvement, without civil society keeping an eye on the political elites and wielding its voice, no "true" democracy was possible.

Some scholars claim that from its very conception the idea of a "civil society" in Poland was conceived as the nonpolitical sphere whose objective is to complement the deficiencies of the neoliberal state and economy (Załęski 2012). Załęski states that such an understanding of the concept of civil society was totally opposed to the social philosophy of the Solidarity movement, and stresses that Solidarity activists did not use the concept of civil society at all, building their vision of society on more "republican" ideas of self-governance and community. Whether Załęski is right or wrong as to the neoliberal bias in Poland's post-1989 use of the idea of a civil society, there is no doubt that it has been introduced into Polish public discourse from above and from outside.

The challenge of transformation was to *build* civil society, not to *revive or adapt* an existing one to the new circumstances. In fulfilling this task one was supposed to break all links with the (corrupt) past. There was nothing of value to be found in the past (Czapliński 2009; Giza 2013). On the contrary, past experiences could easily spoil the new, fragile institutions.

The concept of the third sector came to Poland along with the transformation of the 1990s. It was accompanied by notions such as "nonprofit organization" or "nongovernmental organization" that *soon replaced the exploited and historically compromised concept of social organization* (associated with the "social actions" of the communist era) (Wygnański and Frączek 2007. Thus, not only was the model of social activism new, but so was the vocabulary describing the civil sphere, as new terms were imported from another cultural and economic world.

The problem of local embeddedness of a civil society is valid for all transforming countries in Central and Eastern Europe. There are similarly valid questions about what types of actors took part in the process of articulating the new civil society project, the extent to which this project was rooted in local culture and history, and the extent to which it fits the needs and competencies of the society that was to be transformed. It was also not clear how to implement the ideal model of civil society—how to broaden social participation, increase interest in public affairs, and strengthen the voice of the previously silent citizens. Załęski (2012) goes as far as suggesting that the "civil society" concept was introduced by postcommunist milieus, as he found the first mentions of civil society in *Trybuna Ludu* (the official newspaper of the party), and not in Solidarity's publications. In addition, Kolankiewicz brings to light the very fact that "[c]ivil society has a tendency to be captured by the educated middle class who are more vocal and thus may contribute to the marginalization and disenfranchisement of the less articulate and those devoid of social capital" (Kolankiewicz 2006: 53). He observes that such a tendency can be seen in the Polish third sector, which became dominated by 2 percent of the most powerful NGOs in the late 1990s, controlling 60 percent of resources. Economic disparities are accompanied by a strong tendency toward the formation of oligarchic structures, political clientelism, and the control of civil society structures by ex-nomenklatura and other well-organized groups (Kolankiewicz 2006: 53).

These debates demonstrate that the problems of power and inclusion/exclusion, as well as language and translation, are of crucial importance for analyzing existing civil society. In this chapter, I explore the consequences of the changes in the semantic field of social activism that have been reintroduced under the notion and principles of civil society. My thesis is that the problem with translating key concepts and terms, such as "volunteer," is one of the main reasons the project has not fulfilled its promise, or at least why the prevailing view is that Polish civil society is weak and underdeveloped. To be clear, we cannot be sure at this point whether civil society "is" weak in absolute terms, or whether it merely seems weak due to the way it is defined and measured. The fact that almost everybody repeats the lament that civil society in Poland is weak reveals the expectations and assumptions that accompanied the process of forming the current model, but that do not necessary reflect reality.

My analysis is based on data that comes from various research projects and workshops I led for more than ten years, working with many nongovernmental organizations in Poland.[3] The main body of the data comes from the Social Action 2012 project, financed by the Trust for Civil Society in Central and Eastern Europe, aimed at using the preparations for the European Football Championship 2012 (hosted by Poland and Ukraine) to initiate social change. Within the frame of this project, we have conducted research and workshops on sport volunteering, sport organizations (the "old" third sector), the social role and potential of sport, the first series of research on famous Orlik football fields, and the first deliberative poll on social use of stadiums built for Euro 2012.[4] A network of organizations and public institutions was created under the auspices of the Social Action 2012 project, which became responsible for coordination of voluntary activities in Poland. Regular workshops and meetings of this group, named Voluntary Action 2012+, resulted in a lot of initiatives and recommendations implemented by both public authorities such as the Ministry of Sport, which initiated a program of social animators working at Orlik football fields, and NGOs, e.g., folk sports associations, which started regular trainings to organize volunteering for their sport clubs.[5] My knowledge of voluntary action in Poland comes both from research and from working with people and organizations deeply engaged in its advancement.

Is Polish Civil Society Actually Weak?

Most scholars and commentators agree that, compared to the economic and political objectives of the Polish transformation, introducing a free market and democratic procedures did not achieve the civil society objective to a satisfactory degree. Civil society structures in Poland are seen as underdeveloped and relatively weak. Scholars claim that "they are enclave-like, and are not coequal partners to the spheres of business and politics" (Gliński 2010: 2). The relative weakness of Polish civil society is often interpreted as one of the main reasons for the more general weakness of Polish democracy. This pessimistic diagnosis is widely accepted among scientists, journalists, politicians, leaders of the NGOs, and public opinion (e.g., Gliński 2010;

Gumkowska et al. 2006). Symptomatic was the reaction to the January 2010 article in *Gazeta Wyborcza* published by Agnieszka Graff, a scholar and well-known feminist theorist and activist. Graff's text entitled "Clerks with No Heart, No Soul" depicted the third sector in Poland as bureaucratized and weak, diverting its energy from its civil society mission to "hunting for grants."[6] The text instigated widespread animated discussion. However, the majority of discussants accepted the negative view of civil society, simply adding more evidence to support Graff's thesis rather than challenging it.

According to the common view, the key weakness of the third sector is its diminished ability to mobilize social resources, create networks, and build a social mandate. Contrary to funding plans and hopes, the weakest aspect of Polish civil society is the low level of engagement in public affairs. Quantitative studies such as the European Social Survey show that Poland is below the European average in all categories, such as signing petitions or joining demonstrations. In some, Poles occupy the last position among European countries. The same pertains to membership in organizations: "the percentage of Poles that belong to at least one CSO (Civil Society Organization) varies between 12 percent and 20 percent depending on the study. The National Advisory Group, which is the panel of experts involved in research on the Civil Society Index, estimates the real level of participation in organizations to be even lower" (Gumkowska et al. 2006: 89).

Numbers showing that only a small percentage of Poles are members of formal organizations are undoubtedly worrisome, but it is worth stressing that "engagement of citizens in public affairs" is defined here as the level of involvement in nonpartisan political actions and membership in CSOs and does not encompass informal groups and types of organizing. Here, the focus is on civil society institutionalized within the frameworks of nongovernmental organizations and regulated by law, which is implicitly perceived as instrumental for democracy. The main goal is enabling and broadening social participation in an organized, rational way, providing citizens with a "training ground" for democratic skills and competencies (Putnam 2000). Thus, one may gain the impression that civil society's main goal is to improve democracy and turn people into better citizens, not to emancipate society, cater to social needs, or increase people's well-being.

Another widely recognized and discussed failure of civil society is the very low level of social capital in Poland, or to be more specific, the dominance of binding social capital over bridging capital (Putnam 2000; Czapiński 2007). Apparently, the expected output of civil society has been to build broad, heterogeneous social networks, to open up communities, and to increase the circulation of ideas, information, and good practice. This is why a lot of effort has been invested in creating organizations, such as volunteer centers, citizens' advice bureaus, and others that are supposed to enhance cooperation and networking.[7] However, despite all the investment, the majority of these new networks remain weak or are even decaying, and the level of social capital remains among the lowest in Europe (Czapiński 2007).

It also seems that NGOs have little power to increase the level of sensitivity toward the public (social) good, improving morality that would translate, for example, into paying taxes, thus encouraging people to cover the costs of producing public goods. Nongovernmental organizations face a serious problem of "a lack of people willing to selflessly support their activities" (Gumkowska et al. 2006: 89). This low ability to attract volunteers and collaborators, together with the overall lack of awareness of the existence, role, and achievements of NGOs, suggests that the third sector has not managed to build a social mandate, making us question its power to transform society.

The third sector is also institutionally and economically weak, still striving for stability and independence. According to studies, when Polish nonprofit organizations "enter into cooperation with the state, they tend to develop a dependency on public funding, to the detriment of their civic character" (Evers and Guillemard 2013: 324). The vast majority of NGOs do not create jobs, and the average number of employees per NGO is three. Only 30 percent of organizations are able to attract collaborators, very few use new technologies to manage projects and social networks, and the majority lack resources for communication and promotion (Gumkowska et al. 2006). Moreover, many NGOs are dependent on strong leaders who are not willing (or able) to plan succession or to turn their charismatic type of legitimate leadership into an institutional one.

Despite a favorable legal environment that makes registering organizations easy, which supposedly encourages philanthropy and volunteering and aims to create strong incentives for cooperation between NGOs and public administration, the third sector in Poland has not yet achieved its aims. The authors of the report presenting the Polish context in comparison to other European countries state that while Polish NGOs appear to have strong positions as defenders of the values essential for civil society, such as democracy, transparency, tolerance, nonviolence, gender equity, and poverty eradication, it does not necessarily mean that they apply them in everyday practice. They also have a limited impact on society, which appears consistent with the common perception about the weakness of civil society in the country. The main challenge that Polish civil society organizations face is to "increase the sector's influence on holding the state and private sector accountable" (Gumkowska et al. 2006: 92–93). In short, the authors say that the existing model does not work, and that the values and intents of NGOs "as defenders of the values essential for civil society" do not have enough impact on the state and the market.

It seems that NGOs also do not have enough impact on society itself, which still is not "civil" enough. As a result, the picture of Poland that arises from the literature is one of "democracy without citizens" (Ekiert 2012: 63). This means that the elites have succeeded in implementing democracy, understood as the rule of law, basic civic rights, and democratic procedures, but have failed to encourage voluntarism at the grassroots level and to strengthen citizens' participation. The explanation for the lack of citizens' engagement in the new democracies is usually found in recent history, especially in the socialist period. *"Homo sovieticus"* supposedly has no skills, no competencies, and no will to become an active citizen, preferring instead to remain a passive observer.

Thus, there is wide consensus that the third sector is weak. However, it is weak when measured against a certain "ideal model" and when using a specific set of indices. There are a lot of potential doubts as to whether this model is valid. What if the current way in which civil society is defined and measured actually conceals the reality of social activism in Poland?

There is ample evidence that the "weakness" thesis does not pass the empirical test. Ekiert (2012) discusses a few paradoxes that undermine the "weakness" thesis, like the inconsistency between the low level of membership as reported in surveys and the official registries from individual countries that show phenomenal growth in listed groups and organizations. This is also the case in Poland, where the number of registered NGOs grew by 400 percent in the first five years after 1989. Thus, Ekiert proposes to "abandon any simplistic generalizations regarding the 'weakness' of post-communist civil society or its 'demobilization' following democratic transition" (2012: 69–70).

Another puzzle of "democracy without citizens" is that support for democracy, even though it is declining, is still robust.[8] There are also many signs that Poles are undertaking social initiatives, although not necessarily channeled through NGOs. Recent examples include mass spontaneous mobilizations of right-wing groups (see Płatek and Płucienniczak in this volume), mass protests of the Anti-Counterfeiting Trade Agreement (ACTA) (Jurczyszyn et al. 2014), the revival of "rural housewives' circles" (see Matysiak in this volume), and urban activism (see Polanska in this volume). To summarize, there is some evidence that CSOs are weak, at least in comparison with the expectations of the "fathers" of the Polish postsocialist third sector, but that does not necessarily mean that civil society in general is weak.

The second line of reasoning against the "weak civil society" thesis relates to its definition, and relatedly to the methodology of its measurement. Participation in civil society is usually measured as membership in formal third-sector organizations, and semiformal or informal social circles are not included. Thus, some types of social activism, typical especially for rural

Poland, such as volunteer fire brigades, parish councils, women's clubs, and school committees, are consistently excluded from civil society. The same goes for measuring volunteering when it is understood as work for some kind of formal organization. Focusing on involvement in formal organizations leads to the exclusion of self-help activities, which are still strong in rural Poland and in small neighborhoods. Recently, new questions were introduced, intended to measure informal activities, but they still remain in the realm of "helping."[9] As a result, a skewed picture of activism in Poland is produced that, for example, "systematically underestimates the bottom-up organizational capacity in rural areas" (Gąsior-Niemiec 2013: 171).

Some civil society leaders quite openly state that Poland remains under the strong influence of the Anglo-Saxon (particularly American) tradition of defining and measuring the third sector, which is hardly surprising given that the future leaders of the Polish third sector were trained mainly by American foundations, and the initial inflow of grants (money) to develop civil society came mainly from American funds (Wygnański and Frączek 2007). Nevertheless, this means that the ideas, models, and even words that are used have been brought from a different culture and tradition of active citizenship, as part of some kind of "peaceful colonization." Imposing those concepts on the local context and habits might have resulted in promoting organizations that, without a corresponding "embeddedness" in local society, remain weak. At the same time, that imposition might have blinded us to different forms of civil society, embedded in society, but not matching the Western ideals and deemed "unfit" to respond to the new challenges that post-1989 Poland faced.

The Divide: The "Old" and the "New" Third Sector

Let us start with a very strong statement: it is not true that Polish society had no experience with civil society prior to 1989. The tradition of Polish cooperatives stretches back to the eighteenth century, with millions of members in agricultural, financial, or trade networks. A significant number of them survived under socialism, although they were deprived of independence and subjugated to the state. Thus, in 1989 in Poland there were thousands of organizations that, from a purely formal point of view, were "nongovernmental," some of them covering all of Poland and in possession of substantial wealth. The activists of the "new" civil society used to call them the "old third sector," and as a matter of principle tended to exclude them from the realm of the newly formed ("proper") civil society (Herbst and Przewłocka 2011).

The reasons behind the marginalization of the "old" sector were complex. First, it was perceived as distorted, skewed, and spoiled due to the prolonged influence of socialism. The agenda of the socialist organizations was shaped, or at least heavily controlled, by the state (the party), not by the citizens. Like all organizations under socialism, they were dependent on public money (as in the case of sports associations), contaminated by politics (e.g., volunteer fire brigades, controlled by the United Peasants' Association), and infiltrated by activists steeped in the old regime (*homo sovieticus*). Second, the organizational culture that developed during the socialist era was perceived as antithetical to the ethos of civil society and dysfunctional for democracy. There was widespread belief that the principles governing so-called social organizations under socialism were composed of hypocrisy, clientelism, authoritarian power, strong hierarchy, etc. Not surprisingly, the organizational habits resulting from prolonged exposure to those principles were recognized as being lethal to the spirit of civil society.

Finally, in the broader public's view, these so-called social organizations abused and corrupted the very ideas connected to social activism, as shown by the ambiguous meaning of the old Polish words for social activism, including "volunteer" (*ochotnik*), "social activist" (*działacz społeczny*), and "community action" (*czyn społeczny*). These old-fashioned words were supposed to evoke negative connotations of forced and false mock "citizens' involvement" as in the old days when people were forced to volunteer and when community actions were compulsory. After fifty years of socialism, using the words that had lost their true meaning was perceived as risky.[10]

Thus, the thesis that in 1989 civil society in Poland simply did not exist can be considered true only if one accepts the view that the "old" third sector was not "genuine" or true to its nature. This is, however, not true materially: there were tens of thousands of cooperatives, associations, and even foundations. New leaders of the civil society could either try to reform the existing organizations or leave them behind and create a new third sector. In the 1990s, the latter seemed easier and more efficient. Thus, the "old" sector was left without support and supposed to gradually wither away. And a new civil society was to be established, both in real and symbolic terms.

Furthermore, the "civil society absence" thesis does not hold when put up against the Solidarity movement, or at least against the way it is presented. The events of 1980 ("the first Solidarity"), and then those of 1989 were unequivocally presented as civil society movements of the emancipatory nature that finally triumphed over the socialist state. Accepting this view of Solidarity, and the social mobilization of the early 1990s (especially the so-called Citizens Committees), we have to admit that there was indeed a civil society in Poland under the cover of superficial passivity and hypocrisy.[11] If so, there was no vacuum to be filled by the "new civil society." To the contrary, accepting the vacuum thesis means denying the emancipatory nature of Solidarity. Thus, either Solidarity was the emanation of civil society, or, and this is often claimed by the representatives of postcommunist circles in the 1990s, it was just a reflection of a popular desire for an increased supply of goods and more economic equality as reflected in the popular slogan "we all have the same stomachs."

The "new" civil society was imagined by its leaders to be the heir to Solidarity, carrying its mission forward. That is why it had to be built from scratch, to avoid contamination with the old, corrupt world: "the term 'nongovernmental organization' seemed to be, for historical and political reasons, the easiest to accept and the best fitted to express the emancipatory nature of the Polish civil society movement of the early 1990s" (Wygnański and Frączek 2007: 18). As stated by the authors, the old notion of "social organizations" was to be superseded by the new one, that of the "NGO." Even though awareness of this term is growing (in 2005, 30 percent of respondents declared they had heard of it; ibid.: 18), it is still far from being well embedded in common knowledge. The same goes for another social activism key word, "nonprofit organization," which is used interchangeably with the term "NGO." It should be noted that both terms may bring somewhat negative connotations as both start with the prefix "non," which demarcates the concepts from the state, on the one hand, and from the market (profit) on the other. Later, the concept of the third sector started to be used as an effort to bring some order to this terminological confusion (and perhaps partly to mask it).

In the abovementioned process of terminological evolution, the concept of the third sector practically excluded the so-called old social economy, and cooperatives in particular (Frączak and Skrzypiec 2011). In the prevailing view, they were indiscriminately perceived as part of the "ancient regime" and were not accepted as genuine third sector representatives because at the time they seemed neither nongovernmental nor nonprofit. It needs to be stressed, however, that some of the "old" third-sector organizations, e.g., folk sports associations, continued to receive public money after 1989, often without having to compete for grants with other NGOs. Thus, the divide, and the negative feelings between the "new" and the "old" organizations, are rooted also in a quite clear and measurable conflict of interests. Either way, the new third sector was to be built from scratch, with new rules, new tasks, and a new language.

Volunteer and *Ochotnik*: The Fight for Words

After 1989, the new reality was founded on rejecting socialism. It was widely believed that socialism not only turned people into "anti-citizens" suffering from *homo sovieticus* syndrome, but it also ruined many institutions and compromised the meaning of the terms essential for civil society. Such compromised terms included: "social activity," marked by forced social actions; "social organization," taken over by the party, and "social activist," which lost its meaning given that many people were forced to be affiliated with the Association of Socialist Youth or another type of organization friendly to the party. It was assumed that citizens identified these exact words with the socialist order, and that broad networks, which from a purely formal point of view constituted the "third sector," e.g., volunteer fire brigades and folk sports associations, not to mention other kinds of cooperatives, had no social mandate whatsoever to act.

The result of the assumption described above was a belief that the beginning of the new paradigm of civil society required launching and adopting of new words. There was a fear that the old words would conceal the fundamentally new content; that, for instance, "social organization" would automatically be identified with the phony Association of Socialist Youth, and "social activity" with the forced planting of trees. This was a very justified fear: words have the power to numb and conceal. On the other hand, though, one might think that despite the negative experience people were still able to distinguish a social activity from its caricature, and that restoring the real deep meaning of the words together with the values hiding within them may turn out to be easier than building a new lexicon. After all, nobody rejected elections because the wording used was the same as before 1989, and we did not even wonder how to update the law on elections, damaged by years of socialism, with new wording.

I would like to analyze the social consequences of the attempt to replace the old words with new ones using as an example the term "volunteer activity" (*wolontariat*). In the past, Poland had more than enough activities, people, and organizations that were undoubtedly of a voluntary nature, defined as voluntary and unpaid activities performed for the benefit of others, and going beyond family and friendship relationships. The "old" social associations, such as volunteer fire brigades, Volunteer Mountain Search and Rescue (GOPR), or sports clubs that were members of the popular sports associations all recruited, trained, and benefited from the unpaid work of volunteers. Broad networks of mutual social aid were of a voluntary nature as were "political" support networks formed during the years of underground activity, for a moment institutionalized in the form of Citizens Committees. An old-fashioned *ochotnik* ("volunteer") was basically doing the same type of work as today's *wolontariusz*. What is more, it appears that *ochotnik* as a term has survived to this day without any pejorative meaning, since completely new voluntary organizations, such as the Volunteer Rescue Group (OGR), decided to use it.

However, a decision was made to introduce the term "voluntary activity" (*wolontariat*) into the public sphere. In 1993, based on study tours in the

United States and United Kingdom, and a pilot study, the first Voluntary Activity Center was created. The leaders of the third sector, in cooperation with the government (Ministry of Labor and Social Policy) started to develop the definitions and the special act regulating voluntary activities. The Act on Public Benefit and Volunteer Work was finally issued in 2003, but the new terminology is still under construction (Moroń 2009; Karasińska 2009; Włodarczyk 2011). The word "volunteer" was not completely unknown but it was still a bit alien sounding, "fresh," and thus, it seemed potentially incredibly catchy. The term "voluntary activity" did not sound at all negative; thus, it seemed that it would be relatively easy to imbue it with modern content reflecting a readiness for voluntary (and unpaid) work for the benefit of other people and/or for the benefit of the social good. However, the term was not completely neutral: *wolontariusz* was associated mainly with the nursing and medical professions as well as with the activities of the Red Cross, and the expression "volunteers under the flag of the Red Cross" was widely used in the media. It was precisely because of this tradition that the word *wolontariusz* and not *ochotnik* was used: this was a result of simply taking over the term "volunteer" from the parent organization, the International Red Cross. The Polish Red Cross Association (PCK) was established in 1919, and before the outbreak of the war in 1939 it managed to develop into a sizable organization: it amounted to about 400,000 adult members and 450,000 young people, over 1,300 health service and social care units, technical equipment, and a well-trained staff of emergency service nurses of the PCK. Such a big and important organization that was very active during the war must have created strong connotations for the term *wolontariusz* via its nursing care, or more generally by its activities such as taking care of the ill, the elderly, and the disabled. The word *wolontariusz* thus acquired a slightly different meaning from the term *ochotnik,* or words such as "social activist" or "community worker" (*działacz społeczny* or *społecznik,* respectively).

In the connotational field of the Polish language *ochotnik* stresses individual freedom to put yourself forward to perform a certain task, while "community worker" (*społecznik*) or "social activist" (*działacz społeczny*) emphasizes involvement in matters relating to the social community and selfless activities for the common good or simply for other people. In the case of the term *wolontariusz*, the main emphasis is put on helping those who are weaker (Adamiak 2014). Obviously, becoming an *ochotnik* does not exclude being voluntarily involved in social matters and may entail helping; community workers do things voluntarily in the sense that they undertake them on their own volition and unprompted, and the *wolontariusz* works in the community. Nevertheless, the semantic fields and possible interpretations of these terms are significantly different. Replacing all of them with the term "voluntary work" (*wolontariat*)—understood in the most general sense as any voluntary and unpaid activity for the benefit of others—is in fact an extremely difficult undertaking. Studies still instinctively associate volunteering with "dedication," the word *ochotnik* stubbornly continues to be present in the names of the most prestigious voluntary organizations, and *społecznik* is returning in the form of "social activist" (*aktywista społeczny*). It appears that the term *aktywista* has completely broken away from its socialist understanding and today appears to have no pejorative connotations whatsoever.

Another source of difficulty proved to be new and extremely popular social actions in which, from the get-go, the word *wolontariusz* has been used to define people offering themselves to work as *ochotnik*. This concerns the Great Orchestra of Christmas Charity (WOŚP), a foundation whose main statutory objective includes activities in the field of health care by gathering money to help sick people, especially children, as well as activities aiming to promote health and preventive care. Once a year WOŚP organizes an event called "the grand finale," a media and entertainment event accompanied by the large-scale collection of donations for a specific purpose related to health care. WOŚP involves a huge number of volunteers, mostly young people, whose role is to go around collecting donations in marked cans. The mass scale of the event, along with the publicity surrounding WOŚP's drive, resulted in the identification of a new type of *wolontariat* with one-time activities that do not require any qualifications or long-term commitment. As a result, the term *wolontariusz* now extends from the old image of a selfless carer leaning over the sick in a hospice to that of a young man with a can collecting at a shopping center one day a year. Where in this spectrum does a rural sports activist fit who voluntarily, and without any payment, trains a girls football team, often donating private funds for them to travel to matches? Or young people who, at their own expense, organize a place to rollerblade?

In research, too, both quantitative and qualitative semantic confusion about volunteering appears.[12] The qualitative in-depth study of the sample of sports activists, mountain rescuers from the GOPR, and rangers working for free in national parks, conducted for the Voluntary Action 2012+ group, showed that they did not want to be called *wolontariusz*.[13] On the one hand, they distance themselves from one-time volunteering because to become a rescuer one has to undergo a long training period, gain competences, and earn the confidence of a group. The term *wolontariusz* would put them in the same group as young people collecting money for several hours for WOŚP. On the other hand, they distance themselves from being associated with care and social help, highlighting the diversity of their tasks and competences. Sports activists, in turn, think the concept of *wolontariusz* misses the emphasis on "service to the community," which they understand as a long-term, consistent commitment to a certain mission that is not of a helping nature, but rather involves development. The notion of a social activist, in their opinion, better conveys the meaning and essence of their work.

Recent studies also show that different understandings of the terms related to social activism depend on the ages of respondents and activists. Warsaw secondary school students still identify voluntary work primarily with "bringing help," responsibility, and a time burden.[14] Thus, while the older generation prefer the term *ochotnik* as they distance themselves from one-time activities and temporariness, young people are afraid to make a substantial commitment, something that they do not feel ready to undertake. Is it really possible to use one word to label all those who voluntarily undertake certain actions for the benefit of others and who are not being paid for it?

There are even more problems related to volunteering in practice, which may translate into the results of quantitative studies. Is someone who helps an elderly lady with her shopping a volunteer (*wolontariusz*), since he does not operate within any organization, he is not insured, and no one has signed an agreement with him or her? How are small organizations working with a large number of volunteers supposed to deal with the formalities, e.g., when organizing a festival or sporting event? Is the *wolontariusz* not allowed to gain any benefit at all from his or her activities, including things like obtaining a diploma or a certificate of acquiring specific competence? Can social activities such as organizing evening parties for neighbors' children, feeding stray cats, or taking care of courtyard vegetation be considered volunteering? All these questions attest to the problems concerning definitions and practices one encounters when assessing the level of people's actual engagement in different forms of social activism in the local context.

Conclusions: Models and Reality

The case of introducing and promoting the term "volunteering" in Poland illustrates a conscious effort to shape reality according to a certain intellectual and ideological plan. And the post-1989 transformation is just part of a much longer process. As I discussed elsewhere, Poles were forced three times during the last century to re-create themselves, rejecting past habits and values and adopting a certain model form of "proper" society (Giza 2013). After regaining independence in 1918, three territories that differed in terms of cultural, economic, and social development had to be put together, while the citizens living in them, despite enormous cultural, philosophical, and identity-related differences, were expected to become not only citizens of the same country, but also of one society. After World War II, Polish society had to reject the legacy of the previous republics of Poland and turn into a "socialist" (and ultimately communist) one. And finally, in 1989, after almost fifty years, society was supposed to reject its socialist heritage and become civic-minded, open, and autonomous.

The specificity of the Polish situation, however, lies not just in such rapid and fundamental changes of the desired model of collective life. It also lies in the fact that this desirable model did not emerge organically from ongoing experiences and challenges, from understanding the potential of changes, or using existing resources. The problems of Polish "civil society" result from, among other things, the fact that the concepts introduced in the discourse, concepts that are supposed to describe it, i.e., the third sector, nongovernmental organizations, and volunteering, do not fit the experiences, language habits, or ways of thinking of most people. Undoubtedly, the "old" third sector is doing well; it is even possible that in some respects it is stronger than the "new" one. But even in the case of the "new" types of social activism it seems that some groups and activities remain invisible. Thus, it is difficult to discern the extent to which Polish civil society is weak or underdeveloped, and the extent to which such a view results from the inadequacy of the indicators used and the survey questions asked.

There are signs of the new approach to measuring and defining civil society, as well as the signs of diminishing the divide between "old" and "new" third sector. As to the new paradigm emerging in research and theory development, the indices of informal volunteering realized outside NGOs introduced, and we witness, the growing interest in such organizations as the voluntary fire brigades or rural housewives circles.[15] As to the divide between the two segments of the third sector, we can see both the trend to modernize among the "old" organizations (e.g., folk sports associations) and many examples of the cooperation between the two. It seems that we get closer to grasping the reality of the civil society in Poland as it is, slowly abandoning a priori normative assumptions.

Anna Giza-Poleszczuk is Professor of Sociology at University of Warsaw. She has vast experience both in researching social activism and in working with and for NGOs in developing and implementing programs of social change. Her current interest is in managing social change and participation. She has recently published two books—one on the sources and processes of shaping the self-consciousness of the Polish society, and the second on key trends in contemporary Poland.

Notes

1. This self-image is present both in public discourse led by opinion leaders (politicians, journalists, experts) and in public opinion surveys (Giza 2013).
2. A content analysis of *Gazeta Wyborcza* (a renowned Polish daily) demonstrates that journalists of this daily believe secularization is a necessary condition for modernization (Giza 2013).

3. I conducted research and worked as an expert for the Polish American Freedom Foundation, the Academy for the Advancement of Philantropy in Poland, the Polish Children and Youth Foundation, the Amos Komensky Foundation, and many others. Together with Jakub Wygnański I am cofounder of the "Shipyard" Foundation. My knowledge and understanding of the Polish third sector comes from many sources, including personal experience and scientific literature.

4. Donald Tusk, then prime minister of Poland, initiated the action to build small football fields for Euro 2012 all over Poland, but especially in rural areas. In 2011, the research conducted by the Social Action 2012 was the first evaluation of the social impact of Orliks. Moreover, there were three stadiums built and one modernized for Euro 2012, all financed by the state.

5. The full list of participants is published here: http://www.ps2012.pl/co-robimy/pr ojekty-spoleczne/projekt-spoleczny-2012/grupa-wolontariat-spoleczny-2012/index .html. Retrieved 12 October 2015.

6. The title of the article is a parody of the iconic excerpt from Polish national writer Adam Mickiewicz's poem "Ode to Youth," which epitomizes the essence of Polish romanticism.

7. In 1998, the nonprofit network of citizens' advice bureaus was established to broaden access to the law, giving citizens free legal advice. The bureaus do give advice for free, but only a few are still active and hardly anybody is aware of their existence.

8. According to CBOS (Centre for Social Opinion Research), the percentage of Poles believing democracy is the best political regime is consistently above 66 percent. See http://cbos.pl/SPISKOM.POL/2014/K_105_14.PDF. Retrieved 14 November 2015.

9. In CBOS's report *Aktywność społeczna Polaków,* the question was framed as follows: "Have you devoted, during last 12 months, your free time voluntarily and without payment, to help an unknown person or persons? I mean the activity you have undertaken individually, and not via an organization or institution" (CBOS 2014).

10. There is no research measuring people's reactions to such notions as "community action" or "social activist" that were and still are present in everyday language as they became an element of everyday experience. Under state socialism everybody, from schoolchildren to pensioners, was forced to "volunteer" and take part in "community actions." With time, the latter became a metaphor for mediocre, feigned activity, without sense or goal.

11. Before the first free election in Poland, Solidarity decided to create the network of Citizens Committees, to mobilize supporters, prepare lists of the candidates, etc.

12. Qualitative research carried out by the "Stocznia" Foundation of Social Research and Innovations for the "Dobra Sieć" Foundation among volunteers. For the report on this research see http://www.projektor.org.pl/uploads/184_1.pdf, retrieved 14 November 2015.

13. More information about this research and its findings can be found in the conference presentation retrieved 14 November 2015 from at:https://d1dmfej9n5lgmh .cloudfront.net/msport/article_attachments/attachments/10488/original/Wolon tariat___Sport___Zaangazowanie_-_Aleksandra_Goldys.pdf?1334721204, and the recommendations prepared based on this research: http://bibliotekawolontar iatu.pl/wp-content/uploads/wolontariat_2012_REKOMENDACJE.pdf, retrieved 14 November 2015.

14. See for example http://chikwadrat.pl/wp-content/uploads/2011/11/badanie_akty wnosci_licealistow1.pdf, retrieved 4 June 2015.
15. See, e.g., the research report on the issues of rural housewives circles by the Stocznia Foundation. Retrieved 14 November 2015 from http://stocznia.org.pl/wp-content/ uploads/2014/09/KGW_nie_tylko_od_kuchni_raport.pdf, or the research report on voluntary fire brigades issued by the Klon/Jawor Association in 2012, retrieved 14 November 2015 from http://www.ngo.pl/OSP_2012_raport/ebook/content/ OSP_raport.pdf.

References

Adamiak, P. 2014. *Zaangażowanie społeczne Polek i Polaków. Wolontariat, filantropia, 1% i wizerunek organizacji pozarządowych. Raport z badań 2013* [Social Engagement of Poles: Voluntary Activities, Philanthropy, 1% and the Image of the Nongovernmental Organizations]. Warszawa: Stowarzyszenie Klon/Jawor.

CBOS. 2014. *Aktywność społeczna Polaków–poziom zaangażowania i motywacje* [Social Activity among Poles: Level of Engagement and Motivations]. Komunikat Badan BS/62/2011. Warszawa: CBOS.

Costa, E., L. Parker, and M. Andreaus. 2014. *Accountability and Social Accounting for Social and Non-Profit Organizations.* Emerald Group Publishing.

Czapiński, J. 2005. "Kapitał społeczny" [Social Capital], in *Diagnoza społeczna 2005* [Social Diagnosis 2005], ed. J. Czapiński and T. Panek. Warszawa: Rada Monitoringu Społecznego, 201–214.

Czapiński, J. 2007. "Kapitał społeczny" [Social Capital], in *Diagnoza społeczna 2007* [Social Diagnosis 2007], ed. J. Czapiński and T. Panek. Warszawa: Rada Monitoringu Społecznego, 257–267.

Czapliński, P. 2009. *Polska do wymiany. Późna nowoczesność i nasze wielkie narracje* [Poland to Be Replaced: Late Modernity and Our Grand Narratives]. Warszawa: Wydawnictwo W.A.B.

Ekiert, G. 2012. "The Illiberal Challenge in Post-Communist Europe: Surprises and Puzzles." *Taiwan Journal of Democracy* 8, no. 2: 63–77.

Ekiert, G., and R. Foa. 2011. "Civil Society Weakness in Post Communist Europe: A Preliminary Assessment." *Carlo Alberto Notebooks* No. 198 (January).

Evers, A., and A.-M. Guillemard. 2013. *Social Policy and Citizenship: The Changing Landscape.* Oxford: Oxford University Press.

Frączak, P., and R. Skrzypiec. 2011. *Kondycja spółdzielczości pracy oraz wizje jej rozwoju. Raport z badań* [The Condition of Labour Cooperatives and the Vision of Their Development: The Research Report]. Warszawa: Spółdzielnia Kooperatywa Pozarządowa. Retrieved 12 November 2015 from http://ofop.eu/sites/ofop.eu/files/biblioteka-pliki/ spoldzielczosc_pracy_2011_www.pdf.

Fuszara, M., M. Grabowska, J. Mizielińska, and J. Regulska, eds. 2008. Współpraca czy konflikt. Państwo, Unia i kobiety [Cooperation or Conflict? The State, the EU, and Women]. Academic and Professional Publishers, Warsaw.

Gąsior-Niemiec, A. 2010. "Lost in the System? Civil Society and Regional Development Policy in Poland." *Acta Politica* 45: 90–111.

———. 2013. "Social Capital in Rural Poland: Between Tradition and Social Engineering," in *Social Capital and Rural Development in the Knowledge Society,* ed. H. Westlund and K. Kobayashi. Cheltenham, U.K.; Northampton, MA: Edward Elgar Publishing, 156–179.

Giza, A. 2013. *Gabinet luster. Kształtowanie samowiedzy Polaków w dyskursie publicznym.* [The Mirrors' Cabinet: Shaping of Poles Self-Consciousness in the Public Discourse]. Warszawa: Wydawnictwo Naukowe Scholar.

Gliński, P. 2006. *Style działania organizacji pozarządowych w Polsce. Grupy interesu czy pożytku publicznego?* [Styles of Operating Non-Governmental Organizations in Poland: Interest Groups or Public Utility?]. Warsaw: IFiS PAN Publishing.

———. 2010. "Civil Society: Twenty Years of Change: The Third Sector." *Academia: Focus on Sociology* 1, no. 25: 4–7.

Graff, A. 2010. "Urzędasy, bez serc, bez ducha" [Clerks with No Heart, No Spirit]. *Gazeta Wyborcza* (6 January).

Gumkowska, M., J. Herbst, J. Szołajska, and J. Wygnański. 2006. *The Challenge of Solidarity: CIVICUS: Civil Society Index Report for Poland.* Retrieved 6 November 2015 from http://www.civicus.org/new/media/Poland_Country_Report.pdf.

Herbst, J., and J. Przewłocka. 2011. *Podstawowe fakty o organizacjach pozarządowych. Raport z badania 2010* [The Basic Facts About the Nongovernmental Organizations: The Research Report]. Retrieved 6 November 2015 from http://civicpedia.ngo.pl/files/civicpedia.pl/public/raporty/podstawowefakty_2010.pdf.

Jurczyszyn, Ł., J. Kołtan, P. Kuczyński, and M. Rakusa-Suszczewski, eds. 2014. *Obywatele ACTA* [Citizens of ACTA]. Gdańsk: Europejskie Centrum Solidarności.

Karasińska, A. 2009. "Wolontariat jako nowe zjawisko w Polsce" [Voluntary Activity as the New Phenomenon in Poland]. *Praca Socjalna* 2: 122–129.

Kolankiewicz, G. 2006. "Democracy, Inequality and State Crisis," in *Building Democracy and Civil Society East of the Elbe: Essays in Honor of Edmund Mokrzycki,* ed. S. Eliaeson. London: Routledge, 47–60.

Mancwel, J., K. Milczewska, and J. Wiśniewski. 2014. *Koła Gospodyń Wiejskich nie tylko od kuchni. Raport z badania.* [Rural Housewives Circles Not Only from the Kitchen Side. Research Report]. Warszawa: Pracownia Badań i Innowacji Społecznych "Stocznia."

Moroń, D. 2009. *Wolontariat w trzecim sektorze. Prawo i polityka* [Voluntary Activity in the Third Sector: The Law and the Politics]. Wrocław: Wydawnictwa Uniwersytetu Wrocławskiego.

Projekt Społeczny. 2012. http://www.ps2012.pl/index.html, retrieved 12 October 2015.

Putnam, D. 2000. *Bowling Alone: The Collapse and Revival of American Community.* New York: Simon & Schuster.

The Economist. 2001. "Limping Towards Normality. Report from Poland" 21 October 2001. Retrieved 14 November 2015 from http://www.economist.com/node/821360.

Włodarczyk, E. 2011. "Odcienie i cienie wolontariatu" [Tints and Shadows of the Voluntary Activity]. *Kultura i edukacja* 3, no. 82: 26–50.

Wygnański, J., and P. Frączek. 2007. *Social Economy in Poland: Definitions, Application, Expectations and Uncertainties.* Retrieved 6 November 2015 from http://www.ekonomiaspoleczna.pl/files/ekonomiaspoleczna.pl/public/socialeconomyinPL/wygnanski_openning_report.pdf.

Załęski, P. 2012. *Neoliberalizm i społeczeństwo obywatelskie* [Neoliberalism and Civil Society]. Toruń: Wydawnictwo Naukowe UMK.

Zimmer, A., E. Priller, and H. Anheier. 1997. "Der Nonprofit-Sektor in den neuen Bundesländern: Kontinuität, Neuanfang oder Kopie." *Zeitschrift für öffentliche und gemeinwirtschaftliche Unternehmen* 20, no. 1: 58–75.

Chapter 3

RETHINKING CIVIC PRIVATISM IN A POSTSOCIALIST CONTEXT
INDIVIDUALISM AND PERSONALIZATION IN POLISH CIVIL SOCIETY ORGANIZATIONS

Kerstin Jacobsson

Introduction

Polish civil society is an intriguing case. On the one hand, Poland has long traditions of civic activism, had a relatively developed associational sphere during state socialism, and was one of the few countries in the region in which regime change was brought about by the struggle of a grassroots movement, Solidarity. On the other hand, since 1989 the country seems to have followed the general pattern in the region: people in former state-socialist countries are less likely to participate in voluntary organizations, less likely to contribute financially to organizations, and less likely to trust fellow citizens. This also pertains to Poland, according to both Polish studies (e.g., Czapiński and Panek 2012; Kościański and Misztal 2008) and international surveys, which display comparatively low levels of Poles' participation in protest activities, participation in voluntary organizations, and social trust (see, e.g., European Social Survey 2010).

At the same time, however, myriad civil society organizations exist. According to the Klon/Jawor report of 2012, there were about 11,000 registered foundations and 72,000 associations in Poland in 2012 (the voluntary fire brigades not included), of which about three-fourths were estimated to be active (Przewłocka 2012). According to the Polish statistical office, of 82,500 organizations registered in the National Court register in 2013, about 73,000 had the special status of Public Benefit Organizations.[1] Add to this picture the civil society mobilizations that take place in a less structured format, such as temporary mobilizations or informal forms of activism (e.g., Polanska and Chimiak 2016). Examples include the mobilizations against the ACTA agreement, the yearly feminist Manifa demonstrations, the lively field of urban activism (e.g., Kowalewski 2013; Polanska and Piotrowski 2015), the mobilizations of right-wing groups (see Płatek and Płucienniczak in this volume) as well as the anti-government protests following the 2015 election.

Somewhat paradoxically, then, the Global Survey of the State of Civil Society could conclude that in Poland "a rather well-connected and well-structured organized civil society exists in the context of weak civic engagement" (Heinrich 2007: 300). This raises the question of how we can make sense of Polish civil society, which appears as weak in terms of participation (as conventionally measured), but which is characterized by a large number of active civil society organizations and a lively sphere of informal activities.

A related paradox was formulated by the Polish sociologist Gliński (2004: 429), observing that there is "[o]n the one hand, a peculiar hyperactivity in the day-to-day resourcefulness of our citizens and on the other hand, there is a great passivity in the public sphere ... in the sphere of the public good or common welfare." He concluded that citizenship virtues are deficient in Polish society, a remark that resonates with Sztompka's argument that "civilizational incompetence" is a "trap of post-communist societies" (Sztompka 1993; see also Czapiński 2008).

Like other chapters in this volume, this chapter challenges the view of a weak and incapacitated civil society, arguing that in many ways Polish civil society is lively, dynamic, and entrepreneurial. Nevertheless, the chapter argues that civic engagement displays some distinctive features, such as a certain preference for individualist forms of action. Later I will show how an individualist action orientation features prominently in the self-understanding of activists interviewed for this research, and that organizational representatives seem to envision their civic engagement as part of their personal affairs, even though the (organizational) aim is directed at realizing a common good (see also Chimiak 2006a). Thus, the research problem that this chapter addresses is how to understand this paradoxical combination of individual initiative and resourcefulness, and what Gliński (2004) called a lack of classical civic virtues, or, as I prefer to put it, the inclination to pursue collective aims in individualist and privatist forms. For instance, is people's civic activism based on the citizen role in the classical sense, characterized by participation in public life, or should their engagement rather be understood in relation to other citizen roles, like representing a hybrid of the *homme* (human being, member of the domestic sphere), *bourgeois* (economic citizen, participant in the market sphere), and *citoyen* (political citizen, citizen in relation to the state)? Or is their civic (self-)understanding merely permeated by a (neo)liberal conception of agency?

The chapter suggests a new perspective on Polish civil society by investigating what is here conceptualized as the "civic privatism" of Polish civil society organizations. This feature is characterized first by an individualist orientation to one's civic engagement (whereby collective aims are pursued in individualist forms) and the spirit of enterprise (a "business-mindedness" and power of individual initiative). And, second, it is characterized by a preference for individual resourcefulness, informality, and the personalization of civic relationships. The chapter argues that action logics from both the domestic sphere and the market sphere tend to "spill over" to the civil sphere in everyday practices of social engagement.[2] It is suggested that both of these aspects of "civic privatism" have historical roots and result in a type of "privatization" of the civil sphere.

Thus, to explain this attitude of "civic privatism," pre–state socialist, state socialist, and post–state socialist experiences are relevant. While the roots of entrepreneurialism and individual resourcefulness stem from pre–state socialist times, and these habits (and habits of the heart) became a survival strategy during state socialism, they have subsequently become a strategy of success (or necessity) in postcommunist and capitalist Poland. It is proposed that some traditions of the presocialist time, such as entrepreneurialism, and some legacies of the socialist time, most importantly the lack of generalized trust, fit well and are reinforced by the current neoliberal ideology.

However, in contrast to the more negative accounts of civic privatism as a threat to civic virtues, it is argued that the Polish version of civic privatism is also an expression of civicness, in the sense of embracing a concern for a greater good and a willingness to commit to its realization.

The chapter illustrates empirically how civic privatism can play out in Polish civil society, drawing on a case study of animal rights and animal welfare activism.[3] It is based on thirty-five interviews conducted in 2010–2013, and some followup interviews in 2015–2016, with activists representing the most salient Polish animal rights and animal welfare organizations.[4] The analysis focuses on the self-understanding of the activists and their way of reasoning about their social engagement. In addition, the analysis draws on existing research on civil society in Poland. Polish civil society is well surveyed; the Klon/Jawor Association publishes regular reports on the structure, activities, and funding patterns of Polish civil society, and both the Social Diagnosis and The Public Opinion Research Center (CBOS) regularly present surveys of, inter alia, attitudes on social engagement. As a complement, this chapter provides an interpretation and discussion of some *quali-*

ties of Polish civil society making. A remark on delimitation is in order: while civil society cannot be reduced to formalized civil society organizations or the third sector, this chapter is primarily concerned with this organized civil society, namely nonprofit organizations.

Rethinking Civic Privatism

The concept of civic privatism usually refers to a citizen's attitude of turning away from political life and collective projects in favor of personal, individualist concerns (e.g., Peterson 1984). The most well-known formulation is probably Habermas's in the book *Legitimation Crisis* (1975). Habermas uses the concept of civic privatism to denote what he sees as a syndrome of modern capitalist societies, consisting of political abstinence and mass loyalty in combination with an orientation to career, leisure, and consumption (1975: 37). He divides the concept of civic privatism into civil [*sic*] and familial-vocational privatism, where civil privatism refers to an orientation of low participation in public life corresponding to a structural depoliticization of the public sphere. Familial-vocational privatism complements civil privatism and refers to a family orientation with a developed interest in consumption and leisure on the one hand, and a career orientation and orientation toward status competition on the other hand (1975: 75). Habermas saw familial-vocational privatism as determined by the specifically bourgeois value orientations of possessive individualism and utilitarianism, and by tradition, for instance religion. For Habermas, both the achievement-oriented vocational ethos of the middle class and the fatalism of the lower class are secured by tradition and transposed through educational structures and child-rearing (1975: 77). Thus, he saw the motivational structures as class-specific: an individualistic achievement orientation among the bourgeoisie and external superego structures and a conventional work ethic in the lower class (ibid.).

Howard (2003: 154) picked up Habermas's concept of civil privatism in his discussion on civil society in postcommunist Europe (even if Poland was not in focus in his study). He asked the provocative question of whether civil privatism serves as a functional equivalent to civil society in these countries. He found that citizens in postcommunist Europe typically had highly developed and lively private networks while being much less active and engaged in public and political life. He also found that civil society organizations were often developed on the basis of private networks. While Habermas saw civil privatism as a form of mass loyalty able to produce a form of system legitimation, Howard (2003: 154) argued that the postcommunist private networks do not contain this type of implicit support for the public sphere. One reason is the low levels of social trust as well as trust in public institutions; another is the strong distinction between private and public, with the public being negatively associated with the state and seen as antagonistic to the private sphere.

I suggest that it is useful to distinguish between privatism (in general) and *civic* privatism. While privatism indeed entails a retreat to the private sphere (whether to family life or to the market sphere as consumers or to professional life) at the expense of public engagement, and the pursuit of individual concerns (or narrow interests) rather than a public/common good, I use *civic privatism* to connote an *attitude of active individuals to their engagement in civil society* and thus based on a *civic/citizen identity.* What I am arguing in this study of animal rights/welfare activists in Poland is that *the ethos of the private sphere is readily brought into their civil society engagement.* One manifestation of this is that the individualistic, achievement-oriented vocational ethos and status competition of the middle class also colors social engagement (at least as far as the third sector is concerned). Indeed, this can go hand in hand with the fatalism and passivity of other social classes, as Habermas (1975) noted, as well as with a widespread general privatism of prioritizing consumption, leisure, or family life over engagement in the public sphere.

Ever since Hegel, the modern member of the middle class has often been seen as a combination of two people, the *citoyen* being active in the public or political sphere, and the *bourgeois* being active in the economic sphere. Hegel and many others feared that the self-seeking identity of the *bourgeois* would pose a threat to civic virtues as self-concern poses a risk of overshadowing the drive for the common good (e.g., Gawin 2006). In relation to these citizen roles, my suggestion is that the civic privatism I describe represents a hybrid of the *bourgeois* and the *citoyen* roles and ethos, with a certain fusion of action logics of both political and economic/market citizenship. This results in a distinctive combination of individualism and engagement for the common good. This argument is, in fact, in line with Ost's remark that civil society and bourgeois society became conflated by Polish intellectuals in their embracement of neoliberal economic reform in the first decades of transition (Ost 2005: 192). It is also in line with Rukszto's (1997) observation that the entrepreneurial virtues of the market sphere also permeate the citizenship model in capitalist Poland. And it helps shed light on Rychard's findings (2009: 228); he contrasted the weak participation in political life in Poland with the much stronger participation in the market, and asked: "Could it be that Poles are consumers (and producers) to a greater degree than they are citizens?" Rychard envisaged a gradual erosion of the differences of the two roles (consumers and citizens), with the parallel process of making consumption more civil and marketizing citizenship with political marketing and use of public figures, which have little to contribute to political substance (Rychard 2009: 232). However, in contrast to the more negative accounts,

I argue that the fluid boundaries of the civil and market spheres have both pros and cons.

The second manifestation of the ethos of the private sphere being brought into citizens' social engagement involves action logics from the domestic sphere (personal networks) coloring organizational life, which I conceptualize as a personalization of civic relationships. This, I suggest, represents a hybrid of the *homme* and *citoyen* roles and ethos. My argument here is that individual and family-centered resourcefulness, and the social world of private arrangements, informal economies, and personal networks are also reproduced in the civil sphere, as these action logics are drawn on when building organizations and organizing day-to-day work. Gliński asked: "Why are there two distinct Polands, the powerful Poland of day-to-day resourcefulness and the rather rickety civil Poland?" and he added "And why would our Polish resourcefulness be only a demonic trait?" (2004: 429–430). While acknowledging that individual resourcefulness could potentially benefit civil society, he still concludes that the form it takes is basically anti-civic (as individual strategies are typically preferred over collective action). My contention in this chapter is that Polish resourcefulness colors civil society activity, too, and contributes to its entrepreneurial character, albeit, as we shall see, not without side effects for cooperation and collective action.

The following analysis illustrates the porous borders and interdependency between the domestic sphere, the market sphere, the civil sphere, and political society, in real-life civil society making in Poland.

Civic Privatism in Poland: Forms and Expressions

Below, I describe some empirical dimensions of civic privatism and illustrate how it may play out in Polish civil society. The illustrations are based on an interview study of activists engaged in animal rights and animal welfare issues, while also relating to previous research on the third sector in general, where relevant. First I give a brief description of the study.

Animal *welfare* activism is focused on improving animal protection rather than rejecting the instrumental use of animals for human needs, while animal *rights* activism takes the more radical position. I count both branches as belonging to the wider animal rights movement, and Polish activists recognize each other as parts of the same movement even if there are ideological tensions between the two factions (see also Jacobsson 2012, 2013).

Poland has a long history of animal welfare and hosts one of the oldest active organizations in the world, namely, TOZ (*Towarzystwo Opieki nad Zwierzętami*), founded in 1865 (see Plach 2012). TOZ is the only one of the organizations that existed during state socialism; all the others have developed since the late 1980s and most of them since 2000. Animal *rights* activism, on the other hand, developed in Poland in the late 1980s and early 1990s. While the movement in the 1990s consisted mainly of an informal network of activist groups all over Poland, it has meanwhile undergone an institutionalization process. This was, in part, an accommodation to legal regulations and funding opportunities, namely, the Act on Public Benefit and Volunteer Work of 2003 and the provision of 1 percent tax donations (see Jacobsson 2013). The movement has remained small-scale and fragmented; the studied organizations have less than fifty members or participants, with the exception of TOZ, which is the only large-scale animal welfare organization, with ninety-six branches operating all over Poland, even if their level of activity varies. For an analysis of the mobilization and action strategies of the movement, see Jacobsson (2012, 2013) and Fröhlich and Jacobsson (forthcoming). The analysis in this chapter focuses on the self-understanding, motivations, orientations, and ways of thinking, acting, and being (ethos) of the activists.

Individualism and the Spirit of Enterprise: Action Logics from the Market Sphere

Individual initiative in response to perceived opportunities is of utmost importance for the dynamism of Polish civil society. The animal-oriented organizations in Poland have mostly come about through the initiative of single individuals or a small group of friends who want to "realize their dreams," which they feel can be more easily done by starting their own organization. *"I've just got my goal and I want to realize it,"* as one interviewee explained her decision to start her own organization. Her friend, who is also engaged in the organization, said: *"She has always dreamed about having a foundation and to have more possibilities, better tools for helping animals, for instance having more opportunities for gaining financial support for our activities."*

This achievement orientation, realization of personal ambitions, and self-actualization through one's civic engagement, in combination with a lot of hard work and determination, are some features of what I call the entrepreneurialism of Polish civil society. This is also supported by Chimiak's study on the motivations of Poles engaged in NGOs; self-actualization and accomplishment, along with the desire to realize one's ideas, were the most common motivations (Chimiak 2006a: 190ff.). A good citizen is "a self-reliant initiator and good worker," is Chimiak's description of the civic self-understanding of her informants (Chimiak 2006a: 250). Starting one's own "organization business" appeals to activists, despite the fact that it requires more work, and entails more responsibilities, than joining existing organizations.

The "spirit of enterprise" and "small business" ethos feature strongly in the interview narratives. The activists typically have a strong internal drive and use their creativity and decisiveness to achieve their goals. Related to this is efficiency orientation; the organizations tend to be highly task- and efficiency-oriented. For this reason members are seen by some interviewees as a potentially complicating factor in the smooth running of one's "business": *"the fewer members, the better,"* and *"fewer people, less work,"* as one founder of an animal welfare organization expressed it. This is in contrast to an organizational logic in which numbers mean power.

Entrepreneurial culture, including elements such as innovative push, achievement orientation, and individualistic competitiveness, is no doubt important for the dynamism of Polish civil society organizations. Another aspect of the spirit of enterprise is the culture of competitiveness. The animal welfare organizations join hands occasionally, mostly around specific campaigns (discussed below). However, in between they compete for resources and for attention in public space, a necessity for resource mobilization through tax donations (the 1 percent tax allowance; see Jacobsson 2013). As one respondent put it: *"I think in Poland there is no solidarity between organizations. There also are no sponsors ... Apart from the lack of solidarity and lack of sponsors, there is also a lack of media attention."* Competition plays out both as competition for material resources and as competition for status. While previous research on Polish civil society tended to emphasize the competition for scarce resources and its detrimental effects (e.g., Gliński 2006; Schimanek 2010), my analysis stresses that status competition—competition for recognition as an important actor—is just as much at stake (a theme further developed later in this chapter). In fact, in the case of animal rights and welfare activism in Poland, material incentives are not the most important incentives for starting one's own organization.

Entrepreneurs in the market sphere and actors in the civil sphere have different objectives: profit versus a greater good (in the present case of animal welfare). This does not preclude the use, by some social activists in Poland, of engagement as a way of securing an income as well as pursuing a meaningful cause. It should be noted, however, that there is little evidence that Polish animal rights or welfare activists are motivated by such material incentives. Running an animal welfare organization is typically not a profitable business in the Polish context—there are very few public grants available for animal welfare, and the Polish organizations (with the exception of Klub Gaja) do not have the organizational capacity to apply for international grants. TOZ is the only one of the organizations that is very successful in mobilizing income from the tax allowance (the 1 percent rule). In fact, several of the interviewees for this study invest their own private money in their organizations for the sake of the cause. Rather than stressing material gain, the argument here is that some values associated with business life (such as individual initiative, achievement orientation, and efficiency) also color organizational life. Thus, the ethos of the market sphere is partly transplanted into the civil sphere, which is what I mean when I refer to activists' outlooks representing a hybrid of the *bourgeois* and the *citoyen* role and ethos. Also, Koralewicz and Malewska-Peyre pointed to the similarity in outlook between social activists and businesspeople in Poland, especially in their individualistic attitude (quoted in Chimiak 2006a: 136). Likewise, Rukszto's earlier study (1997) found that the entrepreneurial virtues of the market sphere permeate the citizenship model in capitalist Poland, which led her to speak of "citizen entrepreneurs."

Another example of such "business-mindedness" in my study is the concern with protecting the organization's brand that some animal welfare organizations display, and where keeping the organization small and in tight control is a way of preserving the organization's good name. Another example is marketing strategies, where attempts at external resource mobilization and marketing by using celebrities take precedence over recruitment of members or volunteers. That "organizations turn their back on members" (Papakostas 2011: 10), moving away from large membership stocks toward other forms of resource mobilization, is a general trend in the Western world and not unique to the postsocialist context (e.g., Skocpol 2003). Nevertheless, I suggest that in Poland this trend is further compounded by state-socialist experiences and memories.

An individualist orientation to their social engagement features strongly in the self-understanding of the interviewed activists. Independence, autonomy, and self-reliance are cherished values, while embarking on collective projects and collaborating with others are often associated with "troubles." Poland, along with other postsocialist countries, shares collective memories of the time when membership in organizations was forced or strongly encouraged by the state (e.g., Howard 2003), making autonomy an embraced value. In addition, a neoliberal ideology has served to compound individualist orientations and the notion of the "entrepreneurial self."

Apart from a sense of achievement, in starting one's own organization one gains independence and control. Chimiak, too, found that Polish activists want to be masters of their own fate (2006a: 250). Starting one's own organization or working together with friends is one way of achieving this, while joining an already existing organization or building alliances with others is often associated with "complications." Thus, just as the search for independence was found to be an important motive for starting one's own business in Poland (Sobczuk, quoted in Rychard 2009: 227), the search for independence is an important motive for starting one's own civil society organization.

The new animal-oriented organizations have typically come about when activists who have been active in other organizations broke away to start their own organizations. The aim was often to become more independent and to be able to do one's own thing without others interfering: *"It is easier to be independent"* with *"no one to rule over you,"* as one of the interviewees put it. Another interviewee explained that activists had left the organization where he is employed to start their own organizations because they: *"desire independence in their activities; working for a strongly hierarchical and large organization makes them feel restricted and uncomfortable."* He gave the example of a person who *"wanted to be independent because that is easier, as then he would not have to obtain authorizations or settle accounts with the board. So he does not have anyone above him."* Another respondent from the same organization explained: *"Sometimes they don't like the fact that they have to take others into consideration and you're not independent. Usually it's all about independence."*

To be part of a larger collective is associated with others ruling over one's head. As noted elsewhere (Jacobsson 2013: 41f.), given that the studied organizations tended to be quite hierarchically organized or organized around a strong leader, the chances for an individual to actually exert power by using internal channels for a "voice" may be limited and the exit option quite rational from the individual point of view. Even so, the attitude that cooperation with others complicates one's life seems quite prevalent not only among the interviewees for this research. As Gliński noted, "Poles tend to prefer individual adaptive strategies rather than collective, civic protest, or conflict-generating behavior" (Gliński 2004: 442). Interpersonal conflicts within the previous organization appeared in the interviews as an especially important motive for breaking away and starting one's own group, an organizational logic I have elsewhere formulated as "multiplication by conflict" (Jacobsson 2013: 40). As a representative of the largest animal welfare organization (TOZ) put it: *"So people come in and at some point they come to the conclusion that basically they can try to act on their own, and so they start up their own organizations. Sometimes it also comes to conflicts due to different views on cooperation."* Another interviewee explained her decision to set up her own foundation: *"It's also a bit like part of the Polish NGO world to compete, to play tricks on one another. I don't want to get involved in interpersonal conflicts. I'm just not interested in that."*

This power of individual initiative results in a dynamic, but at the same time fragile, organizational sector characterized by many small-scale initiatives and start-ups of new foundations or associations. For example, in an average year about 4,000 associations and about 1,000 foundations are started in Poland (Herbst and Przewłocka 2011). Dependence on single individuals, however, means that some organizations may have a short life span; thus, organizations survive as long as the individual initiators retain their motivation.

Another consequence of the preference for starting up "one's own" organization is that the leaders of the smaller animal welfare organizations especially seem to conceive of their organizations as their own private projects. These leader-activists typically want to be in control in order to be able to realize their goals efficiently and avoid "troubles" with members and volunteers wanting to have too much say in the running of the organization. This also means that organizational—and financial—transparency is not always a priority; some, as mentioned, even invest their private money in the work, which reinforces the feeling that the organization is their business. The aim of the organizational activity is still oriented toward a greater good (animal welfare), but the forms in which activity is pursued are colored by a logic of personalization of organizational matters.

Personalization and Informality: Action Logics from the Domestic Sphere

An expression of the porous boundaries between the domestic sphere and the civil sphere is that civil society organizing is often built on personalized organizational structures. This preference for informality (which is also common in political life in Poland; see, e.g., Rychard 2009: 226), and personalization of organizational relationships represent another dimension of civic privatism in Poland (one that Poland shares with other postsocialist countries).

In Poland, a civil society also existed under state socialism even though it was not autonomous in relation to the state; apart from the state-controlled associational life (sport clubs, youth clubs, professional associations, etc.), the church, family, and informal groups existed (e.g., Buchowski 1996; Ekiert and Kubik in this volume). The family-centered and informal networks in everyday life were extremely important for the struggles to satisfy day-to-day needs (e.g., Wedel 1986). In many cases these family and acquaintance networks provided the basis for the new organizational life that developed during and after the transition.

Observations that civil society organizations in postsocialist countries are often developed on the basis of personal networks (e.g., Howard 2003, Chimiak 2006a) are supported by this interview study. As one activist who had recently started a foundation described it: "*I am the president of the foundation, my husband is the vice president, and a friend of mine sits on the board. I've had some bad experiences with people in the past, and this time I just wanted to avoid it all.*" Working only with people from one's own circle, who can be trusted, is one way of retaining control and seems to many of the interviewees to be a very natural way of organizing. As Chimiak argues: "participation in the third sector is sometimes an extension of social activists' private lives. It is an instance of an overlap of the public and private sphere" (2006a: 224).

The traditional family-centeredness of Polish society, and/or concern with one's own small social circle rather than society at large, has given rise to a debate about "amoral familism" in Poland (following Tarkowska and Tarkowski 1991). For these authors, such an orientation is not conducive to civic engagement and prevents a strong civil society from developing (e.g., Czapiński 2008). My point is rather that *logics from the private/domestic sphere are readily brought to the public sphere* (norms, expectations, and action logics) and tend to *color one's social engagement* as well, but this does not prevent people from engaging (see also Korolczuk in this volume).

Another aspect of personalization of civic relationships, and, I would suggest, a distinctive feature of civil society functioning in Poland, is the role played by charismatic leadership, that is, strong individual-leaders with "extraordinary qualities" (charisma) or "star qualities." This is supported by a Klon/Jawor study from 2012, which found that one-fourth of the Polish NGOs were small, hierarchical, and formed around a strong leader (Przewłocka et al. 2012). (Two other organization types were enterprise-like NGOs and more spontaneous and flexibly organized associations.) The leaders in my study gathered followers/volunteers (rather than members), invested their own time and resources, were often well connected, and could use informal contacts as well as media contacts to forward the organization's cause. Several of the country's most salient animal welfare organizations are organized around such charismatic leaders. Organizations that are not led by such individuals may still try to mobilize celebrities for marketing purposes and to draw on this type of legitimacy.

Charismatic leadership is a more general feature of postcommunist civil society, and sometimes appears to function as a replacement for internal democratic and depersonalized power structures and legal-bureaucratic rationality.[5] The structures that exist in the organizations, such as boards, are often populated by people from one's own network, while there are fewer structured participation opportunities for members or volunteers (see also Gumkowska et al. 2006). The organizations are not necessarily membership-based, and even if they are, the informal power structures seem more decisive than the formal ones. Well-functioning structures for internal decision making, especially in relation to members, do not seem to be a top priority. Several of the studied organizations were not even interested in increasing the membership stock or the number of volunteers, as expressed in the *"the fewer members, the better"* quote above. *"Volunteers are unreliable,"* as another interviewee opined. Charismatic leadership and personalized organizational structures also go well with the efficiency orientation, as leaders can make the decisions they feel are called for. However, it is less conducive to a participatory organizational culture and thus makes membership less attractive than starting one's own organization.

The informality and personalization mean that the conception of the organizations tends to be mixed with the people/leaders who make them up. For instance, when asked about other civil society organizations, the respondents quickly came to talk about their leaders, their personal attributes, and their qualities as individuals as much as about their agendas or organizational functions, and often in negative terms. Conflicts within the movement have been a recurrent topic in the interviews (which is probably compounded by the small size of the animal rights movements in Poland where all key activists know each other in person). *"Maybe looking from outside it may seem ridiculous, very similar goals and so much tension ... in my view it is not about competition, it is about different views."* The conflicts often have an ideological basis, for instance, vegans are critical of animal welfare activists engaged in animal adoption or shelters who might not even be vegetarians, for not being radical enough. As an activist from a vegan organization said: *"I can't imagine cooperating with [Organization B]. They are so welfarist, like from another planet."* However, the ideological conflicts often seem to be intermixed with conflicts between strong personalities.[6] Just to illustrate: *"[A] is also in conflict with [B] ... And on the other hand she's on good relations with [C]. She likes her, but I can't listen to her, because she's a very particular sort of person and collaboration with her is very difficult."*

The Polish animal-oriented organizations frequently criticize each other in public. In the following example, one organization has tried to discredit another in a letter to the media. An interviewed journalist said: *"[Organization A] plots against [Organization B] by writing to journalists things that they absolutely should not be writing, devaluating [Organization B's] activities ... saying that in the media one can see 'alleged animal defenders' who attempt to legalize the murdering of fish."* Internal ideological disputes are typical for the animal rights movement in many countries. Even so, my interpretation is that there is a dimension of interpersonal conflicts as well as personal status competition in the Polish movement that make collective action more challenging; the fact that many organizational representatives see their organizations as individual projects plays a role here.

Thus, personal stakes and honor seem to color life in the organizations as well as interorganizational relationships, impeding collaboration. Interviews reveal that organizing a meeting with representatives of several organizations requires a careful act of balancing between strong personalities that all expect their share of attention and acknowledgement of their importance.

I suggest that it is in light of the personalization of organizational structures and civic relationships that the prevalence and role of interpersonal conflicts can be understood. As already mentioned, for several of the interviewees, the way to get out of interpersonal conflicts was to start their own organization; thus, instead of engaging in collective problem solving they opted out. Another expression of the personalized relationships is the recurrent suspicion that others have personal agendas and motives, which makes them not trustworthy of collaboration or worthy of credit for their work.

The personalized organizational structures and charismatic leadership are connected to the low levels of generalized trust (in strangers) that Poles in general display while being more inclined to place their trust in individuals. In the Social Diagnosis survey of 2011, only 13 percent of the Poles agreed that most people can be trusted, which is one of the lowest levels of generalized trust in Europe (Czapiński and Panek 2012). However, as we saw, lack of trust in concrete individuals can also prevent more impersonal interorganizational collaboration from developing. Collaboration between animal-oriented organizations of course takes place, but most often in the form of informal and ad hoc networking rather than based on more structured or formalized cooperation.

The role of informal networking among animal-oriented organizations is confirmed in my study. Interestingly, despite the conflicting discourses within which activists from different organizations and groups discuss each other, they have well developed informal networks among them and have at times collaborated successfully around specific campaigns. A recent example was the mobilization in 2010 and 2011, where a loose Coalition for Animals (*Koalicja dla Zwierzat*), coordinated by Viva!, enlisted the backing of more than thirty animal-oriented organizations for a civic law proposal to amend the 1997 Animal Protection Act, for which it managed to collect more than 200,000 signatures (see Jacobsson 2012, 2013). This temporary coalition was a relatively rare event. At present, informal networking rather than formal institution building is the way to achieve coordinated action capacity.

Part of the informal pattern of organizing is also the frequent use of personal contacts and informal ways of solving problems and getting by. Using personal contacts is also connected to the efficacy of purpose discussed earlier. In my analysis, both informality and individual resourcefulness play an important role in Polish civil society making. Informality is a problem-solving strategy and a way to "get things done" in the context of low social trust and trust in formal institutions (e.g., Hayoz 2013: 1), and limited organizational resources. Informality can thus be enabling as it allows for the building of collective action capacity despite these constraints.

While acknowledging that individual resourcefulness could potentially benefit civil society, Gliński concludes that the form it takes is basically anti-civic, as individual strategies are typically preferred over collective action (cf. Gliński 2004, 2006). My contention is that Polish resourcefulness colors civil society activity, too, and contributes to its entrepreneurial character.

This is not to deny that civic privatism may also weaken civil society. For instance, the preference for starting on one's own may make for a more efficient and more easily controlled organization but at the expense of the power and action capacity that large organizations can achieve with the power of bigger numbers. The dependence on personal connections also makes it difficult to build organizational strength, which requires more programmatic and less personalized orientations and structures. The propensity for conflicts that readily follows from personalization is also detrimental to the achievement of collective action.

Civic Privatism in Poland:
Postsocialist Legacies and Marketization Logic

The argument thus far has been that the entrepreneurialism and individualism of Polish civil society activity stems, in part, from a "spillover" of action logics from the market sphere to the civil sphere, while the personalization and informality stem from action logics from the domestic sphere (including friendship networks) being transposed to, and drawn on, in the civil sphere. Both "inclinations" result in a certain privatization of the civil sphere. I argue in this section that legacies from the state-socialist time, and the subsequent neoliberalization of Polish society, are mutually reinforcing in producing and sustaining this effect.

Key to understanding how civic privatism plays out in Poland is the relationship between public and private: both the relationship of the private sphere to the state and—within the broadly conceived private domain—the relationship between the domestic sphere, the market sphere, and the civil sphere. A legacy that Poland shares with other postsocialist states is a persistent public-private divide, in the sense of a marked border between the private/domestic sphere (family and friendship networks) as opposed to the institutional-official (state-controlled) sphere, which developed during the state-socialist time. This legacy is still consequential for citizens' relationship to the political sphere, characterized by negative attitudes toward institutional politics. It also helps explain the positive views of many Poles toward the market (e.g., Rychard 2009).

The negative view of the public arising during state socialism stood in stark contrast to the private sphere as the arena outside state control where freedom could be "lived." The two spheres were governed by different logics. In her well-known study of life in Poland during the last decade of state socialism, Wedel (1986) wrote: "Poles lead two lives, the public and the private ... Poles shape themselves to mesh with the varying demands of private and public worlds. ... One moral code is reserved for the private world of family and friends, another one for the public" (1986: 15–16).

Several decades after the regime change, the state is still generally perceived as antagonistic to the private; state representatives—whether politicians or officials—evoke negative associations, distrust in public institutions, and political elites are marked (e.g., Gliński 2006). For instance, according to EES (European Social Survey) data from 2010, more than 90 percent of Poles have little or no trust in political parties and over 80 percent mistrust the parliament. The government tends to be seen as an arena of cynicism, deceit, or incompetence. As Sztompka remarked, any contact with the public (state) sphere is "polluting," while activities carried out in the private realm are elevated and idealized (1993: 90).

In my interviews, the sense that activists would get "dirty hands" from having too close of a relationship with politicians was salient: the activists were (with only a few exceptions) not interested in developing relationships with political parties. If they had any contacts with the political sphere, it was with individual politicians who were judged to be trustworthy and interested in their issues. Thus, relationships tended to be personalized while institutional channels were undeveloped. This is a rather typical quote: *"We are not connected to politicians but on our demo about seals last year a member of the European Parliament appeared and we talked to her ... So incidentally yes, but on a regular basis we don't have contact with politicians."*

About pursuing change the political way, another interviewee said: *"I think in Poland it would not be successful because politicians would not treat us seriously when we talk about veganism and vegetarianism ... I don't think legal actions would bring much change now. First, it is important to change people's minds, then to change legislation."*

A third person confirmed the futility of lobbying for legal change: *"We try sometimes to go into legislation, for instance about horses or transportation of animals in general. But it is very very hard to go into legislation because people in politics are also involved in businesses that exploit animals ... I think that is why we do not tend to do it in the way of changing legislation, it won't be effective. As a citizen you don't really have an influence on the people elected because they do what they want."*

A fourth interviewee explained her decision not to try to approach politicians with: *"Here most of the councilors are rather not pro-animal. For example once we had a petition directed at the mayor of Cracow. He responded in such an unpleasant manner and just brushed us off, that it is clear that it makes no sense."*

Thus, politicians are best kept at arm's length. Occasionally, organized meetings with invited politicians have resulted in quarrels, partly because the organizations started to quarrel among themselves. An exception happened in 2011, when representatives of a couple of the Polish organizations managed to convince a group of "animal-friendly" parliamentarians to propose an amendment to the Animal Protection Act, which, against expectation, resulted in a minor legal change (entering into force on January 1, 2012). Another part of the movement instead mobilized for a more radically formulated civic law proposal, while a third faction abstained from demanding legal change (see Jacobsson 2012, 2013), also illustrating the difficulty in achieving coordinated action.

If anti-political orientations were salient in the interviews, contacts with public officials were considered even more futile and rarely happened, according to the interviewees. The animal welfare organizations tend to be highly critical of the way the Veterinary Inspectorate, as the main implementing agency for animal protection, functions locally, taking aim at widespread "friendship corruption" between vets and meat producers. A former plenipotentiary for animal welfare, a function that existed during 2009–2010 in the president's office (but was closed down partly because of criticism from animal welfare organizations of its mainly symbolic function), here testifies that there are few connections between the activists and officials: *"The biggest problems are connected with the total lack of cooperation between the veterinary inspection and the organizations, as well as between the organizations and the Ministry of Environment."*

Apart from the oppositional/confrontational orientation toward the political sphere, another orientation (which was present but less salient among the interviewees) was the development of clientelistic relationships with the political sphere. Gliński (2006: 284) interprets the tendency of Polish civil society organizations to form clientelistic relationships with the political sphere as a more or less forced acceptance of the clientelistic character of the social and political environment. For pragmatic reasons, organizations seek the benefits that patronage may give. In my interpretation, this is but one expression of the private action logics being transposed to, and reproduced in, other spheres.

The personalized relationships within the civil sphere, as well as between the civil sphere and the political sphere, thus stem from another persistent legacy of the state-socialist time, that of individual and family-centered resourcefulness and the centrality of personal networks. As illustrated above, this social world of private arrangements, informal economies, and personal networks tends to be also reproduced in the civil sphere, as these action logics are also drawn on when building organizations and organizing the work. Thus, when civil society organizations were built during and after the transition, they, too, were often based on personal relationships, and trust still tended to be placed on people. Tarkowska and Tarkowski's (1991: 103) remark still seems to hold true: "Polish society is divided into 'the world of people' and 'the world of institutions.'"

The fact that trust is personalized rather than generalized and institutional has huge implications for civil society's functioning, a view shared by

Polish scholars. According to Czapiński (2008), due to the low level of social capital, Poland develops at the "molecular level" of individuals and small groups rather than at the level of society. In his view, individual resourcefulness is strong but does not translate into increased cooperation or an inclination to think beyond one's own interests or those of one's own circle. As a result, twenty years after the transition to democracy "we still live in a culture of envy and distrust," Czapiński writes (2008: 193; see also Gliński 2006). In my interview study, distrust in "unknown others" was expressed in the attitudes toward potential members and volunteers who were better avoided unless you knew they were reliable, and suspicion that others had hidden agendas dressed in work for the common good, which was recurrent in the interviews.

While legacies of state socialism are still consequential, I suggest that they gain their force partly by interplaying with marketization and economic liberalization. Thus, neoliberalism as an ideal and policy practice "hooks" into, and reinforces rather than challenges, the legacies of postsocialism on ways of thinking and acting, including the anti-political orientations. This is in line with Hirt's argument that socialism paved the ground for what she calls the "post-1989 privatism" by "inflating but debilitating the public, besieging the private, and erecting a firm, cruel border between them" (Hirt 2012: 22). She concludes that "socialism did not obliterate the private; it obliterated the public—not as an institution but as an *ideal*" (ibid.). Here, Hirt is concerned with what I called above general privatism, understood as "a culture that entails diminishing appreciation of broad-based collective narrations and actions, and a growing interest in issues centered on the personal and the domestic, the individual, the family, and the narrowly defined interest group" (Hirt 2012: 17–18). While sharing many features of privatism in North America or Western Europe, including a weakened state, a transfer of assets and responsibilities from the public to the private sector, and a declining appeal of collectivist narratives, Hirt argues that postsocialist privatism also has its own locally embedded dynamics: its rootedness in the state-socialist attempts to subdue the private realm and the failure to establish a viable noncorrupt public realm after 1989 (Hirt 2012: 27).

The primary interest in this chapter is not in such general privatism (even though it is prevalent in Poland, too) but in what I call civic privatism, that is, a privatist orientation to one's social engagement. Nevertheless, the legacies discussed above are important background factors as to *why* the logic of the private sphere, in terms of patterns of behavior and thinking, tends to be reproduced in the civil sphere. The experiences of the recent (state-socialist) past explain not only the informality and personalization, as an action logic from the domestic sphere, but they can also explain the openness to the pervasive expansion of market rationality in postcommunist Poland. Thus, the relationship to the market sphere is also highly relevant to understanding the Polish version of civic privatism, as the entrepreneurialism, status competition, and achievement orientation of the market sphere tend to "spill over" to the civil sphere. As also noted by Polish scholars, it is the liberal version of civil society and a middle-class ethos that the actors of the Polish third sector typically embody (Gliński, quoted in Chimiak 2006b: 294).

The influx of management ideas in civic life is also a visible trend in other capitalist societies, such as the United States, as is the trend toward other forms of resource mobilization than building membership organizations (e.g., Skocpol 2003). Likewise, political skepticism and "disavowal" of institutionalized politics is not unique for the postsocialist world but prevalent, for instance, among civic actors in the United States (Eliasoph 1998; Baiocchi et al. 2014). However, postsocialist legacies serve to compound these orientations, according to their "locally embedded dynamics" (Hirt 2012: 27).

Thus, in a context with prevalent negative attitudes toward institutionalized politics, drawing on the market as a (role) model is close at hand. This is also in line with Rychard's finding that it is in the market that Poles feel they can exert freedom and agency (2009). In my vocabulary, the rationality of the *bourgeois* (economic citizen) also readily penetrates civic life, as exemplified above by the individualist values and entrepreneurial thinking among activists (see also Rukszto 1997). Powerful neoliberal political discourse in turn serves to legitimize this trend (see also Jezierska in this volume). Thus, the individualist inclination is not merely an expression of neoliberal conceptions of agency but has longer traditions and a rootedness in the social past in Poland. Nevertheless, traditions of individual resourcefulness and public mistrust fit well and are mutually reinforced by neoliberal ideals of "self-made" men/women.

To sum up, while a very lively and dynamic civil society has developed in Poland, it is functioning on the one hand according to ways of thinking, acting, and organizing "imported" from the private sphere of personal networks and, on the other hand, according to the business logic of the market sphere. The result is a fusion of private and public logics, and of individualism and personalization *and* working for the common good. Thus, it is *not* that Poles feel solidarity only with their closest circle but rather that these networks are used when building civil society organizations and private/personal action logics are drawn on.

Unlike the more negative accounts, such as the debate on amoral familism and its consequences for Polish civil society, the civic privatism that I have described has its pros and cons. It is the source and engine of civic initiatives by dedicated individuals, and the entrepreneurial activity that it spurs is a source of grassroots change in Poland, as Chimiak also argued (2006a: 294). Nevertheless, civic privatism is also a source of civil society fragmentation;

many individual initiatives are undertaken in isolation from each other, leading scholars to speak of the "enclave character" of Polish civil society initiatives (Gliński 2006: 274; Gumkowska et al. 2006: 19). More recent studies indicate that contacts between civil society organizations are increasing (Herbst and Przewłocka 2011), which is supported by the case study reported in this chapter. Nevertheless, the interviews also point to the detrimental effects of individualism and personalization of organizational life for the mobilization of collective action capacity.

Conclusion

"Real" civil societies may diverge from ideal-type models provided by political theory; the nature of civil society rather reflects diverse realities in different social contexts (e.g., Hann and Dunn 1996). In this chapter, I analyzed Polish civil society in an inductive fashion, departing from real-life experiences, practices, and processes. Doing so enabled me to capture what the chapter has conceptualized as civic privatism.

In contrast to privatism as a retreat from common concerns and public engagement in favor of the pursuit of private interests, I used the term "civic privatism" first to denote an individualistic attitude toward, and orientation for, one's civil society engagement. In the organizations studied, this attitude was expressed in a preference for a civic engagement in individualist and privatist forms of action rather than more collectively oriented forms, in the spirit of enterprise, and in striving for independence in one's civic work. The second feature concerned the reliance on individual resourcefulness rather than on building organizational strength, a preference for informality, and a tendency to personalize civic relationships and distrust unknown others. This case study illustrates the self-understanding of Polish animal rights/welfare activists; future research would have to confirm the extent to which this attitude of civic privatism is prevalent in the third sector more generally. Nevertheless, it is likely that the small scale of the animal welfare organizations compounds the degree to which civic privatism can play out.

Moreover, I have argued that the distinct version of civic privatism captured in this chapter must be understood against the background of the specific relationship among the domestic sphere, the market sphere, and the civil sphere in Poland as it has developed over the last century. Legacies from state-socialist times, such as low levels of social trust, here interplay with and are reinforced by marketization processes and neoliberal economic discourses, also affecting activist subjectivity and self-understanding. Action logics from the private sphere are transposed to the civil sphere and to public engagement, resulting, inter alia, in a hybrid of the *bourgeois*, *hommes*, and the *citoyen* roles and ethos, as well as a distinctive combination of individualism and engagement for the common good. This activist "inclination" contributes to a dynamic and entrepreneurial civil society, but certainly at the price of civil society fragmentation and difficulties in acting collectively.

My interpretation of the state of civil society in Poland is that conclusions such as "our journey toward civil society has not yet started" (Czapiński 2008: 193) or "the Poles suffer from deficient civic virtues" (Gliński 2004, 2006) are far too pessimistic. Civic privatism is also an expression of civicness, in the sense of embracing a concern for a greater good and a willingness to commit to its realization. I support Chimiak (2006a: 252) when summarizing her own findings as well as research by Domański and Dukaczewska: individualism is not inimical to institutionalized civic activity (Chimiak 2006a: 252). As Chimiak concludes, individualists make solidarity work in Poland.

However, if the strength of Polish civil society consists of the rich diversity of individual initiatives and efforts, the failure to develop impersonal and institutional relationships with members and volunteers, with other organizations, and with political actors stands out as a major weakness. In building a civil society, not only do interpersonal relations matter—relationships with unknown others are as critical. Moreover, a fragmented civil society that fails to develop collective action capacity and organization building will have limited chances to exert influence on the political sphere. Following Habermas (1989), the role of the civil sphere is not only civic self-organization, but also exerting control over the political sphere as well as mediating demands of the political sphere. The case of the Polish animal rights movement serves well to illustrate the entrepreneurial and self-organizing capacity of Polish civil society as well as its limited capacity when it comes to fulfilling these more political roles.

Kerstin Jacobsson is Professor of Sociology at University of Gothenburg. She works on political sociology, including studies of civic activism in Central and Eastern Europe. Recent publications include *Animal Rights Activism: A Moral-Sociological Perspective on Social Movements* (coauthored with Jonas Lindblom, Amsterdam University Press, 2016) and the edited volumes *Urban Grassroots Movements in Central and Eastern Europe* (Ashgate 2015) and *Beyond NGO-ization: The Development of Social Movements in Central and Eastern Europe* (the latter coedited with Steven Saxonberg, Ashgate 2013).

Notes

1. The Polish statistical office has a more inclusive definition of civil society association than the Klon/Jawor report, including trade unions and political parties.

2. I use the civil sphere and civil society as synonyms denoting an associational sphere of solidaristic action by citizens (Alexander 2006). I see the private domain as encompassing the domestic sphere (family and friends), the market sphere, and the civil sphere; however, the civil sphere is a public component of the private domain (*Öffentlichkeit* in Habermas's (1989) terms).

3. This research was funded by the Swedish Research Council (Grant 421/2010/1706). I am grateful for the collaboration with Renata Hryciuk in data collection.

4. One or several representatives of the following organizations were interviewed: TOZ (*Towarzystwo Opieki nad Zwierzętami,* or the Association for Animal Welfare); Viva! (*Fundacja Viva! Akcja dla zwierząt*); Klub Gaja, Empatia (*Stowarzyszenie Empatia* or Empathy Association); TOZ Kraków; Animal Guard (*Straż dla Zwierząt*); the Association of Animal Defenders ARKA (*Stowarzyszenie Obrońców Zwierząt ARKA*); Rabbits—Rabbit Welfare Association (*Króliki–Stowarzyszenie Pomocy Królikom*); the Polish Foundation for the Protection of Animals (*Polska Fundacja Ochrony Zwierząt*); The Shelter under Canine Angel Wings Foundation (*Biuro Ochrony Zwierząt Fundacji: Azyl Pod Psim Aniołem*); the Animal Is Not an Object Foundation (*Fundacja 'Zwierzę nie jest Rzeczą'*); Mr. Cat's Black Sheep Foundation (*Fundacja Czarna Owca Pana Kota*); Animal Friends' Association Amicus (*Stowarzyszenie Przyjaciół Zwierząt Amicus*); and the Arc Foundation (*Fundacja Arka*). In addition, several individuals engaged in animal rights issues but not belonging to an organization were interviewed.

5. Compare Kitschelt's (1995) discussion of party cleavages in postcommunist states, where he distinguishes between charismatic parties, clientelistic parties, and programmatic parties. The former are built on personalized relationships, while the latter are built on legal-bureaucratic and depersonalized organization and more ideologically based programs.

6. Interestingly, historian Plach (2012) found internal tensions to be prevalent in the Polish animal welfare movement during the interwar period as well.

References

Alexander, J. 2006. *The Civil Sphere.* Oxford: Oxford University Press.

Baiocchi, G. Bennett, E. Cordner, A. Klein, P. T. and S. Savell. 2014. *The Civic Imagination: Making a Difference in American Political Life.* Boulder: Paradigm Publishers.

Buchowski, M. 1996. "The Shifting Meanings of Civil and Civic Society in Poland," in *Civil Society: Challenging Western Models,* ed. C. Hann and E. Dunn. London: Routledge, 79–98.

Chimiak, G. 2006a. *How Individualists Make Solidarity Work.* Warsaw: Ministerstwo Pracy i Polityki Społecznej.

———. 2006b. "What Are NGOs and What Do They Have in Common with Civil Society? The Case of Post-Communist Countries and Poland," in *Civil Society in the Making,* ed. D. Gawin and P. Glinski. Warsaw: IfiS, 289–330.

Czapiński, J. 2008. Molekularny rozwój Polski [The Molecular Development of Poland], in *Modernizacja Polski. Kody kulturowe i mity* [Poland's Modernization: Cultural Codes and Myths], ed. J. Szomburg. IBnGR: Gdańsk, 95–102.

Czapiński, J., and T. Panek, eds. 2012. *Social Diagnosis: Objective and Subjective Quality of Life in Poland.* Warsaw: The Council for Social Monitoring.

Eliasoph, N. 1998. *Avoiding Politics: How Americans Produce Apathy in Everyday Life.* New York: Cambridge University Press.

European Social Survey. 2010. Round 5. Retrieved 16 June 2016 from http://www.euro peansocialsurvey.org/download.html?file=ESS5e03_2&y=2010.

Fröhlich, C. and K. Jacobsson. Forthcoming. "States Shaping Civic Activism: Comparing Animal Rights Activism in Poland and Russia." *The Sociological Quarterly.*

Gawin, D. 2006. "European Civil Society: The Citizens' or Eurocrats' Project?," in *Civil Society in the Making,* ed. D. Gawin and P. Gliński. Warsaw: IfiS, 77–88.

Gliński, P. 2004. "How Active Are the Social Actors? Deficient Citizenship versus Day-to-Day Resourcefulness in Poland." *Polish Sociological Review* 4, no. 148, 429–450.

———. 2006. "The Third Sector in Poland: Dilemmas of Development," in *Civil Society in the Making,* ed. D. Gawin and P. Gliński. Warsaw: IfiS, 265–291.

Gumkowska, M., J. Herbst, J. Szołajska, and J. Wygnański. 2006. *The Challenge of Solidarity: CIVICUS Civil Society Index Report for Poland.* Warsaw: Klon/Jawor Association/CIVICUS.

Habermas, J. 1975. *Legitimation Crisis.* Boston: Beacon Press.

———. 1989. *The Structural Transformation of the Public Sphere: An Inquiry into a Category of Bourgeois Society.* Cambridge: Polity Press.

Hann, C., and E. Dunn, eds. 1996. *Civil Society: Challenging Western Models.* London: Routledge.

Hayoz, N. 2013. "Observations on the Changing Meaning of Informality," in *Informality in Eastern Europe: Structures, Political Cultures and Social Practices,* ed. C. Giordano and N. Hayoz. Bern: Peter Lang, 47–65.

Herbst, J., and J. Przewłocka. 2011. *Podstawowe Fakty o Organizacjach Pozarządowych raport z badania 2010* [Basic Facts on Non-Governmental Organizations: Report from Research 2010]. Warszawa: Stowarzyszenie Klon/Jawor.

Heinrich, V.F. 2007. *CIVICUS Global Survey of the State of Civil Society. Volume 1: Country Profiles.* Bloomfield, CT: Kumarian Press.

Hirt, S. 2012. *Iron Curtains: Gates, Suburbs and Privatization of Space in the Post-socialist City.* Chichester: Wiley-Blackwell.

Howard, M. 2003. *The Weakness of Civil Society in Post-Communist Europe.* Cambridge, U.K.: Cambridge University Press.

Jacobsson, K. 2012. "Fragmentation of the Collective Action Space: The Animal Rights Movement in Poland." *East European Politics* 28, no. 4, 353–370.

———. 2013. "Channelling and Enrollment: The Institutional Shaping of Animal Rights Activism in Poland," in *Beyond NGO-ization: The Development of Social Movements in Central and Eastern Europe,* ed. K. Jacobsson and S. Saxonberg. Farnham: Ashgate, 27–47.

Kitschelt, H. 1995. "Formation of Party Cleavages in Post-Communist Democracies: Theoretical Positions." *Party Politics* 1, no. 4, 447–472.

Kościański, A., and W. Misztal. 2008. *Społeczeństwo obywatelskie. Między ideą a praktyką* [Civil Society: Between Idea and Practice]. IFiS PAN Publishers, Warsaw.

Kowalewski, M. 2013. "Organizowanie miejskiego aktywizmu w Polsce: Kongres Ruchów Miejskich" [Organizing Urban Activism in Poland: Congress of Urban Movements]. *Social Space Journal.* Retrieved 30 September 2015 from http://socialspacejournal.eu.

Ost, D. 2005. *The Defeat of Solidarity.* Ithaca: Cornell University Press.

Papakostas, A. 2011. "The Rationalization of Civil Society." *Current Sociology* 59, no. 1: 5–23.

Peterson, S. 1984. "Privatism and Politics: A Research Note." *The Western Quarterly* 37, no. 3: 484–489.

Plach, E. 2012. "The Animal Welfare Movement in Interwar Poland: An Introductory Sketch." *The Polish Review* 57, no. 2: 21–43.

Polanska, D., and G. Piotrowski. 2015. "The Transformative Power of Cooperation between Social Movements: Squatting and Tenants' Movements in Poland." *City* 19, no. 2–3: 274–296.

Polanska, D. V., and G. Chimiak. 2016. "Organizing without Organizations. On Informal Social Activism in Poland." *International Journal of Sociology and Social Policy* 36, no. 9–10: 662–679.

Przewłocka, J. 2012. *Polskie organizacje pozarzadowe 2012* [Polish Nongovernmental Organizations 2012]. Warszawa: Stowarzyszenie Klon/Jawor. Retrieved 20 October 2015 from http://civicpedia.ngo.pl/files/civicpedia.pl/public/FaktyNGO_broszura_full.pdf.

Przewłocka, J., P. Adamiak, and A. Zajac. 2012. *Życie codzienne organizacji pozarzadowych w Polsce* [Everyday Life of Nongovernmental Organizations in Poland]. Warszawa: Stowarzyszenie Klon/Jawor. Retrieved 30 September 2013 from http://civicpedia.ngo.pl/files/civicpedia.pl/public/2012_Klon_ZycieCodzienneNGO.pdf.

Rukszto, K. 1997. "Making Her into a 'Woman': The Creation of Citizen-Entrepreneur in Capitalist Poland." *Women's Studies International Forum* 20, no. 1: 103–112.

Rychard, A. 2009. "Entrepreneurs, Consumers and Civility: The Case of Poland," in *Markets and Civil Society: The European Experience in Comparative Perspective*, ed. V. Pérez-Díaz. New York: Berghahn Books, 222–239.

Schimanek, T. 2010. "Plusy i Minusy Polskiego Grantodawstwa" [Pros and Cons of Polish Grantmaking]. *Trzeci Sektor* [Third Sector] 20: 40–47.

Skocpol, T. 2003. *Diminished Democracy: From Membership to Management in American Civic Life*. Norman: University of Oklahoma Press.

Sztompka, P. 1993. "Civilizational Incompetence: The Trap of Post-Communist Societies." *Zeitschrift für Soziologie* 22, no. 2: 85–95.

Tarkowska, E., and J. Tarkowski 1991. "Social Disintegration in Poland: Civil Society or Amoral Familism." *Telos* 89, no. 3: 103–109.

Wedel, J. 1986. *The Private Poland*. New York: Facts on File Publications.

Chapter 4

DEFINING IN/DEFINING OUT
CIVIL SOCIETY THROUGH THE LENS OF ELITE NGOS

Katarzyna Jezierska

Introduction

Civil society continues to be an essentially contested concept. It is used in widely diverse contexts, from the right to the left. It is recalled by republicans as a source of community and moral obligations, by liberals as a symbol of holding the state accountable, by students of deliberative democracy as a sphere of dialogue and consensus formation, and by radical democrats as a space of contentious political action. In Central and Eastern Europe, civil society used to be interpreted as a source of hope and the means to obtain regime shift, but after 1989 its radical promise has been severely blunted. When civil society materialized into civil society organizations, it recalibrated its goals—it lost the critical potential of "antipolitical politics" (Havel 2010; Michnik 1985), being the source of alternatives to the current political and socioeconomic system, and settled into the role of auxiliary infrastructure legitimizing the existing neoliberal system.

This chapter contributes to this debate about civil society in Central and Eastern Europe with a critical investigation of what the "rebirth of civil society" (Siegel and Yancey 1992) entailed in the Polish context. More precisely, it focuses on the discursive aspects of civil society, a task that is conducted in three steps of analysis. First, the chapter reconstructs existing frames of civil society in the Polish public discourse through the eyes of elite civil society actors. Second, it investigates the extent to which these actors reproduce or challenge the existing frames. And third, it discusses political implications of these discursive formations, i.e., what exclusions these frames bring about, what actors and actions are left out when certain perceptions of civil society prevail.

Frames are here seen as part of discursive structures. Just as all other discursive formations, frames are not solid, but should rather be perceived as floating constructions. They are not mutually exclusive, even though it is possible to distinguish them analytically and claim that some entities are hegemonic, some marginal, and others aspire to a counter-hegemonic position, i.e., to openly challenge the hegemonic link. This reflects an often repeated, but nevertheless important truism about framing—that frames never function in a vacuum. They always exist in a wider discursive surrounding; they are positioned against or in line with other frames. Differently put, frames are not detached and should always be analyzed in a context. This is not to deny the fact that while occupying a hegemonic position (in the sense of leadership, among other ideas), this surrounding tends to be obscured.[1] Adapting what Steven Lukes has written about political rituals (1975), I will stress the cognitive, constitutive component and the exclusionary work of framing. In this sense, a frame, just like a political ritual, has a "cognitive role, rendering intelligible society and social relationships, serving to organize people's knowledge of the past and present and their capacity to imagine the future. In other words, it helps to define as authoritative certain ways of seeing society: it serves to specify what in society is of specific significance, it draws people's attention to certain forms of relationships and activity— and at the same time, therefore, it deflects their attention from other forms, since *every way of seeing is also a way of not seeing*" (Lukes 1975: 15, emphasis added). The questions investigated in this chapter read: What are the forms of civic relationships and activity that are assigned special significance in different frames? And what forms of collectivities and activities are excluded?

Framing processes are seen as "strategic efforts by groups of people to fashion shared understandings of the world and of themselves" (McAdam et al. 1996: 6).[2] Methodologically, identifying frames boils down to finding an adequate label for the observed set of opinions, ideas, and attitudes toward the studied phenomenon and its relationship with other relevant phenomena (here for example the state). A hegemonic claim is formed through the establishment of a chain of equivalence (Laclau and Mouffe 2001: 127), an alignment of particular meanings and the exclusion of others that do not fit into the chain. In effect, the chain of equivalence gains the position of a leading association—seemingly rupture-free and obvious; it is a product of negotiation and adjustment, that is, work of power. It is important to keep in mind that framing is not a pure act of naming but it is a process of establishing a representative, which temporarily settles the meaning and also involves inclusions/exclusions. This process could be theorized with the help of the concepts of "defining in" and "defining out," developed by Thomas Mathiesen to make sense of two strategies that the state applies toward radical advocacy groups—either of which results in their taming (Mathiesen 2015; cf. Rice 2012). In this chapter "defining in" and "defining out" are used more literally, as discursive mechanisms that establish the accepted, legitimate content of the studied phenomenon (civil society), at the same time delegitimizing some forms of activism and actors. The two are hence seen as coexisting and codetermining rather than separate logics. Linguistically this process could show itself in a synecdoche—a reduction of a greater phenomenon to a smaller one—that establishes the part as representative of the whole (*pars pro toto*). It lies in the nature of any hegemony that its position is contingent but it presents itself as fixed and natural, as the only possible option.[3] Otherwise put, the hegemonic frame is an attempt at decontesting the field (cf. Freeden 2005), in this case presenting one clear-cut definition of what civil society is and should be and at the same time occluding the fact that alternative understandings are possible, as well as the fact that what actors and actions are included in the definition is far from given.

The chapter is structured as follows: first the empirical focus of the study, i.e., think tanks, is presented. The following analysis of elite NGO discourses on civil society in Poland identifies four frames, one of which is by my interviewees ascribed a hegemonic position in the broader public discourse. The frames will be examined with regard to both what they include and what they exclude. The chapter ends with a summary of the results interpreted from a radical democratic perspective.

Empirical Focus: Think Tanks

Poland cherishes a leading position in the region with regard to the development and sustainability of civil society.[4] It has also attracted great attention of civil society scholars; however, research dedicated to the discursive aspects is still rather scarce.[5] This chapter aims to partly fill this gap by focusing on civil society frames spread by elite NGOs, here represented by think tanks. This is not to argue that think tanks are the sole actors shaping the hegemonic understandings of civil society.[6] As the analysis will show, they rearticulate certain frames that already circulate, sometimes adding new components. Nevertheless, the voice of think tanks is arguably strong as they have the resources (in the form of both economic and cultural capital) and their explicit task is to influence policy processes, and sometimes also to shape the terrain of civil society by grant making and training of local civil society organizations. The postulation is that, given the influential position think tanks aspire to and to a certain extent occupy, the way they frame civil society plays an important role in delimiting the space of possible actions not only for think tanks themselves, but for other civil society organizations as well. In this sense, frames of civil society spread by think tanks become part of the wider discursive opportunity structure, i.e., part of the enabling and constraining contextual factors that influence (and are influenced by) collective actors (cf. Jacobsson 2012). The hegemonic understandings of civil society shape the available repertoires of collective action (cf. Koopmans 1999), influencing what is possible to think and do politically in a given society.

A prominent commentator on think tanks in Central and Eastern European (CEE) region, Ivan Krastev (2000a; 2000b), points to the specific role these organizations play in this part of the world. He calls think tanks "a new strategy for the institutionalization of the liberal political agenda," because their main efforts since the 1990s have been directed toward keeping the reformist agenda moving ahead when the burdens of transformation made the public turn their back to transition reforms. Krastev (2000a, 2000b) claims that it is partly due to think tanks in the region that the track of neoliberal reforms was kept even after communist successor parties won elections in Poland and Lithuania in 1993 and in Hungary and Bulgaria in 1994. It might as well be argued that the neoliberal policy consensus that think tanks helped to solidify successfully blocked alternative projects of transition, and any non-neoliberal imaginaries of economy, society, and state functioning. Think tanks have hitherto not been in the focus of civil society researchers in CEE. Studies dedicated to Polish think tanks are rather scarce and mostly of inventorial character, concentrating mainly on mapping the phenomenon and identifying the functions, organizational forms, and size of think tanks in Poland (Bąkowski and Szlachetko 2012; Zbieranek 2011; Ziętara 2010). This chapter will treat think tanks as representatives for elite NGOs and will engage in a critical examination of their perspective on civil society.

Think tanks were chosen for identifying elite discourses, which is justified by their status as experts. "Think tanks are by definition elite institutions whose assertion of a voice in the policy making process is based on their claim to expertise rather than as a vox populi" (Weaver and McGann 2000: 17). There is no clear definition of think tanks, but most commonly they are described as independent public policy research institutes, engaged in both research and advocacy.[7] They seek to influence decision makers and, cherishing their status as experts, have some power to set the agenda, shape discourses, and sanction certain knowledge about concrete matters under public discussion. In this sense, think tanks are political institutions. Their history has been traced back to World War II and military experts' planning groups in United States (Weaver 1989; Rich 2004; McGann 2007). The aim and scope as well as the geographic spread of think tanks has gradually expanded since 1960s.

In the CEE context, think tanks are a relatively new phenomenon—most of them were created in the 1990s and early 2000s. Poland is no different in this respect. Depending on the definition applied, the reported number of think tanks in Poland differs slightly, but usually oscillates around forty.[8] Organizationally, think tanks are part of the third sector (in Poland they take the legal form of either foundations or associations), and they operate on the boundary between the third and the first sector, often using methods similar to lobbying.

My interviews show that some employees of Polish think tanks lack a third-sector identification and rather perceive themselves as academics who want to have a more tangible impact on the policy process. Even though they do not deny the fact that their organizations formally belong to the third sector, they underline their distinct characteristics and status. It should also be noted that some respondents were opposed to being classified as think tanks and underlined their identity as "think-and-do tanks," stressing the activist component of their mission. However, the literature mentions "ink tanks" and "think and do tanks" as two common subtypes of think tanks (Stone 2007: 262), the former being more oriented toward publishing books and reports with analyses of policies and the latter being more engaged in grassroots activities and projects. The operative definition used in this chapter, which guided the selection of interviewees, was the inclusion of a research component in the organization and actions directed at influencing public policies (both directly—preparing law proposals—and indirectly—changing the mindset, attitudes, and knowledge about a certain public issue). Think tanks' main targets, or intended recipients, are decision makers and opinion builders (Zbieranek 2011; Rich 2004). My interview material shows that Polish think tanks increasingly perceive the general public (and mass media in their role as transition channels) as one of their targets, as a strategy of consciousness raising and pushing decision makers toward preferred policy change. Additionally, part of their actions consists of training other, smaller civil society organizations that lack the material and intellectual resources they cherish. This puts think tanks in the higher stratum in relation to other NGOs as well.

The analysis in this chapter relies on fourteen semi-structured interviews with directors and project leaders of nine major Polish think tanks.[9] All the interviews were done in the spring of 2013.[10] Even though every interview was unique, the average length was one hour and they all followed more or less the same trajectory, rooted in the interview guide. Complementary data consisted of material published by the contacted think tanks as well as secondary literature on civil society and think tanks in Poland. The think tanks chosen for this project vary significantly when it comes to the size, scope, funding and access to decision makers and mass media. Some of them are linked to political parties; others strive for an independent image as an expert base for anyone who is willing to listen.[11] Regarding the ideological profiles of the interviewed institutions, three of them (Political Critique, Ferdinand Lassalle Centre for Social Thought, and Green Institute) are outspokenly leftist, one (Sobieski Institute) is right-wing (declaring Sarmatist and republican inspirations) and the remaining five (Batory Foundation, Civic Institute, Civil Development Forum, The Institute of Public Affairs, and The Unit for Social Innovation and Research—Shipyard) deny any ideological profile except a general pro-democratic, pro-reform, and pro-European orientation. As I argue elsewhere, such a "neutral," anti-ideological positioning is rather typical of Polish civil society in general (Jezierska forthcoming).

Identifying Civil Society Frames

Strikingly, many Polish NGOs, think tanks included, have "promotion of civil society" as a statutory goal or part of their mission. This propensity to speak of civil society in formal NGO documents can, at least partly, be explained by their catering to the expectations of potential grant givers. Using such a broad and empty (in the sense of an empty signifier) aim, they can claim expertise in a wide spectrum of tasks. This enables them for example to take part in public contests or grant application procedures. Hence, it is seldom clear what particular understanding of civil society they want to promote and what types of actions and actors are defined as part of the preferred vision of civil society. The analysis below aims to provide answers to these questions.

In the CEE context, the answer to the question of what civil society is and what it does is not self-evident. As is widely acknowledged, in the 1990s the term "civil society" was used (both by academics and activists) as a means to conceptualize the resources engaged in abolishing the communist regime through the "rebirth of the civil society." Its usefulness is often ascribed to a double function—civil society described both the process and the proclaimed aim of change.[12] As one of my interviewees put it: "[T]he concept of civil society ... was powerful and important, because it is one of the few terms that contains both the aim and the method. In this sense it was really important. Because it was both our aspiration and our vehicle, the way we did it" (The Unit for Social Innovation and Research—Shipyard).[13] The original Eastern European (and South American if we follow Glasius 2012) contribution to the debate about civil society was the acknowledgement of civil society as a political space, as a space of contention and alternative to the system. What the dissident movements in the 1970s and 1980s opposed was the regime, not the ruling party. They did not aspire to a shift in government, but a turnover of state-society relations and a remodeling of the system. This aim was supposed to be obtained by a broad coalition of different demands, and an association of various actors—mainly a grassroots mobilization. The Solidarity movement of the 1980s became a symbol of successful mobilization and a model for how to peacefully overturn an oppressive regime. However, despite that tradition, the Polish civil society that emerged after 1989 significantly transformed itself. The new civil society sought recognition from the democratic state, broader society, and the international community of founders, and here the Western concept of "third sector" came in handy and was imported to the Polish realm.

The analysis below distinguishes current understandings of civil society as presented by its elite representatives twenty-five years after the caesura of 1989. Based on the interview material four frames have been identified: civil society as third sector/provider of public services; civil society as moral blueprint; civil society as a control on power; and civil society as neoliberal gobbledygook (see also Jezierska 2015). These will be discussed in the following sections of the chapter.

Civil Society as Third Sector/Provider of Public Services

Civil society as third sector is undoubtedly the most often recurring frame in the interviews. First, civil society is here equated with NGOs as a vehicle for aggregating interests. Asked about their understanding of civil society, the respondents most commonly answered with an explanation of the role of NGOs in the Polish system. Not only did they present it as the hegemonic understanding in the wider public perception, but they also seemed to reproduce this frame in their own perception and actions. Those think tanks, which have "promotion of civil society" in their goals and/or mission statements, clarified that their actions are almost exclusively directed at NGOs. It must be noted that such an equation is a widespread, typically liberal view, enforced by the influential data collection on civil society, and thus reproduced by many practitioners and scholars in the field (cf. *CIVICUS Civil Society Index* and *The John Hopkins Global Civil Society Index*). There are numerous examples in the (Polish) academic literature in which NGOs stand in for civil society. As Zbigniew Zagała puts it "One of the most common ways of translating the ambiguous idea of civil society into the language of social practice is equating it with the third sector ... The dominant role in this sphere is played by associations, social organizations and foundations" (Zagała 2008: 219). Attitudes toward NGOs, or the third sector, are for instance studied as representative of the parties' attitudes toward civil society (Piotrowski 2006). Number of NGOs is used as an indicator of civic initiatives in different Polish regions (e.g., Wendt 2007) and conditions of development of civil society are operationalized as interpersonal trust and number of registered NGOs (Czapiński 2006).

Not only is civil society equated with NGOs, but in a second step (double synecdoche) NGOs are reduced to providers of public services (*realizatorzy zadań publicznych*). This commonly agreed on important function of NGOs is presented as their hegemonic role in the interviews. The chain of equivalence "civil society = NGOs = service providers" is ascribed either a positive or a negative normative load. Some of my respondents, reproducing what they present as a commonly shared perception, picture NGOs as more suitable providers of the services than the state—better versed in local needs, more adaptable and flexible in their performance, and/or simply cheaper. Seen through such a lens, NGOs nicely complement the inefficient "small" state. At the same time, these respondents approve of the state backing off from its totalizing aspirations identified with the state-socialist times. "According to me, the third sector can be inspiring for the government, for politics. In the sense that it is smaller, more flexible and more efficient. And I try to facilitate the cooperation between the third sector and the ministries, so that the ministries will transfer their policies or realization of certain tasks to the third sector. My impression is that it is much more efficient than state agencies. I would like the third sector to partake in designing policies" (Civic Institute). Hence, NGOs are foremost pictured as a welcomed substitute in the task of providing public services, but, as this quotation shows, they are also presented as wished-for contributors in decision-making processes.

The opposite normative judgment of this equation that came through in the interviews is the critical stance toward this all-pervasive function of the NGOs and the hegemonic position of this frame in the public discourse. These interviewees expressed their concern that NGOs are almost exclusively seen as service providers at the expense of other important functions they should fulfill in Polish society. "Such a great focus on this service function [means that] a huge number of organizations, especially local ones, are not civic [*obywatelskie*], or social [*społeczne*] but rather service [*usługowe*] organizations. They conduct tasks that the local administration doesn't want or cannot fulfill. ... They have no advocacy functions at all, they do not represent anybody" (Batory Foundation). Another interviewee pointed out that the reduction of NGOs to "efficient implementers of the public good" [*sprawni realizatorzy dobra publicznego*] results in them forgetting the function of control of the state. In effect, civil society gets colonized by the state and we witness a "nationalization [*upaństwowienie*] of civil society, that is, pushing it in the direction of creating services financed by public means" (The Institute of Public Affairs).

We can distinguish different grades of criticism here. Some argued that this substitution process is problematic only because it leads to no substantial change in the services provided by NGOs or the state. Tasks are delegated, but performed in exactly the same manner as before. Here the critique is directed at the way public tasks are conducted rather than the process of ceding state functions per se. In this narrative, instead of contributing to social change through a different philosophy of welfare, NGOs simply legitimize the system. Other respondents had more principal objections, arguing that "NGOs should not substitute the state in its functions towards the citizens—social security and prevention of exclusion" (Political Critique).

Overall, the interviewees were in agreement that the NGO/service-provision frame has no real contender in the public discourse today. The explanation for the hegemonic position of this reduction of NGOs to the service-provision function can be sought in the historical development of the third sector in Poland. In the late 1990s, the discursive field around civil society was still not set, and there had been certain competition between two ideas about civil society—the service-providing initiatives [*inicjatywy pomocowe*] and the associational movement [*ruch stowarzyszeniowy*] (Frączak 2013). The decisive question structuring this debate read: Should organizations focus on service provision and receive funding from (local) government, or should they fulfill the critical democratic role of watchdogs, controlling rather than complementing government? The solution came with money. Pre-accession grants as well as American funding were both geared toward concrete projects involving collaboration between emerging organizations and (local) administration (Frączak 2012, 2013). This orientation and basic understanding of civil society in Poland was further solidified by the Public Benefit and Volunteer Work Act adopted in 2003 (Act of Law 2003), which lists a number of public benefit tasks that can be delegated to NGOs by local government. One interviewee explains: "Citizens associated in organizations were supposed to substitute the state in some public functions, where they have better knowledge and specialize ... This was the purpose of the Public Benefit Act; it created frames and rules for transmitting money for public tasks to NGOs" (The Institute of Public Affairs).

In effect, the service-provision frame, supported by the structure of available funding and the letter of the law, cherishes an unquestioned position. Some scholars, analyzing this development in Polish society, argue that instead of the term "civil society organizations" it would be more accurate to use "welfare organizations," as welfare is actually their main function (cf. Załęski 2012).[14] In place of being motors for social change and critical references for the current socioeconomic system, NGOs have become a support structure for the system (Jezierska 2015). They deliver the services that the state does not (Leś et al. 2000). The state's retreat from certain areas of wel-fare policies resulted in NGOs' overtaking of these spheres of activity. The response is a given—instead of building and supporting movements aspiring to systemic social change, NGOs focus on covering up the deficiencies of state activities. Barbara Einhorn (2000), trying to explain the situation of voluntary engagement of women in CEE after 1989, calls this a "civil society trap."[15] Other scholars point to how this situation might be a peril to democ-racy, arguing that the tendency to let NGOs substitute for state functions should be seen as a sign of the weakness of state institutions rather than of the strength of civil society. "When associationism and communitarian activities flourish in such a context, it would seem that there is cause, not for celebration, but rather deep concern about the failure of the commu-nity's political institutions" (Berman 1997: 428). It is worth noting that the prevalence of the "civil society as NGOs/service providers" frame is not exclusive to Poland. Discussing the state of South American civil societies, Evelina Dagnino underlines the view on civil society as service providers. She concludes that within this perspective "civil society is conceived in a selective and exclusionary way, recognizing only those actors who are able to carry out these tasks" (Dagnino 2011: 128).

This brings me to the exclusionary work of framing and the implications of this particular understanding of civil society. As noted above, not only is the reduction of civil society to service-providing NGOs presented as the hegemonic frame of civil society in public discourse, but some of the in-terviewed think tanks reproduce this frame, also defining civil society in terms of NGOs. Such a move obviously excludes nonformalized associations and civic engagement not channeled through institutionalized forms (see Matysiak in this volume on how it plays out in the case of rural women's organizations). These are either overseen in the funding activities conducted by some of the think tanks, or (partly) ignored in their reports about the different aspects of civil society. By "defining in" NGOs, other types of actors are "defined out." Additionally, the second step of the reduction that was observed in the interviews—the focus on one particular function of NGOs—brings with it further exclusions. By prioritizing service, the provision of other functions and activities of NGOs is overshadowed. Hence, for exam-ple, watchdog organizations and advocacy groups are not prioritized as part-ners, beneficiaries, or objects of analyses.

Civil Society as Moral Blueprint

Another frame identifiable in my interview material, apparently more sa-lient in the older generation of think tank workers, is the normative, aspirational perspective on civil society. Here, civil society is presented as a sphere of civility. In the CEE context it can be traced back to the writings of Václav Havel (2010) and his famous idea of "anti-political politics." In his formulation the concept was largely tainted by an ethical dimension of an alternative way of conducting politics, not the instrumental (Jürgen Habermas would say rationally strategic), but rather politics as a way of taking responsibility for fellow citizens. In the interviews many respondents referred to the importance of values and ethical consciousness in civil society. Some even stated that civil society organizations bear more responsibility and should be an example to the rest of the society and other spheres (market and state) with their ethical conduct: "Civil society is a society, in which civic values have their proper place, and are linked to taking responsibility for others and identifying with common goals ... concern for public good" (The Institute for Public Affairs). Aligning with this perspective, one respondent explicitly paraphrased Habermas, calling civil society an "unfinished project," noting that it can never be fully realized and should rather be seen as a sphere of constant betterment and moral transformation. In this sense, the socialization function of civil society is alluded to, as these are the specific values that are supposed to be fostered in the civil sphere. Hence, this frame helps explain motivational aspects, i.e., why people engage in the work of civil society organizations. Defined as a sphere of ethical conduct, civil society offers an alternative to the crude world of business and the routinized world of state administration. One interviewee argued that civil society in this understanding is almost a religious enterprise. "There is a clearly identifiable way of thinking about civil society stemming from thinking about values, and this civil society is partly supposed to substitute religion, so that people will feel that it is a value and will engage in action for this common good" (The Institute for Public Affairs).

This moral frame of civil society is by some respondents linked to a consensual perspective on the public sphere in which the ultimate goal is social cohesion and consensual decision making. The idea of a deliberative society oriented to consensus seems to be in front of the eyes of many Polish civil society researchers as well. These studies rest on a Habermasian vision (Habermas 2001) of a rationally organized public sphere as a regulative idea (e.g., Misztal and Kościański 2011). Civil society is then expected to conform to the rules of consensual forms of action, contrasted with strategic, particularistic and/or violent actions. "[C]ivil society is not about building factions against someone, but it's an all embracing quality, that either exists or doesn't" (The Institute for Public Affairs). It is in the idea of communicative action oriented to consensus that the emancipatory potential is sought. Within this perspective, the citizens and the state are expected to find a route to peaceful and smooth coexistence, which is supposed to be facilitated by different intermediate organizations. What follows is that contentious actions directed at a shift in the socioeconomic status quo do not have a place in this vision. As my interview material shows, this Habermasian perspective is shared by think tanks situated in the mainstream, liberal space of the ideological spectrum. They are closer to the establishment and less prone to accept disruptive politics.

The exclusions that operate in this frame partly overlap with the debate in the literature on the uncivil or rebellious civil society, that is, groups and organizations that on conceptual and/or normative grounds are excluded from civil society because of their presumably undemocratic orientation and confrontational strategies of action (Chambers and Kopstein 2001; Kopecký and Mudde 2003). Hence, radical right-wing organizations and movements are often ignored in the studies of civil society or treated as its specific subgroup—the "dark side" of civil society (see Płatek and Płucienniczak in this volume). Additionally, defining civil society as a sphere of civility automatically excludes a category of actors who act in an uncivil, disruptive manner.

The further link identified with the moral frame—reliance on a consensual vision of social order—also carries with it some exclusions. If civil society is perceived as the sphere of consensus building, then contentious actions are not seen as (a desirable) part of it. Here a good example can be provided by labor unions and their protest activities. Even though the broad definition of nongovernmental organizations provided in the Act of 2003 (Act of Law 2003) does not exclude labor unions,[16] they are habitually excluded in analyses of civil society in Poland and are continuously delegitimized by mass media as disruptive, uncivil, and nondemocratic (there are also recurring negative depictions of labor unions in such influential media as the weekly *Polityka* and *Dziennik. Gazeta Prawna*).

Civil Society as a Control on Power

Yet another frame, although not as widespread, that came forth in my interviews was the classic liberal perspective on civil society as the source of empowerment of the citizens, who thereby gain the knowledge and capacity necessary to hold authorities accountable for their actions. As one interviewee from the neoliberal Civil Development Forum put it: "The confrontational way of holding the executive to account is also a way to engage citizens."

Civil society is thus pictured as a sphere in which citizens realize their collective interests and through professional organizations gain the necessary knowledge and tools to put the state in its rather limited place. Civil society organizations are here seen as citizens' tools in their fight against the state, and "should serve to limit the state's arbitrariness" (Sobieski Institute). Such a perspective resonates with the CIVICUS guidebook, which states that civil society should provide possibility for "limiting the inherent tendency of governments to expand their control" (Holloway 2001).

In the literature, this frame of civil society as a control on power usually appears in the context of foreign-aid donors who believe that "a strong civil society can prevent the agglomeration of power that threatens autonomy and choice, provide effective checks against the abuse of state authority, and protect a democratic public sphere in which citizens can debate the ends and means of governance" (Edwards 2009: 15). Hence, civil society, usually even where equated with NGOs, is pictured as a counterweight to the state (and market powers) and a guarantee of "good governance," as NGOs are supposed to perform monitoring actions toward power holders. This watchdog function is deemed necessary for proper state functioning. In Poland, even though it has been slowly changing for the better in recent years, this function still remains underdeveloped (Batko-Tołuc and Izdebski 2012). Importantly, think tanks that put forth this understanding of civil society link it very clearly to the vision of a liberal, small state. In effect, the watchdogs are supposed to ensure that the state keeps to its current, rather limited, manège.

What does this frame fail to include by seeing the watchdog, controlling function as the most important? Unsurprisingly, other functions of civil society are toned down. Here, Bob Edwards and Michael Foley's (2001: 5) typology will be useful for highlighting what is "defined out." They list three different functions of civil society. First, civil society is an arena of *socialization*—through associations members learn citizenship skills and public attitudes (this approach is usually labeled the neo-Tocquevillean, or "school of democracy" approach). Second, civil society has a *public or quasi-public function* in terms of providing services such as shelters, elderly care, education aid, culture preservation, etc. (here civil society is often called the "third sector" or "voluntary sector"). Third, civil society has a *political function* insofar as social organizations and social movements mobilize, give identity and voice to the distinct interests and points of view stimulating public debate, press government for action, and in extreme cases stimulate change of regime (this approach could be labeled neo-Gramscian). The "civil society as a control on power" frame prioritizes the political function, toning down both the socialization and the quasi-public role of civil society. Hence, for example, both service-providing organizations and community-building associations are deemed less important in the task of being a strong opposition to the (minimally understood) state.

Civil Society as Neoliberal Gobbledygook

Interestingly, there were some think tanks that objected to the very term civil society and explained their reluctance to use it: "We don't use this word [civil society], it's a buzzword [*słowo wytrych*]. It significantly contributed to the liberalization of the political course and to a certain vagueness [*nie-dookreślenie*]" (Political Critique). Similar thoughts can be heard from the Wrocław-based left think tank: "I see it as an element of liberal gobbledygook in Poland, a key word to realizing grant politics, that's it ... It is dangerous, that under the slogan of civil society, the state resigns from many functions. For example in Poland the concept of civil society is used to justify transformation of public schools into private ones" (Ferdinand Lassalle Centre for Social Thought). Both of these organizations shun the term civil society because they perceive it as used up and misused by the (neo)liberal elites.[17] Hence, they point to a link between the (neo)liberal orientation of Polish politics and the popularity of the term civil society that has been engaged in order to legitimize the political agenda. Moreover, they claim that the term is used purely instrumentally, without any genuine intention to promote broader civic participation: "As I see it, the liberal elites who use this term talk a lot about the development of civil society and at the same time, they do a lot in order to limit civic participation in the public sphere. Very often those who use this slogan [*frazes*] also support further narrowing of social rights or flexibility of the labor market, that is, they contribute to people having less resources and time to participate in public life, so they act to the detriment of civil society. They do not enhance civic participation" (Ferdinand Lassalle Centre for Social Thought). The critique is directed at the effects of the all-pervasive service-provision frame, which has led to gradual dismantling of the state, here identified with a neoliberal orientation of politics. As discussed above, the leftist think tanks also observe that the hegemonic frame has managed to marginalize the understanding of civil society as broad civic participation in public life.

Some interviewees pointed to the dilution of an initially powerful and important concept. From the great mobilizing potential it had in the late 1980s and early 1990s, civil society has become an empty slogan. "[T]his word has such a great value, that it almost makes you fly, or it slips down to idle chatter [*paplanina*]" (The Unit for Social Innovation and Research—Shipyard). Today it only gains momentum in the situation of grant seeking—it is a buzzword used to obtain funding: "I've always been fed up with this theme. A lot of money is spent and a lot of institutions were created only in order to get grants for civil society" (Sobieski Institute). Hence, here it is even more visible that aversion toward the term civil society at least to some extent could be read as a critique of equating civil society with the so-called third sector, or NGOs. Some interviewees argue that the concepts of activism and civil participation or civic engagement should replace civil society in the public discourse, because its current hegemonic understanding occludes actions that are not institutionalized or service-provision–oriented.

The "neoliberal gobbledygook" frame even more strongly highlights what is "defined out" by the hegemonic "NGO/service provision" frame. To highlight the exclusions, the interviewees evoke an idea of a contentious space of civic engagement on local basis, generally disregarding the existing structures of NGOs, which are seen as corrupted by the current socioeconomic system, or simply part of the establishment. It is widely acknowledged that organized civil society, the formalized NGOs, are only the tip of the iceberg, shadowing a wide variety of civic activism of less formal and more elusive character. Aside from traditional forms of civic engagement such as rural women's organizations (see Matysiak in this volume), hobby groups, and self-help groups, recent years have witnessed increased activity of neighborhood movements, rural and urban activism, and activism of parents (see Polanska and Korolczuk in this volume). All these are seen as "defined out" of the hegemonic frame of civil society, which leads these interviewees to reject the term civil society altogether, as polluted, misused, used up and in this sense useless in mirroring the real spectrum of civic engagement for social change.

Concluding Lessons from a Radical Democratic Perspective

Civil society continues to be a catchall term in Poland. It is applied in many, sometimes contradictory, contexts. This chapter, through mapping of the available frames of civil society figuring in the elite NGO discourses, has offered a critical perspective on the direction into which the discourse and practice of civil society in Poland has developed. The focus has not only been on what is included in the existing frames but also on the exclusions that follow. Hence, the intricate work of inclusions/exclusions is highlighted.

The analysis of the material revealed that the "civil society as service-providing NGOs" frame is perceived as hegemonic by the interviewed think tanks, and also reproduced by some of them. In the elite discourse studied here, civil society is often reduced to NGOs, which are further reduced to service provision (double synecdoche). Even though this discursive link was not set until the early 2000s, it was successfully solidified as a chain of equivalence by the Public Benefit and Volunteer Work Act in 2003, constituting part of the existing political opportunity structure for Polish civil society organizations. Creating certain possibilities for funding and enrolling NGOs in the welfare tasks, the Act strengthened the perception of service provision as the fundamental role of NGOs.[18] It was also observed that this frame has no real contender, even though three other frames ("moral blueprint," "control on power," and "neoliberal gobbledygook") are pointed to by the interviewees as coexisting in contemporary Poland.

Departing from the basic theoretical observation that hegemony necessarily involves closure, the task for this chapter was to further identify the specific exclusions put in force by the existing frames. The exclusions were traced by the strategy of pinpointing what is "defined in" and what is "defined out." The empirical analysis leads to the conclusion that different types of inclusions/exclusions are at work in the process of elite framing of civil society: frames (and especially the hegemonic frame) recognize certain *actors* (organizational types) as preferable, simultaneously omitting others; certain *actions* are put forth as either included or excluded; and finally, certain *functions* of civil society are either highlighted or occluded. The hegemonic frame sets NGOs as the principal actors of civil society, marginalizing nonformalized and noninstitutionalized actors; the "moral blueprint" frame clearly privileges consensual actions for the unspecified common good, simultaneously delegitimizing contentious civic action; and finally, the hegemonic focus on service provision also marginalizes other functions that civil society is ascribed in the literature (for example, political). Needless to say, the exclusions discussed here obviously do not mean that these actors, actions, and functions are nonexistent. It is also evident that some exclusions of the coexisting frames have reinforcing effects. Hence nonformal organizations (excluded mainly by the "NGO/service-provision" frame) and contentious actions (excluded by the "moral blueprint" frame) together contribute to double marginalization of contentiously oriented nonformalized actors of civil society.

The double move of inclusion/exclusion has been well theorized by students of radical democracy (see, e.g., Thomassen 2005). One basic lesson from this perspective is that hegemony must be paired with sensibility toward its own contingency and the resulting exclusions (Thomassen 2005: 115). Exclusions as such cannot be eliminated as they are part of the political game, but actual exclusions are always up for scrutiny. Another lesson is that relations between inclusion and exclusion are always to some extent antagonistic. By framing civil society in a particular way, creating a certain chain of equivalence that constitutes a hegemonic understanding of civil society in a given context, those that are subsequently excluded form a threat to the inside (NGOs, service-providing function). In this sense, the dividing line creates a separation between the privileged (not only conceptually, but also economically) and the delegitimized actors and actions of civil society.

Another important lesson is that chains of equivalence can (empirical possibility) and will (theoretical necessity) be broken, and the hegemonic position or understanding will be questioned, shaken, and eventually replaced. "A discursive totality never exists in the form of a simply given and delimited positivity, the relational logic will be incomplete and pierced by contingency" (Laclau and Mouffe 2001: 110). This creates an opening for new articulatory practices, for setting a new chain of equivalence and hence for new understandings of civil society, involving different actors, actions, and functions of civil society as legitimate (and also delegitimizing others). So, even though in contemporary Poland the hegemonic perception of civil society, equating it with NGOs that provide services, seems quite solid, this understanding is only a historic, contingent occurrence that will be contested. The empirical question is when it will happen, as well as what new chain of equivalence will be created (what new actors, actions, and functions of civil society will take the hegemonic position). The analysis shows that within elite discourse there is already a critique of the hegemonic frame of civil society. However, the leftist think tanks skeptical of this understanding of civil society choose not to engage in a discursive battle and thus give up the semantic field to the hegemonic frame. Many authors in this volume, focusing on mobilizations from below, document and analyze a new direction in the working of civil society, such as a vibrant grassroots engagement. The examples of urban and rural activism happening across Poland could potentially form a new counter-hegemonic frame, the success of which remains to be seen.

Katarzyna Jezierska is Postdoctoral Researcher at the Centre for European Research (CERGU) and Department of Political Science, University of Gothenburg, Sweden. Her research focuses on theories of radical democracy, civil society in Central Europe, and interface between democracy and civil society. She has recently published *Dialogue in Democracy, Democracy in Dialogue* (Ashgate, 2015), coedited with Leszek Koczanowicz.

Notes

1. See Laclau and Mouffe (2001) on the intricacies of hegemonic claims.
2. It should be mentioned that McAdam, McCarthy, and Zald (1996) use framing processes in a social movement perspective, which is not how they are examined in this chapter.
3. This is one of the differences between hegemony and domination—hegemony is always only partial, as counter-hegemonic projects always exist (Jezierska 2011: 115ff.). See also Gramsci (2005: 55f.) on the distinction between hegemony (as leadership) and domination.
4. According to *The 2012 CSO Sustainability Index for Central and Eastern Europe and Eurasia,* conducted since 1997 under the auspices of USAID and including twenty-nine countries, Poland scores second best, right after Estonia (*The 2012 CSO Sustainability Index*).

5. Some exceptions deserve to be mentioned here. Załęski (2012) studies the different traditions of the idea of civil society, and both Galasińska and Krzyżanowski (2009) and Czyżewski, Kowalski, and Piotrowski (2010) focus on discursive changes linked to the broader transformation processes.

6. In order to present a fuller picture of the political framing process, this study would need to be complemented by the politicians' discourse, the media discourse around civil society, and mass public opinion attitudes (cf. Matthes 2012).

7. Each one of these attributes can be qualified, and a common strategy in think tank research is to estimate the "independence" aspect and the time and resources dedicated to research versus other activities.

8. For example, the *2013 Global Go to Think Tank Index* lists forty-one think tanks for Poland (McGann 2014: 22).

9. Batory Foundation (*Fundacja Batorego*), Civic Institute (*Instytut Obywatelski*), Civil Development Forum (*Forum Obywatelskiego Rozwoju*), Ferdinand Lassalle Centre for Social Thought (*Ośrodek Myśli Społecznej im. F. Lassalle'a*), Green Institute (*Zielony Instytut*), Political Critique (*Krytyka Polityczna*), Sobieski Institute (*Instytut Sobieskiego*), The Institute of Public Affairs (*Instytut Spraw Publicznych*), and The Unit for Social Innovation and Research—Shipyard (*Pracownia Badań i Innowacji Społecznych "Stocznia"*).

10. The interview material suffers from clear educational, gender, and geographic biases. A huge number of my interviewees have a Ph.D. but only three of these are women. This also reflects the general picture of think tank leadership in Poland. According to the *Social Diagnosis 2013,* highly educated citizens more often engage in civic actions and Ph.D.s are significantly overrepresented in nongovernmental organizations in general (Czapiński and Panek 2013). All but one (Ferdinand Lassalle Centre for Social Thought) of the interviewed think tanks are Warsaw-based, which is also typical for Polish think tanks.

11. Here Civic Institute stands out as an organization that does not have an independent legal form and obtains all its funding from the Civic Platform Party. Some other organizations gain part of their funding from a political party (Polish or foreign) but claim independence based on income diversity and intellectual autonomy.

12. Importantly, as some scholars have shown, the term only came about as an a posteriori interpretation and self-identification of the movement (cf. Szacki 1997; Załęski 2012).

13. Quotes referring to Polish civil society organizations are taken from the interviews. All interviews were conducted in Polish and all the quotes were translated to English by the author. I would like to thank Magdalena Wójcik for help with transcriptions.

14. Interestingly, some NGOs (e.g., those working with women's issues) claim that it is difficult to get funding for direct help (e.g., Fuszara et al. 2008; Korolczuk 2014).

15. Einhorn uses this term to describe the situation of women in Eastern Europe, whose unpaid voluntary engagement compensates for the deficiencies of state provision, which at the same time keeps them out of the work market. I believe the term can be used more broadly to express the paradoxical situation of NGOs substituting for state provision while at the same time discouraging the state from adjusting its activity to local needs.

16. The legal definition of nongovernmental organizations in the *Act of Law on Public Benefit and Volunteer Act* is quite broad, encompassing "entities which do not form

part of the public finance sector … [and] which do not operate for profit" (Act of Law 2003, Art. 3).

17. Compare Szacki's claim that civil society is an element of the democratic "gobbledygook" (Szacki 1997: 7).

18. Cf. Jacobsson's (2013) conceptualization of relations between the state and civil society in terms of "channeling," i.e., indirect influence that the state exerts through institutional opportunity structures, and "enrollment," i.e., direct involvement of civil society actors in the policy implementation work.

References

Act of Law of 24 April 2003 on Public Benefit and Volunteer Work. Retrieved 4 October 2013 from http://www.pozytek.gov.pl/Law,534.html.

Bąkowski, T., and J.H. Szlachetko, eds. 2012. *Zagadnienie think tanków w ujęciu interdyscyplinarnym* [The Question of Think Tanks in an Interdisciplinary Perspective]. Gdańsk: Wydawnictwo Uniwersytetu Gdańskiego.

Batko-Tołuc, K., and K. Izdebski. 2012. *Organizacje Strażnicze w Polsce. Stan Obecny, Wyzwania, Perspektywy* [Watchdogs in Poland: Current Condition, Challenges, Prospects]. Warszawa: Fundacja Instytut Spraw Publicznych. Retrieved 10 January 2014 from http://www.isp.org.pl/uploads/pdf/1444484346.pdf.

Berman, S. 1997. "Civil Society and the Collapse of the Weimar Republic." *World Politics* 49, no. 3: 401–429.

Chambers, S., and J. Kopstein. 2001. "Bad Civil Society." *Political Theory* 29, no. 6: 837–865.

CIVICUS Civil Society Index. Retrieved 30 September 2013 from https://civicus.org/csi/.

Czapiński, J. 2006. "Polska–państwo bez społeczeństwa" [Poland–A State without Society]. *Nauka* 1: 7–26.

Czapiński, J., and T. Panek, eds. 2013. *Diagnoza Społeczna 2013. Warunki i jakość życia Polaków* [Social Diagnosis 2013: Objective and Subjective Quality of Life in Poland]. Warszawa: Rada Monitoringu Społecznego.

Czyżewski, M., S. Kowalski, and A. Piotrowki, eds. 2010. *Rytualny chaos. Studium dyskursu publicznego* [Ritual Chaos: A Study of Public Discourse]. Warszawa: Wydawnictwa Akademickie i Profesjonalne.

Dagnino, E. 2011. "Civil Society in Latin America," in *The Oxford Handbook of Civil Society*, ed. M. Edwards. Oxford: Oxford University Press, 122–133.

Edwards, B., and W.M. Foley. 2001. "Civil Society and Social Capital," in *Beyond Tocqueville: Civil Society and the Social Capital Debate in Comparative Perspective*, ed. B. Edwards, M.W. Foley, and M. Diani. Hanover, NH: University Press of New England, 1–14.

Edwards, M. 2009. *Civil Society*. Cambridge: Polity Press.

Einhorn, B. 2000. "Gender and Citizenship in the Context of Democratisation and Economic Reform in East Central Europe," in *International Perspectives on Gender and Democratisation*, ed. R. Shirin. London and Basingstoke: Macmillan, 103–124.

Frączak P. 2012. *Trzeci sektor w III Rzeczypospolitej. Wybór artykułów 1989-2001* [Third Sector in the Third Republic of Poland: Selected Articles 1989–2001]. Warszawa: Fundusz Współpracy.

———. 2013. *W poszukiwaniu tradycji. Dwa dwudziestolecia pozarządowych inspiracji* [Searching for Tradition: Two Decades of Non-Governmental Inspirations]. Warszawa: OFOP.

Freeden, M. 2005. "What Should the 'Political' in Political Theory Explore?" *The Journal of Political Philosophy* 13, no. 2: 113–134.

Fuszara, M., M. Grabowska, J. Mizielińska, and J. Regulska, eds. 2008. *Współpraca czy konflikt. Państwo, Unia i kobiety* [Cooperation or Conflict? The State, the EU, and Women]. Warszawa: Wydawnictwa Akademickie i Profesjonalne.

Galasińska, A., and M. Krzyżanowski, eds. 2009. *Discourse and Transformation in Central and Eastern Europe.* Basingstoke: Palgrave Macmillan.

Gawin, D., and P. Gliński, eds. 2006. *Civil Society in the Making.* Warsaw: IFIS.

Glasius, M. 2012. "Dissident Writings as Political Theory on Civil Society and Democracy." *Review of International Studies* 38: 343–364.

Global Civil Society Index 2004. Retrieved 30 September 2013 from http://ccss.jhu.edu/publications-findings?did=360.

Gramsci, A. 2005 [1971]. *Selections from the Prison Notebooks,* ed. and transl. Q. Hoare and G. Nowell Smith. New York: International Publishers.

Habermas, J. 2001. *Between Facts and Norms: Contributions to a Discourse Theory of Law and Democracy.* Cambridge: MIT Press.

Havel, V. 2010 [1985]. "The Power of the Powerless," in *The Power of the Powerless: Citizens against the State in Central-Eastern Europe,* ed. V. Havel et al. New York: Routledge, 23–96.

Holloway, R. 2001. *Using the Civil Society Index: Assessing the Health of Civil Society: A Handbook for Using the CIVICUS Index on Civil Society as a Self-Assessment Tool.* Retrieved 28 September 2013 from https://civicus.org/view/media/IndexHandbook.pdf.

Jacobsson, K. 2012. "Fragmentation of the Collective Action Space: The Animal Rights Movement in Poland." *East European Politics* 28, no. 4: 1–18.

———. 2013. "Channeling and Enrollment: The Institutional Shaping of Animal Rights Activism in Poland," in *Beyond NGO-ization. The Development of Social Movements in Central and Eastern Europe,* ed. K. Jacobsson and S. Saxonberg. Farnham: Ashgate, 27–47.

Jezierska, K. 2011. *Radical Democracy Redux: Politics and Subjectivity beyond Habermas and Mouffe.* Örebro: Örebro University Press.

———. 2015. "Moral Blueprint or Neoliberal Gobbledygook? Civil Society Frames among Polish Think Tanks." *East European Politics and Societies* 29, no. 4: 831–849.

———. Forthcoming. "Performing Independence. The Apolitical Image of Polish Think Tanks." *Europe-Asia Studies.*

Koopmans, R. 1999. "Political. Opportunity. Structure. Some Splitting to Balance the Lumping." *Sociological Forum* 14, no. 1: 93–105.

Kopecký, P., and C. Mudde. 2003. *Uncivil Society? Contentious Politics in Post-Communist Europe.* London and New York: Routledge.

Korolczuk, E. 2014. "Promoting Civil Society in Contemporary Poland: Gendered Results of Institutional Changes." *VOLUNTAS: International Journal of Voluntary and Nonprofit Organizations* 25, no. 4: 949–967.

Krastev, I. 2000a. "The Liberal Estate: Reflections on the Politics of Think Tanks in Central and Eastern Europe," in *Think Tanks and Civil Society: Catalysts for Ideas and*

Action, ed. J. McGann and R.K. Weaver. New Brunswick: Transaction Publisher, 273–291.

———. 2000b. "Post-Communist Think Tanks: Making and Faking Influence," in *Banking on Knowledge, The Genesis of the Global Development Network,* ed. D. Stone. London and New York: Routledge, 145–163.

Laclau, E., and C. Mouffe. 2001 [1985]. *Hegemony and Socialist Strategy: Towards a Radical Democratic Politics.* London and New York: Verso.

Leś, E., S. Nałęcz, and J. Wygnański. 2000. "Defining the Nonprofit Sector: Poland." *Working Papers of the Johns Hopkins Comparative Nonprofit Sector Project* 36, Baltimore: The Johns Hopkins Center for Civil Society Studies, 1–27. Retrieved 15 June 2015 from http://ccss.jhu.edu/wp-content/uploads/downloads/2011/09/Poland_CNP_WP36_2000.pdf.

Lukes, S. 1975. "Political Ritual and Social Integration." *Sociology* 9: 289–308.

Mathiesen, T. 2015. *The Politics of Abolition Revisited.* Abingdon and New York: Routledge.

Matthes, J. 2012. "Framing Politics: An Integrative Approach." *American Behavioral Scientist* 56, no. 3: 247–259.

McAdam, D., J. McCarthy, and M. Zald. 1996. "Introduction: Opportunities, Mobilizing Structures, and Framing Processes—Toward a Synthetic, Comparative Perspective on Social Movements," in *Comparative Perspectives on Social Movements: Political Opportunities, Mobilizing Structures, and Cultural Framings,* ed. D. McAdam, J. McCarthy, and M. Zald. New York: Cambridge University Press, 1–20.

McGann, J. 2007. *Think Tanks and Policy Advice in the United States. Academics, Advisors and Advocates.* New York: Routledge.

———. 2014. *2013 Global Go to Think Tank Index and Abridged Report.* Philadelphia: University of Pennsylvania. Retrieved 10 July 2014 from http://gotothinktank.com/dev1/wp-content/uploads/2014/01/GoToReport2013.pdf.

Michnik, A. 1985. *Letters from Prison and Other Essays.* Berkeley: University of California Press.

Misztal, W., and A. Kościański, eds. 2011. *Rozdroża praktyki i idei społeczeństwa obywatelskiego* [Crossroads of the Practice and Idea of Civil Society]. Warszawa: Wydawnictwo IFiS PAN.

Piotrowski, J. 2006. *Politycy wobec społeczeństwa obywatelskiego 2005/2006. Raport z monitoringu obietnic wyborczych z pierwszego roku funkcjonowania Sejmu V kadencji* [Politicians versus Civil Society 2005/2006: A Report Monitoring Electoral Promises after the First Year of the Fifth Term of Polish Parliament]. Warszawa: OFOP.

Rice, S. 2012. "Are CLCs Finished?" *Alternative Law Journal* 37, no. 1: 17–21.

Rich, A. 2004. *Think Tanks, Public Policy, and the Politics of Expertise.* Cambridge: Cambridge University Press.

Siegel, D., and J. Yancey. 1992. *The Rebirth of Civil Society: The Development of the Nonprofit Sector in East Central Europe and the Role of Western Assistance.* New York: The Rockefeller Brothers Fund.

Stone, D. 2007. "Recycling Bins, Garbage Cans or Think Tanks? Three Myths Regarding Policy Analysis Institutes." *Public Administration* 85, no. 2: 259–278.

Szacki, J. 1997. "Wstęp. Powrót idei społeczeństwa obywatelskiego" [Introduction: The Return of the Idea of Civil Society], in *Ani książę, ani kupiec: Obywatel* [Neither Prince, nor Merchant: Citizen], ed. J. Szacki. Kraków: Znak, 5–62.

The 2012 CSO Sustainability Index for Central and Eastern Europe and Eurasia. Retrieved 30 September 2013 from http://www.usaid.gov/sites/default/files/documents/1863/2012CSOSI_0.pdf.

Thomassen, L. 2005. "In/exclusions: Towards a Radical Democratic Approach to Exclusion," in *Radical Democracy: Politics between Abundance and Lack*, ed. L. Thomassen and L. Tønder. Manchester: Manchester University Press, 103–119.

Weaver, K. 1989. "The Changing World of Think Tanks." *Political Science and Politics* 2, no. 3: 563–578.

Weaver, K., and J. McGann. 2000. "Think Tanks and Civil Societies in a Time of Change," in *Think Tanks and Civil Society: Catalysts for Ideas and Action*, ed. J. McGann and R.K. Weaver. New Brunswick: Transaction Publisher, 1–35.

Wendt, J. 2007. *Wymiar przestrzenny struktur i aktywności społeczeństwa obywatelskiego w Polsce* [The Spatial Aspect of the Structures and Activities of Civil Society in Poland]. Warszawa: IGiPZ PAN.

Zagała, Z. 2008. "Miejskie społeczeństwo obywatelskie i jego przemiany" [Urban Civil Society and Its Transformations], in *Społeczeństwo obywatelskie między idea a praktyka* [Civil Society between Idea and Practice], ed. A. Kościański and W. Misztal. Warszawa: Wydawnictwo IFiS PAN, 219–234.

Załęski, P.S. 2012. *Neoliberalizm i społeczeństwo obywatelskie* [Neoliberalism and Civil Society]. Toruń: Wydawnictwo Naukowe Uniwersytetu Mikołaja Kopernika.

Zbieranek, P. 2011. *Polski model organizacji typu think tank* [The Polish Model of the Think Tank Organization]. Warszawa: Wydawnictwo Naukowe Scholar.

Ziętara, W. 2010. *Think tanks na przykładzie USA i Polski* [Think Tanks in Case of USA and Poland]. Lublin: Wydawnictwo Uniwersytetu Marii Curie-Skłodowskiej.

PART II

(De)legitimization of Civic Activism:
New Actors and Marginalized Groups

Chapter 5

WHEN PARENTS BECOME ACTIVISTS
EXPLORING THE INTERSECTION
OF CIVIL SOCIETY AND FAMILY

Elżbieta Korolczuk

Introduction

On 4 June 2015, a delegation of Polish parents presented Ewa Kopacz, the then prime minister, with a petition signed by 330,000 citizens protesting the reduction of the age at which children were required to begin formal schooling from seven to six. Parental activists used the slogans "Save the Little Ones!" and "Don't Take Childhood away from the Children!" to voice their opposition. The action was initiated by *Fundacja Rzecznik Praw Rodziców* (Parents' Rights Ombudsperson Foundation) a nongovernmental organization that underscores its claims to represent the broad public with the inclusion of "ombudsperson" in its name (Elbanowska and Elbanowski 2015; see also Hryciuk and Korolczuk 2015; Polkowska 2014). Founded in 2009 by Karolina and Tomasz Elbanowscy, a young couple concerned about the well-being of their own six children, the foundation managed to attract considerable media attention, mobilized hundreds of thousands of Polish parents, and secured the support of the then opposition party Law and Justice. Despite this extensive mobilization and media attention, neither the then ruling Civic Platform nor the Ministry of Education agreed to discuss the issue any further and the law remained in effect until the elections of October 2015, when the new right-wing government overturned the decision to make schooling compulsory at the age of six.

Neither the scale of the mobilization against school-age reform nor its success in changing the law are unique: parents' activism is increasingly visible and influential in Poland (e.g., Hryciuk 2008; Hryciuk and Korolczuk 2013; Korolczuk 2014; Polkowska 2014; Wojnicka 2013). A broad range of parental movements has also emerged in other postsocialist countries, including soldiers' mothers' activism in Russia, mobilizations of conservative parental groups against legal and discursive changes that would affect gender equality in Ukraine and Russia, Czech and Polish fathers focusing on custody rights, or persons affected by infertility demanding state support for in vitro fertilization in Bulgaria (e.g. Dimitrova 2017; Fábián and Korolczuk 2017; Jagudina 2009; Saxonberg 2017). However, parents' activism has been the subject of relatively little research and is seldom mentioned in the civil society literature. This relative lack of interest can be explained by the theoretical separation of the family and civil society, which were often imagined to occupy different and separate spheres—the private and the public (Nautz et al. 2013; Hagemann et al. 2008). Most definitions of civil society mention the family, usually stressing that—analogous to the state and the market—it is a separate sphere, yet interconnected to the others. The nature of this interconnectedness is seldom explored, however. In their widely discussed book *Civil Society and Political Theory,* Jean Cohen and Andrew Arato (1992) suggest that the family should be conceptualized as the basic unit of civil society, "the voluntary association par excellence," but in contemporary literature on civic activism this issue is often left out (Ginsborg 2013; Hagemann 2008).

Moreover, social activism is routinely interpreted as an alternative to family engagement, while "family-civil society relationships were often narrowly reduced to nepotism, corruption and a lack of transparency" (Nautz et al. 2013: 5). Somewhat analogous to the NIMBY (Not in My Backyard) type of urban social movement, people mobilizing to fight for specific goals, or social provisions they would benefit from, are often perceived as egoistic and their activism as self-serving since they allegedly pursue their own rather than the common good. Therefore, their efforts are not seen as part of civil society, which is defined as based on "responsibility, solidarity and commitment to the well-being of the larger community" (Gawin and Gliński 2006: 8).

This interpretation of the relationship between civil society and the family is repeated in Polish debates on civil society. Problems such as low civic engagement, corruption and nepotism, and underdeveloped organizational culture are often attributed to people's orientation toward the good of their immediate social circles, an orientation that Elżbieta and Jacek Tarkowscy (1994) interpret as a local variation of "amoral familism."[1] Scholars claim that people's "individual resourcefulness" in the private sphere correlates with "deficient citizenship" regarding the public (Gliński 2004). The predominance of the orientation toward family and friends is interpreted as a factor that hinders social activism and slows down the emergence of wider civic networks, attitudes, and practices in Poland (Czapiński 2008).

While these views may, in some respects, be accurate, the assumption that the orientation toward the welfare of one's family is antithetical to acting on behalf of a common good and that people either pursue the interests of their family and immediate social circle *or* engage in activism on behalf of the whole society does not necessarily reflect reality. The cases of social activism coalescing around issues concerning the family, such as mothers' and fathers' mobilizations around alimony and custody rights, schooling reform, access to new reproductive technologies, and high-quality perinatal care, which emerged during the last decade in Poland (and in many other countries worldwide), show that people often transgress the public/private divide and mobilize on the basis of their identities and experiences as parents with the goal of introducing changes pertaining to their families *and* to society in general.

While it has been acknowledged that before 1989 in Central and Eastern Europe the family and focus on the private sphere did not necessarily weigh negatively upon civic engagement but provided sustenance that encouraged it (e.g., Nautz et al. 2013), today this recognition seems to be lost. Social scientists interested in contemporary Polish civil society have paid very scant attention to the role of family in the development and functioning of civil society in the country (see e.g., Gawin and Gliński 2006; Kościański and Misztal 2008; Raciborski 2010). Parental activism has been under-researched and under-theorized within mainstream Polish sociology and has only recently became an object of study (e.g., Charkiewicz 2009; Fábián and Korolczuk 2017; Hryciuk and Korolczuk 2013, Korolczuk 2014; Wojnicka 2013).

This chapter aims to fill the gaps in existing scholarship by examining the intersection of family and civil society in the Polish context.[2] I focus on recent initiatives whose participants position themselves as citizens by way of accountable parenthood and I stress that their social engagement stems from parental experiences and identities. Specifically, I am interested in how the activists become mobilized and how they conceptualize their civic engagement in terms of the goals they pursue. The aim is to reflect back on existing definitions of civil society, and to address the question of what understandings of civil society and political engagement are reflected in these mobilizations as well as how to conceptualize local understandings and practices.

The emergence of such groups and organizations demonstrates that the division between the public and private spheres (understood here as the nondomestic and domestic spheres) are porous and negotiable, and suggests that even if parental activism is often initiated around practical interests and issues connected to people's immediate socioeconomic realm, it easily develops into mobilization oriented toward broadly defined social change.

Thus, parental activism challenges the "field approach" in civil society studies, which presupposes a clear separation between the private/domestic and public/political spheres, as well as the "normative approach" to civil society, which values orientation toward common good as opposed to private/familial orientation (Hagemann 2008). The cases studied here show also that civic participation is a gendered process, as are the definition of the political and the shape of the public/private divide.

Data and Methodology

This analysis is based on five case studies of social mobilizations around issues concerning mothers' and fathers' rights in contemporary Poland. Due to space limitations these cases will not be described in detail (see Korolczuk 2014; Hryciuk and Korolczuk 2013). Rather, the focus is on participants' motivations, their claims and goals. The following cases are analyzed:

- A national campaign advocating a new approach to pregnancy, birth, and perinatal care, which in 1994 turned into the Childbirth with Dignity Foundation (*Rodzić po ludzku*). Its primary strategies comprise social campaigns, media releases, workshops for parents-to-be, and cooperation with authorities, media, and experts. Its activities led to the introduction of the new birth care standards approved by the Ministry of Health in 2011.[3]
- The AF movement—a national movement of single mothers for the re-establishment of the Alimony Fund, which was a state institution that paid child support in cases where the parent who was supposed to pay could not, and collecting the debt from him later (see also Hryciuk in this volume). The movement was most active between 2002, when the authorities announced the liquidation of the Fund, and 2007, when it was finally re-installed. The activists used different tactics, including demonstrating, sending protest letters, cooperating with MPs and politically active groups, and finally, preparing the civic law proposal that was submitted to the parliament by the single mothers and their political allies and served as the basis of the bill re-installing the Alimony Fund in September 2007.
- The local feminist nongovernmental organization MaMa Foundation (*Fundacja MaMa*), focused mainly on changing the discourse on mothering, access to public space, and equal treatment, and which was established in 2006. The types of action they employed are very diverse (demonstrations and picket lines, campaigns via social media, workshops, debates and conferences, cooperation with local authorities

as well as publications and trainings), e.g., the first initiative called "I can't enter with a pram here!" took the form of a public event showing the many architectural barriers in the capital city of Warsaw. The action stressed the fact that mothers with prams, as well as people in wheelchairs, have limited access to public space, which violates their civil rights and is in contradiction to the social justice principles. It attracted considerable media attention and social support especially via the Internet.

- The conservative Mother and Father Foundation (*Fundacja Mamy i Taty*), which focuses on countering cultural and social changes interpreted as endangering the well-being of Polish families and children (e.g., the proliferation of divorce, abortion, and "homosexual propaganda" in schools and media). It was established in 2009, and its main slogan is "The whole of Poland protects the children." Its most well-known initiatives included a social campaign initiated in 2011, "Divorce? Think about it!," which involved spots on TV and the outdoor media, the main message being that divorce should be avoided because it causes a range of long-term negative consequences in children, such as alcoholic tendencies and violent and anti-social behaviors; and the 2015 campaign, "Don't delay motherhood!," with TV and online commercials warning women against the dangers of focusing on career, traveling, and pleasures rather than becoming mothers. According to representatives of the organization, the campaign aimed to show that motherhood is "a natural desire of many women that the contemporary world limits in significant ways" and to "portray contraception in a new light ... not as a source of freedom but as a source of women's oppression, thwarting their desire to become mothers."[4]
- Campaign "Save the Little Ones!," coordinated by *Stowarzyszenie & Fundacja Rzecznik Praw Rodziców* (Parents' Rights Ombudsman Foundation & Association) and initiated in 2009 by Karolina and Tomasz Elbanowscy, successfully opposing the governmental plan to reduce the age at which children were required to begin formal schooling from seven to six. Over the years the activists managed to gather over 1,600,000 signatures under three consecutive projects involving changes in the education system, and in 2015 the Polish weekly *Wprost* awarded them the title of People of the Year for their tenacity in mobilizing Poles and building civil society. The foundation became also involved in efforts to ban gender-equality education from schools, to oppose the ratification of the Council of Europe Convention on preventing and combating violence against women and domestic violence, and to lobby for "family friendly" social policies. According to the leaders of the movement and commentators, this mass mobilization

also had important political consequences, because its well publicized critique of the then ruling Civic Platform became one of the factors leading to electoral success of the populist right-wing Peace and Justice Party in October 2015.

The cases were purposely selected to vary by scale (both mass mobilizations such as the AF movement and "Save the Little Ones!" and small-scale initiatives such as MaMa Foundation were included), the ideological orientation of the activists (both feminist and conservative organizations were studied), as well as the types of issues they focus on (e.g., health care, education, work-life balance, law enforcement, and cultural changes). Most of the activists are women, but in three out of five cases fathers are also involved, and mobilizing men and women alike is often stressed as an important goal of the studied initiatives, hence I use the term "parental activism" rather than "motherist movements" (cf. Jaquette 1994).[5]

The paper draws on qualitative analysis of over thirty individual interviews with people involved in these mobilizations (mostly female leaders and activists who are engaged in the day-to-day functioning of groups and NGOs) conducted between 2011 and 2015 in different Polish cities. Another important data set regards textual analysis of websites of the specific organizations and groups, printed materials, and media reports concerning their activism. This chapter also refers to previous studies on civil society and on the conditions of mothering and fathering in Poland, which serve as the background against which the outcomes of the present study will be viewed.

In this analysis I am interested in the ways in which the activists link their "private" identities, experiences, and claims they make as parents to their "public" civic engagement within the cultural, social, and political context of Poland. Thus, I examine how the activists motivate their engagement, how they frame their goals, and on whose behalf they claim to act—themselves? Their children? Polish mothers or fathers? Parents in general? Or the whole society? I focus specifically on the analysis of the goals these groups and organizations claim to pursue, and the identities of the activists as presented in the interviews, in the organizations' mission and vision statements, in media reports, and in other texts, as well as during public debates, conferences, and protests.

Conceptualizing the Relationship between Civil Society and Family

The definition of civil society has been the subject of ongoing discussion internationally (Lane 2010: 311), as well as in the Polish context (Gawin and Gliński 2006). Most scholars follow what historian Karen Hagemann (2008) terms a "field approach" and conceptualize civil society as a sphere that is separated from, even if in practice interconnected with, the family, the state, and the market (e.g., Lane 2010; Ginsborg 2013).[6] Another approach distinguished by Hagemann is a "normative" one, which includes a strong normative content, undergoing alterations in different historical and geographical contexts. Such a definition has been outlined, e.g., by British scholar Paul Ginsborg, who follows Jürgen Kocka in defining civil society as a force that is supposed to: "… foster the diffusion of power rather than its concentration, to use peaceful rather than violent means, to work for gender equality and social equity, to build horizontal solidarities rather than vertical loyalties, to encourage tolerance and inclusion" (2013: 31). In other words, the normative basis for the emergence of civil society networks is seen as related to people's willingness to think and act beyond their own interests, even though the criteria for differentiation between individual egoistic goals and the abstract category of the common good are seldom explicitly addressed. Such conceptualizations of civil society have their advantages, but hardly seem suitable for the purpose of analyzing parental activism that transgresses the public/private divide, appears as oriented primarily toward the good of one's family and friends, and sometimes opposes liberal values such as tolerance, gender equality, and minority rights.

My goal is to reconstruct local understanding of social activism and civil society that the activists adhere to, rather than to verify whether the types of activism I study fit the hegemonic definitions promulgated by scholars and practitioners (see also Jacobsson and Korolczuk in this volume). Thus, I adopt an "action-logical approach" that is practice-based and focuses on what groups and communities do (independent from the state) as they bind "citizens together in matters of common concern, and by their existence and actions" (Hagemann 2008: 21). According to Hagemann (2008), such an approach allows for including a wider range of initiatives based on family relations and local neighborhood networks within civil society. It also seems more fitting to examine types of activism that oppose liberal values, e.g., conservative parental organizations and groups.

Parental activism focuses on the issues concerning motherhood and fatherhood and the well-being of children and family, but as I will show in the analysis, the ways in which specific groups and organizations define family or children's needs differ significantly. The problem with the definition of family is also observable in scholarship on civil society. According to Okin (1998; cf. Michel 2013), terms such as *family, private sphere,* and *home* are often used interchangeably, and the gendered consequences of this conflation have often been omitted in mainstream debates. In my analysis I focus on practices and ways in which the activists construct their goals and claims, thus, I adopt a view on the family proposed by U.S. historian Sonya Michel, who asserts: "By family I do not mean a 'natural,' transhistorical biological unit but rather a social formation that emerges at the intersection of law, institutions, economic and demographic trends, ideologies, custom, convention and practice" (2013: 67).

Scholarship exploring the intersections of civil society and the family is scarce. In the book "The Golden Chain: Family, Civil Society and the State" one of the editors, Paul Ginsborg, points to the fact that "The relationships between family, civil society and the state are still both under-theorised and under-researched. There are almost no works which assume these relationships as their central methodological point of departure, or utilize this framework in their reconstruction of societies and phases in history" (2013: 17). Existing studies and theoretical considerations focus mostly on the family as part of the cultural context and structural basis for people's engagement, and examine issues such as socializing people into being good citizens, or the question of what kind of family culture, structure, or system leads individuals toward an active role in civil society. For example, Kerbner (1997) and Alexander (2006) debated the concept of the Republican Mother and the role of mothers in facilitating the development of civic attitudes through proper upbringing and education. Banfield's (1958) study showed that atomized and strong families, which have little or no ties with the outside world and focus on their own survival and well-being, contribute to under-developed and isolationist community life, while Reher's analysis of family systems in Europe demonstrated "the broad correlation between the flourishing civil society and a family system where the individual counts more," and where intergenerational ties are not too strong (Reher 2004, in Ginsborg 2013: 29).

Regarding Central and Eastern Europe, there are suggestions that "certain forms of family solidarities and kinship supplied important conditions for the rise of civil society" before 1989 (Nautz et al. 2013: 5). This concerns the use of private resources, relying on the networks of family and friends as well as creating a semipublic sphere in private homes where debates, education, and other dissident activities took place (e.g., Kubik 2000; Penn 2003). Under the authoritarian state the family (understood as a domestic space) became the only space where people could meet, cooperate, and discuss freely, thus, it has been interpreted as "a besieged or nascent civil society" (Ginsborg 2013: 22). Under a democratic state, such an interpretation of the relationship between family and civil society would be difficult to sustain, but "private" identities and recourses remain of crucial importance for the development of a civil society. Recent studies show, for example, that social activism in Poland is often based on extended private networks, and that there is a tendency to pursue collective aims in privatist and individualist forms (e.g., Chimiak 2006; Jacobsson in this volume). While this trend has been interpreted as the legacy of state-socialist times, strengthened by recent neoliberal influences, some scholars suggested that it also reflects the ways in which the public/private divide was already constructed in Poland in the nineteenth and early twentieth centuries. During the times of partitions, when Poland lost sovereignty, family not only had to serve "private" purposes but also had certain political and public functions, e.g., in the area of education, art, and religion (Matynia 2003). Under this period "the public/private distinction was often less sharply gendered, boundaries were drawn differently than in some Western liberal thought, and the relations between the public and private were sometimes even explicitly discussed" (Funk 2004: 711). Consequently, the ways in which some aspects of family life have become a matter of public concern in the nineteenth century (e.g., teaching national values or reproducing the nation) have consequences for the politicization of certain issues in Poland after 1989 (e.g., abortion, which is interpreted as weakening the nation) (Korolczuk 2013).

The relationship between activism and "private" identities, roles, and interests has been recognized and theorized mostly by scholars who work at the intersection of gender and social movements, especially those who examined "motherist movements" (Jaquette 1994; Hryciuk in this volume). Such movements, understood as mobilizations of women who asserted their claims as mothers responsible for the well-being of their families, emerged as early as the nineteenth and early twentieth centuries, but became most visible in Latin America, the United States, and other parts of the world during the 1970s and 1980s (Molyneux 1985; Naples 1998; Yuval-Davis 1997). The term "motherist movements" concerns various types of initiatives, most of which were triggered by social and economic changes resulting in deterioration of working and living conditions, scarcity of food, and/or retrenchment in social provisions (Jaquette 1994; Michel 2013; Molyneux 1985; Werbner 1999). Worsening living conditions often led to mobilizations of women who were not previously engaged in public life. Maxine Molyneux explains that "[b]y virtue of their place within the sexual division of labor as those primarily responsible for their household's daily welfare, women have a special interest in domestic provision and public welfare. When governments fail to provide these basic needs, women withdraw their support; when the livelihood of their families, especially their children, is threatened it is women who form the phalanxes of bread rioters, demonstrators, and petitioners" (Molyneux 1985: 233).

Such mobilizations of working, often economically underprivileged, women who took to the streets claiming they needed to feed their children and care for their families also emerged in Poland under state socialism (Fidelis 2010; Mazurek 2010), and after 1989 due to dismantling of welfare provisions and increasingly precarious living and working conditions

(Charkiewicz 2009; Hryciuk and Korolczuk 2013; Maciejewska 2010).[7] Results of the studies on mothers' mobilizations have not yet been integrated into the studies of civil society. Thus, I argue for the need to integrate the theoretical developments proposed by scholars in the field of social movements and gender into civil society studies in contemporary Poland.

From Parents to Activists: Transgressing the Private/Public Divide

The analysis of parental activism in contemporary Poland suggests that although in general young parents, especially mothers, are the most likely to be oriented toward the good of their families and the least likely to be politically engaged (Ginsborg 2013), there are exceptions to this rule. In all cases studied here, the activists envisioned their social engagement as stemming first and foremost from personal experiences connected to family life, such as giving birth, providing for the family financially, or raising children in an increasingly pluralized society. In the case of many female activists, the sole experience of getting pregnant and becoming a mother led to a sort of political awakening, initiating a process of "political becoming" (Gunnarsson Payne and Korolczuk 2016). The process of becoming a parent involves a crucial shift of perspective that leads to re-interpretation of individual problems with child care, access to public space, or the decision as to when the child should enter education system as collective issues, and to redefine parental identities as political rather than individual and emotional. At the same time, having a child strengthens a sense of entitlement and empowerment, which often results in a continuous engagement.

Excerpts from the interviews show how "private" experiences and roles translate into public engagement. An important element of this process, often seen in the case of civic engagement, is the experience of difference, which is interpreted as unjust. In the words of Karolina Elbanowska, the leader of the Parents' Rights Ombudsman Foundation: "We are discriminated against as parents in this country. We feel oppressed by the state."[8] While she referred to parents of both genders being marginalized and not listened to by the authorities, in the case of mothers who are associated with the domestic sphere, discrimination is often connected to daily experiences concerning child care, including the quality of early childhood education and limited access to public spaces such as streets, buses, and municipal buildings. One of the founders of the MaMa Foundation, who had not been an activist before, declared that after giving birth, her perspective fundamentally changed: "All of a sudden I realized that I am, in some sense, discriminated against, that there is discrimination against mothers, they are excluded from the public sphere, that in theory a mother can enter the public space, but is not given a voice … I realized that I am not treated seriously as a mother, not to mention practical issues such as not being able to cross the street, not being able to enter the municipal office with a stroller" (2012, Warsaw). The representative of the Birth in a Dignified Way Foundation expressed a very similar view on the motivations behind becoming an activist. In her case, the long-term social engagement was triggered when she encountered the inhumane and humiliating conditions in Polish hospitals. In her view, individual experiences with the Polish health-care system instigated the process of "political becoming" of a whole generation of men and women who had children in the early 1990s: "The whole group that started this movement, all women and men who got involved, did so because of their personal experiences. And there is nothing unusual in that. I talked to many people from different countries and organizations, and usually it is what one lives through that counts, it is not an academic choice … we were all somehow affected by the perinatal care system, which was really inhumane under this period" (2012, Warsaw). Being personally affected by the health care or education system proved to be an eye-opening experience for many people, making women and some men aware of the conditions of mothering and fathering in the local context and leading them to a conclusion that significant change in this area is needed—thus giving them motivation to engage in collective action.

Parental experiences are clearly gendered, and appear much more significant in the case of women, who are going through potentially difficult events such as birth and early motherhood. It is not a coincidence that in her speech delivered in the lower chamber of the Polish parliament in March 2015 Karolina Elbanowska began speaking on behalf of all parents but quickly moved to stressing the specificity of mothers' experiences and motivations: "As mothers we love our children from the moment they are the size of a pinpoint, we are ready to give our lives for them, we take care of them when they are sick, we give up our dreams and plans in the name of their health and happiness. On behalf of our children we are ready to gather as many as 1,600,000 signatures supporting civic law proposals that our children will benefit from."[9] The embodied character of parenting experiences also enables women to identify with others who went through similar experiences and suffered from discrimination, neglect, and abuse. Working together with other mothers (and fathers) not only gave the respondents personal satisfaction, but it offered the possibility of making their difficult experiences and feelings meaningful.

For some of the activists parenting is also an empowering experience: they claim that becoming a mother opens up new possibilities and is a source of motivation to engage. In short films featuring the founders of the Mother and Father Foundation (three women and one man) explaining why they became engaged and why the viewer should support the Foundation financially, all four activists refer to their parental roles and identities as positive and rewarding. A male funder described a conversation with his son as the turning point when he realized how important it is to "make the world more friendly toward our children." Parental activists stress that having kids makes parents, despite of their gender, focused on the common good, more responsible and future-oriented: "Nothing sharpens your social sensibility as becoming a parent. Thanks to our children we look at the world around us with new eyes, asking ourselves what has or can have influence on children's upbringing, safety, and their future. Thus, it is not a coincidence that mothers and fathers often become leaders of different, very active social movements or consumer groups, motivated by honest concern for their children and their future."[10] Acting on behalf of children and with their best interest in mind allegedly guarantees that the activists work on behalf the whole society: Who if not parents would ensure that we all have a better future?

While the activists usually present having children as a universal and unifying experience, class matters for parental activism as much as it matters for parenting itself. Whereas working-class poor mothers protesting against welfare cuts are delegitimized in the media as emotional and demanding (Hryciuk and Korolczuk 2013), middle-class parents are seldom accused of selfishness or criticized for making claims vis-à-vis the state. Furthermore, middle-class parents have significant resources, financial and otherwise, that are needed to engage in any sort of collective action. Thus, it is hardly surprising that the majority of parent activists represent the urban middle-class or intelligentsia. For example, in their mission statement, available on the website of the organization, the representatives of the Mother and Father Foundation stress that their commitment to the cause stems also from their education and/or professional experience, e.g., from having higher education or working as a family counselor. These declarations confirm the activists' middle-class status that is indicated by their neat clothes and elegant interiors in which the material was filmed. Moreover, stressing their activism as connected to professional lives helps to present civic engagement as an activity that bridges the public/private divide separating work and family life without challenging the gender hierarchy inscribed in this division.

Becoming parents gave the activists three fundamental reasons for participation, which Bert Klandermans refers to as instrumentality, identity, and ideology: "*Instrumentality* refers to movement participation as an attempt to influence the social and political environment; *identity* refers to movement participation as a manifestation of identification with a group; and *ideology* refers to movement participation as a search for meaning and an expression of one's views" (2008: 361, emphasis in original). Although they can be analytically separated, in practice these three types of motivation are interrelated and seldom manifest themselves separately. The example of the women fighting for the restitution of the Alimony Fund demonstrates that even if the motivation behind the activism is at first instrumental, other factors also play a role. In the beginning, the focus of the mobilization was on influencing politicians and changing their decision on the Fund, as the plan to eradicate it was experienced by most single mothers as illegitimate inequality and evident injustice, requiring a swift correction. At the same time, the sense of a shared identity based on similar experiences and emotions connected to these experiences turned out to play an important role in mobilizing women (Hryciuk and Korolczuk 2013; see also Hryciuk in this volume). Importantly, the activists often explicitly discuss the connection between their activism and dominant citizenship ideals, stressing that fighting for one's rights is not only a right but an obligation. One of the AF movement's leaders states: "I teach history at school, so I always believed in the idea of a civil society, and the strength of the citizen's engagement. So (when I heard about the Fund) the first thought was, 'yes, we need to pressure the MPs but we need to do something ourselves, for ourselves; surely there are more people in the same situation, and we need to reach out to them!'" (2012, south of Poland). This quotation shows that the activists consciously position their actions as an expression of engagement in civil society and see the public sphere as a space where issues that in the Polish context are considered private, such as the economic security and financial stability of the family, can and should be addressed.

The cases studied here also highlight the role of ideological factors, related to the specificity of the Polish cultural and social context and characterized by a heightened debate on what constitutes the right, "moral" way of living. By stressing the analogy between being a responsible parent and an active citizen, activists legitimize efforts for social change and present themselves as oriented toward the common good and the best possible future. To some extent, such a frame confirms Cohen and Arato's (1992) vision of the family as the basic unit of civil society. At the same time, in the cases of the Mother and Father Foundation and the Parents' Rights Ombudsperson Foundation it is used to legitimize the promulgation of a neoconservative agenda, including opposition to gender-equality education (aka "homosexual propaganda") in schools or portraying motherhood as necessary for women's fulfillment. Presenting such actions as stemming from civic engagement and reflecting high levels of social responsibility of the activists, rather than as linked to religious beliefs and right-wing political affiliations, can be interpreted as an attempt to gain legitimacy and attract more supporters. Somewhat ironically, conservative views on gender roles and discriminatory views on sexual minorities are promulgated using the discourse of civil society, which is supposedly based on values like gender equality and social equity (e.g., Ginsborg 2013: 31).

The emergence of conservative groups and movements that oppose liberal values by democratic means, claiming to represent the "true civil society," is not specific to Poland (e.g., Graff and Korolczuk 2017; Fábián and Korolczuk 2017; Kováts and Põim 2015). Höjdestrand (2015) shows that the so-called Russian Parents' Movement, which opposes sex education in schools and promotes patriarchal family values, uses the notion of civil society to construct itself as an authentic voice of the people. Similar trends also emerged in other countries, such as France, where in 2013 citizens, many of them parents with young children, went to the streets in protest against the legalization of marriage for homosexual couples, which they interpret as a danger to the "natural family" (Fassin 2014); or in Germany, where in 2014 an alliance called Concerned Parents was formed to oppose the new sex education curriculum (Blum 2015). This trend toward redefining normative foundations of civil society "from below" demonstrates that civil society is a contested ground, which poses a challenge for scholars and practitioners alike. Destabilizing the normative tenets of civic activism broadens the scope of activities that should be studied, but at the same time blurs the definitional clarity as to what norms and values form the basis of civil society, and may pave the way for populist right-wing forces.

"Practical" and "Strategic" Interests in Parental Activism

Parental mobilizations also help us to examine the problematic differentiation between activists' orientation toward their own versus the common good, which is often taken for granted as a defining feature of civil society engagement. As already indicated, most definitions of civil society stress that people's activism should be oriented toward a common good, although what exactly separates the common from the individual good is seldom explicitly stated. Thus, in the present analysis, I propose a more precise conceptualization of what may separate the two, following Maxine Molyneux's (1985) separation between "practical" and "strategic" interests. In her well-known study of the women's movements in Nicaragua, Molyneux defined practical interests as "a response to an immediate perceived need, (which) does not generally entail a strategic goal such as women's emancipation or gender equality," while strategic interests "… are derived in the first instance deductively, that is, from the analysis of women's subordination and from the formulation of an alternative, more satisfactory set of arrangements to those which exist" (1985: 233). Thus, the practical interests are oriented mostly toward achieving immediate, tangible effects that concern the good of one's family and immediate social circle, while strategic interests can be interpreted as related to a more abstract category of social change. In the following section I will discuss the types of interests that parental mobilizations in contemporary Poland coalesce around and show how practical and strategic interests become intertwined.

Both the Parents' Rights Ombudsmen Foundation and the AF movement are examples of mass mobilizations against specific policy changes, which later expanded the claims to include other issues. The AF movement demanding the restitution of the Alimony Fund is probably the most vivid example of a movement that coalesced mostly around "practical" interests (Hryciuk and Korolczuk 2013). From the very beginning the movement activists—almost exclusively women—focused on a single issue, which was the preservation of the Alimony Fund. Its liquidation endangered the economic survival of their families and most efforts focused on this immediate threat. Importantly, the fact that the women made claims on behalf of their families was also one of the reasons why a large part of the general public did not support their fight (Charkiewicz 2009; see also Korolczuk 2014; Hryciuk in this volume). Content analysis of online discussions shows that the majority of commentators considered women's social claims illegitimate and perceived the activists as irresponsible "welfare queens": "The protesters—especially the mothers—were perceived as irresponsible, lazy and immoral, mostly because they decided to have children despite their difficult economic situation. They were referred to as 'pathological mothers,' 'post-communist leftovers,' and some people went as far as expressing the opinion that poor mothers should be sterilized and their children taken away" (Hryciuk and Korolczuk 2013). The activists' gendered identity as mothers in combination with their class status had a detrimental effect on the social resonance of their claims. Social activism of economically underprivileged single mothers was interpreted as an expression of their particularistic interests and egoistic orientation toward the well-being of their families at the expense of other citizens who have to pay taxes to cover social expenditures. Thus, the mobilization was seen by part of the public as an expression of "amoral familism" (Tarkowscy 1995) rather than as a case of civic engagement (cf. Charkiewicz 2009).

Partly due to those negative reactions, and partly due to the fact that they did not manage to put a stop on the liquidation of the Fund, the activists changed their strategy, a shift that can be interpreted in terms of "frame transformation" (Snow 2008: 394–395). Instead of stressing their goals as connected to "private" maternal responsibilities, they started to present themselves as rightful citizens who demand the state fulfill its obligations concerning court orders (see also Hryciuk in this volume). Their goals changed as well, from practical—securing the financial survival of their families, to strategic—changing the relationship between citizens and the state and defending mothers' civil rights. This strategy turned out to be more successful, and finally resulted in the restitution of the Alimony Fund in 2007.[11] The case of the AF movement shows that even if the activists initially focus on particular issues that mostly concern their families and children, the scope of their goals may expand with time to include more general social changes. It also suggests that such a change may be driven by the lack of resonance that issues such as the economic problems of single mothers have in the Polish context.

Often, parent-activists see their engagement as oriented toward broader social change from the very beginning. The representatives of the MaMa Foundation and the Birth in a Dignified Way Foundation stress that their aim was never limited to securing the interests and rights of a particular, narrowly defined social group. In mission statements on their websites, in press releases, and in the conducted interviews, the activists declare that they want to facilitate a widespread social change, or at least significant change pertaining to health care, education, or management of public spaces. Therefore, they include mothers, fathers, and whole families, as well as decision makers, educators, the media, and the general public in their activities, so that the results of their actions affect Polish society at large. Significantly, in their actions they show that parenting, especially mothering, is not limited to the domestic sphere, but that it also takes place in public spaces such as hospitals, schools, public transportation, the streets, and museums. Changing the public spaces and state regulations to meet the needs of parents also affects other social groups, as seen in social campaigns such as "O Mamma Mia! I cannot drive my pram in here!," a campaign that not only concerns architectural barriers that lead to social isolation of young mothers, but opens up more general issues, such as for whom the city is built, who should have access to public spaces, and how city management is intertwined with citizenship. Similarly, the campaigns initiated by the Birth in a Dignified Way Foundation address not only the standards of perinatal care and the conditions of giving birth in Polish hospitals, but also the detrimental effects that privatization and neoliberal management of health care have for the health and well-being of all citizens.

The goals of the Mother and Father Foundation also concern a more general change in discourses, ideologies, and practices of parenting in Poland. The stance of this organization bears a clear resemblance to goals of "the Fathers' Rights Movement" (Flood 2012) in the United States and other countries, as well as various types of conservative groups that mobilize against women's liberation, new forms of family life, and emancipation of sexual minorities. This trend is also present in Poland, where fathers' activism around custody rights often addresses the need for revival of "true masculinity" and "normal family" (Korolczuk and Hryciuk 2017; Wojnicka 2013). Such groups aim not only at facilitating the changes of the juridical system to ensure that men will be able to get custody rights, but also at restoring the social position of the father and patriarchal hierarchy within the family.

For the representatives of the MF Foundation (as for the fathers' rights movement in the United States and to some extent in Poland), the main enemy is "family relativism." The activists strongly oppose the notion that all family structures and arrangements may be equally good for children, asserting instead that children fare best when reared by heterosexual couple: a mother and a father bound in marriage. The MF Foundation interprets new forms of familial arrangements, such as single-parent or same-sex families, as the ultimate source of all social evils. A vivid example of such a stance is the report produced by the foundation entitled "Against Freedom and Democracy—Political Strategy of LGBT Lobby in Poland and in the World: Goals, Tools and Consequences," where tolerance toward non-normative relationships and lifestyles is equated with an attack on "normal" families and the well-being of children.[12] In this case, the activists are not necessarily oriented toward the welfare of specific families but rather toward securing the well-being or the survival of the Family, which in their world view is the most precious common good by definition. Consequently, they present initiatives such as fighting against gender equality education in schools as an expression of "responsibility, solidarity, and commitment to the well-being of the larger community" (Gawin and Gliński 2006: 8).

The Parents' Rights Ombudsperson Foundation, apart from opposing education reform, also promotes "traditional family values," allegedly endangered by equality and sex education in schools. What links the two conservative organizations is not only their ideological orientation and resistance toward "progressive" changes, but also the tendency to reinforce the public/private division understood as the distinction between public and domestic spheres (Hagemann 2008: 29). Although the leaders demand the state to "protect the family" they also promulgate the idea that domestic life and children's upbringing should be free from the interference of the state and parents should retain the right to have a "free choice" or in fact, to control their children. Whereas in other cases of parental mobilizations studied here, the activists tend to oppose what they see as bad laws and ineffective regulations, defending the rights of specific family members (usually mothers), conservative parental groups demand that the state keep away from families, refusing to acknowledge unequal power relations within them and the consequences of this inequality, including domestic violence. "The little ones" need to be saved from the intrusive and oppressive state in the name of parents' rights to have "free choice," which shows how conservative ideological orientation is reinforced by neoliberal validation of individual choice and strict separation of the public and private spheres (cf. Jacobsson in this volume).

In all cases studied here the goals of the activists went beyond the well-being of their immediate social circle and their claims concerned broad social change, although the ways in which these goals and claims were constructed differ. In some instances, e.g., in the case of the AF movement, social mobilization began with the focus on "practical interests" and the activists moved to address more general issues, such as the state's responsibility for enforcing court orders and the social consequences of modernization, in order to gain wider social support. In other cases, specific problems encountered by mothers (and fathers) have been redefined by the activists as public issues, e.g., access to the public space, reform of the education system, or the quality of health care. Alternatively, the focus on family and the children is equated with opposition to social and cultural changes, presented as stemming from familial responsibilities rather than religious or ideological positions (cf. Graff and Korolczuk 2017).

Conclusions

Concentration on the private sphere and on one's immediate social realm is often associated with apathy in the public sphere and a specific type of privatism that is detrimental to the development of the civil society. It is often assumed in literature on Polish civil society that in a "privatized" society minding one's own business becomes a widespread social norm, while the category of a common good—the normative basis of civil society—is lost. Contrary to this view, the analysis of parents' mobilizations in contemporary Poland reminds us that people's "private" experiences, identities, and interests can, and often do, stimulate civic engagement. Moreover, experiences and identities connected to parental roles may lead to civic activism, which is oriented not only toward the practical interests of one's family or a specific group, but social change in general. In practice, focusing on one's role as a parent, and the well-being of one's family, may be conducive to civic engagement and not antithetical to it.

These findings have interesting consequences for the conceptualization of Polish civil society. They show that we should look closer at family–civil society relationships and place these relationships in the wider context of connections between individuals, the state, and civil society. Parental activism demonstrates that although "very rarely do families as a whole move onto the terrain of civil society (and) it is individuals who compose" it (Ginsborg 2013: 24; cf. Kok 2002), people enter the public sphere and engage *as* family members. Thus, instead of studying citizens as individuals—free from specific types of bonds and obligations related to their domestic responsibilities and private lives, entering the sphere of politics, voluntary associationism, and civic participation of their free will, and driven by civic orientation—a more intersectional perspective should be employed. Citizens should be viewed as embodied and embedded in a set of relationships and various types of identification (Fraser 1997; Okin 1998; Kwiatkowska 2010).

Another issue is that civic participation is a gendered process, as is the definition of the political and the shape of the public/private divide. This perspective helps us understand why women often choose to enter the public sphere as mothers, representing the family and children. As in many other countries, e.g., in Latin America, in the Polish context this is simply one of the few legitimate ways women can enter it (Mazurek 2010; see also Michel 2013). This, in turn, has an effect on the type of claims that can be voiced, on the ways that goals can be framed, and on the type of social response they get. In practice, motherist movements as well as parental movements often subscribe to essentialist notions of gender roles and responsibilities for strategic reasons, or because such a stance reflects their ideological affiliations (Jaquette 1994; Werbner 1999). This does not mean that valorizing maternal qualities and building collective identity around a conservative vision of motherhood necessarily helps to legitimize their fight. It may bring ambiguous results, as the social resonance depends not only on the parental status of the claimants, but also on their class, sexuality, and level of ability, as well as dominant discourses on motherhood and citizenship. Previous analyses of mothers' movements in Poland (e.g. Hryciuk and Korolczuk 2013) shows that in the local context the resonance of the claims concerning the social and economic rights of mothers is seriously limited, as they clash with the neoliberal vision of citizens as economically self-sufficient entities. Consequently, conceptualizations of civil society should consider not only gender relationships, but also structural hierarchies, such as class, sexuality, and ethnicity.

Last, but not least, civic activism that originates from, and is related to, familial obligations, identities, and roles exposes the need to pay more attention to the normative basis of the definitions of civil society that we use. We should keep asking what constitutes the common good, what differentiates it from particularistic interests of individuals and/or groups, and how we can operationalize it in the studies of social activism. Hopefully, conceptual differentiation between practical and strategic goals as an analytically distinct but interconnected set of objectives, which are relational and evolve over time, will help us to rethink the category of common good in ways that would make the definition of civil society more practice-oriented and inclusive.

Elżbieta Korolczuk holds a Ph.D. in Sociology and is currently working as a researcher at Södertörn University, Sweden. She also teaches at University of Warsaw and the Institute for Advanced Study, Political Critique in Warsaw, Poland. Her research interests include social movements, civil society, and gender (parenthood, new reproductive technologies and gendered knowledge). Recent publications include the volumes *Dangerous Liaisons: Motherhood, Fatherhood and Politics*, coedited with Renata E. Hryciuk (in Polish, WUW, 2015) and *Rebellious Parents: Parental Movements in Central-Eastern Europe and Russia*, co-edited with Katalin Fábián (Indiana University Press, 2017).

Notes

1. The concept of "amoral familism," proposed by Edward Banfield (1958) to characterize the atomized social structure of the Italian South and adopted by Elżbieta and Jacek Tarkowscy (1994) to describe the Polish context, is based on the assumption that focusing on the interests of one's immediate social realm is detrimental to civic activism. Within this framework the existence of close relationships and trust among neighbors or within the family does not necessarily translate into strengthening of social ties in the society in general. To the contrary, it hinders cooperation, not only with the state but with other social groups. As a result, only small "islands of integration," such as associations and self-help groups, based on existing close social ties, emerge from the sea of apathy and distrust (Tarkowscy 1994; see also Gliński 2004; Czapiński and Panek 2013). For contemporary debates on amoral familism in Poland, see, e.g., http://www.polityka.pl/rynek/ekonomia/220401,1,polska-wciaz-tkwi-w-glebokim-sredniowieczu.read; http://www.batory.org.pl/programy_operacyjne/debaty/2012/zawlaszczanie_panstwa_klientyzm_korupcja_nepotyzm. Retrieved 2 October 2015.

2. This research has been enabled by a research grant from the Swedish Research Council (Grant 421/2010/1706). I wish to thank Kerstin Jacobsson, participants of the conference "The Challenge of Collective Action: New Perspectives on Civil Society and Social Activism in Contemporary Poland," organized at University of Warsaw, and participants of the project workshop in Gdynia for comments and suggestions regarding earlier versions of this analysis. Any mistakes are of course mine.

3. More information on the new standards of perinatal care is available at http://www.rodzicpoludzku.pl/Standard-opieki-okoloporodowej/Do-czego-mam-prawo-nowy-standard-opieki-okoloporodowej.html. Retrieved 2 October 2015.

4. More information on the campaign is available at http://www.mamaitata.org.pl/wiadomosci/ruszamy-z-nowa-kampania-spoleczna-nie-odkladaj-macierzynstwa-na-potem. Retrieved 2 October 2015.

5. I use the term "parental activism" rather than "parents' rights activism" because the activists studied here address not only legal changes concerning custody or welfare, but have a broader agenda, including social and political issues, such as gender order or citizens' relationships to the state (cf. Fábián and Korolczuk 2017).

6. As to the relationship between civil society and social movements, I am inspired by Paul Ginsborg, who sees civil society as "characterized by a myriad of self-forming and self-dissolving voluntary organizations, circles, clubs, rank-and-file networks, social movements, and so on" (2013: 31). In other words, I conceive of social movements as a type of social activism that active citizens may engage in, along with participation in NGOs, taking part in elections or petitioning the authorities. That being said, I acknowledge that social actors may identify with one type of activity

and not the other, and that they may see engagement in civil society as contradictory to social movement participation.

7. Acting on behalf of one's children was often used as the rationale for women's social activism, the well-known examples including Mothers Against Drunk Driving in the United States and Mothers De Plaza de Mayo in Argentina, but in the case of the parental movements studied here, the maternalist argument that women, due to their social role as caregivers (or in an essentialist version, due to their natural altruism and kindness), are predisposed to care for the world at large (Michel 2013), is also extended to men.

8. Video available at https://www.youtube.com/watch?v=UioB8laAyoE. Retrieved 7 October 2013.

9. Recording of Elbanowska's speech is available at https://www.youtube.com/watch?v=UioB8laAyoE. Retrieved 7 October 2013. Author's translation.

10. Mother and Father Foundation mission statement, available at http://www.mamai-tata.org.pl/o-mamie-i-tacie/o-mamie-i-tacie.html. Retrieved 23 October 2015.

11. For a more detailed discussion on the strategies employed by the AF movement, the framing employed, and the ultimate outcomes of the mobilization, see Hryciuk 2008; Hryciuk and Korolczuk 2013.

12. Report "Przeciw wolności i demokracji—Strategia polityczna lobby LGTB w Polsce i na świecie: cele, narzędzia, konsekwencje." Retrieved 2 October 2015. http://www.mamaitata.org.pl/raporty/przeciw-wolnosci-i-demokracji.html.

References

Alexander, J. 2006. *The Civil Sphere.* Oxford: Oxford University Press.

Banfield, E. 1958. *The Moral Basis of a Backward Society.* Glencoe, IL: Free Press.

Blum, A. 2015. "Germany," in *Gender as Symbolic Glue: The Position and Role of Conservative and Far Right Parties in The Anti-Gender Mobilizations in Europe,* ed. E. Kováts and M. Põim. Retrieved 20 October 2015 from http://www.feps-europe.eu/assets/cae464d2-f4ca-468c-a93e-5d0dad365a83/feps-gender-as-symbolic-glue-wwwpdf.pdf.

Charkiewicz, E. 2009. "Matki do sterylizacji. Neoliberalny rasizm w Polsce" [Mothers Should Be Sterilized: Neoliberal Racism in Poland]. *Biblioteka On-line Think Tanku Feministycznego.* Retrieved 12 November 2014 from http://www.ekologiasztuka.pl/pdf/f0053charkiewicz_szkic2.pdf.

Chimiak, G. 2006. *How Individualists Make Solidarity Work.* Warsaw: Ministerstwo Pracy i Polityki Społecznej.

Cohen, J., and A. Arato. 1992. *Civil Society and Political Theory.* Cambridge and London: MIT Press.

Czapiński, J. 2008. "Molekularny rozwój Polski" [The Molecular Development of Poland], in *Modernizacja Polski. Kody kulturowe i mity* [Poland's Modernization. Cultural Codes and Myths], ed. J. Szomburg. Gdańsk: IBnGR, 95–102.

Czapiński J., and T. Panek, eds. 2013. *Diagnoza Społeczna.* Retrieved 12 June 2015. http://ce.vizja.pl/en/issues/volume/7/issue/4.

Dimitrova, I. 2017. "(Un)deserving Parents: Constructing Parenthood and Nation in Bulgaria through New Reproductive Technologies," in *Rebellious Parents: Parental*

Movements in Central-Eastern Europe and Russia, ed. K. Fábián and E. Korolczuk. Indiana University Press. Forthcoming.

Elbanowska, K., and T. Elbanowski. 2015. *Ratuj maluchy! Rodzielska rewolucja* [Save the Little Ones! Parental Revolution]. Warszawa: Znak.

Fábián, K., and E. Korolczuk, eds. 2017. *Rebellious Parents: Parental Movements in Central-Eastern Europe and Russia.* Indiana University Press.

Fassin, É. 2014. "Same-Sex Marriage, Nation, and Race: French Political Logics and Rhetorics." *Contemporary French Civilization* 39, no. 3: 281–301.

Fidelis, M. 2010. *Women, Communism and Industrialization in Postwar Poland.* New York: Cambridge University Press.

Flood, M. 2012. "Separated Fathers and the Fathers' Rights Movement." *Journal of Family Studies* 18, no. 2–3: 235–245.

Fraser, N. 1997. *Justice Interruptus: Critical Reflections on the "Postsocialist" Condition.* New York and London: Routledge.

Funk, N. 2004. "Feminist Critiques of Liberalism: Can They Travel East? Their Relevance in Eastern and Central Europe and the Former Soviet Union." *Signs: Journal of Women in Culture and Society* 29, no. 3: 695–726.

Gawin, D., and P. Gliński. 2006. "Introduction," in *Civil Society in the Making,* ed. D. Gawin and P. Glinski. Warsaw: IfiS Publishers, 7–15.

Ginsborg, P. 2013. "Uncharted Territories: Individuals, Families, Civil Society and the Democratic State," in *The Golden Chain: Family, Civil Society and the State,* ed. J. Nautz, P. Ginsborg, and T. Nijhuis, New York: Berghahn, 17–42.

Gliński, P. 2004. "How Active Are the Social Actors? Deficient Citizenship Versus Day-to-Day resourcefulness in Poland." *Polish Sociological Review* 4, no. 148: 429–450.

Graff, A., and E. Korolczuk. 2017. "'Worse than Communism and Nazism Put Together': War on Gender in Poland,'" in *Anti-gender Campaigns in Europe: Religious and Political Mobilizations against Equality,* ed. R. Kuhar and D. Paternotte. Lanham: Rowman and Littlefield (forthcoming).

Gumkowska, M., J. Herbst, J. Szołajska, and J. Wygnański. 2006. *The Challenge of Solidarity: CIVICUS Civil Society Index Report for Poland.* Warsaw: Klon/Jawor Association/CIVICUS.

Gunnarsson Payne, J., and Korolczuk, E. 2016. "Reproducing Politics: The Politicization of Patient Identities and Assisted Reproduction in Poland and Sweden." *Sociology of Health and Illness* 38(7): 1–18.

Hagemann, K. 2008. "Civil Society Gendered: Rethinking Theories and Practices," in *Civil Society and Gender Justice: Historical and Comparative Perspectives,* ed. K. Hagemann, S. Michel, and G. Budde. New York, Oxford: Berghahn Books, 17–42.

Hagemann, K., S. Michel, and G. Budde, eds. 2008. *Civil Society and Gender Justice: Historical and Comparative Perspectives.* New York, Oxford: Berghahn Books.

Höjdestrand, T. 2015. "Moralne odrodzenie i obywatelski aktywizm: ruch społeczny rodziców we współczesnej Rosji" [Moral Resurgence and Civic Action: The Russian Parents' Movement], in *Niebezpieczne związki. Macierzyństwo, ojcostwo i polityka* [Dangerous Liaisons: Motherhood, Fatherhood and Politics], ed. R.E. Hryciuk and E. Korolczuk. Warsaw: Warsaw University Press, 299–326.

Hryciuk, R.E. 2008. *Kulturowy kontekst macierzyństwa. Na przykładzie Meksyku* [Motherhood and Culture: Continuity and Change: The Case of Mexico]. Unpublished Ph.D. thesis, Graduate School for Social Research, Polish Academy of Sciences, Warsaw.

Hryciuk, R.E., and E. Korolczuk. 2013. "At the Intersection of Gender and Class: Social Mobilization around Mothers' Rights in Poland," in *Beyond NGO-ization: The Development of Social Movements in Central and Eastern Europe,* ed. K. Jacobsson and S. Saxonberg. Farnham: Ashgate Press, 11–44.

Hryciuk, R.E., and E. Korolczuk, eds. 2015. *Niebezpieczne związki. Macierzyństwo, ojcostwo i polityka* [Dangerous Liasons: Motherhood, Fatherhood, and Politics]. Warsaw: Warsaw University Press.

Jacobsson, K., and S. Saxonberg, eds. 2013. *Beyond NGO-ization: The Development of Social Movements in Central and Eastern Europe.* Farnham: Ashgate.

Jagudina, Zaira. 2009. *Social Movements and Gender in Post-Soviet Russia: The Case of the Soldiers' Mothers NGOs.* Göteborg Studies in Sociology, Department of Sociology: University of Gothenburg.

Jaquette, J.S. 1994. "Conclusion: Women's Political Participation and the Prospects for Democracy," in *The Women's Movements in Latin America: Participation and Democracy,* ed. J.S. Jaquette. Boulder: Westview Press, 109–130.

Kerbner, L.K. 1997. *Women of the Republic: Intellect and Ideology in Revolutionary America.* Williamsburg: University of North Carolina Press.

Klandermans, B. 2008. "The Demand and Supply of Participation: Social-Psychological Correlates of Participation in Social Movements" in *The Blackwell Companion to Social Movements,* ed D.A. Snow et al. Malder, MA and Oxford, UK: Blackwell Publishing, 360–379.

Kok, Jan, ed. 2002. *Rebellious Families: Household Strategies and Collective Action in the Nineteenth and Twentieth Centuries.* New York and Oxford: Berghahn Books.

Korolczuk, E. 2013. "Gendered Boundaries Between the State, Family and Civil Society—The Case of Poland after 1989," in *The Golden Chain: Family, Civil Society and the State,* ed. J. Nautz, P. Ginsborg and T. Nijhuis. New York: Berghahn, 240–259.

———. 2014. "Ruchy społeczne a płeć—perspektywa intersekcjonalna. Kongres Kobiet i ruch na rzecz przywrócenia Funduszu Alimentacyjnego" [Social Movements and Gender–Intersectional Analysis: The Congress of Women and the Alimony Fund Movement]. *Kultura i społeczeństwo* 1: 97–120.

Korolczuk, E., and R.E. Hryciuk. 2017. "In the Name of the Family and Nation: Framing Fathers' Activism in Poland," in *Rebellious Parents: Parental Movements in Central-Eastern Europe and Russia,* ed. K. Fábián and E. Korolczuk. Indiana University Press (forthcoming).

Kościański, A., and W. Misztal. 2008. *Społeczeństwo obywatelskie. Między ideą a praktyką* [Civil Society: Between Idea and Practice]. Warsaw: IFiS PAN Publishers.

Kováts, E., and M. Põim, eds. 2015. *Gender as Symbolic Glue: The Position and Role of Conservative and Far Right Parties in the Anti-Gender Mobilizations in Europe.* http://www.feps-europe.eu/assets/cae464d2-f4ca-468c-a93e-5d0dad365a83/feps-gender-as-symbolic-glue-wwwpdf.pdf.

Kubik, J. 2000. "Between the State and Networks of 'Cousins': The Role of Civil Society and Noncivil Associations in the democratization of Poland," in *Civil Society Before Democracy,* ed. N. Bermeo and P. Nord. Lanham: Rowan and Littlefield Publishers, 181–207.

Kwiatkowska, A. 2010. "Koncepcja obywatelstwa w teorii feministycznej" [The Concept of Citizenship in Feminist Theory], in *Praktyki obywatelskie Polaków* [Civic Practices of the Poles], ed. J. Raciborski. Warsaw: IFiS Publishers, 185–220.

Lane, D. 2010. "Civil Society in the Old and New Member States." *European Societies* 12, no. 3: 293–315.

Maciejewska, M. 2010. *Odzyskać obywatelstwo.* "*Kobiety i warunki życia w Wałbrzychu*" [Re-claiming Citizenship: Women and Living Conditions in Wałbrzych]. *Biblioteka Online ThinkTanku Feministycznego.* Retrieved 12 November 2015 from http://www .ekologiasztuka.pl/think.tank.feministyczny/readarticle.php?article_id=369.

Matynia, E. 2003. "Provincializing Global Feminism: The Polish Case." *Social Research* 70, no. 2: 499–530.

Mazurek, M. 2010. *Społeczeństwo kolejki. O doświadczeniach niedoboru 1945-1989* [Queuing Society: On the Experience of Shortages 1945–1989]. Warsaw: TRIO Publishers.

Michel, S. 2013. "The Family, Civil Society and Social Policy: A US Perspective," in *The Golden Chain: Family, Civil Society and the State,* ed. J. Nautz, P. Ginsborg, and T. Nijhuis. New York: Berghahn, 66–85.

Molyneux, M. 1985. "Mobilization without Emancipation? Women's Interests, the State and Revolution in Nicaragua." *Feminist Studies* 11, no. 2: 227–254.

Naples, N.A. 1998. *Grassroots Warriors: Activist Mothering, Community Work, and the War on Poverty.* New York and London: Routledge.

Nautz, J., P. Ginsborg, and T. Nijhuis, eds. 2013. *The Golden Chain: Family, Civil Society and the State.* New York and Oxford: Berghahn Books.

Okin, S. 1998. "Gender, the Public and the Private," in *Feminism and Politics,* ed. A. Phillips. Oxford and New York, 116–141.

Penn, S. 2003. *Podziemie Kobiet* [National Secret: The Women Who Brought Democracy to Poland]. Warszawa: Rosner & Wspólnicy.

Polkowska, D. 2014. "Parental Movements in Poland as the Bottom-up Forms of Action: Success or Failure? The Cases of First Quarter Mothers and Save the Little Ones." *Warsaw Forum of Economic Sociology* 1, no. 9: 55–68.

Raciborski, J., ed. 2010. *Praktyki obywatelskie Polaków* [Civic Practices of the Poles]. Warsaw: IFiS Publishers.

Saxonberg, S. 2017. "Down and Out in a 'Femo-Fascist' State: The Czech Fathers' Discussion Forum," in *Rebellious Parents: Parental Movements in Central-Eastern Europe and Russia,* K. Fábián and E. Korolczuk. Indiana University Press (forthcoming).

Snow, D.A. 2008. "Framing Processes, Ideology, and Discursive Fields", in *The Blackwell Companion to Social Movements,* ed D.A. Snow et al. Malder, MA and Oxford, UK: Blackwell Publishing, 380–412.

Tarkowscy, E., and J. 1994. "Amoralny familizm, czyli o dezintegracji społecznej w Polsce lat osiemdziesiątych" [Amoral Familism: On the Social Disintegration of Poland in the Eighties], in *Socjologia Świata Polityki Tom 1. Władza i społeczeństwo w systemie autorytarnym* [Sociology of the World of Politics: Part I: Power and Society in the Authoritarian Regime], J. Tarkowski. Warszawa: Instytut Studiów Politycznych PAN, 263–282.

Werbner, P. 1999. "Political Motherhood and the Feminization of Citizenship: Women's Activism and the Transformation of Public Sphere," in *Women, Citizenship and Difference,* ed. N. Yuval-Davis and P. Werbner. London and New York: Zed Books, 221–245.

Wojnicka, K. 2013. "Męskie ruchy społeczne we współczesnej Polsce: Wybrane ustalenia i wnioski" [Men's Social Movements in Contemporary Poland: Conclusions]. *Acta Universitatis Lodziensis Folia Sociologica* 47: 87–103.

Yuval-Davis, N. 1997. *Gender and Nation,* London: Sage.

Chapter 6

ON THE DISAPPEARING MOTHER
POLITICAL MOTHERHOOD, CITIZENSHIP, AND NEOLIBERALISM IN POLAND

Renata Ewa Hryciuk

Introduction

The first social movement of mothers in Poland emerged in 2002. It was a grassroots mobilization rallying single mothers, most of them poor, to protest against the shutdown of the Alimony Fund (AF). Despite the movement's overwhelming popularity and widespread support, the women, who were given the moniker of *Alimonaries* by the media, were only partially successful. The height of the movement was between 2002 and 2007. At that time I was carrying out research on the transformation of the cultural representations of motherhood and the social practice of mothering in the urban culture of Mexico. Immersed in the Latin American literature on women's movements, and strongly influenced by the general belief in the powerful hold of the archetypal Polish Mother myth, as well as the first gender and feminist analyses of the gender contract in Poland, I fully expected the Polish single mothers to take as their point of reference the figure of the Polish Mother and motherhood as a unique cultural value, using strategies similar to those employed so effectively by women in Argentina or Mexico. I carefully followed every development, awaiting the spectacular success of the mothers' movement in the country of the Polish Mother. However, the protesters taking a stand from their marginalized position as "bad neighborhood" dwellers, representatives of so-called "Poland B," and single mothers, proved more effective than a middle-class researcher from the capital city at recognizing the hegemonic model of motherhood and the resulting—limited—potential for a grassroots movement created by women perceived as "secondhand" mothers.

Recent sociological studies proved that motherhood remains at the core of the identity of Polish women (Budrowska 2000; Titkow 2007). The central figure in the hegemonic discourse of womanhood still appears to be the archetypal Polish Mother, reproduced and reinforced by a set of mutually reinforcing elements: the Catholic doctrine, nationalism, and neoliberal ideology. The myth of the Polish Mother is not only the principal point of reference for social actors, and thus a common stereotype, but also a model employed by male and female researchers analyzing the gender contract in Poland (Hryciuk and Korolczuk 2010, 2012). However, the actual political power and cultural capital associated with this model were put into question by the first spontaneous and independent mothers' mobilization after the political transformation of 1989.

In this chapter I examine the Single Mothers for the Alimony Fund Movement and, in particular, their strategies and positions with respect to motherhood.[1] I analyze the nature of changes that occurred in the cultural construct of motherhood during the socioeconomic transformation, the power of maternal capital, and its potential as the basis for political action and legitimization of demands raised by women in Poland's public sphere.

Polish and Latin American cultural contexts share a common patriarchal-Catholic component that glorifies motherhood, as well as a political culture based on collective values (Funk 2004). For that reason, in my analysis of the strategies employed by mothers defending their social rights in the past decades in Poland, I invoke the models of women's mobilization, mechanisms of politicizing motherhood, and mothers' activities in the public domain in Latin America.[2] By juxtaposing the uses of symbols and discourses of motherhood by women's movements in both contexts I aim to capture and interpret the nature of mothers' mobilization in post-transformation Poland.[3] Finally, the case of the single mothers' mobilization is telling of the conditions under which women can legitimately raise claims in the public sphere in Poland and, conversely, what types of claims are likely to be delegitimized in the process of claim making.

The Pioneers: Mothers' Movements in Latin America

From the 1970s, Latin America has been the seedbed for local and transnational social movements, emerging as a response to the universal "crisis of modernity" and global shift toward postmodernity (Escobar 1992). One of the characteristic features in the process of democratization and formation of civil societies in the region has been mass participation of women in multiple social mobilizations (including women's movements), which resulted in their inclusion into active citizenship (Jaquette 1994). Latin American women are active in human rights movements, mobilizations aiming to improve living conditions in rural and urban areas (including environmental movements in recent decades), campaigns for the autonomy and rights of indigenous communities, students' movements, reclamation of land rights, trade unions, missing persons' organizations, and feminist movements (including those fighting for reproductive and abortion rights) (Luna 2006).

It should be noted that women in postcolonial states often possess a sizeable and typically female cultural capital, one that is not available to the women of Europe or the United States (Werbner and Yuval-Davis 2005). Its key aspect across multiple cultural contexts, including Latin America, is the unique maternal capital generated from the available cultural material in the course of nation-state formation. This resource is deeply ingrained in national ideologies, and further upheld and transformed by modernizing government policies. It is the source of strength and power used to legitimize women's demands in the public domain and it may serve as a strong foundation for their political identity (Craske 2003; Hryciuk 2008). As Jane Jaquette notes:

> It makes sense for women to organize as mothers and to emphasize collective values within political cultures where motherhood is sacred, where men's and women's roles are sharply distinguished and considered both natural and normatively appropriate, and where the political cultures rest on a Catholic concept of community rather than on an individualistic social contract. The rhetoric of political motherhood is thus a rational and powerful collective action frame that avoids the costs of a frontal attack on traditional values while leaving considerable room to maneuver in the public sphere (1994: 227–228).

Analyses of the Latin American women's movements confirmed that motherhood identity constitutes a strategic and useful factor in the mobilization of the region's female inhabitants: a starting point toward a broader political participation, and frequently for taking subversive action against the state. In light of research, motherhood proves a rather flexible political strategy at times of "disrupted" relations between the public and the private spheres, when gendering of the public discourse or politicizing of the domestic sphere comes into play. On such occasions, women resort to available means to attain their goals either by adapting to social norms or by questioning and undermining them (Craske 1999, 2003; Jaquette 1994; Hryciuk 2008).

It is commonly accepted that making political use of women's maternal roles in Latin America is a universal rule. Local constructs of motherhood, which provide a symbolic basis of both revolutionary and reactionary social movements, are utilized by all political discourses, parties, and regimes.[4] This was emphasized by Nikki Craske in the introduction to *Women and Politics in Latin America*: "Although motherhood may underpin certain forms of women's political action, there is no direct relationship between motherhood and particular political agendas, actions and ideologies: motherhood does not determine women's interests within traditional political discourses such as left-right or progressive-reactionary. Furthermore, parties and regimes of all political hues have embraced the idealization of motherhood. This idealization tends to essentialize the mothering experience, seeing it as "destiny" for women, and reinforces the links between womanhood and social reproduction" (1999: 5–6).

Motherhood movements have played a decisive part in the democratization of political processes in Latin America, leading to the emergence of a new type of citizenship "inclusive" of the previously shunned group, namely, women originating from a range of social and ethnic groups (Álvarez 1990; Craske 1999, 2003; Goddard 2000; Jaquette 1994; Logan 1990; Schirmer 1993; Stephen 1997; Werbner 2005).

The new forms of mothers' involvement in the political domain have come to be known as "political motherhood."[5] Pnina Werbner (2005) defines it as a form of active citizenship of women founded on the culturally defined areas of women's authority—the right to property and responsibility for the fate of a community. She stresses that such movements are usually characterized by a certain degree of opportunism: they valorize maternal qualities—caring, compassion, and responsibility for the vulnerable—as encompassing and well anchored in democratic values. This new discourse of motherhood questions established notions of citizenship, leading to its feminization and reconstruction in terms of values associated with women's roles as mothers, carers, and defenders of the family and community. Additionally, it brought about a more "inclusive" definition of citizenship. In the opinion of the British scholar, the strength of political motherhood is in the introduction of new values into the public domain, those recognized as rightful foundations of a political community.

The mobilizing and self-organizing of women has had an undeniable impact on the transformation of gender roles, the image of a mother, and the performance of motherhood, as well as on women's participation in the public sphere. For instance, the statements recorded during ethnographic studies in the *colonias populares*[6] of Mexican cities made by mothers-activists who had been taking part in diverse mobilizing actions since the 1970s, as well as statements made by their children, indicate that women's involvement in political or social activities became an integral part of the social practice of motherhood in those local contexts. These processes changed the perception and enriched the model of the Mexican mother with new elements: mother-activist, mother involved in the public realm, and actively participating in local politics. It has also boosted the sense of empowerment and self-esteem, modified gender consciousness (both on the individual and collective levels) of women taking part in social movements and mobilizations, and, in effect, led to a broader participation of women in the public sphere in Mexico (Gutmann 1996; Hryciuk 2008; Logan 1990; Massolo 1992).[7]

Thus, Latin American women have deliberately employed techniques that put emphasis on the cultural role of mothers, thereby making use of "strategic essentialism" (Spivak 1989), which proved an effective strategy of women's mobilization during the times of political and economic crises. Given these experiences of mothers' mobilizations in Latin America, we now turn our attention to the Polish case: to what extent could the single mothers in Poland draw on motherhood as a cultural resource in their struggles?

Mobilizations of Polish Mothers

First, it should be emphasized that the mobilization of women in defense of the AF has not been the only popular mass mobilization of the Polish mothers. The hunger marches organized in the city of Łódź in the summer of 1981 could be considered one of the first attempts at making use of maternal capital in the Polish context. Manifestations held by the male leaders of the "Solidarity" movement gathered tens of thousands of people in the city center. Female textile workers, accompanied by their children, chanted slogans and brandished banners saying: "We want bread," "We won't eat ration coupons," "More bread, more milk, less queuing" (Mazurek 2010: 143). Their attitude expressed fatigue and anger exacerbated by an increasing scarcity of food supplies, in particular further reductions of meat rations. The women's manifestation was meant to bolster the protests organized by the "Solidarity" and, at the same time, serve as a buffer against violent actions on the part of the police force. As Małgorzata Mazurek reported: "Regional 'Solidarity' boards expected that the participation of women in the protests of the "starved" would relieve the tense atmosphere among the female blue collars whose frustration related to the 'queuing nightmare' made itself distinctly felt. Trade unionists also hoped that the Polish Mother figure would act as a radical and meaningful weapon of the society aimed at the indolence of authorities and, simultaneously, prevent the women on strike against the state system of violence" (2010: 143).

The next grassroots, spontaneous, and mass mobilization of mothers did not surface until twenty years later, in the autumn of 2002, when the media announced the plan to abolish the Alimony Fund (Hryciuk and Korolczuk

2013a). It was intended as part of the so-called "Hausner's Austerity Plan", providing for cuts in public expenditure including social welfare spending in order to meet the requirements of joining the European Union. The purpose of the Fund, established in 1974, was to pay child support to single parents in cases where the other parent defaulted on the required payments. The effectiveness of alimony collection, which in the 1980s reached 90 percent of amounts due, fell dramatically in the 1990s as an effect of growing unemployment, the pursuit of jobs in the grey economy, neglect on the part of bailiffs who perceived the recovering of alimonies as insufficiently profitable,[8] and also—or probably first and foremost—because of the social consent to the fathers' avoidance of financial responsibility for the upbringing of children (Alimentare 2008).

The shutdown of the Fund marked the climax in the process of deterioration of living standards for many families, and the general plight of women in the period of the so-called transformation of the political system. By the early 1990s, a kind of backlash occurred in the form of attacks launched by consecutive governments against the position of women in society. Its primary manifestations included the limitation of women's reproductive rights and their participation in the labor market (Titkow 2001). These developments were accompanied by the state's withdrawal from a range of social benefits, diminishing expenditures in the field of education, health care, and child care, resulting from the shift toward a market economy.

With media support, the mobilization in defense of the Fund quickly reached countrywide popularity, and some sixty associations uniting three hundred thousand single parents (90 percent of whom were mothers) came into being. The self-organizing of women was supported by feminist organizations (e.g., in Kraków and Łódź), journalists, some of the Catholic Church clergy, trade unions (NSZZ "Solidarity"), as well as female and male politicians, primarily of right-wing affiliation. The Single Mothers for the Alimony Fund Movement, shortened by the media to *Alimonaries*, which was established at the time, was considered the first mass social movement to emerge after Solidarity (Ostałowska 2004). Its membership included women of diverse backgrounds: educated teachers, office workers, and accountants, as well as women with little education, working poor women, and inhabitants of small towns and larger cities across Poland. The mobilizing factor was shared dependence on the benefits paid out from the Fund, while the proposed changes in the law entailed, for the majority of women, sudden impoverishment or even a direct threat to the physical survival of their families.

All around Poland, single mothers initiated actions to prevent the shutdown of the Fund. They organized protests, picket rallies, and demonstrations intended to attract attention to the situation of single-mother families;

they sent letters to the members of Parliament, the Polish Ombudsman, the Children's Rights' Ombudsman, the Polish Plenipotentiary for the Equal Status of Men and Women (at that time it was Magdalena Środa, a renowned scholar and feminist), and President Aleksander Kwaśniewski. They cooperated with local and national media and organized information campaigns in their neighborhoods. In addition, they collected signatures on the petition for a presidential veto against the act on the abolition of the Fund and, in December 2003, representatives of the movement delivered a petition signed by three hundred thousand people to the Chancellery of the President. Nevertheless, their efforts failed to produce the expected result, and ironically the act on the abolition of the Alimony Fund came into force on the 1 May 2004, the day of Poland's accession to the European Union.

The mass, nationwide mobilization of women criticizing the effects of the government's neoliberal policy, demanding that fundamental social rights be respected and guaranteed, and opposing the gradual shifting of financial responsibility for social reproduction onto their shoulders, failed to attract the attention of most politicians. Mothers initiated their protests at the least opportune moment, one and a half years before Poland's admittance to the European Union, an event that was perceived as a kind of "reward" for successful socioeconomic transformation. In 2003, 63 percent of the Polish population favored the accession and, in contrast to the women taking part in the mobilization, expected their standard of living to improve.[9] For the Single Mothers, 1 May 2004 had a completely different significance and indicated the beginning of the struggle, often in the literal sense of the word, for the survival of their families.

After the shutdown of the Fund, a dozen picketing actions and demonstrations were organized across the country, including two of the largest events in Warsaw on Mother's Day, which was 26 May 2004, and in March 2005. They became, as I will demonstrate, a space for expressing feelings and emotions, condemning the decisions made by politicians, and for subversive acts in the public sphere. At the same time, on the initiative of a group of leading activists headed by Renata Iwaniec, a history teacher from Tarnów (a city in southern Poland), a change in the strategy was in progress. The Single Mothers started to invoke the civil rights they were entitled to as well as the constitutional provisions regarding the protection of families. With the assistance of female and male politicians of the rightist Law and Justice (PiS) party that, as on many other occasions, seized the opportunity to take advantage of social unrest and distress of marginalized groups ignored by the elites (see Ost 2005), the Legislative Initiative Committee was established. A group of experts immediately got down to writing the citizens' draft act to reinstate the Fund; some three hundred thousand signatures were collected and the draft was presented to Parliament in autumn.

When the PiS Party—favorably disposed toward the movement—eventually won the election, the Fund was reinstated. It happened in 2007 on the very last day of the right-wing coalition of Law and Justice, Self-Defense, and the League of Polish Families. The proposed solutions and subsequent changes in the calculation and distribution of benefits fell short of the expectations of some Single Mothers, who decided to continue their actions. The leaders of the movement vested with the largest social capital became involved in political lobbying, and in 2008 and 2009, in Toruń, two rallies were held in the course of which the leaders of eight of the most active associations established an umbrella organization Godność i Rodzina (Dignity and Family).[10] With time, however, most women discontinued their activities in the public sphere, and certain mothers' associations, for instance "Damy Radę" (We'll Make It), based in Warsaw, took up self-help activities (Elas 2008). The new regulations resulted in restricting access to the Fund for mothers who had some income, so a number of the mothers struggling for restoration of the AF decided to emigrate in a quest to provide for their families, joining the group of mobile "long-distance" mothers (Urbańska 2010; see also Keough 2006; Hryciuk and Korolczuk 2013b).

Political Motherhood the Polish Way

The case of the single mothers' mobilization is interesting from the perspective of processes of legitimization and delegitimization of claims and claim making in Polish civil society. An analysis of the discourse employed by the protesting single mothers, names of associations, and changes in the strategy and self-presentation of the movement demonstrates that women politicized motherhood in a particular manner that stemmed directly from the contemporary, hegemonic construct of motherhood in Poland. Women from lower social strata, from the circles characterized by the feminization of poverty, and from regions with high unemployment rates performed their maternal roles by protesting against the policies of the state that entailed deterioration of the living standards of their families. They did not do it in a straightforward way, though. Unlike Latin American women, they did not invoke the central element of national gender imagery, the Polish Mother figure, nor did they make reference to any other popular images of motherhood or representations of Saint Mary.

Contrary to the motherhood movements in Latin America, explicitly referred to in this way by their female members, in Poland the name Single Mothers for the Alimony Fund Movement was devised to refer to that phenomenon by the media and a handful of researchers who wrote about the protesting mothers (see Desperak 2008; Hryciuk and Korolczuk 2013a; Korolczuk 2014). The colloquial moniker *Alimonaries* was popularized by the media reports (see Ostałowska 2004, 2005, 2007a, 2007b, 2007c) and also adopted by some researchers/activists, e.g., Iza Desperak, a sociologist from Łódź (Desperak 2008). From the very start, the word "mother" only rarely appeared in the names of organizations or on the banners of manifesting women and the term, seemingly catchy and infused with clear meaning, "the Polish Mother" was even less frequently seen during protests. Mothers protested in defense of their children and families, organized themselves, and established associations, but all the time kept placing themselves symbolically in the background.

Words like "children," "parents," and "persons" prevail in the names of associations included in the Single Mothers' movement, such as: "Aid to the Alimony Fund Children" (Brodnica, Toruń), "Parents to Children" (Kalisz), "Children of the Fund" (Lubań, Milejów, Świdnik), "Children of the Fund Association" (Lublin, Siedlce), "Children's Rights" (Łódź), "Decent Life for Children" (Mielec), "For Our Children Association" (Ostrowiec Świętokrzyski, Poznań), "Threatened by the Shutdown of the Alimony Fund" (Tarnów), "Association of Persons Aggrieved by the Abolition of the Alimony Fund" (Bytom), "Single Mothers Community Association" (Cracow), and "Committee of Single Parents in the Podkarpackie Region" (Rzeszów). Some of the names made reference to the situation of mothers: "Threatened" (Bydgoszcz, Opole), "Distress Association" (Wrocław), or "We'll Make It" (Warsaw) (Elas 2008). Other names included: "For a Decent Life of Children," "Single Mothers Community," "Caring for Our Kids," and "Association for the Rights of Responsible Parents" (Ostałowska 2004).

Even if the word "mother" appeared in the name of an organization at the start of the protest, it was subsequently changed, as was the case with the Toruń-based "Single Mothers' Association," established by Daria Cieplik, one of the movement's leaders, in 2003. After the Fund's closure, she merged her organization with another local association, namely, "Threatened," created by Irena Dąbrowska, to form an association named "Helping Women" that is still in operation, but that joined an umbrella organization "Dignity and Family" in 2008.

The tendency to not expose single mothers or those with "incomplete" families, but rather to conceal or obscure the predicament in broader categories such as "woman," "parent," or "family" finds its confirmation in the following example. The mobilization of Single Mothers in Cracow was initiated by the local Women's Rights Center, and a local activist, Beata Zadumińska, coined the term "independent mothers," which was later picked up by part of the movement (e.g., the feminists from Łódź struggling for the reinstatement of the Fund). In effect, a website was launched under the name of "Independent Mothers," but an association was registered under a modified name, the Association for Independent Parents.[11]

The female mobilization participants I interviewed admitted they had not been previously interested in politics, had not followed changes in legislation, and could not tell the party affiliation of individual politicians. They started to act because as the ones responsible for the well-being of their families, they were "forced to the wall." What is more, they wanted to express their anger, frustration, despair, and fear about their children's future. Also, the language of the demonstrations was highly emotional. It expressed their disapproval of the deteriorating living conditions of families and child care. And again, while women assumed their maternal role during manifestations, they hardly ever referred to it explicitly. The slogans and images that the protesters used during demonstrations and demonstrations are very telling: "Single mothers are patching up the budget gap," "Poland goes to Europe, children go to Africa," "For a governmental limousine many families could have a decent cuisine," "Poland is a mother, not a father," "Hitler was held to account and so will be Hausner," and "Militant Warsaw." Hunger, impoverishment, and the resulting extreme despair run through the demonstrators' slogans and statements: "Africa is starving and Poland is following," "They took bread away from children to have more for war in Iraq," "Jolanta, you and the president lack nothing, we and our children have no bread," "Five hundred thousand children will perish of hunger—shame on the nation," "Gas the children! Hausner, I'm starving!" (Elas 2008: 39; Ostałowska 2004).

Film documentaries shot during the demonstration on 26 May 2004 (available on YouTube), are full of statements about the inability to provide health care to children, the need to discontinue higher education by older children who had been deprived of benefits, giving children up into foster care under the threat of starvation, and even suicidal thoughts.[12] The women are speaking in raised voices, crying, many of them bringing their children along to demonstrations, including disabled children, which reinforced the message. Polish anthropologist Marta Elas, who witnessed that event, wrote: "*During the demonstration on the 26th of May 2004, people were carrying a black plate with an image of a coffin under an inscription saying 'May 26th, the Mother's Day' and many participants were holding black flags. During the protest held at the beginning of March 2005, a gallows with a hanged doll was set up next to banners stuck in the snow*" (2008: 37). In the course of the same demonstration, women composed their own lyrics for the national anthem: [there is money] *Enough for bonuses, balls and governmental salaries / But not enough for poor children / March, march to the heart of stone / May this new anthem bring a change in it.*

Street actions, demonstrations and blockades of roads and offices had been staged from the very start of the mobilization by the most radical groups of the poorest women. The angry protest of mothers shouting out anti-government slogans was disregarded by the politicians from the ruling coalition as an expression of irrational behavior of hysterical women. Moreover, the subversive nature of protests did not suit the slightly better off and well-educated leaders who attempted to "calm the emotions" and modify the image of the movement, especially after the autumn of 2004, when the citizens' draft law was submitted to Parliament (see also Hryciuk and Korolczuk 2013a, Korolczuk 2015). In 2004, in a press interview, Renata Iwaniec said: "The girls want to vent their fears because it helps. To block! The access road! At the lights! Puncture a tire! Go onto the railway track! Onto the office! Hunger strike! With those who can do it. Join Lepper! Join the Self-Defense Party! When I went to Cracow and saw their banners, I was dumbfounded. Children in prison-style striped uniforms, with bleeding wounds, walking skeletons. And the slogans: 'Gas the children!', 'Hausner, I'm starving!'. We have to moderate them. Lublin is the most determined, but it is the most frivolous as well" (Ostałowska 2004).

Actions taken to temper the behavior of the most radical groups inside the movement, shifts in the strategy, and framing mothers' demands as civil rights were meant to prevent the consolidation of a negative image of single mothers popularized by the politicians from the ruling coalition. This was related to the accusations that money from the Fund was spent on reproducing "social pathology," that it promoted passive attitudes and ended up in the hands of a narrow group of "female con artists." During the Mother's Day demonstration in 2004, one of the leaders explained to a TV camera: *That is how we are referred to, female con artists. . . . We are no pathology, we have single-parent but healthy families. We are responsible parents struggling for the good of our children.*[13] Symptomatically, only words like "family" or "parents," rather than "mother," can be heard in that statement.

The Single Mothers, who had been intuitively shifting emphasis away from the maternal role, did not manage, however, to avoid the criticism of their life choices. Single motherhood, especially in the case of poor women, does not fit the nationalist and neoliberal construct of the "Polish family" and is perceived as a social ill. The claims for social rights put forward by the Single Mothers were characterized as reflecting a "demanding attitude" and Joanna Banach, a left-wing MP, the leader of the Parliamentary Women's Group, and the author of the act on the abolition of the Fund, explained in Parliament that "the state is not the father" and, therefore, it should be free of financial obligation when fathers do not want to or cannot pay child support. At best, women faced indifference and lack of interest, but they frequently had to cope with contempt and sometimes were subjected to public humiliation. In their interviews, representatives of the movement quoted the opinion of one of the left-wing female deputies, which was also referred to in press articles: *"you shouldn't have spread your legs and you wouldn't have children now"* (Ostałowska 2004: 28).

As a strategy, renouncing the extreme forms of protest and legitimization of demands by referring to the discourse of mothers as citizens struggling for improved living conditions of their families, as well as the use of the social capital of the leaders (most of them teachers) as representatives of the movement, proved effective. It secured at least a partial success for the movement. Eventually, all those effortful actions taken by women led to the restoration of the Fund (although in an unsatisfying form), brought issues related to motherhood and mothers' rights into the public discourse, and initiated a debate about fatherhood and fathering. Consequently, the mobilization of single mothers revealed the collective agency of marginalized groups and their political potential, and contributed to the introduction of new elements to the Polish debate on citizenship (see Lister 2005).

On the other hand, the modified strategy within the movement itself revealed class-based differences and divisions. The leaders of the movement—well-educated persons, mostly employed and not relying on welfare benefits—aspired to the middle-class lifestyle and the model of "intensive mothering" characteristic of that group (Hays 1996; Urbańska 2012). For that reason, they wished to be perceived as rational persons and competent partners in the discussion. In the interviews, they stressed that the accusations of "demanding attitude" and "parasitism" were particularly painful as they targeted their sense of dignity (see Lister 2005). What is more, they frequently perceived the behavior of politicians, even those allegedly in support of the cause, as condescending. Opting for a strategy in which they were acting primarily as citizens allowed them a higher sense of self-worth, while contacts with politicians informed them about the mechanisms of politics and even offered them an opportunity to start their own political careers. Some of the leaders have subsequently decided to run in local and national elections.

Legitimization and Delegitimization of Claims in the Public Sphere

The fate of the next mobilization of poor mothers and its social impact demonstrated why the strategy employed by the leaders of the Single Mothers Movement, consisting of politicizing single motherhood without emphasizing the mother figure, tempering the radical actions of the poorest women, and focusing on civil rights, turned out to be effective. A couple of months after the reinstatement of the Fund and disbanding of the Single Mothers movement, in May 2008 in the city of Wałbrzych, a group of poor mothers, the majority of them in permanent relationships, some visibly pregnant, started a hunger strike after their gas and electricity supplies had been cut off and after some of them had been brutally removed from the uninhabited flats they had occupied in the Biały Kamień district (Maciejewska 2010).

Mothers from a "fallen" town, stricken with structural unemployment, themselves jobless or recruiting from the so-called working poor, tried to draw attention to the dramatic situation of their children and families and to the threat of homelessness. They emphasized their maternal role, related obligations, and the particular situation they found themselves in. They invoked social rights, such as the right to housing. Eventually, they decided to stage a protest when, similar to *Alimonaries,* they were "forced to the wall" and literally thrown out into the street. Their protest, however, ended in a fiasco because as unemployed persons dependent on welfare benefits, or simply poor, they were counted among the "social pathologies" and their stance was likened to the "demands of welfare-dependent pathological forms of families." They were threatened with administrative penalties, arrest, and even seizure of their children.

Ewa Charkiewicz investigated the reactions to that protest found on the Internet, and instead of understanding for the female "managers of poverty" (Tarkowska 2002) or respect for the hardships of motherhood she found mostly invectives. The poor mothers were perceived as "thieves" and "swindlers" stealing from the city and hard-working taxpayers, "vicious and irresponsible mothers who should be sterilized" (Charkiewicz 2009: 3). The analysis of the actions taken by the city authorities, of social organizations, and of the related Internet discourse, conducted as a project of the Feminist Think Tank, clearly demonstrates that the fight the poor mothers waged for their social rights did not receive public legitimization and, moreover, led to their disempowerment (Charkiewicz 2009; Maciejewska 2010).[14]

The public response to these mobilizations of poor mothers illustrates the character of sociocultural changes in post-transformation Poland, including, in particular, the significance and consequences of *a restructuring of the perception of social inequalities by the hegemonic liberal ideology* (Buchowski 2006: 464). In the public discourse, the poor, including poor mothers, are perceived as internal, "uncivilized" Others, a potential source of moral corruption, a threat, an economic burden, and an object of pity. The reaction to the protests of mothers in defense of their social rights reveals the processes of stereotyping and orientalizing and, therefore, the ways in which cultural differences come into being in contemporary Poland (see Lister 2005). Michał Buchowski pointed out that internal societal orientalization proceeds on three planes and in relation to three dichotomies: urban vs. rural, educated vs. uneducated, and winners vs. losers of the transformation (2006: 466). As a result, ideological and essentializing images of single or destitute mothers as con artists, lazy women living off welfare benefits, or irresponsible migrant mothers are produced in the public discourse (see Charkiewicz 2009; Urbańska 2010). Destitute or impoverished women, poorly educated, working poor, or employed in professions of low prestige, speaking from the position of the province or a neglected district of a "fallen" city, situated on the side of losers of the transformation are presented as uncivilized. They are clearly unaware of the "new deal" and, therefore, classed among the "new Others" of the transitions (Buchowski 2006: 467). That is why their voice, like the voice of so many others, "... *the voice of the powerless and the poor[,] rarely make it through the accepted democratic procedures. Subalterns have to resort to radical methods if they want to articulate their interests and are afterword accused of demagoguery"* (2006: 467).

The protests of destitute mothers from Wałbrzych failed to attract broad public support.[15] To the contrary, they were silenced and marginalized because the motherhood of poor women does not fit in the hegemonic construct of individualistic intensive mothering; it constitutes an offense, reprehensible behavior, and is by no means a desired mode of accomplishing the "female calling" (Charkiewicz 2009; Maciejewska 2010). Going on strike, solidarity actions, and the subsequent self-organization of women all failed to produce changes in the city's housing policy, and the participants continued to pay compensation to the city (double rent) for occupying apartments without a contract. They were sentenced to imprisonment, excluded from access to council housing, and presented as uncaring mothers (Charkiewicz 2012).[16]

Concluding Discussion

Some sociologists believe that a social movement can be successful when the collective action frames, including discourses, symbols, and patterns followed by their members, fit the broader system of convictions and cultural notions regarding a given phenomenon and thus meet with broad public resonance (Snow and Benford 1988; Williams 2008). Even so, it must be remembered that the choice of strategies and notions around which mobilizations take place depends not only on the shape and dynamics of cultural constructs, but also on the political and social history of a given country, social, or ethnic group. Thus, some types of claims and collective identities are delegitimized in public discourse. In the case of mothers' mobilizations, local ideals and practices of gender and motherhood are crucial to the movement's strategies and ultimately its success or failure.

Latin American women continue to use strategic essentialism in their political struggle, more often than not with good results. They use political motherhood in their strife against social exclusion and violence as well as the unilateral, neoliberal logic of social development and its social and economic effects (see Stephen 1997; Hryciuk 2008). Using symbolic imagery of motherhood promotes an active attitude among women and attaches a new significance to the resistance against the received situation, thus legitimizing the mobilizations of women in the public sphere (Hryciuk 2008). Mother-activists in Latin America refer to the hegemonic construct of motherhood characteristic of the social groups to which the protest is addressed. With time, mothers' mobilizations have modified the nature of women's participation in the public sphere, enriched the model of a mother with an element of political activism, and led to the emergence of a new, gendered type of citizenship. All those factors are behind the fact that despite the neoliberal policies embraced by the majority of states in the region, including practices emphasizing individual responsibility for the fate of individuals and families, actions taken by mothers continue to resonate strongly with societies in the region. References to motherhood legitimize protests in defense of political, civil, and social rights and remain the fundamental tool in the political struggle of Latin American women.

Contrary to the Latin American context, the political history of Poland does not provide models for grassroots mobilizing of mothers. Under state socialism, women's and mothers' interests were officially represented by the party and the League of Polish Women. Despite the moderate reinforcing of maternal identity by the state policies, including the symbolic celebration of Mother's Day on one hand, and the use of gender equality rhetoric on the other hand, it was still not possible to freely articulate the interests of women (see Fidelis 2010). Also, women's participation in social mobilization against the state, in the "Solidarity," is often marginalized (see Penn 2005).

Today, despite some significant changes in the cultural construct of motherhood and women's identity over the last thirty years in Poland, certain elements remain unaltered. One of the components of exceptional permanence is the imperative of self-reliance and self-sufficiency of mothers as well as the conviction that readiness to make sacrifices and provide for children is part and parcel of the construct of good mothering (Titkow 2007).[17] That perception of the maternal role, shared by women themselves, has been always exploited by the state, which imposed on them the role of a "buffer" cushioning the social costs of political or economic crises (see Lister 2005). This trend undermines the legitimacy of demands (based on social or economic rights) put forward by women and, consequently, thwarts collective actions of emancipative character (Hryciuk and Korolczuk 2013a). Actually, this culturally specific and deeply rooted conviction about mothers' obligations falls in line with the ongoing global process of neoliberalization of citizenship where "the neoliberal subject is not a citizen with claims in the state but a self-enterprising citizen subject who is obliged to become an entrepreneur himself or herself" (Ong 2006: 14). The changes in framing mothers' rights and ambiguous outcomes of their mobilization clearly reveal the vernacular character of this process in the Polish context. In the period of transition toward the so-called "market democracy," when the shrinking of the welfare state and privatization of care as well as the retraditionalization of gender roles were presented as a "return to normalcy" or to the natural order of things (see Gerber 2011; Graff 2008), the social costs involved in that process were laid on the shoulders of women, the poorest of them in particular.

The initial criticism that the AF movement was met with can be explained by the fact that their actions targeted the process that began after 1989, especially the dismantling of the remaining welfare state institutions that supported underprivileged groups. It was also the first mass movement interested in the economic standing of women and one that proposed an alternative narration regarding the supposedly successful transformation after 1989. In the eyes of the elites and a large part of society, mobilization of mothers in defense of social rights represented the "demanding attitude" and "*homo sovieticus* mentality" characteristic of the communist times (see also Buchowski 2006). Single motherhood of impoverished teachers, the working poor, or unemployed women did not grant legitimization to their demands. To the contrary, it could become a reason for limiting their civil rights as illustrated by the threats to take away the children of protesting mothers, as was the case in Wałbrzych.

The strategies for the politicizing of motherhood that, more or less deliberately, were employed by women struggling to keep the Alimony Fund attest to the increasing class-based and cultural stratification of the contemporary model of motherhood in Poland (Hryciuk and Korolczuk 2013a). Single motherhood of destitute women does not fit in the nationalist-neoliberal-expert definition of family: nuclear, heteronormative, and coresidential (see Mizielińska 2012; Młodawska 2012; Urbańska 2010, 2012). In order to be at least partially successful and to achieve the exercise of practical interests, in the name of which the Single Mothers took action, they not only avoided the use of the Polish Mother or the Mother of God figures, but they also symbolically effaced the mother figure from their discourse and replaced it with a neutral citizen fighting for the rights that she and her family were constitutionally entitled to.

The analysis of the emergence, development, and moderate success of the movement provokes numerous questions: first and foremost about the "mythical" power of the maternal capital and the symbolism of motherhood in the Polish culture including, in particular, the myth of the Polish Mother—which, as the fate of the Single Mothers' mobilization clearly demonstrated, has a normative and exclusive character that, among others, rules out the motherhood of poor women. Other important issues concern women's rights more generally, new forms of citizenship, and the participation of Polish women in the public sphere and civil society. Despite the fact that traditional images of motherhood linger on in the realms of culture and politics (propagated, among others, by politicians), they do not effectively reinforce women's individual and collective agency and, therefore, do not legitimize their actions in the public sphere. The Polish Mother seems to be merely an exalted figure that is all too frequently referred to in scholarly debates and the public discourse to explain the complex, ambiguous role and position of the mother/mothers in contemporary Poland. Most of all, however, the case of the Single Mothers' mobilization sheds light on processes of delegitimization of certain claims and social groups and, more specifically, the conditions under which women can legitimately formulate resonant claims and become recognized civil society actors in contemporary Poland.

Renata Ewa Hryciuk is Assistant Professor at the Institute of Ethnology and Cultural Anthropology, Warsaw University. She is the coeditor of five edited volumes in Polish: (with Agnieszka Kościańska): *Gender: Anthropological Perspective: Social Organisation* (Warsaw University Press, 2007), *Gender: Anthropological Perspective: Femininity, Masculinity, Sexuality* (Warsaw University Press, 2007); (with Elżbieta Korolczuk) *Farewell to the Polish Mother? Discourses, Practices, and Representations of Motherhood in Contemporary Poland* (Warsaw University Press, 2012) and *Dangerous Liaisons: Motherhood, Fatherhood, and Politics* (Warsaw University Press, 2015), and (with Joanna Mroczkowska) *Food: An Anthropological Perspective. (Post)socialism* (Warsaw University Press, 2017).

Notes

1. The empirical basis of the article comes from the analysis of the media discourse related to the Single Mothers for the Alimony Fund movement and from the results of fieldwork (interviews with activists and leaders of the movement) conducted in 2011–2012. The article presents the results of studies conducted under the project titled "Institutional Constraints and Creative Solutions: Civil Society in Poland in Comparative Perspective," funded by the Swedish Research Council (Grant 421/2010/1706), as well as the outcomes of the research visit to Södertörn University in Stockholm as part of the scholarship of The Swedish Institute Baltic Sea Region Exchange Program (Visby Program).

2. To draw this comparison, I refer to the literature on the subject and to the results of fieldwork conducted in 1999–2006 in *colonias populares* of Mexico City (Hryciuk 2008), and follow-up mini research conducted in 2009, 2011, and 2014.

3. Some theses discussed in this chapter were also presented in the chapter published in Polish in Hryciuk and Korolczuk 2012.

4. The topical literature shows the profound diversification of the social mobilizations of mothers. The first movements of that kind in the region emerged by inspiration of the hierarchy of the Catholic Church, right-wing parties, and conservative circles. For instance, the mobilization of Mexican women in the 1930s, intended to stop the introduction of the socialist education curriculum (including sex education) developed by the administration of president Lazaro Cardenas (Hryciuk 2008). Women's right-wing movements in the period of military regimes in Brazil (1964–1985) and Chile (1973–1989), famous for their spectacular actions in the public space: "Marches of the Family, with God and for Freedom" gathering hundreds of thousands of women in the streets of Brazilian cities in the sixties, or "Marches of the Empty Pots" during the rule of Salvador Allende in Chile (Power 2006). The seventies marked the emergence of maternal movements aimed against violence and crimes of military governments, civil wars, and guerrilla activities. They included both apolitical movements like the Argentinean "Mothers of the Plaza de Mayo" (Feijóo 1989), movements heavily influenced by the theology of liberation, e.g., the COMADRES (*Comité de Madres Arnulfo Romeo*) movement established during the civil war in El Salvador in 1977 on the initiative of archbishop Arnulfo Romero (Stephen 1977), or the organizations of indigenous women, e.g., the Guatemalan organization of widows (mainly originating from Mayan groups) CONAVIGUA (*la Coordinadora Nacional de Viudas de Guatemala*) (Schirmer 1993). In the years of economic crises, the majority of (though not all) maternal movements were class-based; the most deprived women from the lowest social strata were mobilized to take collective action.

5. The term is taken from Schirmer (1993). Other expressions used to denote the political activity of mothers in Latin America include: "subversive motherhood" and "militant motherhood," the latter coined by Álvarez (1990).

6. Working-class and lower-middle-class neighborhoods in Mexican cities.

7. See data available at www.inmujer.df.gob.mx and www.ife.org.mx, Retrieved 10 November 2015.

8. Report of the Ministry of Labour and Social Affairs for 2003, www.mpips.gov.pl, retrieved 10 November 2015.

9. See http://ec.europa.eu, Retrieved 10 November 2015.

10. Since 2014, the highly neglected issue of child support enforcement has been again discussed in Polish media and the association Dla Naszych Dzieci (For Our Children) was established by a new group of single mothers. This time feminist organizations and groups got involved (including the Warsaw-based Women's 8 of March Alliance, the Congress of Women, and the MaMa Fundation). The association's efforts were also backed by well-known feminist politicians, such as Małgorzata Fuszara, who was the Plenipotentiary for Gender Equality in 2015, and MP Wanda Nowicka.

11. See http://samodzielne-matki.free.ngo.pl/kontakt.html, Retrieved 12 October 2015.

12. See https://www.youtube.com/watch?v=tEYPxC_8s88, Retrieved 12 October 2015.

13. See https://www.youtube.com/watch?v=tEYPxC_8s88, Retrieved 12 October 2015.

14. See http://www.ekologiasztuka.pl/think.tank.feministyczny/articles.php?article_id=404, Retrieved 12 October 2015.

15. In the city of Wałbrzych, despite the fact that it has a population of one hundred twenty thousand and nearly two hundred NGOs operating, support for protesting women came only from Akcja Lokatorska (Tenants' Action), Kancelaria Sprawiedliwości Społecznej (Social Justice Office), Partia Kobiet (Women's Party), Inicjatywa Pracownicza (Workers' Initiative), and the Feminist Think Tank (Charkiewicz 2012).

16. These issues are discussed by the female protagonists of the film titled *Mothers' Strike*, shot in 2010 by Małgorzata Maciejewska and Magda Malinowska in the course of the participatory action research conducted by the Feminist Think Tank with mothers involved in the protests in Wałbrzych. Meetings held in the offices of one of the local government associations were intended to discuss problems related to living in the poor districts of Wałbrzych, the feminization of poverty, and possible strategies of resistance and further mobilization. The film documents the attitudes of individual women, including those who stressed the need to take action in defense of their social rights, and ends with information that after the completion of the project mothers would continue to meet as part of the Women's Social Initiative "Akademia Malucha" (Toddler's Academy). It seems, therefore, that the destitute mothers from Wałbrzych followed in the steps of the Single Mothers' movement and, instead of emphasizing their maternal role, decided to disguise it strategically. The city authorities offered office space for women to hold self-help meetings on condition that they would focus on matters related to the upbringing of children and culture and not to existential issues, such as the availability of labor and housing (Charkiewicz 2012).

17. However, not all of the "survival" or "coping" strategies intended to ensure the physical continuation of families are socially acceptable, e.g., migrants were presented in the public discourse as immoral and irresponsible mothers (see Urbańska 2010; Keough 2006).

References

Alimentare znaczy jeść [Alimentare Means to Eat]. 2008. Report, CPK Kraków, in *Homofobia, mizoginia, ciemnogród. Burzliwe losy kontrowersyjnych ustaw* [Homophobia, Misogyny, and Backwardness: Controversial Regulations in Poland], ed. I. Desperak. Łódź: Omega–Praksis, 194–237.

Álvarez, S.E. 1990. *Engendering Democracy in Brazil: Women's Movements in Transition Politics.* Princeton: Princeton University Press.

Buchowski, M. 2006. "The Specter of Orientalism in Europe: From Exotic Other to Stigmatized Brother." *Anthropological Quarterly* 79, no. 3: 463–482.

Budrowska, B. 2000. *Macierzyństwo jako punkt zwrotny w życiu kobiety* [Motherhood as a Turning Point in a Woman's Life]. Wrocław: Monografie FNP.

Charkiewicz, E. 2009. *Matki do sterylizacji. Neoliberalny rasizm w Polsce* [Mothers to Be Sterilized: Neoliberal Racism in Poland]. Retrieved 20 June 2014 from www.ekolo giasztuka.pl/pdf/f0053charkiewicz_szkic2.pdf.

———. 2012. *Partycypacja nie dla wszystkich* [Participation Not for All], in *Partycypacja. Przewodnik Krytyki Politycznej* [Participation: A Krytyka Polityczna Guide]. Warsaw: Wydawnictwo Krytyki Politycznej, 329–341.

Craske, N. 1999. *Women and Politics in Latin America*. New Brunswick, NJ: Rutgers University Press.

———. 2003. "Gender, Poverty and Social Movements," in *Gender in Latin America*, ed. S. Chant and N. Craske. New Brunswick, NJ: Rutgers University Press, 46–70.

Desperak, I. 2008. "Podwójnie samotne—wykluczenie ze społeczeństwa rodzin niepełnych" [Double Exclusion: Social Marginalization of Single-Parent Families], in *Homofobia, mizoginia i ciemnogród. Burzliwe losy kontrowersyjnych ustaw* [Homophobia, Misogyny and Backwardness: Controversial Regulations in Poland], ed. I. Desperak. Łódź: Omega–Praksis, 160–180.

Elas, M.G. 2008. *W obronie praw, w obronie dzieci. Ruch samotnych matek w stowarzyszeniu 'Damy Radę'* [In the Name of Law, in the Name of Children: Single Mothers' Association "We Will Make It"]. Unpublished M.A. thesis, Institute of Ethnology and Cultural Anthropology, Warsaw University.

Escobar, A. 1992. "Culture, Practice and Politics: Anthropology and the Study of Social Movements." *Critique of Anthropology* 12, no. 4: 395–432.

Feijóo, M.C. 1989. "The Challenge of Constructing Civilian Peace: Women and Democracy in Argentina," in *The Women's Movements in Latin America: Participation and Democracy*, ed. J.S. Jaquette. Westview Press, 72–94.

Feijóo, M.C., and M. Gogna. 1990. "Women in the Transition to Democracy", in *Women and Social Change in Latin America*, ed. E. Jelin. London: Zed Books, 79–134.

Fidelis, M. 2010. *Women, Communism and Industrialization in Postwar Poland*. New York: Cambridge University Press.

Funk, N. 2004. "Feminist Critique of Liberalism? Can They Travel East? Their Relevance in Eastern and Central Europe and The Former Soviet Union." *Signs: Journal of Women in Culture and Society* 29, no. 30: 695–726.

Gerber, A. 2011. Cultural Categories of Worth and Polish Gender Policy in the Context of EU Accession. *Social Politics* 18, no. 4: 490–514.

Goddard, V.A. 2000. "'The Virgin and the State': Gender and Politics in Argentina," in *Gender, Agency and Change: Anthropological Perspectives*, ed. V.A. Goddard. London and New York: Routledge, 221–249.

González de la Rocha, M. 1994. *The Resources of Poverty: Women and Survival in a Mexican City*. Cambridge, Manchester, and Oxford: Basil Blackwell.

Graff, A. 2008. "The Return of Real Men and Real Women: Gender and EU Accession in Three Polish Weeklies," in *Global Empowerment of Women: Responses to Globalization, and Politicized Religion*, ed. C. Elliott. London and New York: Routledge, 191–212.

Gutmann, M.C. 1996. *The Meanings of Macho: Being a Man in Mexico City*. Berkeley: University of California Press.

Guy, D.J. 1997. "Mothers Alive and Dead: Multiple Concepts of Mothering in Buenos Aires," in *Sex and Sexuality in Latin America*, ed. D. Balderstone and D.J. Guy. New York, London: New York University Press, 155–193.

Hays, S. 1996. *The Cultural Contradictions of Motherhood*. New Heaven, London: Yale University Press.

Hryciuk, R.E. 2008. *Kulturowy kontekst macierzyństwa. Na przykładzie Meksyku* [Motherhood and Culture: Continuity and Change: The Case of Mexico]. Unpublished Ph.D. thesis, Graduate School for Social Research, Polish Academy of Sciences, Warsaw.

Hryciuk, R.E., and E. Korolczuk. 2010. "Poland," in *Encyclopedia of Mothering*, vol. 3., ed. A. O'Reilly. Thousand Oaks: Sage, 990–991.

Hryciuk, R.E., and E. Korolczuk. 2012. "Wstęp. Pożegnanie z Matką Polką?" [Introduction: Farewell to the Polish Mother?], in *Pożegnanie z Matką Polką? Dyskursy, praktyki i reprezentacje macierzyństwa we współczesnej Polsce* [Farewell to the Polish Mother? Discourses, Practices, and Representations of Motherhood in Contemporary Poland], ed. R. Hryciuk and E. Korolczuk. Warszawa: Wydawnictwo Uniwersytetu Warszawskiego, 7–26.

Hryciuk, R., and E. Korolczuk. 2013a. "At the Intersection of Gender and Class: Social Mobilization around Mothers' Rights in Poland," in *Beyond NGO-ization: The Development of Social Movements in Central and Eastern Europe,* ed. K. Jacobsson and S. Saxonberg. Farnham: Ashgate, 49–70.

Hryciuk, R.E., and E. Korolczuk. 2013b. "Ruchy społeczne kobiet" [Women's Social Movements], in *Encyklopedia Gender.* Warsaw: WAB, 492–496.

Hryciuk, R.E., and E. Korolczuk. 2015. "Konteksty upolitycznienia macierzyństwa i ojcostwa we współczesnej Polsce" [Motherhood, Fatherhood, and Politics in Contemporary Poland: An Outline], in *Niebezpieczne związki. Macierzyństwo, ojcostwo i polityka* [Dangerous Liaisons: Motherhood, Fatherhood, and Politics], ed. R. Hryciuk and E. Korolczuk. Warszawa: Warsaw University Press, 11–44.

Jaquette, J.S. 1994. "Conclusion: Women's Political Participation and the Prospects for Democracy," in *The Women's Movements in Latin America: Participation and Democracy,* ed. J. S. Jaquette. Westview Press, 223–238.

Keough, L.J. 2006. "'Globalizing 'Postsocialism': Mobile Mothers and Neoliberalism on the Margins of Europe." *Anthropological Quarterly* 79, no. 3: 431–461.

Korolczuk, E. 2014. "Ruchy społeczne a płeć—perspektywa intersekcjonalna. Kongres Kobiet i ruch na rzecz przywrócenia Funduszu Alimentacyjnego" [Social Movements and Gender: Intersectional Analysis: The Congress of Women and the Alimony Fund Movement]. *Kultura i społeczeństwo* 1: 97–120.

———. 2015. "Musimy pokazać swoja siłę. Rozmowa z Elżbietą Dyś, w latach 2002–2007 aktywistką zaangażowaną w ruch na rzecz przywrócenia funduszu alimentacyjnego" [We Need to Show Our Strength: Interview with Elżbieta Dyś, an Activist of Single Mothers for the Alimony Fund Movement in 2002–2007], in *Niebezpieczne związki. Macierzyństwo, ojcostwo i polityka* [Dangerous Liasons: Motherhood, Fatherhood, and Politics], ed. R. Hryciuk and E. Korolczuk. Warszawa: Warsaw University Press, 343–356.

Lister, R. 2005. *Poverty.* Cambridge: Polity Press.

Logan, K. 1990. *Women's Participation in Urban Protest,* in *Popular Movements and Political Change in Mexico,* ed. J. Foweraker and A.L. Craig. Boulder, London: Lynne Rienner Publishers, 150–159.

Luna, L.L. 2006. "Mujeres y movimientos sociales," in *Historia de las mujeres en España y América Latina, Vol. IV Del Siglo XIX a los umbrales del XXI,* ed. I. Morant, G. Gómez-Ferrer, G. Cano, D. Barrancos, and A. Lavrin. Madrid: Ediciones Cátedra, 653–674.

Maciejewska, M. 2010. *Odzyskać obywatelstwo. Kobiety i warunki życia w Wałbrzychu,* Wstępny raport z badań [Reclaiming Citizenship: Women and Living Conditions in Wałbrzych]. Biblioteka Online ThinkThanku Feministycznego. Retrieved 12 June 2015 from http://www.ekologiasztuka.pl/think.tank.feministyczny/readarticle.php?article_id=369.

Massolo, A. 1992. *Por amor y coraje: mujeres en movimientos urbanos en la ciudad de México.* México: COLMEX/PIEM.

Mazurek, M. 2010. *Społeczeństwo kolejki. O doświadczeniach niedoboru 1945-1989* [Queuing Socjety: On the Experience of Shortages 1945–1989]. Warsaw: Trio Publishers.

Mizielińska, J. 2012. "Czy macierzyństwo jest już od zawsze heteroseksualne? Próba refleksji" [Is Family Always Already Heterosexual? Some Reflections], in *Pożegnanie z Matką Polką? Dyskursy, praktyki i reprezentacje macierzyństwa we współczesnej Polsce* [Farewell to the Polish Mother? Discourses, Practices, and Representations of Motherhood in Contemporary Poland], ed. R. Hryciuk and E. Korolczuk. Warszawa: Wydawnictwo Uniwersytetu Warszawskiego, 235–266.

Młodawska, A. 2012. "Tradycyjna polska stygmatyzacja czy ponowoczesne neoliberalne wykluczenie? Analiza internetowego dyskursu kobiecej bezdzietności" [Traditional Polish Stigmatization or Postmodern Neoliberal Exclusion? The Analysis of Internet Discourse of Women's Childlessness], in *Pożegnanie z Matką Polką? Dyskursy, praktyki i reprezentacje macierzyństwa we współczesnej Polsce* [Farewell to the Polish Mother? Discourses, Practices, and Representations of Motherhood in Contemporary Poland], ed. R. Hryciuk and E. Korolczuk. Warszawa: Wydawnictwo Uniwersytetu Warszawskiego, 97–124.

Nash, M. 2004. *Mujeres en mundo. Historia, retos y movimientos.* Madrid: Alianza Editorial.

Ong, A. 2006. *Neoliberalism as Exception: Mutations in Citizenship and Sovereignty.* Duke University Press.

Ost, D. 2005. *Defeat of Solidarity: Anger and Politics in Postcomunist Europe.* Cornell University Press.

Ostałowska, L. 2004. "Batalia o Alimenty" [The Fight for Alimony]. *Gazeta Wyborcza: Wysokie Obcasy,* 8 May.

———. 2005. "Alimenty. Przegrana Walka?" [Alimony: Lost Battle?]. *Gazeta Wyborcza: Wysokie Obcasy.* 6 June.

———. 2007a. "Porzucone przez mężów i polityków?" [Abandoned by Husbands and Politicians?]. *Gazeta Wyborcza: Wysokie Obcasy.* 10 April.

———. 2007b. "Alimenciary contra feministki?" [Alimonaries against Feminists?]. *Gazeta Wyborcza: Wysokie Obcasy.* 11 April.

———. 2007c. "Feministki kontra kobiety" [Feminists against Women]. *Gazeta Wyborcza: Wysokie Obcasy.* 9 June.

Penn, S. 2005. *Solidarity's Secret: The Women Who Defeated Communism in Poland.* Ann Arbor: University of Michigan.

Power, M. 2006. "Las mujeres conservadoras en Brasil y Chile," in *Historia de las Mujeres en España y América Latina del siglo XX a los umbrales del XXI,* ed. I. Morant, G. Gómez-Ferrer, G. Cano, D. Barrancos, and A. Lavrin. Madrid: Cátedra, 633–650.

Schirmer, J. 1993. "The Seeking of Truth and the Gendering of Consciousness: The Comadres of El Salvador and the Conavigua Widows of Guatemala," in *'Viva': Women and Popular Protest in Latin America,* ed. S. Radcliffe and S. Westwood. London: Routledge, 30–64.

Snow, D.A., and R.D. Benford. 1988. "Ideology, Frame Resonance, and Participant Mobilization," in *International Social Movement Research. T. 1, From Structure to Action: Comparing Social Movement Research Across Cultures,* ed. B. Klandermans, H. Kriesi, and G. Tarrow. Greenwich, CT: JAI Press, 197–217.

Spivak, G. 1989. "In a Word: Interview with Ellen Rooney." *Differences* 1, no. 2: 124–156.

Stephen L. 1997. *Women and Social Movements in Latin America: Power from Below.* Austin: University of Texas Press.

Tarkowska, E. 2002. "Intra-household Gender Inequality: Hidden Dimensions of Poverty among Polish Women." *Communist and Post-Communist Studies* 35: 411–432.

Tiano, S. 2001. "From Victims to Agents: A New Generation of Literature in Latin America." *Latin American Research Review* 36, no. 3: 183–203.

Titkow, A. 2001. "On the Appreciated Role of Women," in *Women on the Polish Labor Market,* ed. M. Ingham, H. Ingham, H. Domański. Budapest: Central European University Press, 21–41.

———. 2007. *Tożsamość polskich kobiet. Ciągłość, zmiana, konteksty* [Identity of Polish Women: Continuity, Change, Contexts]. Warsaw: IFiS PAN Editors.

Urbańska, S. 2010. "'Cała Polska liczy Eurosieroty'. Panika moralna i płeć w wykluczeniu oraz stygmatyzacji rodzin migrantów" ["All Poland Counts Euro-orphans": Moral Panic, Gender and Social Exclusion and Stigmatization of Migrant Families]. *Kultura i Społeczeństwo,* LIV 3: 59–88.

———. 2012. "Naturalna troska o ciało i moralność versus profesjonalna produkcja osobowości. Konstruowanie modelu człowieka w dyskursach macierzyńskich w latach 70. (PRL) i na początku XXI wieku" [Caring for the Natural Body and Morality vs. Professional Personality Production: Mothering Discourses under State Socialism and in Post-transformation Poland], in *Pożegnanie z Matką Polką? Dyskursy, praktyki i reprezentacje macierzyństwa we współczesnej Polsce* [Farewell to the Polish Mother? Discourses, Practices, and Representations of Motherhood in Contemporary Poland], ed. R. Hryciuk and E. Korolczuk. Warszawa: Wydawnictwo Uniwersytetu Warszawskiego, 49–70.

Werbner, P. 2005. "Political Motherhood and the Feminisation of Citizenship: Women's Activisms and the Transformation of the Public Sphere," in *Women, Citizenship, and Difference,* ed. P. Werbner and N. Yuval-Davis. London and New York: Zed Books, 221–245.

Werbner, P., and N. Yuval-Davis. 2005. "Introduction. Women and the New Discourse of Citizenship," in *Women, Citizenship, and Difference,* ed. P. Werbner and N. Yuval-Davis. London and New York: Zed Books, 1–37.

Williams, R.H. 2008. "The Cultural Contexts of Collective Action: Constraints, Opportunities, and the Symbolic Life of Social Movements," in *The Blackwell Companion to Social Movements,* ed. D.A. Snow, S.A. Soule, and H. Kriesi. Malden, MA and Oxford, U.K.: Blackwell Publishing, 91–115.

The Yearly Report of the Ministry of Labour and Social Policy. 2003. Retrieved 2 November 2015 from www.mpips.gov.pl.

Chapter 7

MARGINALIZING DISCOURSES AND ACTIVISTS' STRATEGIES IN COLLECTIVE IDENTITY FORMATION
THE CASE OF THE POLISH TENANTS' MOVEMENT

Dominika V. Polanska

Introduction

This chapter examines an increasingly important and interesting type of civil society activism, tenants' activism, which has been understudied thus far and whose members struggle for legitimacy for their claims in the public sphere. The aim is to study how this kind of activism has been delegitimized in public discourse and how tenants' activists struggle for legitimization. The ambition is to broaden the understanding of civil society activism by studying how conventionally excluded forms of activism and groups function and struggle for change.

The first tenants' organization in Poland, the Polish Association of Tenants, was founded in 1989 and throughout the 1990s several other tenants' organizations and coalitions were initiated in the country as a reaction to the ongoing changes in the housing system.[1] In the first decade after the systemic change these organizations and groups were mainly active in the field of legislation. Forming coalitions among tenants' groups and owners, pensioners, trade unions, homeless groups, residents of cooperatives, business representatives, and researchers enabled them to improve and clarify the legal situation of the involved groups, which led to several attempts to reform tenancy law in the country. The Act on the Protection of Tenants'

Rights of 2001 has stood at the center of these reforms to clarify regulation on tenants' rights, but the outcomes have been heavily criticized by tenants' organizations (the act has been amended repeatedly) and caused the emergence of more tenants' organizations in the early 2000s (although these organizations are no longer working with owners' organizations).

At present there are about forty tenants' organizations in the country, but their ability to recruit members and sympathizers is still limited for reasons that will be discussed later in this text. Cities like Warsaw, Kraków, Poznań, Łódź, Gdańsk, Radom, Mińsk Mazowiecki, Bielsko-Biała, and Białystok are the locations of tenants' formal and informal mobilizations in the country. Tenants' organizations' main activities cover: providing legal counseling for tenants; organizing protests, demonstrations, meetings, campaigns and eviction blockades; disseminating information on housing issues (to the media, to the authorities, to tenants, and so on); and writing petitions and amendments to legal acts. Polish tenants' activism is a hybrid of transactional activism, characteristic of the postsocialist world, where activism is mainly concentrated on building networks and ties between nonstate actors (Petrova and Tarrow 2007; Cisar 2013), and self-help activism, in a society where the public housing stock is gradually shrinking and the percentage of municipal (public) dwellings amounted to 8 percent of the total stock in 2009 (Polish Statistical Office 2014).[2]

The number of tenants in Poland is therefore quite small, and the majority of these reside in the municipal stock. Tenants are a minority in the housing sphere; they are represented by the older parts of the Polish population, and their economic position is rather weak (see Audycka-Zandberg 2014). Many tenants have also experienced marginalizing practices and stereotypical attitudes related to their housing arrangements. Audycka-Zandberg's (2014) study of Polish tenants of municipal, company-owned, and social housing shows that the main problems experienced by such tenants are, besides high rents, different types of harassment directed toward them. The anti-social attitudes of local authorities and civil servants toward tenants, along with repressive eviction measures toward residents of public housing, are highlighted in media reports (Urbański 2010). In this light, the mobilization and organization of tenants is facing some difficulties that need to be overcome, or at least met and reflected on, by the tenants' activists. This is why tenants' activism, and in particular the question of how these marginalizing attitudes and practices are reflected on by tenants, is the focus of this study.

Another notable feature that impedes tenants' activism in the Polish context is the lack of economic support. Previous studies discuss donor dependence as the main feature of activism in postsocialist societies (see for instance Mendelson and Glenn 2002), but these organizations and groups do not usually receive financial support from donors. Polish tenants' mobilization is particularly interesting, as previous studies show that economically weak groups are less likely to act together with others, or to choose collective action before individual solutions (Pickvance 2001; Vihavainen 2009). Polish tenants' activism goes against the assumptions of who is more likely to act collectively due to age, economic position, lack of financial support, and the postsocialist citizens' preference for family- and friend-based networks (Sztompka 2004; Gliński 2004). This makes their activism interesting to study, as it can contribute to knowledge in the field of social movement studies by enriching the understanding of social mobilizations of people in weak social and economic positions and the strategies they develop to overcome marginalization. The specific cultural context serves as an example where tenants—despite stigmatizing discourses[3]—mobilize and organize at a grassroots level and contest these discourses in their struggle.

The objective of this study is thus to examine how Polish tenants' activism has been delegitimized in public discourse, how this delegitimation is reflected in tenants' activists' collective identity formation, and which strategies are employed to challenge this trend. I reconstruct the hegemonic public discourse on tenants as reflected in the largest Polish liberal newspaper (*Gazeta Wyborcza*) and on the basis of twenty semistructured interviews with tenants' activists, I analyze the process of collective identity formation in the movement and discuss how it relates to the discourse on tenants in the newspaper media. I specifically focus on the self-presentation of tenants as a collective and strategies used in their collective identity formation to legitimize the claims of the movement.

Data and Research Methods

The empirical base for this study consists of two parts: newspaper articles on tenants and interviews with tenants' activists. The newspaper articles were selected according to specific criteria in order to give a representative picture of the discourse on tenants from 1989 to 2014. All of the articles include the main keyword "tenant(s)." In the archive of *Gazeta Wyborcza*, the country's largest newspaper with a liberal orientation, there were more than three thousand articles including the word "tenant." The next step in the selection process was to select articles that included descriptions of tenants (excluding those covering the legal and material conditions of tenants at the local or national level). An additional step was to read the remaining eighty-nine articles, but limiting the basis for analysis to about fifty articles that contained the longest and richest descriptions. In the selection process, I have focused on the last decade (2004–2014) (thirty articles), but the years 1989–2003 are covered in the material as well (twenty articles). The texts were analyzed with a qualitative focus on the representations of tenants and the attributes used to describe this group (for instance, the use of metaphors, active versus passive actors, positive versus negative characteristics, voice versus no voice) answering the questions "What is said about tenants?," "Who is saying this?," "To whom?," and "What arguments are used to legitimize what is said?"

The twenty interviews were conducted with activists in 2013. The majority of the respondents were leaders and other activists involved in the four biggest tenants' associations (the Warsaw Tenants' Association, the Committee for the Defence of Tenants, the Social Justice Office and the Polish Union of Tenants) (for more detailed information on data collection, see Polanska 2014). Three of these twenty interviews were conducted with representatives from other, much smaller associations (at neighborhood or even building level) and five of the respondents were "loosely" connected to the big associations, without any formal membership in any of them, but actively working with tenants' issues. The interview questions encompassed information on individual motives, experiences with tenants' issues and collective strategies, practices, internal and external relations within the organization, and the organization's general characteristics. Where possible (depending on the length of the interviewees' activism), the questions even covered respondents' interpretations of changes over time in, for instance, practices, relations, attitudes, and so on. All respondents are anonymous in the material and the quotations used are designed not to reveal any sensitive data about the respondents. (A numbering system is used.)

Previous Research on Social Movements and Collective Identity Formation

In this review of previous studies on collective identity making among social movements, I will concentrate on research that connects to discourses and the way discursive practices affect the process of collective identity formation. According to Jasper, "libraries have been written about collective identities and politics" (2011: 294), but there is a limited number of relevant studies concerning marginalized and de-legitimized identities employed by collective actors in order to change or resignify the stigmatizing labels (for instance Berbrier 1998; Dowse 2001; Kaplan and Liu 2000; Taylor 2000). Movements ranging from the women's movement (Taylor 2000), to the gay and lesbian movement (Van Dyke and Cress 2006), to the AIDS movement (Gould 2009), to the disability movement (Dowse 2001), to the white supremacist movement (Berbrier 1998) are among these. Kaplan and Liu (2000) studied the so called "spoiled" identities, a term coined by Goffman, examining why people choose to cope with these stigmatized identities in social movements. Their explanation is based on the assumption that the stigmatization/disapproval/devaluation experiences of a certain social group have accumulated over time and might lead to the disposition to participate in collective action/social movements. In the case of the Polish tenants' movement, the delegitimation of tenants' activism in public discourse has emerged along with the formation of tenants' associations since the systemic change in the 1989. The interesting question here is: "How have these images been challenged by the activists?"

Scholars observe that participation in social movements provides individuals with new sets of norms, which makes it possible to reject the conventional devaluing labels. It may lead to some changes in terms of collective identity and result in a more positive self-evaluation of the individuals involved. However, as convincing as these arguments might sound, the picture is more complex, and it is not enough to study marginalized identities and experiences of devaluation to explain the formation of collective identities. Taylor (2000) and Gould (2009) emphasize the emotional dimension in the study of social movements and their collective identitymaking by examining the work involving emotions among women's self-help movements and AIDS activists. Gould argues that "to understand the sources and character of political action requires tangling with emotion" (2009: 439) and Taylor (2000) emphasizes that emotions do not belong to individuals but to specific organizational contexts. According to Gould, political opportunity structures and other external factors result in collective action only when they are interpreted and responded to emotionally by people. The collective identity of the activists included differences in gender, race, sexualities, and even HIV/AIDS status (HIV-negative individuals included), and the differences were overcome by the formation of a common enemy: the state and social institutions along with a strong sense of belonging based on the shared experience of living with AIDS and "a shared queer sensibility" (2009: 333). In the study of Polish tenants' activists' collective identity formation I will therefore pay attention to emotions and how they are processed collectively and in particular how they function as triggers for collective action.

Berbrier (1998) adds to the literature on how movements frame and legitimize their claims by studying white separatists' rhetoric. Berbrier's ambition is to bridge the gap between the macro and the micro level in his study, and he focuses on the cultural contexts and the agency of the studied individuals. He develops two interesting strategies in this marginalized group's desire to legitimize its claims and win broader support: equivalence and reversal. The first, equivalence, aims to frame the group's position as equivalent to other minority groups and the second, reversal, involves reversing the label put on the group externally by those denying the group's position as a minority. In the examination of the Polish tenants' activists' collective identity processes, the strategies of equivalence and reversal will be given particular attention, as they allow for empowerment in collective action.

Furthermore, changes in political opportunities and their consequences for social movements' collective identities are explored in the study by Van Dyke and Cress (2006). By focusing on the gay and lesbian movements, the authors show that political opportunities, the actions of the movements' opponents, public opinion, internal movement conflicts, and other external threats affect the composition of a movement and therefore its collective identity. Collective identity formation is a complex process, and as the focus of this study is on how marginalized collective identities are formed and legitimized, it is interesting to further investigate the issues of overcoming differences, handling emotions, strategically framing and positioning groups, and the role of internal and external threats and conditions in the case of Polish tenants' movement.

Collective Identities and the Contestation of Discourses: Theoretical Framework

The starting point of this study is that identity is a process in which meaning is created, a process that is not fixed, but continually created and recreated. Identities may be many and sometimes contradictory, but are different from roles or functions in that they are internalized by social actors (Castells 1997). Identities, including collective identities, define the meanings that social actors assign to their actions and are powerful sources of meaning. They are constructed in specific contexts (space, time, and social structures) and are always produced in relation to power structures. Power structures, in turn, might be maintained or transformed by specific discourses, as discourses are intimately connected to conceptions of power. Discourses are understood in this study as processes and practices of knowledge creation, by which we understand and represent the world. Discourses are the processes of knowledge production, sharing, negotiating, and imposing, and are constituted and constituting societal processes and practices. In this study the focus is on how discourses are reproduced, contested, and changed in the collective identity formation of a specific group, namely, tenants. The starting point is shared with Foucault (1977): language is a reflection of power relations in a given society, as it both gives power and makes it real by producing meaning about our social life that encompasses social relations, subject positions, and identities. Fairclough (1992, 1995) has further illuminated the link between language and social and political change. For him, discourses are forms of social practices/social actions that reflect social structures and social change. They might also be used as mechanisms of social control.

Melucci defines collective identity as a process that is not singular or fixed but "constructed through interaction and comprises different and some-times contradictory definitions" (1996: 72). The prerequisite of collective identity is, according to Melucci, a network of relations between actors who are involved in interactions, communicating, influencing each other, nego-tiating, and making decisions. Collective identity is, according to Melucci, based on a collective perception with an orientation toward the goal, the means, and the relationships with the environment. Melucci's contribution to the field is to provide cultural, sociopsychological, and emotional aspects for the field of social movement studies, which had previously focused mainly on structural and rationalistic explanations of social movements' emergence and persistence.

Melucci stresses resource mobilization ability and political opportuni-ties for collective identity formation within the systems of opportunities and constraints (1988: 332). Mobilization of actors in collective action is closely connected to the development of a collective identity, and, I would like to argue, in accordance with Della Porta and Diani's (1999) contention that collective action requires a presence of a "we" that is characterized by common features and solidarity. Moreover, as the "we" is constructed, it is always constructed in relation to the "other" or "others," as will be argued below. The "other" might be an adversary that is attributed the responsibility for/causes behind the condition of a particular group of actors and "against which the mobilization is called" (Della Porta and Diani 1999: 94).

Social movements are conditioned in several ways by discursive practices, as they are situated not only socially and politically but also culturally (Fine 1995). The specific cultural context affects what social movements and other actors define as acceptable (and unacceptable), how social movements frame their claims, and how they create collective identities. Della Porta and Diani argue that the construction of identity involves both negative and pos-itive identifications and should be understood in the light of not only pro-cesses of exclusion, but equally processes of active opposition. The reference given is to the "protagonists, antagonists and audiences" (Hunt et al. 1994: 186) and the role they play in identity formation. Melucci's contribution that is important to the field of collective identity formation—and for the purposes of this study—is his recognition of adversaries and their role in terms of collective identity.

This study's contribution to the theoretical field of collective identity formation in social movements lies in the development of three strategies among social movement actors in their collective identitymaking, perme-ated by emotional investments and reflexive discursive practices. The first strategy is the process of forming a collective identity based on *positive identi-fication*; the second is to form the collective identity based on *negative identi-*

fication by defining common enemies and internal others; and the third is to *recognize the sources of negative images,* the sources of power. It will be argued that, in the case of the first strategy, interactions with other social movement actors have a consolidating function (Melucci 1988, 1989, 1996; Flesher Fominaya 2010). The focus is shifted from an individual perspective to a collective perspective, and continued interactions result in emotional ties between the activists. The second strategy of defining "the ones we are not" involves both external and internal "others" from whom the activists distinguish themselves. As other scholars have pointed out, collective identity formation is a negotiation of boundaries not only between different groups but also within groups (Gamson 1997), and this negotiation can consist of different and even contradictory definitions (Melucci 1995). I argue in this chapter that the marginalizing discourses on tenants are reflected in this practice of distinguishing oneself from internal others. This categorization of internal others functions as a buffer, where all of the undesirable descriptions of one's own group can be distanced from the group's collective identity and self-presentation. The consolidation of the group is thus facilitated by the boundary-making practices and the creation of others. The third strategy in collective identity formation is to identify and reflect on the "opportunities and constraints" (Melucci 1988) that characterize activists' field of action. It functions as an identification of the sources of constraints for the collective identity formation of a social movement, and is marked by reflexive explanations among social movement actors on the functioning of these sources of power, a development of a sort of "oppositional consciousness" (Mansbridge 2001).

Collective identity formation is influenced by discourses, frames, and culture. However, it is when social movement actors invest their emotions and engage in reflection on/responding to these influences that collective identity takes form. The temporal character of identity formation, and also the nature of identity per se, are important to take into account in studies of such social phenomena. In the case of Polish tenants, their collective identity formation is strongly connected to the group's economic and social position in society; this is one of the starting points of this study.

Tenants in the Media

The Immoral Nature of Tenants

In the reports on tenants in *Gazeta Wyborcza* since 1989, one can observe one recurrent theme: most journalists questioned tenants' moral orientation, describing tenants as not fulfilling their obligations by not paying their rents. Especially in the early period of the transformation era the tenants were represented as the remnants of the former housing system and the focus was on the problematic situation of the tenants, whose housing was provided by the social housing system of state socialism (*lokatorzy z kwaterunku/decyzyjni*), that is, their dwellings were given to them in housing owned by private persons, but managed by the state or municipality. The authors of the articles condemned rent strikes as a form of protest, encouraging tenants to always pay the rent, regardless of increases, and proposing a solution to the increased rent of letting out some parts of their "relatively large" dwellings to students. The argument on the distribution to tenants of generous dwellings during state socialism has been a recurring theme since 1989. Tenants were here perceived as privileged by the former system, a privilege that was no longer reasonable in the new order.

In most articles tenants were described in relation to housing owners, whose property rights had been reduced due to the old system's redistribution and allocation of social housing in private property and the "impossibility" of eviction of such tenants "due to the limited possibilities of execution of such law" (Article from 5 February 1990).[4] The reports highlighted the perspective of owners and emphasized the importance of property rights in the new order. The following is a quotation from an article from 1990: "The project of housing law is abandoning the hitherto used system of administrative interference in the distribution of housing, rent regulation, and housing management. This system, still in operation, treads on property rights and destroys tenement-house-owners that rightfully consider it to be a Stalinist system" (6 December 1990). In the above quoted text the tenants were described as "poor," "pensioners," and "single persons," but also as "unpunishable," often "wild tenants" destroying the property of private owners. The perspectives of the owners and political representatives of the new system were presented more favorably by the journalists, while the representations of tenants as actors were usually accompanied by condemnation of their unwillingness to adapt to the new system (by not paying rents, thus not taking responsibility): "The Minister of Construction Andrzej Bratkowski concluded that the demands of the tenants' organizations are absurd, and he will therefore not comment on them. He only acknowledged that there might soon be a conference organized by those who do not wish to pay for anything" (18 August 1992). Most media reports presented both tenants' and housing owners' perspectives, but the result was often rather one-sided. The best illustration of the duality of the discourse of this period is the article "A Guide to Increased Rents" (7 October 2002), presenting the recent changes in rent regulation from the perspective of tenants and property owners, but covertly propagating the importance of property rights over tenants' rights. The article tries to convince tenants and owners of their common interests, encouraging tenants that "it is worthwhile to grit one's teeth and pay the highest rates" in order to allow for some renovation of the neglected housing stock. The focus was again not on the tenants' ability to afford higher rents, but on their (un)willingness to pay more. I suggest that the argument about tenants' willingness (to pay rent) was here closely connected to the perception of their (im)morality in the public discourse, as the argument about tenants' unwillingness to pay rent was repeated over and over again.

The pro–property rights argument was covertly embedded in the discourse on tenants and tenants' rights. The overall argument was that the owner "cannot be the tenant's hostage" (7 May 2003) or "the tenants' compulsory private social support" (9 January 2006). Owners were advised to be patient and split rent increases into installments, to justify their increases, to vary increases among the tenants according to their individual incomes, and to inform and help the poorest tenants to apply for housing allowances. The tenants, on the other hand, were advised not to treat the owner as an enemy and to understand that because he or she was entitled to increase rents, the best strategy is to negotiate. Tenants should "choose three well-articulated persons (not aggressive)" to negotiate with the owners, and to consider "gritting one's teeth and paying the highest rates in return for a renovation or thermo-isolation" (7 October 2002).

The depiction of tenants in opposition to the owners reverses the power relations that characterize their relationship in a capitalist society. The tenants were described as powerful enough to refuse to pay rent, move out of a property, or do damage to it. The owners, on the other hand, were depicted as powerless in these kinds of situations. The three forms of resistance among the tenants of not paying, not obeying owners' wishes, or causing damage to the property can be seen as the "weapons" used by the tenants (Scott 1985). However, the moral distinction between what is right to do and which actions are seen as despicable and unacceptable is unfavorable to the tenants in the discourse. These "weapons" are not recognized as means in a struggle, but as immoral behavior of an equal party.

Treating Tenants as Objects

In 2009, the topic of "container neighborhoods" (*osiedla kontenerowe*) was introduced into the discussion on tenants in the studied newspaper. Container neighborhoods, consisting of container modules serving as living spaces, were proposed and built in some Polish municipalities as a solution to the lack of social housing, and it was planned that "the most problematic" households would reside in these. The image of the tenants was even more negative during this period (in the wake of the global financial crisis of 2008), when the solutions for treating tenants were discussed. In an interview with the director of management of the municipal housing stock in Szczecin, the argument was presented in the following way:

> We need to move these people somewhere. We are not allowed to throw them out into the streets. Among these debtors, there are those in difficult situations not caused by their own faults—they have lost their jobs, somebody close to them has died, their child got sick. We offer them support, including financial support, from the Local Centre for Family Support; we offer to divide their debt into instalments or work within the "Work off the debt" programme. If somebody is a little interested, we help him. But there is a group that does not do anything. These people think that the municipality should give them food, housing and money for small expenses. They don't need work, because they don't want to work. They are not following any social norms. (20 August 2009)

The neighborhoods planned on the outskirts of the Polish cities and reserved for the "bad tenants" were defended with arguments such as the one above. The terms "degenerates" (*degeneraci*) (20 August 2009, 22 August 2009) and "pathology" (*patologia*) were used to describe the tenants who did not follow the established social norms of hard work and provide for themselves. Relocating them (like objects, reflected in the expressions of "move these people" or "throw them out" above) to container neighborhoods was seen in this line of reasoning as a punishment: "Barracks are something worse than an apartment—not yet the streets, but a level lower. They will not solve the problem, but they will teach people something" (20 August 2009). Nowhere in these articles were the reasons behind the inability to pay the rent examined in detail. The moving of tenants to the container neighborhoods became a solution to restore the order of power, where the owners and their right to manage their property is more justified than the right to inhabit.

Tenants as Sympathetic Victims

The rather recent media tendency to describe developing business in the sphere of reprivatization of the property nationalized during socialism was often exhibited in the articles on tenants. The notion of tenants as victims appeared with the realization that law firms, banks, and private persons were making great profits by buying claims to buildings and land in Polish cities and replacing them with new investments. The new owners were using brutal and illegal methods in order to get rid of the tenants in their properties, and by the end of the first decade of the 2000s the media started to cover such cases, presenting a sympathetic picture of the tenants as victims, while at the same time condemning the business-oriented owners:

Local authorities are giving back property taken by the state after the war, often after years of dramatic efforts. Justice is being done. Unfortunately for thousands of people it becomes a drama. Local authorities are not giving back empty tenement houses, but houses with tenants. Most often these people are not well off (municipal housing is intended for these). They lived for years with the feeling of security, they improved their living conditions. Overnight, they find out that the building is under private ownership. The rent is increased as nobody wants to add to the maintenance of the building. Those who did not previously have problems paying their rent end up in debt. They have court sentences imposed in connection with debts and evictions. They lose their dwellings and the ground under their feet. And therefore they end up on the streets. (2 October 2011)

The tenants were described as passive victims; however, they continued to be described as unwilling to pay for some expenses related to housing in these articles. In 2011 the murder of the founder of the Warsaw Tenants' Association, Jolanta Brzeska,[5] was widely covered in the media, and not least in *Gazeta Wyborcza*. According to the activists and some media Brzeska was burned to death most likely because of her involvement in the tenants' movement. This murder contributed to the unification of tenants' organizations across the capital city, as well as to solidarity actions all over the country. Brzeska became a symbol (martyr) for the tenants' movement, including in the media, and the source of the new slogan "You will not burn us all." The police investigation into the murder was often questioned in the articles, as the perpetrator had not been convicted as of fall 2016. Brzeska's death marked a change in the discourse about tenants. They were no longer portrayed as passive victims, but as active, sympathetic, and admirable for their dedication.

Strategies in Collective Identity Formation among Tenants

The respondents' self-descriptions in the interviews often reflected the negative images of tenants that have been identified in the analysis of newspaper articles. They all stressed negative stereotypes that they had to relate to in their identity formation. They referred to the dominant opinion while talking about these stereotypes of tenants:

And there is a dominant opinion about the people who have difficulties in paying their rents that they are not paying because they would rather spend their money on other things. Or because they are lazy and don't want to work. Indeed, the majority of these people, especially in Warsaw, work illegally, sometimes for very low wages, for instance in the security business for five złoty an hour. You cannot cover all expenses with that kind of money. ... There is an image created all the time that those who are evicted come from the social margins, that they have alcohol-related diseases, and as a result they are to blame for it, simply like that. It is difficult to fight for the rights of people with such an image. (1)[6]

Due to these negative views, various strategies were developed to counteract them. One of these concerns defining the boundaries of acceptable and unacceptable behavior. The definition of a tenant was based on the signifying difference between "us" and "them" (Hall 1997). The definition of "them" was different depending on the situation or context. The differences between various categories of "them" were used to define undesirable features and behaviors among tenants. There were, furthermore, two kinds of others identified: internal others and external others. Three interconnected strategies were developed in the collective identity formation of tenants' activists that will be described next: (1) defining who "we" are in positive terms, (2) defining the others by finding common enemies and internal others, and (3) reflecting on the sources of negative images. All three strategies are characterized by emotions and constant reflections on the collective actors themselves and other actors in their field of activity.

We, the Tenants

A process of collective identification based on positive qualities was described in the activists' stories of involvement in tenants' issues. Most express initial surprise at the similarities between the people involved in the movement and their "good qualities." The moment when the tenants realize they are not alone is described in the interviews as a moment of revelation; a revelation that after a while is transformed among tenants into a common ground to fight for. Once the negative associations are removed, the positive features are dominant in the formation of a collective identity of activists. The individual identity that is associated with negative features is in the meeting with others transformed to a collective one with positive associations. In the case of Polish tenants' activists, this might be due to the identification of positive features within the group, for instance their dedication, hard work, and enterprising qualities. In the interviews, face-to-face interactions are described as facilitating the process of collective identity formation: "When the first meeting was held between WSL [the Warsaw Tenants' Association] and KSS [the Social Justice Office], people met and realized how much we all are not a bad populace" (4). When the initial common ground is found, some emotional investments develop and transform into collective action (cf. Hunt and Benford 2004; Jasper 1997):

> And it happened that we joined the association and our anger in some way caused a closer contact between us. You might say that both my wife and me, we made

friends quickly. We did not only talk about tenants' issues but also about personal ones. It was strengthened by the fact that we lost a lot of friends at the same time, as we became monothematic. It was like talking to a fisherman: whatever you would discuss you would always end up discussing fish. The same happened to us. Whatever we would talk about, we would always end up discussing housing problems, and people whom we have known for years left us and started to avoid us. We are not surprised, because it is as if we mechanically always end up discussing tenants' topics. From one point of view it is a pity that it happened; from another, there is a good thing in all of this bad luck. We met a lot of nice people, with whom we made friends. (3)

In the quotations above and below, the respondents speak about the emotional investments made among the activists and about the replacement of feelings of anger and guilt with feelings of self-worth and empowerment and readiness to act together:

I think that the very fact that these individuals [tenants] come to meetings and meet other nice people, with the same kind of problems, makes it all better. They don't look down on them, they don't see them as worth any less, as is common in Poland, and they start to realize that they feel guilty unnecessarily. Because the majority feels guilty in this situation. I consider it as our [the tenants' organization's] success to have created an environment where people can feel good and do something. It happens often now that people say that they would like to be involved in some political activity. (1)

Interactions function here as affirmation of the collective identity and collective interests (Melucci 1988, 1989, 1996; Flesher Fominaya 2010). The emotional ties, personal connection, and face-to-face interaction enables the discharging of guilt and shame, and the negativity related to the situation of tenants and makes positive identifications possible (cf. Gould 2009). The emotions of guilt and shame have proven to be more powerful than those of anger in earlier research. The result is that some of the old identities and relations lose their importance, while new ones are formed and strengthened when the new collective identity is constructed. Interactions with others in a similar situation enable a shift from the individual focus to the focus on collective interests and the formation of a collective identity (Melucci 1996).

Furthermore, instead of using the label "poor" and the countless associations it brings with it, many of the tenants' activists used arguments referring to tenants as "people disadvantaged by the system." The label of "poor" was simply associated with individual characteristics (Tarkowska 2009) and above all the "inability to adapt to the new situation" (Stenning 2005: 989) of capitalist order. Or, as formulated by one of the interviewees: "'How are you?' 'Not bad,' said the patient and died. Because if being poor is culpable, then people do not want to plead guilty. Why? Because a culpable act is followed by punishment" (2). Recently, the collective identity of tenants has been further strengthened by the creation of a common symbol and martyr within the movement, Jolanta Brzeska. Tenants interpreted Brzeska's murder as a part of the tenants' resistance against greater powers and interests, such as the interests of the municipality, the interests of real estate owners, the interests of entrepreneurs active in the field of housing, the interests of large corporations, and the interests of the elite. Brzeska reflects all of the positive qualities and attributes that the tenants strive for in their collective identification: she was a tenant in reprivatized housing, she was active, and did not give up despite harassment from the new owner; she was sixty-four years old at the time of her death and despite limited economic resources (she was a pensioner) she acquired legal knowledge that enabled her to help others in similar situations. She has become the ideal that tenants' activists pursue in their collective identity formation, an empowering image, clearly demarcating the ideal category of "who to be," from the category of others, the ones "who to oppose."

Defining the Other

Antagonizing views, or creating *internal others*, could be observed as a common reaction among the activists. Polish anthropologist Buchowski argues that groups stigmatized by dominant discourses tend to "employ the same language in their description used by the others for the description of others" (2006: 474). It is, according to him, a tool of identity reconstruction by those who lack power to influence the dominant image. There were two groups of internal others in particular to be distinguished in the identity formation of tenants' activists. Tenants' activists' distinction covered those who were (1) *dependent on the support of others*, often described as helpless, and (2) *the scammers*, who were driven, but still drawing some specific personal gain from their activity or position as tenants. In distancing themselves from these two types, many of the interviewees stressed their own resourcefulness, their hard work, and their enterprising qualities when describing their involvement in tenants' issues.

Gamson (1997) argues that collective identity formation is a negotiation of boundaries not only between different groups but also within groups. In the "boundary work" of tenants there was a distinction between the "good" and the "bad" activists. Undesirable categories of tenants were created; the first was passive tenants who experienced difficulties in getting by. In the words of one of the founders of a tenants' association on the deciding motives for the foundation of the association: "At some point in time we, together with my colleague, came to the conclusion that 'Listen, there are two of us that are active, that can do things'. And we said to each other: 'We can manage, but these people that come along on every manifestation, we collect their contacts, we text them, they cannot manage by themselves. Let's do some emergency counselling'" (6). A picture of passive and helpless tenants was drawn by some activists in the interviews, and in particular in the quotation above, where the helpless tenants cannot manage without the help of the more active ones.

The other type, that of a driven tenant who wants to profit from the system, was also repeatedly mentioned by the interviewees. A clear boundary was drawn against actions that would be of interest to the activist only; the ideal was that activism had a selfless motivation. Many of the interviewees expressed frustration with the distrust and misunderstanding of their unselfish intentions from others. A common stereotype among the wider public was that tenants were "scammers, pretending to do social work, but are there to gain something" (4). Tenants' activists were aware of this stereotype and frequently gave examples of their dedication to the cause by telling stories about situations where they were offered appealing bribes and rejected them, in this way transforming the stereotypes of egoistical scammers into honest and uncorrupted actors. The negotiation and legitimation of "pure" intentions among tenants' activists are interpreted here as a process of negotiation inherent in collective identity. Melucci (1996) stresses the contradictions and differences when negotiating collective identity and the questioning of intentions behind tenants' activists' involvement functions as a process of negotiation in which qualities and attributes are to be seen as collective values.

Moreover, the vast majority of the interviewees described some categories of tenants as the ones they do not identify with, cooperate with, or help. There were internal rules among the activists concerning the kinds of tenants that should be helped or cooperated with, including the two kinds of "internal others" described above. The rules covered tenants that (1) "in an obvious way brought the situation upon themselves" (6), i.e., tenants who—due to arrogance or reluctance—will not pay the rent when they can afford it, (2) tenants not behaving according to some social norms—i.e., perpetrators of domestic violence or troublemakers, (3) real estate owners or owners of apartments, and (4) criminals. Nevertheless, people with alcohol problems were included in the category of tenants who would obtain help from the activists, even if that help would probably be given on some specific conditions requiring the tenants to show their dedication to the cause. This list of "undesirable" categories of tenants sums up the negative images of tenants in the media discourse (in particular, the image of immoral tenants who do not follow social norms) and the necessary boundaries that tenants' activists draw in their identity as a collective in order to legitimize their existence and claims. The boundaries drawn by tenants' activists serve the purpose of showing the wider public, as well as tenants, that the category of "bad" tenants has been excluded from the collective identity of the group.

Another important strategy in the collective identity formation of tenant activists has been to create common "enemies," the *external others*, and in that way generate unity and solidarity within the group (Melucci 1995, 1996). The main groups include politicians, real estate owners, civil servants, and representatives of the justice system, who are all described by tenants' activists with a list of undesirable, repulsive, and immoral attributes and behaviors. This process functions similarly to the boundary-drawing process of creating internal others described above, but differs in that the line is drawn *between* their own group and some other strategically chosen groups, not *within* the group. Social movement scholars emphasize not only the role of identifying adversaries, by forming exclusive identities, but also the importance of actively opposing them (Della Porta and Diani 1999: 94). In order to understand the basis of the collective identity of tenants, it is important to examine this list of undesirable attributes and behaviors. What are the tenants distancing themselves from in their collective identity formation? Which social groups are excluded? Which attributes and behaviors are regarded as unacceptable?

Politicians were seen by the tenants' activists as immoral and corrupt. So were civil servants, and both groups were referred to equally in the interviews. Sometimes it was even unclear if there were any differences between these groups, as they were associated in their corrupt behavior and referred to in the interviews as the "power-holders" (*władze*). Politicians were described by the activists as representatives of the system. They were seen as corrupt and as serving their own selfish interests. Sometimes they were described as "elites" and most often as a group of people closely connected to each other, and even more disconnected from the problems of the majority of the population. Politicians' behavior was explained by the tenants' activists as a result of the instability of the political system, where those in power had only a limited period of time to take advantage of the privileged position they held. At the same time, the identity of tenants was in that way opposed to the egoistic intentions and corrupt behaviour of politicians. It gave the tenants' collective identity a sense of genuineness and continuity, and most importantly, a feeling of belonging.

Civil servants were described as "uncivil" and "not serving the people" or not fulfilling their obligations as civil servants. Their attitude toward tenants was frequently questioned in the interviews. They were described as disrespectful, haughty, cynical, and disagreeable: "They completely don't give a damn. They despise these people [tenants]. They consider them to be worthless. Can they really realize their legal obligations to satisfy these people's housing needs? How can they do that if they consider these people to be worthless?" (1). The justice system was described as serving the interests of the elite. Courts of law were described as biased, and particular judges as corrupt or incompetent in the field of legal regulations. Examples were often given of particular court cases where regulations and existing laws were not fully followed, or where special interests were favored above the interests of tenants. Tenement house owners or real estate owners were also used in the interviews to demarcate the line between tenants and other groups. This group was frequently mentioned when describing the initial motives for joining the movement. The following quotation sheds light on how the activity of the claimspurchaser(s) motivates collective identity formation (in relation to a common enemy) and triggers tenants' activism:

> We can say that a group of people crystallized among those who had been disadvantaged by that man. It turned out that this man claimed 30 properties, but the number quickly doubled and we talk about a much larger number today. You can see that he is starting to act resiliently in Praga; he was earlier active on the left side of Warsaw. And this group started to support each other as a consequence. We supported each other by attending each other's court cases, and we started to share observations about the activity, so that others will not make the same mistakes, to fight with XX more efficiently. (3)

The identification of internal others and common enemies is one of the most salient strategies in tenants' activists collective identity formation. By identifying enemies, the activists strengthen the solidarity within the group (Melucci 1995; Della Porta and Diani 1999). By questioning and negotiating intentions behind actions, they define the boundaries of immoral behavior that function as shared values and as a base for solidarity. Risks and uncertainties of collective action are consequently perceived as less important when solidarity and collective identity are consolidated (Della Porta and Diani 1999: 94).

Identifying the Sources of Negative Depictions

The third strategy in response to the negative dominant perceptions of tenants was to identify the sources of such perceptions and the people behind them. This third strategy corresponds with activists' process of identifying the power structure in a society, a process that aims to make "visible the operation of power at multifarious levels and produces an awareness of the way power can traverse, produce and construct collective action" (Chesters and Welsh 2011: 51). It also makes it possible to reverse negative images of the tenants from outside the group (cf. Berbrier 1998). The media, politicians, and scientists were frequently mentioned in the interviews as those responsible for the negative image of tenants. The media's representations were described as biased and strictly following the logic of argument, where success depends on making the right choices and hard work. "People here work the longest hours in Europe. It was communicated in the newspaper 'Wprost' that we [the Poles] are workaholics. Do you get it? Or that we prefer to spend vacations in the country. We prefer, we choose, it is all our decision. The fact that we are starving to death is also a matter of choice as a consumer. To eat or to die. And everybody can live under a bridge. Everybody can choose. There is a freedom of choice" (2). While neoliberal logic and narrowness of media representations (reflected in the "elitist" interests of media) were criticized, most of the tenants' activists also reflected on the conditions under which these representations are produced. The activists shared an understanding of the working conditions of journalists, the lack of identification among journalists with the tenants' issues, the pressure on the media to attract readers/viewers, and the "politics" steering the representations.

Nevertheless, once the focus in tenants' descriptions was shifted from individuals and their achievements to the collective interests, more systemic criticism was put forward. The Polish housing system, labor conditions, and welfare system were condemned, along with housing and spatial planning policies. Structural explanations were used to explain the situation of tenants in the country. The use of systemic explanations for the situation of social groups has been observed in other studies of social movements (Della Porta and Diani 1999; Chesters and Welsh 2011). By identifying the sources of negative images, the activists made the production and reproduction of power visible, making it possible for individuals to be exonerated from blame.

Conclusions

The discourse on tenants in the studied newspaper has changed slightly since 1989 and in particular since reports were published on the harassments of tenants in reprivatized stock and the death of the founder of the Warsaw's Tenants' Association in the later part of the first decade of the 2000s. However, the most characteristic feature has remained until today and it is the dehumanizing view, portraying tenants as immoral, victims, and objects that need to be dealt with. Tenants' moral basis has been frequently questioned, and their unwillingness to pay the rent was the focus of most media reports and used as an argument for not considering tenants as well-intentioned and moral human beings. The affordability of rents or explanations of tenants' inability to pay were left aside when the unwillingness to pay the rent was discussed. Moreover, the tenants were persistently portrayed in relation to the past and the past housing system that was partly inherited by the new system (for instance, the system for social housing allocation). It was clearly pointed out in the studied articles on tenants that expectations for housing to be provided by the state or the municipal authorities are outdated and belong to the past. Tenants were perceived in this line of argument as remnants of the old system, limiting the full development of the new system.

The negative and stereotypical depictions of tenants are reflected in tenants' activists' boundary-making practices and the categorization of internal others. The collective identitymaking was in this way centered first and foremost on drawing the boundaries against some specific categories and defining unacceptable behavior and characteristics to be able to define and fill the category of "us" with positive meaning. Those that the tenants' activists distanced themselves from were both internal others and external. The internal category encompassed tenants that did not have altruistic intentions and showed passivity and helplessness. To draw the line between tenants and tenants was necessary in order to strengthen and empower the identity of tenants' activists, as tenants' activists all were tenants, but all tenants were not activists. These internal categories clearly reflect the media discourse on tenants in Poland, in which tenants are depicted as either passive or acting selfishly and immorally (by not paying the rents, living in large apartments, destroying others' property, etc.). The external other, the power holders, were accused of similar immoral characteristics and functioned as a boundary in collective identitymaking against corrupt and elitist behavior.

The collective identity formation was described initially as a revelatory process, in which the positive characteristics are discovered one by one, together with other tenants. The interaction and getting to know others in the same situation opened up the opportunity for emotional investments on the part of tenants' activists and the formation of lifelong friendships. Furthermore, this process was permeated with emotional descriptions of reversing negative feelings of anger and guilt into feelings of empowerment and self-worth. Reflexivity was a significant part of the collective identity formation as tenants frequently reflected on themselves and on others' perceptions of tenants; it was also part of their understanding of other collective actors' behaviors and activity and the conditions behind them.

Buchowski (2006) accurately describes the situation in Poland by arguing that "the new others" of transition are the poor, the workers, the unemployed, and the peasants. He refers to the dominant discourses in the country in the mass media and in academia, arguing that poor and powerless groups are blamed for their situation using arguments about their "subaltern nature," their ignorance, and their incivility. These marginalized groups lack influence in public discourse, writes Buchowski, and are therefore objectified in the Polish context. Other researchers confirm this depiction in their observations of economically weak groups and their treatment in Polish public discourse as "post-communist leftovers" that are useless to society (Hryciuk and Korolczuk 2013). To study how public and academic discourses delegitimize the activism of poor and powerless groups and at the same time how these groups mobilize and legitimize their claims is important in the broader understanding of civil society and how it functions. The case of Polish tenants' activism demonstrates the political and ideological consequences of a narrow understanding of civil society, excluding specific forms of activism from the definition of "legitimate" civic activism. I argue that even if this kind of activism is defined-out from the common understating of what civil society is (see also Jezierska in this volume), it is an important form of activism that empowers less privileged groups to rise up for change.

The ambition of this chapter has been to broaden the understanding of civil society and civic activism in a setting that is often described as following a specific logic in the sphere of collective and collaborative activity. In light of this, the Polish tenants' movement challenges the assumption that civil society activism in the postsocialist setting is created from abroad, and above, dependent on financial support (Mendelson and Glenn 2002) and/or permeated by the socialist past at the low level of interpersonal and interorganizational trust (Gliński 2004; Sztompka 2004) and in Poles' unwillingness to participate in the political sphere. The social and economic position of tenants in Poland should furthermore obstruct their collective action and creation of collective claims and identity. These obstacles, although important, can be effectively challenged due to emotional and reflexive boundary work, providing the tenants with a sense of self-worth and empowerment. I show in this study that the objectification, victimization, and moralization of tenants in the discourse are reflected in the strategies of exclusion and inclusion of specific features and qualities in their collective identitymaking. As a final point, the additional intention of this study has been to give a voice to tenants' activists representing a vulnerable and stigmatized group, in order to provide counter-narratives to the dominant discourses.

Dominika V. Polanska holds a Ph.D. in Sociology and is currently a research fellow at the Institute for Housing and Urban Research at Uppsala University. Her research interests encompass social movements related to the issues of housing and noninstitutionalized forms of organization. She has published in the journals: *City*; *Interface*; *Geojournal*; *Human Geographiy* and *Space and Culture* and co-edited a special issue "Squatting in the East: Exploring Overlooked Contexts" in the journal *Baltic Worlds*.

Notes

1. Polskie Towarzystwo Mieszkaniowe (Polish Housing Society) 1989; Krajowy Ruch Mieszkaniowy (National Housing Movement) 1991; Polska Unia Lokatorów (Polish Union of Tenants) 1994; Ogólnopolski Ruch Ochrony Interesów Lokatorów (National Movement for the Protection of Tenants' Interests) 1995; Krajowy Związek Lokatorów i Spółdzielców (National Association of Tenants and Residents in Cooperatives) 1997.
2. The municipal stock is not entirely representative of the number of rental dwellings in the country, as there are also rental dwellings within the cooperative stock (about 5.8 percent of the total stock consisting of dwellings for rent), social housing (TBS) (0.6 percent of the total stock), company-owned dwellings for rent (unknown number), and privately rented dwellings (unknown number) (Polish Statistical Office 2014).
3. Discourse is defined here as the way a certain issue is represented or communicated (in written and spoken language). The concept is further elaborated on in the theoretical section.
4. From here on, the articles analyzed in the study will be cited by parentheticals containing their date of publication.
5. Brzeska was burned to death and her body found in the Kabaty forest on the outskirts of Warsaw. She was at that time involved in a legal process with the owner of the building she was living in. The conditions of Brzeska's murder are still unclear, and the perpetrator has not been identified. The investigation was dropped in April 2013, despite the expert report that excluded the possibility of suicide in this case.
6. A numbering system from 1 to 20 is used when interviews are cited.

References

Audycka-Zandberg, B. 2014. *Warunki i strategie mobilizacji najemców lokali mieszkalnych w stowarzyszeniach lokatorskich* [Conditions and Strategies for Mobilization among Renters in Tenants'Associations]. Warszawa: Uniwersytet Warszawski.

Berbrier, M. 1998. "'Half the Battle': Cultural Resonance, Framing Processes, and Ethnic Affectations in Contemporary White Separatist Rhetoric." *Social Problems* 45: 431–450.

Buchowski, M. 2006. "Social Thought and Commentary: The Specter of Orientalism in Europe: From Exotic Other to Stigmatized Brother." *Anthropological Quarterly* 79, no. 3: 463–482.

Castells, M. 1997. *The Power of Identity.* Massachusetts: Blackwell.

Chesters, G., and I. Welsh. 2011. *Social Movements: The Key Concepts.* London/New York: Routledge.

Cisar, O. 2013. "Post-Communism and Social Movements," in *Encyclopedia of Social and Political Movements,* ed. D. Snow, D. della Porta, B. Klandermans, and D. McAdam. London: Blackwell, 994–999.

Della Porta, D., and M. Diani. 1999. *Social Movements: An Introduction.* Malden: Blackwell Publishing.

Dowse, L. 2001. "Contesting Practices, Challenging Codes: Self Advocacy, Disability Politics and the Social Model." *Disability and Society* 16, no. 1: 123–141.

Fairclough, N. 1992. *Discourse and Social Change.* Cambridge: Polity Press.

———. 1995. *Media Discourse.* London: Edward Arnold.

Fine, G.A. 1995. "Public Narration and Group Culture: Discerning Discourse in Social Movements," in *Social Movements and Culture,* ed. H. Johnston and B. Klandermans. Minnesota: University of Minnesota Press, 127–143.

Flesher Fominaya, C. 2010. "Collective Identity in Social Movements: Concepts and Debates." *Sociology Compass* 4, no. 6: 393–404.

Foucault, M. 1977. *Discipline and Punishment.* New York: Pantheon.

Gamson, J. 1997. "Messages of Exclusion: Gender, Movements, and Symbolic Boundaries." *Gender and Society* 11, no. 2: 178–199.

Gliński, P. 2004. "How Active are the Social Actors?" *Polish Sociological Review* 4, no. 148: 429–450.

Gould, D. 2009. *Moving Politics: Emotion and Act Up's Fight against AIDS.* Chicago: The University of Chicago Press.

Hall, S., ed. 1997. *Representation: Cultural Representations and Signifying Practices.* London: Sage Publications.

Hryciuk, R.E., and E. Korolczuk. 2013. "At the Intersection of Gender and Class: Social Mobilization Around Mothers' Rights in Poland," in *Beyond NGO-ization? The Development of Social Movements in Central and Eastern Europe,* ed. K. Jacobsson and S. Saxonberg. Farnham: Ashgate, 49–70.

Hunt, S., R. Benford, and D. Snow. 1994. "Identity Fields: Framing Processes and The Social Construction of Movement Identities," in *New Social Movements: From Ideology to Identity,* ed. E. Larana, H. Johnston, and J.R. Gusfield. Philadelphia, PA: Temple University Press, 185–208.

Hunt, S., and R. Benford. 2004. "Collective Identity, Solidarity, and Commitment," in *The Blackwell Companion to Social Movements,* ed. D. Snow, S. Soule, and H. Kriesi. Oxford, U.K.: Blackwell, 461–488.

Jasper, J. 1997. *The Art of Moral Protest.* Chicago: University of Chicago Press.

———. 2011. "Emotions and Social Movements: Twenty Years of Theory and Research." *Annual Review of Sociology* 37: 285–303.

Kaplan, H.B., and X. Liu. 2000. "Social Movements as Collective Coping with Spoiled Personal Identities: Intimations from a Panel Study of Changes in the Life Course between Adolescence and Adulthood," in *Self, Identity, and Social Movements,* ed. S. Stryker, T.J. Owens, and R.W. White. University of Minnesota Press, 215–238.

Mansbridge, J.J. 2001. "The Making of Oppositional Consciousness," in *Oppositional Consciousness: The Subjective Roots of Social Protest,* ed. J.J. Mansbridge and M. Aldon. Chicago: The University of Chicago Press, 20–37.

Melucci, A. 1988. "Getting Involved: Identity and Mobilization in Social Movements." *International Social Movement Research* 1: 329–348.

———. 1989. *Nomads of the Present.* London: Hutchinson Radius.

———. 1995. "The Process of Collective Identity," in *Social Movements and Culture,* ed. H. Johnston and B. Klandermans. Minneapolis: University of Minnesota Press, 41–63.

———. 1996. *Challenging Codes: Collective Action in The Information Age.* New York: Cambridge University Press.

Mendelson, S., and J.E. Glenn, eds. 2002. *The Power and Limits of NGOs.* New York: Columbia University Press.

Petrova, T., and S. Tarrow. 2007. *Transactional and Participatory Activism in the Emerging European Polity: The Puzzle of East-Central Europe.* Ithaca, NY: Cornell University.

Pickvance, C. 2001. "Inaction, Individual Action and Collective Action Responses to Housing Dissatisfaction: A Comparative Study of Budapest and Moscow." *Political Opportunities, Social Movements and Democratization* 23: 179–206.

Polanska, D.V. 2014. "Cognitive Dimension in Cross-movement Alliances: The Case of Squatting and Tenants' Movements in Warsaw." *Interface: A Journal for and about Social Movements* 6, no. 2: 328–356.

Polish Statistical Office. 2014. *Gospodarka mieszkaniowa i komunalna. Zasoby mieszkaniowe wg form własności* [Housing and Municipal Economy: Housing Stock According to Ownership Status]. Retrieved 17 June 2014 from www.stat.gov.pl.

Scott, J. 1985. *Weapons of the Weak: Everyday Forms of Peasant Resistance.* New Haven/London: Yale University Press.

Stenning, A. 2005. "Where is the Post-socialist Working Class? Working-Class Lives in the Spaces of (Post)socialism." *Sociology* 39, no. 5: 983–999.

Sztompka, P. 2004. "The Trauma of Social Change: A Case of Postcommunist Societies," in *Cultural Trauma and Collective Identity,* ed. C.J. Alexander. Berkeley: University of California Press, 155–195.

Tarkowska, E. 2009. "Oblicza Polskiej Biedy" [Forms of Polish Poverty].*Więź* 4, no. 606: 90–100.

Taylor, V. 2000. "Emotions and Identity in Women's Self-Help Movements,"in *Self, Identity, and Social Movement,* ed. S. Stryker, T.J. Owens, and R.W. White. Minneapolis: University of Minnesota Press, 271–299.

Urbański J. 2010. "Polityka wysiedleń po polsku" [The Politics of Evictions in Poland]. *Le Monde Diplomatique* 11/57. Retrieved 17 June 2014 from http://monde-diplomatique.pl/LMD57/index.php?id=1_3.

Van Dyke, N., and R. Cress. 2006. "Political Opportunities and Collective Identity in Ohio's Gay and Lesbian Movement, 1970 to 2000." *Sociological Perspectives* 49, no. 4: 503–526.

Vihavainen, R. 2009. *Homeowners' Associations in Russia after the 2005 Housing Reform.* Helsinki: Kikimora Publications Series.

Chapter 8

VOICE AND INSECURITY
POLITICAL PARTICIPATION AMONG MEMBERS
OF THE PRECARIAT

Anna Kiersztyn

Introduction

The aim of this chapter is to assess the possible impact of precarious employment on civic and political participation among Polish workers. Equality in civic and political participation has long been viewed as one of the cornerstones of civil society and well-functioning democracy. Unequal participation further increases the gap between different social strata, through an under-representation of the problems and needs of the lower-status groups in the public debate and on the political agenda (Marien et al. 2010; Skocpol 2004; Verba 2004). It also precludes the development of social networks that cut across socioeconomic divisions, the crucial building blocks of the "good" civil society (Putnam 2000; Chambers and Kopstein 2001). The problem of the social and political alienation of lower-class citizens is becoming even more important today, due to the increase in various aspects of socioeconomic inequality in many developed countries, including Poland.

Since the early 1970s, there have been many studies consistently pointing to the existence of a participation gap associated with socioeconomic status, age, and gender. Wealthier, better educated people, males, and older generations have been shown to be more politically active (see e.g., Schlozman et al. 2010). More recent research based on data for EU countries found similar relationships (Gallego 2008). Explanations of this gap point to the unequal distribution of resources facilitating participation: knowledge and specific competencies, time and money (Sandovici and Davis 2010; Stolle and Hooghe 2011). These inequalities were to some extent mitigated by the presence of various mobilizing institutions, such as the church, trade unions, and political parties, enabling individuals from lower socioeconomic strata to undertake political activity by providing access to group resources and networks. During recent decades, however, the weakening of these institutions led to a further widening of the participation gap (Acik 2013; Kittilson 2005; Skocpol 2004).

Today, the issue of inequalities in participation is linked to a wider debate, concerning the general changes in the level and forms of civic and political activism in developed countries. Many studies point to declining rates of participation in conventional political activities, ranging from voting, to party membership, to contacting politicians, to attending group meetings (Putnam 2000; see Stolle and Hooghe 2005, for other references). Such data are the basis of well-known claims that citizens, especially the younger generation, are becoming more and more alienated from civic and political life, and social capital is in decline (Putnam 2000). Many scholars, however, reject such pessimistic views, arguing that the indicators of traditional, institutionalized political and civic participation do not take into account the more individualized and informal activities, which are practiced outside of the institutionalized political realm, and which have proliferated in many developed countries during recent decades, replacing the conventional forms of participation (Dalton 2000; Stolle and Hooghe 2005). These so-called emerging forms of civic engagement include internet campaigns and online petition signing, participation in ad hoc demonstrations or protests, as well as choosing to buy or boycott certain products or brands based on political or ethical considerations, a phenomenon referred to as political consumerism (Stolle and Hooghe 2011; Stolle and Micheletti 2013). Such noninstitutionalized forms of participation expand the repertoire of actions available to those who wish to express their views on public issues or influence the democratic process (Dalton 2000). These activities are sometimes also regarded as "a weapon of the weak," offering new opportunities for action to various groups of outsiders, who do not have the means or motivation for conventional participation, who feel distrustful of traditional politics and alienated from the political system (Gaventa 2002; Li and Marsh 2008). Such arguments imply that the difference between people of differing socioeconomic status lies not so much in their general propensity for participation, but rather in their preferred forms of civic or political activism.

Across Europe, insecurity in the labor market has become an important line of social stratification (Standing 2011). This is associated with the growth in the incidence of various nonstandard forms of employment during recent decades, including work on the basis of fixed-term contracts or civil law agreements, or for temporary help agencies. The move toward employment flexibility and corporate downsizing has raised concerns regarding the sustainability of stable, long-term employment relations (Beck 2002; Kalleberg 2009). Lifelong employment is thought by many to be "a thing of the past" (Neumark 2000), replaced by a new, more precarious type of career: movement from one short-term job to another. In addition, there are many studies showing that nonstandard employment is linked to inferior working conditions: lower wages, worse access to employee benefits, fewer training opportunities, and shorter career ladders (Arulampalam and Booth 1998; McGovern et al. 2004; OECD 2014). Given such findings, the impact of changes in the employment relationship may result not in a general decline in job security, but rather foster a two-tier labor market, in which a large group of outsiders remain trapped in precarious, low-quality jobs or cycle between temporary work and spells of unemployment (European Commission 2006; Polavieja 2003). This dimension of social inequality and its possible influence on the civic and political participation of individuals are particularly relevant in Poland, where in the past few years the rate of temporary employment has been around 27 percent—almost twice the EU average (EUROSTAT 2013).

Since nonstandard employees are not a homogenous group and differ by socioeconomic status, the theoretical and empirical analysis presented in this chapter takes into account conditional relationships, assuming that different effects are possible for different categories of workers. Further, it is possible that the difference between the economically insecure and those holding more stable employment lies not so much in their general propensity for participation, but rather in the preferred forms of civic activism: conventional or emerging. Are the latter forms likely to become a weapon for those who suffer from precarious labor market conditions? This question is of particular importance given the allegedly low levels of civic participation in Polish society, observed in quantitative studies over many years (recent examples are offered by Czapiński 2013 and Sułek 2013).

The chapter is structured as follows: the next section reviews the literature on the relationship between precarious employment and civic/political involvement and develops the research hypotheses. Thereafter the data and measures used in the present study are introduced, followed by a presentation of the results, and finally a conclusion.

Voice and Insecurity: A Literature Review

From the point of view of the existing research on participation inequalities in general, it seems reasonable to assume that labor market precarity is likely to have a negative effect on the level of civic and political involvement. The lack of access to stable employment may be regarded simply as another dimension of economic hardship experienced by individuals, limiting their access to the resources necessary for active participation. However, the literature focusing directly on the socioeconomic consequences of the raise in nonstandard employment offers a more complex picture of the possible mechanisms by which labor market insecurity may affect civic and political activism.

The most common claim is that labor market precarity generally weakens attachment to society and lowers the chances of participation. In current policy debates, unstable employment is regarded, along with unemployment, as one of the important aspects and determinants of social exclusion, understood as a multidimensional process involving gradual withdrawal from community life (Atkinson 1998; Mayes 2001). This withdrawal may be related to the negative psychological consequences of prolonged economic insecurity. Numerous studies found that underemployment and inability to plan for the future has a number of adverse effects on individual well-being, causing, for example, depression and health problems (Dooley et al. 2000; Virtanen et al. 2005). Sennett (1998) argues that pervasive labor market precarity and the accompanying ideology of "no long term" undermines interpersonal trust and fosters feelings of needlessness, meaninglessness, and apathy (a process he terms "corrosion of character"), which in turn weakens social bonds. Summing up, the first hypothesis assumes that employment precarity results in a withdrawal from social and civic life, as individuals devote most of their time and energy toward making a living and experience feelings of alienation, disillusionment, and loss of trust in the system. I call this the withdrawal hypothesis.

Conversely, some point to signs of civic and political mobilization among the economically insecure members of the so-called precariat (Standing 2011). Although they are distrustful toward conventional politics, as their problems and interests are not articulated by any mainstream political party, they undertake collective action to express their discontent and common sense of insecurity, as exemplified by the EuroMayDay parades or Indignants movement. Participants in these movements represent many diverse categories of the population and have not developed a coherent political agenda, yet many of them seek to address their problems by self-organizing and gaining voice. Far from being unembedded, they build active social networks via the Internet. This notion is well illustrated by the following quote from a recently published book: "from having an individualist, consumerist and indifferent attitude, from the search for individual solutions that led them to reject politics ..., young Portuguese people, similar to the Spanish, English, French, Greek, Americans and even those who organized the Arab Spring, are showing signs of wanting to have a voice and to return to assert a collective will. To shout out their protests and return to politics" (Estanque and Costa 2012: 277). This is the mobilization hypothesis. It should be noted, however, that the political mobilization of the precariat is based on the emerging, noninstitutionalized forms of participation, which resonates well with the literature treating such activities as "a weapon of the weak."

Another hypothesis that has appeared in the literature points to the civic potential that may be associated with more flexible employment relations. It is argued that precarious employment need not only be a negative experience, but may also open up new possibilities for workers to enhance their personal and professional development, and to achieve a better work-life balance (e.g., Gracia et al. 2011). Some authors note that in reality, the precariat does not seek to return to the predictable world of Fordism, in which people remained tied to one job for their whole working lives (Sennett 1998; Standing 2011). According to critics of the Fordist system, though lifelong routine full-time jobs may have ensured security, they also left little room for the exercise of freedom or meaningful political and civic participation (Arendt 1958). Today's workers in short-term jobs, though suffering from a higher exposure to economic risk, may focus on other aspects of life than only work. According to this hypothesis—which I call the work-life balance hypothesis—in the long run, precarious employment may foster political participation. This reasoning, however, may apply primarily to a relatively limited group of temporary workers in high-status, professional occupations, who are more likely to enter such employment relationships by their own choice, and not by economic necessity (Kiersztyn 2016a).

Notwithstanding the abovementioned specific examples of political mobilization on the part of young members of the precariat, there have been few systematic studies attempting to directly link employment insecurity to civic participation. So far, the results suggest that cases of political activism such as EuroMayDay or the Indignants movement should be treated as an exception rather than the rule. Even in the early 1960s, Wilensky observed that orderly careers, characterized by employment security and following a predictable path of occupational development, are associated with higher organizational membership and activity, along with stronger ties to the local community (Wilensky 1961). According to a multicountry study of 2004 European Social Survey data, working with a temporary contract significantly lowered the chances of voting, and had no effect on the chances of attending a demonstration or political consumerism, although it also appears to have increased the likelihood of working with political parties or action groups (Gallego 2008).

With respect to the emerging forms of participation and political consumerism, there are practically no studies, apart from the one by Gallego (2008), dealing directly with the ways in which employment precarity may affect the chances of engaging in such activities. There is, however, a debate on whether the availability of new forms of political expression indeed narrows the participation gap, or, on the contrary, reproduces or even reinforces inequalities with respect to gender, age, education, and social class. The recent research on socioeconomic correlates of petition signing, political consumerism, and protest activities offer an important insight for the current analysis. These studies have consistently found that the noninstitutionalized forms of activism are more willingly practiced by women and younger people. However, the participatory inequalities persist with respect to education, strongly suggesting that the emerging forms of participation are not as easily accessible as some theorists had presumed (Acik 2013; Marien et al. 2010; Sandovici and Davis 2010; Stolle and Hooghe 2011). Indeed, it has been pointed out that the individualized political activities characteristic of the "new civic culture" (Beck 2002) may require greater personal initiative and a higher level of cognitive skills, making participation even more dependent on social status (Dalton 2000; Skocpol 2004). These findings suggest that the relationship between employment precarity and participation may be a conditional one: among the less educated temporary workers, the withdrawal scenario is likely to prevail, whereas for those with higher education precarity may result in mobilization, though perhaps not of the conventional kind—in accordance with the work-life balance hypothesis. In other words, different hypotheses may be true for differing categories of precarious workers.

Data and Variables

This study is based on quantitative data from two sources: the first six rounds of the Polish edition of the European Social Survey, conducted once every two years since 2002, and the most recent wave of the Polish Panel Survey, POLPAN 2013.[1] Both datasets contain items referring to political participation, as well as variables allowing the measurement of nonstandard employment. The main rationale for using the ESS is the large sample, which can be obtained through pooling the data gathered throughout the whole ten-year period from 2002 to 2012. Large sample sizes are important given the complexity of the studied relationship, as they enable an in-depth study of conditional relationships and interactions between variables. Another important point about the ESS is that the survey item on political participation includes an extensive list of particular actions, allowing for a relatively clear distinction between the traditional, institutionalized forms of participation and the emerging, noninstitutionalized forms. Such distinctions have already been studied using the ESS (Acik 2013; Gallego 2008; Stolle and Hooghe 2011).

POLPAN offers a smaller sample, but a much more accurate measurement of employment precarity, not only at a given point in time, but throughout the entire career of each respondent, either employee or self-employed. In addition, the question on political participation is very different from the one used in the ESS: it contains fewer detailed items, but is partly open-ended. As such, it allows for the capture of any additional forms of participation not covered by the ESS items that the respondents themselves may regard as important. It also asks directly about civic involvement at the local level, as opposed to the ESS question, which explicitly refers to activities intended to affect the situation of the whole country, leaving local matters aside.

The analyses are done on subsamples of productive-aged respondents who were either working during the time of the fieldwork (in the ESS, in seven days preceding the survey), or who had recently lost their jobs. The latter category consisted of jobless people who declared they were working in the year of the survey (in the ESS, such people were included only if they defined themselves as unemployed during the week before the survey). From both samples, I excluded individual farm owners, respondents aged twenty-one to twenty-nine who were still in school at the time of the survey, and respondents receiving pension[2] or disability benefits. These characteristics may be important mediators between precarious employment and its expected negative outcomes, as young people who have not completed schooling are—according to the literature—the most likely to be in nonstandard job arrangements by their own choice (Hipple 2001). People with alternative, stable sources of income, such as pension or disability benefits, may be more willing to enter into temporary jobs, and less able to actively engage in public life due to health problems. Both samples were weighted to correct for imbalances in the sex and age structure.

The final ESS sample consisted of 4,483 individuals (the unweighted sample sizes for the individual rounds of the ESS were: 772 in 2002, 684 in 2004, 721 in 2006, 671 in 2008, 770 in 2010, and 865 in 2012), and the POLPAN 2013 sample consisted of 947 respondents.

Political and Civic Participation

This study uses binary measures of participation. The ESS measure is based on the survey question on whether the respondents, during the year before the study, had undertaken several sociopolitical activities, including contacts with politicians, associational involvement, signing petitions, participation in demonstrations, or consumer boycotts.[3] All the respondents who answered yes to at least one of those items are coded 1. The participation variable for POLPAN is based on the respondents' answers to the following questionnaire items: whether, during the twelve months preceding the survey, they: (a) "participated in a demonstration, gathering, or march," (b) "signed a petition to the government or an open letter in public matters," or (c) "engaged in other kinds of public (social) activity," concerning either matters of the whole country or province (*voivodeship*), or at the local level: district, municipality, or county (*poviat*). The last item is followed by an open-ended question, asking the respondent to describe these other kinds of activity. Respondents who declared they participated in at least one of the activities listed above (a, b, or c), are assigned the value 1; those who responded negatively to all the items, are coded 0.

Overall, 20 percent of the ESS participants reported participation in at least one of the activities covered by the questionnaire. The respective percentage for the full POLPAN 2013 sample was only 14.6 percent. In order to account for these differences and the way they may affect the relationship under study, I include a detailed discussion of the validity of both indicators in the results section. I also provide an in-depth analysis of the forms of participation reported by the POLPAN respondents, paying special attention to the distinction between the conventional and emerging forms of participation in both surveys. Drawing on similar distinctions used in the literature (e.g., Acik 2013; Marien et al. 2010; Stolle and Hooghe 2011), in the conventional category I include working for a political party, contacting a politician, and associational involvement. The emerging forms include: signing petitions, consumer boycott, participation in demonstrations, and displaying or wearing a campaign badge/sticker.

Precarious Employment

The key variable is employment precarity in the respondents' current or last job (in the case of the recently unemployed). Labor market studies commonly associate this phenomenon with employment through temporary contracts (see, however, Kiersztyn 2016b); this was also the approach adopted in this study. For hired employees in both the ESS and POLPAN, employment through open-ended contracts (both full-time and part-time) is considered nonprecarious, and all other arrangements (e.g., temporary contracts, including fixed-term or civil law agreements) as well as unregistered work (without a written contract) are considered precarious.[4]

The situation becomes more complex with regard to the nonfarming self-employed workers. In definitions of precarious employment, the focus is on economic insecurity resulting from a specific employment relationship, while for the self-employed, economic insecurity usually results from the instability and unpredictability of demand for products and services offered by firms; precarious employment by definition does not apply to individuals who are not employed by anyone. However, in practice there can also be cases in which workers are forced into self-employment as contractors by firms aiming to minimize employment costs. Such contractors often perform tasks similar to those of regular employees in the firm, under similar conditions and under the firm's supervision, but are deprived of the rights offered by employment protection legislation. If this is the case, what formally appears as self-employment is, in reality, dependent self-employment, and can be considered precarious (OECD 2014). The POLPAN 2013 database contains detailed information on the situation of the self-employed, making it possible to capture this phenomenon. I adopt two criteria of precarity among the self-employed: respondents who work under the supervision of one person or company and respondents who do not hire nonfamily employees and at the same time have only one client firm are both considered precarious. Since the ESS offers no information on whether self-employed respondents were working under the supervision of another party or had only one client, all self-employed as sole proprietors (not hiring nonfamily members) are treated as precarious. In sum, as much as 33.4 percent of the ESS sample were precarious workers at the time of the survey, while the respective percentage calculated on the basis of POLPAN data is 26.1 percent.[5]

Temporary employment in Poland is a standard feature of entry-level jobs and is commonly used during probation periods for newly hired workers. In such cases, it need not imply actual precarity, but may be a normal phase of the process of labor market entry or re-entry (Kiersztyn 2016a). From this point of view, a potential reason for concern and factor affecting the level of political involvement may not be temporary employment measured at a given moment in time, but rather, persistent labor market precarity, measured over longer periods of time. I use an additional measure of long-term precarity calculated using the POLPAN 2013 data on the respondents' previous employment spells since 2008. From the whole category of respondents whose current or last job was precarious, persistently precarious includes: (1) all those who started the jobs performed in 2013 no later than three years before the survey and (2) all those whose first spell of employment since 2008 started no later than three years before the survey and who had not been employed on the basis of an open-ended contract since 2008.[6] Such a measure focuses on those who either remain in a single precarious job or experience multiple spells of temporary employment, and excludes recent labor market entrants, for whom fixed-term contracts and engaging in short-term jobs may be regarded as a natural and temporary state. The percentage of persistently precarious workers in the POLPAN 2013 sample was 17.1 percent.

Control Variables

Among the control variables, I included basic demographic and social char-acteristics: gender, with males as the reference category, the respondents' age in years (as well as age squared to account for nonlinear relationships between participation and age), and educational attainment. The latter vari-able divides the survey participants into three categories, based on the type of schooling they completed: below secondary (those who completed only primary or middle school, or basic vocational education), secondary educa-tion (graduates of general or vocational high schools, as well as postsecondary schools), and college/university education.

The next three control variables characterize the respondents' house-hold: whether the respondent lives with his/her husband/wife or partner, and whether he/she has children under sixteen years of age who are also current household members. Parenting has been shown to be an important variable influencing civic activism (Putnam 2000), while living in a stable relationship may enhance economic security and access to economic and social resources enabling more active participation despite one's own pre-carious labor market position. On the other hand, it can be hypothesized that individuals preoccupied with their families may be less motivated and have less time to spend on civic and political participation (Standing 2011). Another important characteristic is the total level of household income *per capita*, which is available only in the POLPAN database. The values of the POLPAN income variable in the studied sample range from 175 to 50,000 złoty, with a mean of 1,751, median of 1,333, and standard deviation of 2,092 (N=899). To correct for the skewedness of the income distribution, I use the natural logarithm of this variable in the regression models. The ESS does not ask directly about the household income level, but classifies respondents into income groups. The classification scheme underwent some changes between rounds 1 through 3 and 4 through 6: up to 2006, there were twelve categories defined by stable income thresholds, and starting from 2008, there were ten categories defined by the actual income deciles in a given country. I created a binary variable, identifying respondents with monthly household income below 1,200 złoty for the first three rounds of the survey, and 1,400, 1,500, and 1,600 złoty for the fourth, fifth, and sixth round, respectively. The percentage of respondents falling below this threshold ranged from around 20 to 25 percent (in the years 2006 to 2012) to around 30 to 33 percent (in 2002 to 2004). This measure is not consistent across rounds, and should be treated with caution.[7]

Finally, the analysis includes two characteristics that determine the social context of the respondents' actions: type of residence and church attendance. Both are likely to have an indirect effect on political and civic participation,.

by influencing the scope and nature of social relationships. The first variable distinguishes between three categories: rural, small or medium town, and large city. Research has found that residents in larger communities tend to be less interested in local politics and less active in local civic affairs. This may be partly due to the alienation and social disconnection in large cities: people are less likely to know their neighbors or have mutual friends, which makes political mobilization more difficult and involvement more costly (Oliver 2000). On the other hand, there were also claims that larger cities may offer more resources and opportunities for participation, for example in the form of a larger variety of civic organizations that mobilize citizens for action (see Oliver 2000). In POLPAN, small and medium towns are defined as those with less than 100,000 residents. In the ESS, the residential categories are based on the respondents' own definitions of rural areas, small and medium towns, big cities and suburbs (the latter were included in the big city category). The final control variable identifies the respondents who declared they participate in religious practices at least once a week. Church attendance has been found to be positively correlated with social capital and civic participation (CBOS 2012a; Putnam 2000).

Employment Precarity and Participation

Table 8.1 presents the incidence of various forms of participation by employment precarity, according to POLPAN and the pooled ESS data. There are some differences between the surveys: the POLPAN data suggest that holding a temporary job might have a negative effect on civic and political activism, however, this effect is very weak. According to the pooled ESS, employment precarity has a moderate negative impact on all the forms of participation covered by the survey. In sum, the incidence of any activity among precarious workers is 6.4 percentage points lower than among those in regular employment. With respect to the forms of participation, associational involvement and petition signing appear the most affected by employment precarity. The differences between the ESS and POLPAN results cannot be explained by the fact that the ESS was conducted earlier and covers a longer period—when the ESS sample is limited to respondents from the most recent (2012) round of the survey, the participation gap with respect to precarious employment is even larger than in the pooled sample.

Table 8.2 shows additional descriptive results for political and civic participation according to the ESS, broken down by level of education. The participation indices are grouped into two categories: conventional activities, including contacting politicians, work for political parties and associational involvement, and emerging activities, which include signing a petition, par-

Table 8.1. Civic participation indicators by employment precarity, POLPAN 2013 and ESS 2002–2012.

	Total	Non-precarious	Precarious at time of survey	Long-term precarious
POLPAN 2013				
Involvement in public affairs at least once in the last year	18.2%	19.0%	16.1%	17.1%
ESS 2002–2012				
Any activity at least once last year	24.4%	26.5%	20.1%	
Contacted a politician, government or local government official	9.6%	10.3%	8.2%	
Worked in a political party or action group	3.0%	3.5%	1.9%	
Worked in another organisation or association	7.5%	8.8%	4.7%	
Worn or displayed a campaign badge/sticker	4.7%	5.3%	3.5%	
Signed a petition	10.1%	11.3%	7.6%	
Taken part in a lawful public demonstration	1.8%	2.1%	1.1%	
Boycotted certain products	6.2%	7.0%	4.6%	

Notes. POLPAN and ESS sample weighted according to main socio-demographic categories.

Table 8.2. Civic participation indicators by education and employment precarity, ESS 2002–2012.

	Any activity	Conventional	Emerging	Weighted N
Below secondary education				
Not precarious	14.0%	8.0%	8.5%	1081
Precarious	12.9%	7.1%	7.9%	718
Secondary education				
Not precarious	26.4%	14.2%	18.2%	962
Precarious	22.8%	12.5%	14.5%	470
College / university education				
Not precarious	42.5%	27.7%	31.0%	856
Precarious	34.4%	21.9%	21.7%	267

Notes. Design weights provided in the ESS database were applied to correct for sample imbalances.

ticipation in a demonstration or march, consumer boycott, and wearing a badge. The table presents the percentage of respondents who declared they participated at least once in the year before the survey in any of the respective activities. Interestingly, it appears that the negative association between employment precarity and participation increases with education. Contrary to expectations, the level of participation is the most affected by temporary job holding among college and university graduates, especially with respect to the emerging forms of political expression.

The next step of the analysis is to assess the relationship between employment precarity and participation when other important respondent characteristics are controlled for. This is done by means of logistic regression models. Table 8.3 presents the results for POLPAN. Contrary to the initial bivariate analysis, logistic regression models suggest a weak positive relationship between temporary employment and participation in various protest activities and civic initiatives when age, education, family situation, and income are included in the equation (model 1a). This relationship, however, is statistically insignificant. This finding remains unchanged when the alternative measure of precarity, identifying those who remain in temporary employment over a long period of time, is used (model 1b).

Analogous regression models estimating using pooled ESS data, presented in Table 8.4, do not point to any significant relationships between having a precarious job and political participation, which is consistent with the POLPAN results. However, a slightly different picture emerges when the effects of employment precarity conditional on education are the focus of analysis (model 2b). The descriptive results presented in Table 8.2 are confirmed: insecure work is associated with around 26 percent lower odds of participation, but only among college- or university-educated respondents. This relationship, although quite striking, is not highly significant, and in models not controlling for low household income it drops below significance levels. However, this may be explained by the relatively small size of the college-educated, precarious worker category (unweighted N=283). It is worth noting that the direction and size of the coefficients remain similar regardless of model specification.

As far as the control variables are concerned, the results are mostly consistent with earlier studies, both in Poland and other countries. There are, however, some differences between the POLPAN and ESS results. The most striking difference concerns gender: while the ESS data point to a strong and robust relationship, the odds of participation for women being almost 30 percent lower than those for men, according to POLPAN being a woman has no effect on the likelihood of engaging in civic and political activities. Similarly, age appears to affect participation only in the models estimated using the ESS. The equations suggest a curvilinear relationship between age

Table 8.3. Logistic regression results for civic participation, POLPAN 2013

	Model 1a			Model 1b		
	Coeff	Std. Err	Exp(B)	Coeff	Std. Err	Exp(B)
Precarious employment: yes (ref.: no)	.222	.228	1.249			
Persistent precarious employment: yes (ref.: no)				.104	.250	1.110
Gender: female (ref.: male)	−.034	.190	.967	−.038	.190	.963
Age in years	−.086	.079	.917	−.096	.078	.909
Age squared	.001	.001	1.001	.001	.001	1.001
Educational attainment (ref.: below secondary)						
Secondary	.430	.278	1.537	.408	.277	1.504
college / university	1.320	.282***	3.744	1.294	.280***	3.647
Lives with spouse / partner (ref.: single)	.511	.267^	1.667	.496	.266^	1.642
Has children under 16 living in household (ref.: no children under 16)	.265	.241	1.304	.254	.241	1.290
Log household per capita income	.323	.166^	1.381	.305	.165^	1.356
Church attendance: at least once a week (ref.: less than once a week)	−.029	.197	.971	−.033	.197	.968
Type of residence (ref.: rural)						
small / medium town	−.041	.238	.959	−.035	.238	.965
big city	.521	.233*	1.683	.528	.233*	1.695
Constant	−3.783	1.957^	.023	−3.356	1.896^	.035
Log likelihood		−386.523			−386.905	
Model Chi^2		77.637			76.874	
Cox and Snell R^2		.083			.083	
Nagelkerke R^2		.136			.134	

Notes. Models estimated on a sample of production aged respondents who were working in 2013, N=748. Sample weighted according to gender and age categories. *** p<0,001; ** p<0,01; * p<0,05; ^ p<0,1 (2-tailed).

Table 8.4. Logistic regression results for civic participation, ESS 2002–2012

	Model 2a			Model 2b		
	Coeff	Std. Err	Exp(B)	Coeff	Std. Err	Exp(B)
Precarious employment: yes (ref.: no)	−.067	.095	.936			
Precarious employment by education (ref.: no)						
precarious and below secondary education				.086	.154	1.090
precarious and secondary education				−.030	.152	.970
precarious and college / university education				−.305	.173^	.737
Educational attainment (ref.: below secondary)						
Secondary	.826	.104***	2.285	.871	.127***	2.390
college / university	1.479	.110***	4.390	1.587	.129***	4.887
Gender: female (ref.: male)	−.345	.085***	.708	−.345	.085***	.708
Age in years	.082	.034*	1.085	.081	.034*	1.085
Age squared	−.001	.000*	.999	−.001	.000*	.999
Lives with spouse / partner (ref.: single)	.135	.116	.600	.136	.116	1.145
Has children under 16 living in household (ref.: no children under 16)	−.154	.102	1.145	−.164	.103	.849
Low income households (ref.: income above threshold)	−.510	.142***	.857	−.516	.142***	.597
Church attendance: at least once a week (ref.: less than once a week)	.082	.084	1.085	.085	.084	1.089
Type of residence (ref.: rural)						
small / medium town	.049	.101	1.050	.049	.101	1.050
big city	.229	.104*	1.257	.231	.104*	1.260
ESS round (ref: first, 2002)						
second (2004)	−.159	.137	.853	−.160	.137	.852
third (2006)	−.474	.142***	.622	−.484	.142***	.617

fourth (2008)	−.510	.145***	.601	−.515	.145***	.598
fifth (2010)	−.287	.138*	.751	−.291	.138*	.748
sixth (2012)	−.236	.134^	.790	−.241	.135^	.786
Constant	−3.225	.659***	.040	−3.253	.657***	.039
Log likelihood		−1834.246			−1832.734	
Model Chi²		305.138			308.164	
Cox and Snell R²		.083			.084	
Nagelkerke R²		.123			.124	

Notes. Models estimated on a sample of production aged respondents who were working in 2013, N=3553. Design weights provided in the ESS database were applied. *** p<0,001; ** p<0,01; * p<0,05; ^ p<0,1 (2-tailed).

and participation: people tend to participate more often as they grow older, but at a certain point in life their activity diminishes. In both surveys, the most important predictor for all the dependent variables was the level of education. Higher educational credentials generally increase political participation. Worth noting is also the fact that, net of other variables, higher household income enhances civic and political activism. Even the rather rough income measure available in the ESS is sufficient to allow this relationship to be captured. Living in a big city is another factor positively related to engaging in public matters. All these findings support the resource theory of participation.

With respect to family situation, the results are more mixed. Living with a spouse or partner may be a source of security and stabilization, enabling more active participation. This is, however, a rather weak relationship, and visible only with the POLPAN data. Raising children under sixteen years of age appears to be unrelated to civic and political activity. Finally, regular participation in religious practices does not seem to affect the chances of participation. This is inconsistent with earlier survey results, which suggested that systematic church attendance is an important correlate of social capital in Poland. Such a finding raises interesting research questions concerning the role of the Church as promoting civic engagement in Poland: is it limited only to specific groups of individuals or certain forms of activism? Such questions, however, are beyond the scope of the present analysis.

Venues of Participation

All the regression models presented above explained a single, general measure of political and civic participation: involvement in any type of activity covered by the survey at least once during one year. Such a simple indicator of activism may mask important individual variations in the nature or type of the activity undertaken. This section takes a closer look at the specific forms of participation reported by the respondents in both surveys, paying special attention to the distinction between the conventional and the so-called emerging or individualistic forms of political expression.

The ESS 2002–2012 results pertaining to the percentage of respondents who engaged in various civic and political activities at least once in the year before the survey are presented in Table 8.5. Throughout the studied period, the most common activities were signing a petition and contacting a politician or government official, followed by associational involvement and consumer boycott. The activities that occurred the least often were participation in demonstrations and work in a political party or action group.

It should be noted that the results of other surveys point to similar patterns with respect to the forms of participation—though many indicators are not comparable across the surveys. According to a 2012 Public Opinion Research Centre (CBOS) study, Poles express their views on public matters mainly by signing petitions (13 percent during the preceding year) and consumer boycott (7 percent during the preceding year). These percentages

Table 8.5. Incidence of various forms of civic activism (percentages), ESS 2002–2012.

	Pooled sample	2002	2004	2006	2008	2010	2012
At least one activity	20.0%	20.9%	20.4%	15.3%	18.5%	21.7%	22.4%
Contacted a politician, government or local government official	7.1%	9.6%	7.1%	6.2%	7.2%	8.7%	7.3%
Worked in a political party or action group	2.4%	2.9%	2.7%	1.7%	2.6%	2.2%	2.5%
Worked in another organisation or association	6.0%	5.9%	5.7%	4.3%	5.9%	7.1%	7.1%
Worn or displayed a campaign badge/sticker	3.8%	2.9%	3.8%	2.4%	4.2%	5.3%	4.4%
Signed a petition	8.4%	6.9%	9.3%	5.4%	7.5%	10.7%	10.4%
Taken part in a lawful public demonstration	1.7%	1.3%	1.6%	1.3%	1.5%	2.0%	2.3%
Boycotted certain products	4.6%	3.6%	5.0%	4.0%	4.5%	4.9%	5.7%

Note. Design weights provided in the ESS database were applied to correct for sample imbalances. Data for all survey participants, regardless of age and employment status (N=10815).

are slightly higher than the ones observed in the 2012 ESS, which may be because the question used in the ESS refers to actions undertaken "to improve things in Poland" and thus may not cover instances of participation to resolve more specific or local matters. The CBOS survey also confirms the reluctance of Poles to participate in demonstrations (2 percent) (CBOS 2012b). With regard to associational involvement, the 2013 Social Diagnosis survey found that one out of ten respondents aged sixteen and above are active members of at least one organization. However, only 0.3 percent report working for a political party (Czapiński 2013).[8]

A different picture of civic activism emerges based on the POLPAN results. Looking at the percentage answering "yes" to the survey questions on different types of activity, the most often engaged into are signing petitions (8.9 percent) and active involvement in matters of district, municipality, or poviat (7.3 percent). However, to get a full picture of the activities through which Poles participate in public life, we need to take into account the respondents' more detailed answers to the open-ended question regarding the way they were involved in country-level, regional, or local issues. Overall, 189 respondents (8.6 percent) described at least one activity, among them twenty-four provided information on two activities, and eight of them provided information on three activities. This gives us a total of 221 responses.[9]

The open-ended question referred to forms of participation other than demonstrating and involvement in petitions. Nevertheless, a number of respondents answering this question pointed to these two activities. In fact, petitions were the category mentioned the most often (sixty-two responses).[10] If we combine these responses with answers to the earlier yes-no question, the total percentage of POLPAN respondents who declared signing a petition or gathering signatures is 9.9 percent. Participation in demonstrations and gatherings was mentioned much less frequently—in only nine responses to the open-ended question. Thirteen additional respondents declared participation in protest activities other than petitions or demonstrations, such as strikes, community gatherings, writing a protest letter to the local government, or others.

The respondents also gave examples of actions that can be treated as representing the more conventional, institutionalized forms of political participation. These include membership in local government bodies or neighborhood councils, as well as attending, on a more or less regular basis, various public meetings: *"I participate in a commission, which is part of the neighborhood council," "member of the village council, I did some work on behalf of the village," "meetings of the housing cooperative, suggestions what needs to be done in the neighborhood."* The number of such responses was twenty-seven. In addition, sixteen respondents declared contacting politicians or the local government, usually with the aim of resolving a specific local issue or issues, for example: *"intervenes in public matters, for the construction of a railway bridge," "expressing my opinion on various public issues to one of the [parliamentary] deputies–on a cyclical basis," "dialogue with the authorities, submission of proposals on public matters."* Some perceived themselves as intermediaries between politicians and the general public.

Other forms of involvement in local affairs involve participation in various community initiatives. This is a wide category of activities, including help with the organization of various cultural or sports events, community work, or membership in parental boards of educational institutions: *"I organized voluntary work and social campaigns," "help with the organization of a neighborhood fair," "community work–cleaning up the outdoor area of a community centre in my village," "editor-in-chief of a local newspaper," "head of the preschool's Parent's Board."* Such activities were mentioned in twenty-two responses. An additional eleven responses referred to various activities to benefit specific groups of recipients: *"fundraising campaign for a sick child," "on behalf of the Polish Humanitarian Action–educational fair–collecting aid for Somalia," "help with the distribution of food–Food-bank for the poor."* Another important category is associational involvement, declared by twenty-one respondents. The most commonly mentioned organization was the Volunteer Fire Brigades. Explicit reference to party membership was made by only one person.

With the exception of petition signing, the percentages of respondents reporting various types of activity in the POLPAN survey are very low compared to similar indicators based on the ESS data or results of other recent surveys. The fact that people are more likely to report various activities when confronted with a list of specific items than while answering an open-ended question is, in itself, not very surprising. What is striking is the magnitude of these differences: while the 2013 Social Diagnosis survey suggests that around 10 percent of Poles work in various nongovernmental organizations, only 1 percent of POLPAN respondents spontaneously mention such activities. When asked directly whether they attended a public meeting during the last year, 17 percent of respondents in the Social Diagnosis Survey answered yes (Sułek 2013)–in POLPAN, the respective rate was 1.3 percent. Donating or raising funds for charitable causes was reported by 19 percent of CBOS survey participants in response to a closed-ended question (CBOS 2012b), and mentioned by only 0.6 percent of POLPAN respondents. The confrontation of POLPAN results with those of other surveys suggests that for many people, participation in community activities may occur in the form of rare, isolated events, to which little importance is attached or that are not associated with the more general idea of involvement in public matters—making it more difficult to recall the relevant activities when confronted with an open-ended question. This also suggests that the POLPAN measure of political and civic activism is likely to overrepresent the emerging forms of participation: signing petitions and attending demonstrations. These two categories were more likely to be reported, since they were the only ones covered by closed-ended questions. This observation, coupled with the fact that earlier research has consistently shown the emerging forms to be much more evenly distributed with respect to gender and age than the conventional forms, also explains the different relationships found in regression models based on the POLPAN and ESS data: only the latter point to a gender and age gap in participation.

In the final part of the analysis, I turn to the relationship between employment precarity and the form of activity undertaken by the respondents. I use only ESS data, due to the larger sample and the fact that they include a larger and more diverse set of civic/political activity variables. Table 8.6 presents the coefficients of a multinomial logistic regression model, explaining the likelihood of engaging only in conventional activities (contacting politicians, working for a political party or another association), only in emerging activities (signing a petition, wearing a campaign badge, attending a demonstration or consumer boycott), or in both types of activities. Living with spouse or partner, having children under sixteen years of age, and church attendance are not included in the models presented below, as they do not show any significant relationships with the dependent variable and their inclusion does not improve the final model.

The regression results point to interesting variations with respect to the socioeconomic correlates of various types of participation. First, the gender participation gap was observed only in the case of conventional political and civic activism, and not among those who engaged only in the emerging forms of political expression. This finding is consistent with earlier research results. Second, the distribution of different types of participation is dependent on the type of local community. While signing petitions, wearing campaign badges, demonstrating, and consumer boycotts are more common in large cities, the conventional forms of political and civic activism are more likely to occur in rural areas. These differences are understandable in light of the literature—activities involving more direct interpersonal contact are easier to come by in smaller communities, whose members are more likely to know each other, while big cities encourage the forms of participation that are associated with modernization and individualization. However, the regression coefficients also suggest that both types of activities require access to certain resources: better education and higher income.

Regarding precarious employment, it appears that neither conventional nor emerging forms of participation are, by themselves, determined by this phenomenon. The negative effect of temporary job holding among workers with college or university education works mainly through the reduction in the odds of declaring participation in *both* types of activities, by as much as

Table 8.6. Multinomial logistic regression results for involvement in conventional vs. emerging political activity, ESS 2002–2012

	Conventional forms of participation only			Both conventional and emerging forms of participation			Emerging forms of participation only		
	Coeff	Std. Err	Exp(B)	Coeff	Std. Err	Exp(B)	Coeff	Std. Err	Exp(B)
Precarious employment by education (ref.: no)									
precarious and below secondary education	.204	.233	1.227	-.105	.337	.900	.069	.229	1.071
precarious and secondary education	.111	.240	1.117	-.064	.286	.938	-.151	.209	.860
precarious and college / university education	-.072	.280	.931	-.615	.275*	.540	-.172	.236	.842
Educational attainment (ref.: below secondary)									
secondary	.747	.198***	2.111	1.001	.251***	2.720	.891	.184***	2.438
college / university	1.412	.200***	4.106	2.269	.233***	9.668	1.240	.189***	3.454
Gender: female (ref.: male)	-.378	.133**	.685	-.502	.144***	.605	-.179	.118	.836
Age in years	.078	.050	1.081	.070	.055	1.073	.083	.045^	1.086
Age squared	-.001	.001	.999	-.001	.001	.999	-.001	.001^	.999
Low income households	-.495	.214*	.609	-.665	.292*	.514	-.497	.207*	.608
Type of residence (ref.: rural)									

small / medium town	−.230	.151	.795	.040	.171	1.041	.294	.153^	1.342
big city	−.384	.166*	.681	.029	.177	1.030	.784	.147***	2.189
ESS round (ref: first, 2002)									
second (2004)	−.449	.205*	.638	.127	.244	1.135	−.052	.194	.950
third (2006)	−.661	.210**	.516	−.266	.256	.766	−.428	.207*	.652
fourth (2008)	−.821	.222***	.440	−.336	.258	.715	−.322	.205	.725
fifth (2010)	−.696	.211***	.499	−.008	.237	.992	−.135	.196	.873
sixth (2012)	−.723	.207***	.485	.005	.234	1.005	−.043	.190	.958
Constant	−4.162	1.016***		−4.758	1.116***		−4.197	.897***	

Notes. Models estimated on a sample of production aged respondents who were working in 2013, N=3553. Design weights provided in the ESS database were applied to correct for sample imbalances. Log likelihood= −2670.46, Chi²=403.415, Cox and Snell R² =0.108, Nagelkerke R² =0.133. *** p<0,001; ** p<0,01; * p<0,05; ^ p<0,1 (2-tailed).

46 percent. In fact, additional analyses of ESS data, in which the respondents were divided into nonparticipants, those who declared participation in exactly one of the seven activities covered by the survey, and those who participated in two or more of these activities, showed that precarious employment among respondents with higher education is negatively correlated only with the likelihood of engaging in more than one activity. These findings suggest that, when looking at the possible effects of labor market changes on the state of civil society, an important distinction may be not with respect to the type(s) of activity, but participation intensity and/or diversity. This observation is inconsistent with the notion of labor market flexibility as enhancing work-life balance, but confirms Standing's (2011) description of European precarious workers becoming increasingly preoccupied by "making a living," searching for new employment, and undergoing additional training to enhance their employability. As a result, they have little time for other activities. It should also be noted that this study does not take into account part-time employment, which could improve work-life balance, including among nonregular employees. This, however, is unlikely to happen on a large scale in Poland, where working part-time is relatively rare, compared to in other EU countries (EUROSTAT 2013).

Is the Truth Still Out There? Discussion and Conclusions

In general, the results described above lead me to conclude that both the concerns voiced by theorists arguing that the "brave new world of work" will cause citizens to withdraw from political life and the enthusiasm expressed by those who see flexible employment as promoting civic participation are mostly exaggerated. It appears that political voice is determined mostly by cultural capital, as measured by the educational level of respondents. Economic determinism seems far less important as a factor explaining political and civic involvement, at least in the Polish context. Analyses based on data from two different surveys, using various measures of precarious employment and political participation, do not point to the existence of a direct and significant relationship between these phenomena, when controlling for important predictors of political activism such as education.

However, this does not mean that there are no reasons for concern. First, the statistical analyses revealed a robust positive relationship between household per capita income and civic activism. As precarious employment has been found by many studies to negatively affect income levels (e.g., Comi and Grasseni 2012; Kiersztyn 2012; OECD 2014), it may have an indirect negative effect on the strength of civil society. This mechanism may be stronger in the case of households where precarious employment is the only source of work-related income. In this context, it is worth noting that according to a recent study, in 2008 around 10 percent of the total number of households in Poland met this condition, and these households suffered a much higher risk of poverty compared to those in which stable employment was one of the sources of income (Kiersztyn 2012).

Second, and maybe more importantly, there are reasons to believe that the withdrawal hypothesis is true for one important group of citizens—those with higher education. This finding is surprising and contradicts one of the main hypotheses adopted here, which predicted that withdrawal would be more likely among the *least* educated, while those with better education would tend to mobilize. This, however, is likely to be a Polish specificity. Although there is no research from other countries to directly confirm the latter claim, given the generally low levels of political mobilization in Poland as measured by standard quantitative indicators, access to resources enabling participation for those with lower education is so limited that precarious employment, in a sense, cannot make matters much worse. Conversely, for higher education graduates, who have the necessary competencies and are expected to be more active in the public sphere, precarious employment can really make a difference. This does not mean that educational resources and cultural capital do not matter anymore: respondents with college or university diplomas in precarious jobs are still—on average—more likely to participate than high school graduates with open-ended employment contracts. However, a paradoxical effect of precarious employment could be, to some extent, the equalization of participation rates across people with different levels of education—though, sadly, by leveling down. The analysis of different forms of political participation sheds some light on the possible character of this change. It appears that what is affected is not the percentage of individuals who ever engage in either the conventional or the emerging forms of participation, but rather the degree of involvement, understood in terms of participation intensity or engaging in more than one activity. The highly educated in precarious jobs who decide to become involved in public matters are more likely to choose only one venue of participation, rather than combine differing types of activities. In light of the literature, the latter finding is also likely to apply to countries other than Poland, especially those where temporary employment is not correlated with working part-time.

This also brings us to the more general issue of the state of civil society in Poland. The findings presented above confirm the popular claim of the low level of participation of Poles in public affairs. However, it should be remembered that these analyses are mostly based on simple binary measures of civic and political activism, commonly used in quantitative and international research. Such measures may not capture certain forms of civic involvement that may be specific to the Polish context, and they offer no information on the degree of involvement, the number of acts the respondent participated in, or the time spent on political or civic activities. The results of this study suggest that such time-use data may actually be the key to capturing the relationship between individual employment status and participation.

Since Durkheim's *Division of Labour*, sociologists have regarded work as one of the key institutions attaching individuals to society and maintaining social order. The social consequences of changes in the nature of the employment relationship are likely to be profound and are difficult to foresee. From the point of view of sociological theory, an important drawback of unstable jobs may be their inability to generate bonds of social solidarity (Durkheim 1999). Indeed, in light of the results discussed above, it seems likely that current changes in the labor market, if they persist, may, in the long term and indirectly, turn out to be much more detrimental to civic participation than often debated trends such as the postcommunist legacy of apathy.

Anna Kiersztyn is Assistant Professor of Sociology at the Institute of Sociology, University of Warsaw, and a member of the Research Group of Comparative Analysis of Social Inequalities at the Institute of Philosophy and Sociology, Polish Academy of Sciences. Her current research concerns the dynamics and social consequences of substandard employment, and the relationship between alternative work arrangements and the quality of jobs. She is the author of several research articles analyzing the incidence and correlates of educational mismatch, low-paid employment and unstable employment on the Polish labor market.

Notes

1. The Polish Panel Survey (POLPAN) was conducted on a nationally representative sample of adults aged twenty-one and above, in five-year intervals starting in 1988. Starting from the 1998 wave, the sample was regularly supplemented to include members of the youngest cohorts, aged twenty-one to twenty-five. The most recent 2013 wave was funded by a Polish National Science Centre Maestro grant awarded on the basis of decision number: DEC-2011/03/A/HS6/00238. More information on the POLPAN project, data accessibility, and a list of relevant publications is available on the project website (www.polpan.org).
2. In Poland, until 2006, early retirement options were readily available to many workers who had not reached retirement age. In most cases, people on early retirement could work without losing pension entitlements. Today, early retirement is still available in certain occupations.
3. "There are different ways of trying to improve things in [country] or help prevent things from going wrong. During the last twelve months, have you done any of the following? Have you: contacted a politician, government or local government official, worked in a political party or action group, worked in another organisation or associ-

ation, worn or displayed a campaign badge/sticker, signed a petition, taken part in a lawful public demonstration, boycotted certain products."

4. In the case of POLPAN respondents holding multiple jobs, all individuals who at the time of the survey held at least one nonprecarious job were assumed nonprecarious (even if the stable job was the not his/her main employment).

5. The inconsistent findings regarding the incidence of precarious employment in both surveys may be explained by the fact that the ESS defines as working all the respondents who had a paid job for at least one hour during the week before the survey, while POLPAN includes only those who consider themselves employed (in any type of job). Further, POLPAN uses stricter criteria for the classification of self-employment as precarious.

6. The data on the respondents' earlier jobs do not include any items allowing identification of dependent self-employment, which caused some difficulties in classifying spells of self-employment and farming. Additional analysis found that such spells were relatively rare: among the respondents who met the other criteria of persistent precarity, only six had ended spells of self-employment, and five had been working as farm owners. They were classified based on a detailed, case-by-case analysis of their individual employment histories. Shorter spells of self-employment, which ended involuntarily and were accompanied by a larger number of odd jobs, were treated as precarious. Similarly, spells of work as an individual farm owner were classified according to the number of hours worked per week, length of the spell, and whether farm work was the respondent's main job throughout the duration of the spell (the main job is the one on which the most time is spent).

7. However, it can be argued that this measure roughly reflects changes in the actual income distribution across Polish households, not only changes in the survey methodology. One reason is the inflation rate, which was relatively low in the years from 2002 to 2006, and then, on average, almost doubled in the period from 2006 to 2012 (the data are provided on the Polish Central Statistical Office website: www .stat.gov.pl). Second, although the threshold value for the low-income variable changed the most abruptly between 2006 and 2008 (from 1,200 to 1,400 złoty), I did not observe a corresponding increase in the percentage of low-income households in the sample. In fact, it fell slightly, from 24.7 percent to 22.7 percent.

8. This indicates a widespread distrust toward conventional political parties, and is an important thing to note, as it suggests that a majority of the 2.2 percent of ESS respondents who declared working for a "political party or action group," may, in reality, not be involved in partisan activities at all. In fact, the Polish translation of this survey item covered not only political parties, but also, literally "organizations active in social and political matters."

9. Forty responses were left out of the detailed analysis due to interpretational difficulties. These responses were either too general (e.g., *"active participation"*) or pointed only to the specific issues at which the activity was directed, without any information on the type of activity itself (*"playground for the kids," "construction of a road,"* etc.). Several respondents also mentioned activities that could involve monetary remuneration or be performed in the course of their occupation (e.g., membership in precinct electoral commissions or preparation of expert reports).

10. Interestingly, participation via the Internet was explicitly mentioned only twice (signing an Internet petition and Internet campaigns); both of these cases were also included in the "petition" category.

References

Acik, N. 2013. "Reducing the Participation Gap in Civic Engagement: Political Consumerism in Europe." *European Sociological Review* 29, no. 6: 1309–1322.

Arendt, H. 1958. *The Human Condition.* Chicago: University of Chicago Press (Polish edition).

Arulampalam, W., and A.L. Booth. 1998. "Training and Labour Market Flexibility: Is There a Trade-off?" *British Journal of Industrial Relations* 36, no. 4: 521–536.

Atkinson, A.B. 1998. "Social Exclusion, Poverty and Unemployment," in *Exclusion, Employment and Opportunity,* ed. A.B. Atkinson and J. Hills. CASE/4, Centre for Analysis of Social Exclusion, London School, 1–21.

Beck, U. 2002. *Risk Society: Towards a New Modernity.* Warsaw: Scholar (Polish edition).

CBOS. 2012a. "Aktywność społeczna w organizacjach obywatelskich" [Social Activity in Civic Organizations]. Warsaw: CBOS.

———. 2012b. "Poczucie wpływu na sprawy publiczne i zaangażowanie obywatelskie" [Sense of Influence on Public Affairs and Civic Involvement]. Warsaw: CBOS.

Chambers, S., and J. Kopstein. 2001. "Bad Civil Society." *Political Theory* 29, no. 6: 837–865.

Comi, S., and M. Grasseni. 2012. "Are Temporary Workers Discriminated Against? Evidence from Europe." *The Manchester School* 80, no. 1: 28–50.

Czapiński, J. 2013. "Stan społeczeństwa obywatelskiego. Identyfikacja i aktywność polityczna. Diagnoza Społeczna 2013. Warunki i Jakość Życia Polaków–Raport" [Social Diagnosis 2013: Objective and Subjective Quality of Life in Poland: Report]. *Contemporary Economics* 7 (special issue): 317–320.

Dalton, R. 2000. "Citizen Attitudes and Political Behavior." *Comparative Political Studies* 33, no. 67: 912–940.

Dolado, J., C. García-Serrano, and J. Jimeno. 2002. "Drawing Lessons from the Boom of Temporary Jobs in Spain." *The Economic Journal* 112, no. 721: F270–95.

Dooley, D., J. Prause, and K.A. Haw-Rowbottom. 2000. "Underemployment and Depression: Longitudinal Relationships." *Journal of Health and Social Behavior* 41, no. 4: 421–436.

Durkheim, E. 1999. *The Division of Labour in Society.* Warsaw: PWN. (Polish edition).

Estanque, E., and H.A. Costa. 2012. "Labour Relations and Social Movements in the 21st Century," in *Sociological Landscape–Theories, Realities and Trends,* ed. D. Erasga. InTech, 257–282. Retrieved 10 October 2013 from http://www.intechopen.com/books/sociological-landscape-theories-realitiesand-trends/labour-relations-and-social-movements.

European Commission. 2006. "Employment in Europe 2006." Luxembourg: Office for Official Publications of the European Communities.

EUROSTAT. 2013. "European Social Statistics 2013 Edition." Eurostat Pocketbooks. Luxembourg: Office for Official Publications of the European Communities.

Gallego, A. 2008. "Unequal Political Participation in Europe." *International Journal of Sociology* 37, no. 4: 10–25.

Gaventa, J. 2002. "Introduction: Exploring Citizenship, Participation and Accountability." *IDS Bulletin* 33, no. 2: 1–11.

Gracia, F.J., J. Ramos, J.M. Peiró, A. Caballer, and B. Sora. 2011. "Job Attitudes, Behaviours and Well-Being Among Different Types of Temporary Workers in Europe and Israel." *International Labour Review* 150, no. 3–4: 235–254.

Hipple, S. 2001. "Contingent Work in the Late 1990s." *Monthly Labor Review* 124, no. 3: 3–27.

Kalleberg, A.L. 2009. "Precarious Work, Insecure Workers: Employment Relations in Transition." *American Sociological Review* 74, no. 1: 1–22.

Kiersztyn, A. 2012. "Analiza ekonomicznych konsekwencji zatrudnienia na czas określony dla jednostek i gospodarstw domowych" [Analysis of Economic Consequences of Fixed-Term Employment for Individuals and Households), in *Zatrudnienie na czas określony w polskiej gospodarce. Społeczne i ekonomiczne konsekwencje zjawiska* [Fixed-Term Employment in the Polish Economy. Socio-Economic Consequences of the Phenomenon], ed. M. Bednarski and K. Frieske. Warsaw: IPiSS, 93–121.

———. 2016a. "Fixed-Term Employment and Occupational Position in Poland: The Heterogeneity of Temporary Jobs." *European Sociological Review* Advance Access. DOI: http://dx.doi.org/10.1093/esr/jcw044.

———. 2016b. "Non-Standard Employment and Risk: How Can We Capture Job Precarity Using Survey Data?" Distributed paper prepared for the 3rd ISA Forum of Sociology, Vienna, July 2016.

Kittilson, M.C. 2005. "Changing Patterns of Mobilization, Increasing Bias? Trends in Participation in Established Democracies 1960-2003," *Annual Meeting of the American Political Science Association, Washington, DC, 1-4 September 2005.* American Political Science Association. Retrieved 19 November 2014 from http://www.allacademic.com/meta/p41511_index.html.

Li, Y., and D. Marsh. 2008. "New Forms of Political Participation: Searching for Expert Citizens and Everyday Makers." *British Journal of Political Science* 38, no. 2: 247–272.

Marien, S., M. Hooghe, and E. Quintelier. 2010. "Inequalities in Noninstitutionalized Forms of Political Participation: A Multilevel Analysis for 26 Countries." *Political Studies* 58, no. 1: 187–213.

Mayes, D. 2001. "Introduction," in *Social Exclusion and European Policy,* ed. D. Mayes, J. Berghman, and R. Salais. Cheltenham, Northhampton: Edward Elgar, 1–23.

McGovern, P., D. Smeaton, and S. Hill. 2004. "Bad Jobs in Britain: Nonstandard Employment and Job Quality." *Work and Occupations* 31, no. 2: 225–249.

Neumark, D. 2000. "Changes in Job Stability and Job Security: A Collective Effort to Untangle, Reconcile, and Interpret the Evidence," in *On the Job: Is Long-term Employment a Thing of the Past?,* ed. D. Neumark. New York: Russell Sage Foundation, 1–27.

OECD. 2014. *OECD Employment Outlook 2014.* OECD Publishing, Paris. DOI: http://dx.doi.org/10.1787/empl_outlook-2014-en.

Oliver, J.E. 2000. "City Size and Civic Involvement in Metropolitan America." *The American Political Science Review* 94, no. 2: 361–373.

Polavieja, J. 2003. "Temporary Contracts and Labour Market Segmentation in Spain: An Employment-Rent Approach." *European Sociological Review* 19, no. 5: 501–517.

Putnam, R. 2000. *Bowling Alone: The Collapse and Revival of American Community.* New York, London: Simon and Schuster.

Sandovici, M.E., and T. Davis. 2010. "Activism Gone Shopping: An Empirical Exploration of Individual-Level Determinants of Political Consumerism and Donating." *Comparative Sociology* 9, no. 3: 328–335.

Schlozman, K.L., S. Verba, and H.E. Brady. 2010. "Weapon of the Strong? Participatory Inequality and the Internet." *Perspectives on Politics* 8, no. 2: 487–509.

Sennett, R. 1998. *The Corrosion of Character: The Personal Consequences of Work in the New Capitalism.* London/New York: W.W. Norton & Company.

Skocpol, T. 2004. "Voice and Inequality: The Transformation of American Civic Democracy." *Perspectives on Politics* 2, no. 1: 3–20.

Standing G. 2011. *Precariat: The New Dangerous Class.* London: Bloomsbury Academic.

Stolle, D. and M. Hooghe. 2005. "Inaccurate, Exceptional, One-sided or Irrelevant? The Debate About the Alleged Decline of Social Capital and Civic Engagement in Western Societies." *British Journal of Political Science* 35, no. 1: 149–167.

Stolle, D., and M. Hooghe. 2011. "Shifting Inequalities: Patterns of Exclusion and Inclusion in Emerging Forms of Participation." *European Societies* 13, no. 1: 119–142.

Stolle, D., and M. Micheletti. 2013. *Political Consumerism.* Cambridge: Cambridge University Press.

Sułek, A. 2013. "Doświadczenie, działania dla społeczności i kompetencje obywatelskie. Diagnoza Społeczna 2013. Warunki i Jakość Życia Polaków—Raport" [Social Diagnosis 2013: Objective and Subjective Quality of Life in Poland: Report]. *Contemporary Economics* 7 (special issue): 286–295.

Verba, S. 2004. "Would the Dream of Political Equality Turn Out to Be a Nightmare?" *Perspectives on Politics* 1, no. 4: 663–679.

Virtanen, M., M. Kivimäki, M. Joensuu, P. Virtanen, M. Elovainio, and J. Vahtera. 2005. "Temporary Employment and Health: A Review." *International Journal of Epidemiology* 34, no. 6: 610–622.

Wilensky, H.L. 1961. "Orderly Careers and Social Participation: The Impact of Work History on Social Integration in the Middle Mass." *American Sociological Review* 26, no. 4: 521–539.

PART III

Civil Society Making: Between the Past and the Present

Chapter 9

BETWEEN TRADITION AND MODERNITY
THE CASE OF RURAL WOMEN'S ORGANIZATIONS IN POLAND

Ilona Matysiak

Introduction

Historically speaking, the tradition of rural women's organizations (*Koła Gospodyń Wiejskich*) in Poland can be traced back to the second half of the nineteenth century, when, after the enfranchisement of peasants, the first social and economic rural associations started to emerge. Their main goal was to support the advancement of agriculture and living standards in rural households by turning rural women into active actors in these processes. Since the beginning, rural women's organizations have been initiating many cultural and educational activities for women as well as all people living in villages. Before World War II, their members became the female vanguard of rural development, who set up new and innovative ways of increasing the quality of agriculture and rural families' well-being as well as community life. During the state-socialist period, rural women's organizations were incorporated into the complex system of ideological control over the rural population. At the same time, as female structures, they were perceived as "politically harmless" and managed to continue and even broaden their cultural and educational activities, which were highly appreciated in rural communities. Soon, rural women's organizations became one of the most characteristic and prevalent entities in the Polish countryside. When the systemic transformation began in 1989 rural women's organizations faced new challenges and structural changes.

First, many organizations operating in the state-socialist period not only were discredited as being "infected" by the previous system, but were also deprived of the institutional and financial support that had formerly been provided. Most of the organizations existing at that time, regardless of their activity and the results they achieved, tended to be classified as "bad," irrespective of the fact that the historic traditions of some of them went back much further than the postwar period. At the same time, the concept of civil society, which was basically limited to new nongovernmental organizations (associations and foundations) established after 1989, became dominant. Moreover, civil society in Poland used to be described as universal, ignoring the perspective of the local context—the specific needs, traditions, and expectations in the diversified local communities (see Bartkowski 2003; Ekiert and Foa 2011; Ekiert and Kubik 2014; Kurczewska and Kurczewski 2011). This led to local concerns' exclusion from the debate and research on civil society of many groups and organizations, other than associations or foundations registered after 1989.

Rural women's organizations, which were numerous and active in the state-socialist period, and have an underestimated, rich historic tradition, rooted deeply in the local rural communities, in fact, fulfilled all of the prerequisites for such exclusion. Therefore, during the transformation period of the early 1990s, regardless of their merits, they were commonly depicted as "communist" and "backward" structures that did not fit the new reality. However, not only have many of these organizations survived, but new ones have been established in recent years. This raises the question of why the rural women's organizations still exist—who needs them and why? What are their strategies of action? This chapter explores this phenomenon, focusing on the modes of working adopted by rural women's organizations today. The main aim is to address three basic research questions: (1) What are the characteristics of rural women's organizations' members? (2) What kind of activities are implemented by these organizations? and (3) How do these organizations operate and find their place in the structural conditions shaping the modern civil society in Poland? It is argued that rural women's organizations, despite their shared core of activities, are deeply rooted in the local contexts where they operate. The variety of their forms and modes of action is simply ignored when they are observed through lenses focused on formal structures of nongovernmental organizations. Thus, this study shows the theoretical and empirical limits of using a universalist model of civil society in the assessment of actually existing civil societies.

The chapter starts with a methodological section, presenting the empirical data used in the analysis. Thereafter, the basic mechanisms of narrowing and unification of the concept of civil society in Poland are discussed. This section shows how this has led to unjust belittling of the significance and potential of traditional rural organizations. The following section discusses the specific characteristics of rural women's organizations and the role that these organizations have played in various historic periods. The subsequent parts of this chapter are devoted to the analysis of the empirical data, arranged in sections corresponding to the posed research questions.

Data and Research Method

This chapter is based on the results of analysis of data from two rounds of data collection.[1] The first one was conducted in 2005. It encompassed fifteen in-depth interviews conducted with the leaders and members of four chosen rural women's organizations, which differed in terms of when they were established—one existing since the second half of the nineteenth century, one established in the state-socialist period, and two reactivated in the late 1990s and early twenty-first century. The organizations examined operated in various types of rural communities: an urbanizing village located next to a large city, a village with a significant number of residents living off of agriculture, a village, where the state farm (PGR) operated before 1989. The interviews with the leaders and members of the selected rural women's organizations were complemented by four interviews with the "key informants" in the corresponding village, such as the village representative (sołtys),[2] the head of the local school, or the mayor.

The second source of empirical material consists of results of the analysis of qualitative data collected from ten communes located in different regions of Poland. The communes were chosen because of their different proportions of women serving as village representatives and commune councilors.[3] Two communes—one "feminized" and one "masculinized"—were examined in each of five chosen regions of Poland. The former was based on the percentage of women among village representatives and commune councilors, which was close to 50 percent, and the latter represented communes where the percentage of women village representatives and commune councilors did not exceed 30 percent. Eight individual in-depth interviews were conducted with the leaders of the rural women's organizations. In addition, interviews were conducted with female and male village representatives (fifty-one) and representatives of the local authorities, public institutions, and organizations (forty-nine). One of the topics discussed was the activity of the local organizations, and thus, some of the interviews contained information concerning the rural women's organizations in examined communes. Fieldwork was conducted between November 2008 and December 2010.

In addition, the chapter includes the results of a short survey, which was conducted in May 2005 among the participants of the Conference of Female

Village Representatives "It's time for the countryside!" (N=100). The conference was organized in the Polish Parliament by the Administrative Office of the Governmental Plenipotentiary for Equal Status of Women and Men and the Women's Parliamentary Group. Some of the questions in the survey questionnaire pertained to rural women's organizations.

Collecting the data in the two different time periods allows for capturing the processes of change in terms of the rural women's organizations' modes of working as well as the influence of external factors, such as Poland's accession to the European Union. The chapter also draws on the latest available secondary data.

The Concept of a Civil Society in Poland

According to Lane (2010: 259), most of the definitions of civil society share three main components: "an area between the individual (and family) and the state; an economy based on private ownership and the market; and a particular set of values and norms, which include the legitimating concepts of freedom and democracy." Rather than proposing or imposing a specific definition of civil society, however, the aim of this section is to reconstruct the notion of civil society that became dominant among Polish researchers as well as public opinion leaders.

Due to the complex nature of the concept of civil society, its comprehensive operationalizations, encompassing both structural and normative components, assuming both quantitative and qualitative indicators, are rather rare. In the late 1990s, Szacki (1997: 30) pointed out that: "From the perspective of researchers—empiricists, a civil society is usually perceived simply as the so called third sector, identified on the basis of a relatively simple process of reasoning, where the starting point is the division into private and public entities and public and private objectives of activity. The first sector is the market, where the entities and the objectives are private; the second sector is the government, where the entities and the objectives are public; the third sector is the civil society, where the entities are private and the objectives are public." In the period of systemic transformation, an even narrower concept of civil society caught on in Poland, influencing not only research undertaken in the subsequent years, but also public debate and the practice of supporting citizens' activity. The mainstream way of thinking of civil society was reduced to several types of entities and deprived of a historic perspective, as well as of the local dimension.

First, relating to the experiences of Western countries and concepts, which have become popular in this part of the world,[4] civil society understood as the third sector was identified with nongovernmental organizations, that is, associations and foundations, which, since 2003, have been regulated by the Act of Law on public benefit and volunteer work (see also Jezierska's chapter in this volume). Consequently, entities operating on the basis of other legal provisions—such as various professional organizations, Catholic Church–based nonprofits, and various unregistered organizations like councils of parents or committees building local infrastructure—were by and large ignored (Leś et al. 2000: 13–16).

Second, the "old" organizations, established before 1989, were generally recognized as facade entities, entirely subordinated to the Communist Party and doomed to die out in the new reality. This point of view, however, fails to reflect the complexity of structures "inherited" from the period of the People's Republic of Poland. According to Ekiert and Foa (2011: 9), even mass organizations could not always be boiled down to the "transmission belts" subordinated to the party: "Following de-Stalinization in the 1950s and especially since the mid-1970s, this official institutional sphere experienced a gradual process of pragmatization, de-ideologization, and even pluralization. This happened to a different degree in various countries, with Poland and Hungary leading the way. In the 1970s and 1980s many of these organizations became less ideological, and acquired a degree of autonomy in managing their internal affairs, as well as a growing lobbying capacity."

In addition, as Ekiert and Kubik (2014: 47; see also Ekiert and Kubik in this volume) point out, some of the organizations functioning in the state-socialist period were rooted in much older traditions: "Some pre-communist civil society traditions and even organizations (mostly in the realms of leisure, education, and culture) survived under communist rule, especially at the local level. They served as semi-official carriers of local traditions and provided a modicum of public space somewhat sheltered from direct political interference." Literature on the subject includes a number of publications, presenting historical details on structures and patterns of organized cooperation in Poland in the partition and prewar periods, as well as in earlier times (for example, see Bartkowski 2003; Leś et al. 2000). Poland thus entered the transformation period with some significant assets, including strong professional associations, numerous sports clubs, cultural organizations, as well as organizations associating specific groups, such as farmers, veterans of war, or women. Many of them had such resources as well-developed local structures and experienced activists (Ekiert and Kubik 2014). Thus, seen from a historic perspective, associations and foundations established after 1989 are only one possible type of third-sector entity in Poland.

Third, due to the diversity of such local factors as tradition, character of social bonds, and activity of the local authorities, in Poland we should refer to local civil societies rather than to a single, universal model of a civil society (Kurczewska and Kurczewski 2001; Misztal 2003). However, in the transformation period, the reflection on the meaning of the dimension of locality was clearly insufficient. These tendencies were strengthened by the destinations of foreign aid for Polish civil society. Regulska (1998) has pointed out that American funds for nongovernmental organizations have been received mainly by large entities operating in large cities. On the other hand, expert support for local organizations and institutions, financed by Western countries, has often been delivered by external consultants, who are not familiar with the peculiarities of the local contexts.

Disregarding of diversity of forms of civic engagement, of the historic perspective, and the dimension of locality, typical in the transformation period, has established the framework for defining of the civil society in Poland and the methodology applied to its analysis. This has led to marginalization of the significance of, among other things, traditional rural organizations and the specific character of other collective activities undertaken by rural residents.

The Concept of a Civil Society and Rural Communities in Poland

Poland is characterized by a relatively high share of inhabitants of the rural areas in the total population. According to the results of the National Census of 2011, the percentage of the Polish rural population was 39.2 percent (GUS 2012: 47). In 2009, the share of rural areas of the total geographic area of Poland amounted to 85.4 percent based on the criteria of Eurostat and 90.8 percent based on the criteria of the OECD (Stanny 2011: 105).[5] The agriculture sector is characterized by a great number of small family farms—in 2010, the average area of a farm in Poland was 9.6 hectares (Poczta 2012: 84).

At the same time, the social structure of the rural population has been changing. Due to the progressing de-agrarization of employment, more than 60 percent of rural residents have nothing to do with agriculture, while the percentage of rural households living on farming only has dropped below 10 percent (Wilkin 2011: 117). The education aspirations of the rural population are growing, and the migration flow from the cities to the countryside—in particular, to the suburbs—is increasing. Halamska (2013) indicates that, as a result of all these changes, "the rural middle class," which consists of white-collar workers and specialists, is emerging. Also, the quality of the rural "technical" infrastructure, including roads, sewage systems, etc., has been improving, along with the "social" infrastructure—e.g., public utility buildings (schools, community centers, etc.). It should be underlined, however, that the developmental changes in specific communities differ greatly in terms of their intensity, depending on the characteristics of the local context (ibid.).

At the end of 2011, only 24 percent out of seventy-two thousand associations (excluding the voluntary fire brigades) and eleven thousand foundations existing in Poland were registered in the rural areas (Przewłocka 2013: 2). Focusing on the registered associations and foundations, however, leads to a false conclusion concerning the low level of civic engagement of rural residents. Associations and foundations are just two of many possible types of organizations and collective actions present in local rural communities. Moreover, in the villages, we also deal with the entire spectrum of organization forms, which are not found in the national registers or databases. These are groups and initiatives associated with the local parishes, schools, committees for construction of the local infrastructure (which are usually dissolved after they have completed their task), as well as informal groups established on the basis of economic cooperation or relations with the neighbors (Herbst 2008). A significant indicator of civic engagement in the rural communities is also the activity of the rural self-government (*samorząd wiejski*), which comprises the local initiatives of the village representative (sołtys) and the village council (*rada sołecka*), usually undertaken together with the inhabitants (Matysiak 2014). The rural population is also characterized by various informal activities, undertaken spontaneously in order to solve a specific local problem.

Particularly noteworthy here are the so-called traditional rural organizations, many of which were established as early as the second half of the nineteenth century (Bartkowski 2003). These entities vary in terms of their legal form, and usually are subject to legal provisions other than those regulating the activity of nongovernmental organizations (associations and foundations). The most significant are the voluntary fire brigades (*ochotnicze straże pożarne*), usually established as associations; farmers' organizations and rural women's organizations, formally registered as socioprofessional farmer entities similar to trade unions; and amateur sports clubs. In the state-socialist period, traditional rural organizations were controlled by the state through the complex system of numerous formal vertical and horizontal dependencies. Nevertheless, many of them implemented a great deal of useful initiatives on behalf of the villages and their residents.

The dimension of locality is of key significance for the theory and practice of civil society in Poland. Some authors pointed to the need to "sensitize" the research on the specific character of the rural communities. For instance, Herbst distinguished two models of civil society in Poland—"urban" and "rural" (Herbst 2005, in Bartkowski 2007: 90), Lewenstein (1999) wrote about the "community based model of cooperation," typical for the rural areas, and Fedyszak-Radziejowska (2012: 122) emphasized the significance of traditional informal bonds based on relations in the frame of family and neighborhood circles as well as religious community formed by the local parish. Going even further, Klekotko (2005: 105–116) underlined that the

Polish rural communities were not only different from those in the cities, but also from one another. Therefore, according to Klekotko, we should not construct a universal model of the "rural civil society," but we can speak of "rural civil communities" as civil society manifests itself at the local level, strongly related to the specific social and historic context.

Limiting the operational definitions of civil society to nongovernmental organizations established after 1989 has popularized the false belief that it is a new phenomenon, observed mainly in the urban context. This perspective has turned out to be extraordinarily resistant to change, despite the efforts of some researchers who point to the diversity of types of civic engagement in the rural communities (e.g., Bukraba-Rylska 2011; Herbst 2008; Kamiński 2008). The victims of this way of thinking include the rural women's organizations—traditional entities that are still insufficiently noticed and constantly underestimated.

Rural Women's Organizations: A Historic Sketch

The first organizations of rural women started to emerge in the second half of the nineteenth century, during the period of liquidation of the corvée farm economy. The decline of the patrimonial role of landlords resulted in a growing demand for institutions and collective structures that would support the processes of modernization of agriculture, peasant farms, and conditions of living in the rural areas (Bukraba-Rylska 2008). Such initiatives were undertaken with the assumption that rural women should participate actively in the changes taking place. The first female organizations in rural communities were founded by representatives of the gentry and the clergy, as well as activists of the peasant movement (Kostrzewska 1992). Usually, these were established simultaneously with the farmers' organizations (*kółka rolnicze*)—the peasant socioeconomic associations for men (Sawicka 1996). Before the World War II, rural women's organizations (*Koła Gospodyń Wiejskich*) were the most popular associations for female inhabitants of the rural areas. Under the supervision of full-time female instructors and activists of the peasant movement, their members acquired practical skills associated with household and farm work and they developed rural cooperatives. Another aim was to engage the rural women in the cultural initiatives and draw their attention also to involvement in local self-government and decision-making processes (Kostrzewska 1992). In 1937, there were 4,221 rural women's organizations with more than ninety-nine thousand members in Poland (Marczakiewicz et al. 1992: 19). The membership was not mass, but the significant group of rural female activists was formed within these structures.

In the early postwar years, traditional rural organizations, including the rural women's organizations, tried to continue their activity from before 1939; however, they were quickly "absorbed" by the centrally controlled structures founded by the Communist Party. Their revival took place only after 1956, when the state policy became "softer," including toward the rural organizations. In the state-socialist period, rural women's organizations became a mass structure—in 1959, there were more than eight thousand of these, with almost one hundred and sixty thousand members, and in 1989—more than thirty-five thousand organizations with more than one million members (Marczakiewicz et al. 1992: 27). Before 1989, the rural women's organizations were "fitted into" the system of vertical and horizontal institutional interdependencies controlled by the state. They were an autonomous component of the structure of "male" farmers' organizations, and until 1966, they had also formed a part of the League of Polish Women (*Liga Kobiet Polskich*). Nevertheless, the rural women's organizations performed many activities that were useful on the local level with regard to agriculture (e.g., poultry collectives), education and culture (e.g., courses in cooking, baking, sewing, handicraft, as well as trips for sightseeing, to the movies and theaters), child care (e.g., during intensive agricultural work), health care and hygiene (e.g., by organizing experts' talks and medical examinations), promotion of handicraft, folk culture (e.g., through establishment of singing and acting groups), and agrotourism (Grzebisz-Nowicka 1995). However, involvement in the rural women's organizations also facilitated access to resources and services, which were hindered under the conditions of the "economy of shortage" (Kornai 1985), such as household equipment (e.g., washing machines, irons) and farming devices (e.g., potato lifters), which were distributed or co-used among the members.

In the literature on the subject, it has been noted that unlike the farmers' organizations, the rural women's organizations, perceived as dealing with practical "female issues," largely avoided ideologization and political infiltration. They provided rural women and the rural population in general with needed information and services that were inaccessible otherwise. At the same time, as it has been noted by Siemieńska (2005: 245), during the state-socialist period, rural women's organizations were not feminist structures acting on behalf of women, but rather entities that acted in the best interest of the state through the agency of women.

Rural Women's Organizations Today

The legal basis for rural women's organizations is provided by the Act on Socioprofessional Organization of Farmers of 1982. In the Act, the female structures are referred to as a "separate organizational unit of a farmers' organization" (Art. 22, clause 2). According to official information, the objectives of the rural women's organizations include: providing assistance for the rural families in bringing up and educating children and ensuring their participation in various forms of holiday recreation; activities on behalf of health care and well-being of rural families thanks to development of health-care education; improvement of the sanitary conditions of the farms and whole villages and assistance to the elderly and the disabled; development of various forms of entrepreneurship among rural women; increased efficiency in management of rural households and areas of agricultural production; increasing participation of the rural inhabitants in culture, promotion of folklore, and folk art.[6] It does not mean, however, that the rural women's organizations fit the model of service providers, which is often imposed on nongovernmental organizations. The great majority of these official objectives remained the same as before 1989 and, according to the empirical data presented later, are met only to some extent today.

According to the legal provisions quoted, the rural women's organizations, as before 1989, formally remain a part of the structure of the "male" farmers' organizations, which make up the Association of Farmers, Farming Groups and Organizations (*Związek Rolników, Kółek i Organizacji Rolniczych*). The structures of the Association include those established at the national, provincial (that are, relatively speaking, the most dynamic), and local level (districts and communes) as well as the farmers' organizations operating at the level of villages. The rural women's organizations have their councils at all levels of the Association structure—from the national to local one; individual organizations operate at the level of the village. The "institutional dependence" of the rural women's organizations on the farmers' structures has many significant consequences.

First of all, the rural women's organizations are not entered in any official registers or databases on third-sector organizations, such as those established by the Klon/Jawor Association or Polish Central Statistical Office. Thus, it is not possible even to estimate their number. On the website of the National Association of Farmers, Farming Groups and Organizations, it is stated that there are 25,800 rural women's organizations with more than eight hundred thousand members;[7] however, this number seems to be highly overstated.[8]

The situation becomes even more complicated if we consider the fact that the rural women's organizations survived the transformation period or were revived in the recent years, while a lot of farmers' organizations simply disappeared, being too dependent on the previous state system of support for agriculture (Grzebisz-Nowicka 1995). Thus, many of the rural women's organizations were deprived of their "parent" institutional structure. As a result, some of them, particularly in the areas in which the farmers' organizations no longer exist, function as informal groups. Others, located in the areas in which the farmers' organization structures survived, retained their former legal and institutional format. However, the Association of Farmers, Farming Groups and Organizations, operating dynamically at the national level, but rather weak when it comes to the local structures, is able to control the rural women's organizations operating at the local level only partially. At present, the Association estimates the number of organizations that still "belong" to its institutional network to be around 2,500.[9]

Second, as they officially belong to the farmers' structures, the rural women's organizations are not "independent" legal persons, which substantially limits their ability to apply for funds, e.g., in grant competitions. As a result, women decide to register their organizations as autonomous associations and gain the status of a nongovernmental organization as defined in the Act of Law on public benefit and volunteer work.[10] It must be underlined that the farmers' structures usually do not financially support the rural women's organizations. The National Council of Rural Women's Organizations (*Krajowa Rada Kół Gospodyń Wiejskich*), connected strongly to the Association of Farmers, registered the separate entity called the Association of Rural Women (*Stowarzyszenie Kobiet Wiejskich "Gospodyni"*), which may create local branches that "lend" legal personality to the rural women's organizations operating at the local level. However, no information has been obtained with regard to whether this solution has proven to be effective or not.

It can thus be said that, attempting to find their place in the new reality, today's rural women's organizations select various paths and strategies. The empirical data gathered have allowed for in-depth analysis of their modes of action.

Members of the Rural Women's Organizations

In the rural women's organizations included in the 2005 research, the number of members ranged from seven to thirty-two. In the later research, conducted in 2008–2010, some organizations operating in much larger villages had fifty or even more than one hundred female members. In most cases, women, who were members of these organizations, were older or at least middle-aged (about fifty years old or more) and most of them were no longer employed. Younger women were a minority, usually connected by family ties to the older members (daughters, daughters-in-law, granddaughters). Only two of the examined organizations consisted exclusively of younger women, aged approximately between thirty and fifty. It should be emphasized that the weak engagement of young women is one of the most significant problems faced by the rural women's organizations. In general, the great majority of the analyzed organizations' members were married; most of them had children. It should be noted, however, that among the oldest members, there was a large group of widows whose children had left for the city or gone abroad. In almost all the examined rural women's organizations, their members came from the rural areas, often from the vicinity, or they had lived there since their childhood. In some organizations operating in suburban villages or in areas characterized by good transport connections with the cities and thus attractive for "settlers" from the outside, the members included women who used to live in the city. One of them declared having become a member of the rural women's organization to get to know the local community better and learn about the local traditions: "I got enrolled, because I'd grown up in a city ... first of all, I was curious what it was like. I also attended the meetings gladly, because ... one could find out many interesting things, for instance, how the countryside used to be in the past, how people used to do this or that, for example, the harvest festival" [M.Z.2].[11]

The qualitative research conducted in 2014 by The Unit for Social Innovation and Research—"Shipyard" (*Pracownia Badań i Innowacji Społecznych Stocznia*) contained an interesting case of a rural women's organization established by the female "newcomers" who had moved to the rural areas from the city. Mostly young women, with small or school-age children, not working, organized themselves in order to spend time together, develop their interests and hobbies (mainly sports), and act on behalf of the community, in which they were otherwise strangers. Interestingly enough, the organization encountered distrust and discontent from the "indigenous" elderly population, who felt "robbed" of their rural tradition by the "newcomers." The members of the organization had to prove their sincerity for a long time, and only after they organized the celebration of an anniversary of the establishment of the village did they win the hearts of the elderly (Milczewska et al. 2014: 32).

In terms of the two research projects, it can be concluded that the key role in all of the rural women's organizations examined was played by their leaders (their chairwomen). Their persistence and willingness to preserve the traditions of the organization often served as the main conditions for its existence. It is interesting to note that most of interviewed leaders of the rural women's organizations had unique social resources and life experiences. First, all of them had at least vocational secondary (technical school) education; there were also several university graduates. Some of them had occupations not associated with agriculture (e.g., teachers, accountants), and this group included former holders of managerial positions in local institutions or companies. Some of them had managed family farms, engaging in agricultural work as their husbands worked away from home. Also, most of the interviewed leaders mentioned their activity in youth organizations in which they were involved when they were young—the Rural Youth Association (*Związek Młodzieży Wiejskiej*), the Socialist Polish Youth Association (*Związek Socjalistycznej Młodzieży Polskiej*), or scouting. Some of them pointed to their involvement in the local public life: positions in the local administration, in parents' committees, village councils, etc. A great majority of the interviewed leaders of rural women's organizations also pointed to the patterns of public activity among their closest relatives, e.g., grandfathers, who were the activists of peasant movement; mothers, who were also involved in the rural women's organizations; and fathers, who became village representatives or communal council members. It can thus be said that women leading the rural women's organizations had relatively diverse and rich cultural and social capital (Bourdieu 1986), and they were strongly socialized to public activity both in their family and—in many cases—in the structures of the youth organizations, as well as later in adult life.

Activities of the Rural Women's Organizations

Along with progress of the systemic transformation, which led to a structural change of the rural areas and improvement of their inhabitants' standard of living, the rural women's organizations gradually ceased to engage, e.g., in poultry collectives, rental of household equipment, organizing of courses or trainings related to children's upbringing, maintenance of the household, or talks on health and hygiene. According to the interviewees, all this information is easy to find in women's magazines or on the Internet. It does not mean, however, that they gave up all types of traditional initiatives. The analyzed rural women's organizations continued their activities from the past to a greater or lesser extent, combining them with new concepts and ideas.

Among the organizations examined in 2005, the most visible type of activity was associated with the broadly understood continuation of folk traditions and participation in various local events and celebrations. Female members of the rural women's organizations prepared harvest festival garlands, dishes, and handicraft for the local picnics and other events, and participated in the local contests—e.g., in cooking. Members of three of the organizations examined also created folk singing groups, attending local celebrations and festivities. In addition, the rural women's organizations participated in organization of local cultural events—the female members of one of the examined organizations initiated and then, with the support of the local authorities, co-organized, a two-day festival of folk culture in their village. Members of the rural women's organizations also prepared official treats for the guests visiting their villages, e.g., representatives of state institutions or

Catholic Church authorities. One of the organizations examined was particularly strongly connected with the local parish—women were engaged in
cleaning of the church and caring for the internal decorations.

Another typical field of activity was the organization of meetings and celebrations for the residents of the village, such as a New Year's party, Christmas
party, Women's Day, Children's Day, etc. One of the organizations examined, in which most members were older women, "specialized" in organizing
meetings for the elderly, e.g., Seniors' Day, trips to the movies or the theater.
The leader of this organization pointed out that, thanks to their initiatives,
these events were also accessible to people, who could not afford them independently: "Of course, this is rather for the group of those less affluent,
because ... those, who have cars, I guess they have reached a certain standard
of living ... when there is a trip to a theater or to the movies, or a meeting,
a bonfire, well, for such people, this is not attractive ... we help those, who
stay at home ... we organize this Seniors' Day, or a Christmas party, an Easter
party or a bonfire" [M.Z.1].

In one of the organizations examined, whose members were mostly relatively young women (aged about thirty to fifty), innovative ideas for activities in the near future emerged: organizing of fitness classes for all interested
women, talks on women's health, meetings and discussions with experts in
various fields: "I used to dream of something like aerobics, some exercising
... because everyone complains after the winter. We could do something like
that for the women ... well, we could invite a doctor, organize some lectures,
for instance, these days, those gynecological problems, right? ... We could
invite someone, who would present the issues, which are more, well, I don't
know, in the rural areas, people tend to fall behind, we don't even know
what's happening out there, in the world" [Z.P.2].

The organizations examined in 2008–2010 presented very similar types
of activities—participation in local events and festivals, organization of meetings for the members and inhabitants of the village, management of folk
bands. Some of them were also very strongly connected to the parish and
the church, for instance, they prepared the altars for the Corpus Christi
celebrations or decorated the church for religious celebrations. However, this
time the trainings were mentioned—one of the interviewed leaders pointed
out the free floral and regional cuisine courses open for all interested women
from the village. According to the interviews, these activities enjoyed great
interest among women of various ages, which means that, despite the availability of information, such collective learning through courses and workshops is still needed. Members of the same organization also prepared an
exhibition of old rural household equipment: "for our fiftieth anniversary,
we had this exhibition of old stuff, which people no longer remember, particularly the young ones—they have no idea what a churn looks like, all kinds

of old tools, for spinning, mangling, etc." [L.R.2_k.l][12] In this sense, the rural women's organization should be perceived as a guardian and promoter of local traditions and folk culture.

Similar types of activity of the rural women's organizations were found in quantitative research conducted in 2014 by "The Shipyard" in 300 communes (stratified and proportional sample), where 200 rural women's organizations were randomly selected. The organizations examined (N=139) engaged in cuisine and cooking (92 percent), handicraft and arts (77 percent), folk singing, theatre, and dancing groups (39 percent), organization of classes and workshops (28 percent), promotion of local products (22 percent), organization of trips and pilgrimages (12 percent), reconstruction of the history and tradition of the region (10 percent), and organization of festivities and events (7 percent) (Milczewska et al. 2014: 17).

Statements of the interviewees of 2005, and even more so, of those of 2008–2010, indicate a process of "renaissance" of the women's rural organizations. On the one hand, these organizations are perceived by the local authorities and cultural institutions as excellent "tools" for promotion of the whole community, e.g., during folklore festivals or any kind of local celebrations. On the other hand, rural women's organizations are valuable "operational" resources when the local events are organized. This "renaissance" of rural women's organizations is also due to the growing interest in regional products, local cuisine, and handicraft traditions, etc., which have been strengthened by the availability of EU funds in this area. During the "picnics of local tastes" organized in various villages and towns, the rural women's organizations present the forgotten local dishes and they promote new recipes, which reflect a mix of tradition and modern inspirations.

Modes of Working of the Rural Women's Organizations

None of the rural women's organizations examined in 2005 had the status of an independent legal person, but at the same time only one of them was strongly associated with the Provincial Association of Farmers, Farming Groups and Organizations. Two other rural women's organizations officially belonged to the structure of the Association, but in the face of liquidation of farmers' organizations in their vicinity, they no longer perceived themselves as being a part of it: "the farmers' organizations, which were formerly connected to the rural women's organizations were … well, they are practically diminishing, they are dissolving, they no longer exist, and so we are now 'abandoned', as the rural women's organization." [M.Z.1] The remaining fourth organization was reactivated in 2003 as an informal group operating at the local community center.

As a result, the budgets of all rural women's organizations examined were very limited. The basic sources of funds were membership fees, revenues from the lending of kitchen utensils and dishes for wedding parties, sales of their own products, and awards received for performances and harvest festival garlands. Usually, some small support was provided by the local authorities (e.g., a one-time subsidy of about 100 € for the purchase of products to prepare dishes for the local event). The local authorities provided the rural women's organizations with some support, e.g., rooms for their meetings or buses for trips.

An exception was one of the organizations examined, subsidized with relatively high amounts of money (about 1,000 €) by the local authorities and the Provincial Association of Farmers, Farming Groups and Organizations. Both actors have seen this financial support as an investment that should pay off in terms of their promotion in the region. According to one of the interviewees, the folklore festivals and other events of this kind were extremely popular there and each commune or local institution wanted to be represented: "At first, we just created this singing group, but some of us did not expect it to be such a duty. Well, some say, 'hey, we thought we would just sing a little, just like that.' Because, well, who would give us money to sing only here, in our village, at the community center or the playing field? Well, it is normal, we have to represent our commune, make it famous, so that they know this money isn't wasted" [Z.P.2].

Given the lack of funding, almost all the other examined rural women's organizations searched for a new formula that would allow them to obtain greater funds for their undertakings. A leader of the informal group operating at the community center planned to register the organization as an association. Another leader indicated that she was a cofounder of the District Association of Women and that her aim was to take advantage of this structure to obtain the funds for her rural women's organization as well: "the possibility of having our own account, making money, performing, addressing sponsors, having some real assets, ... because, as a rural women's organization we have no such possibilities." [M.Z.1] Also, in her opinion, in the suburban villages, which were undergoing significant urbanization and "colonization" by newcomers from the cities, a women's association would have more opportunities to act and to survive than would a rural women's organization, which is associated too strongly with tradition and agriculture. A leader of yet another organization was looking for an "umbrella" structure with a legal person status, which is necessary to apply for more significant funds from sponsors other than local authorities. At the time of the research, none of the organizations examined had made an independent attempt to obtain funds from a grant competition, although the leaders were optimistic about such a possibility.

Among the organizations examined in 2008–2010, only two were still connected with the structure of the Association of Farmers, Farming Groups and Organizations. These relations were due to the existence of the still relatively dynamic farmers' structures in their region, but they did not translate to substantial financial support. Most of the remaining rural women's organizations operated as nonregistered informal groups, one of them connected with the local community center.

An exception to the rule was the rural women's organization transformed into the Association of Creative Women: "There was a very dynamic rural women's organization, and the Association emerged, in fact, from this organization." [M.K.4_k.l] In the opinion of the leader, this was mainly due to its willingness to become independent from the local institutions associated with farming, which interfered too much in the activity of the former rural women's organization.

Basic financing of the organizations examined turned out to be similar to the situation in 2005. These included the membership fees, funds, and support provided by the commune authorities and the local cultural institutions. Some of the organizations examined also attained small amounts of money for their activities thanks to introducing fees for celebrations organized in the village (e.g., New Year's parties) or sale of their dishes during the local festivities or events.[13] One of the interviewed leaders, who, despite the lack of legal personhood status for her organization, was the least eager to complain about the financial problems encountered, said this was mainly due to her individual resourcefulness:

> I wrote a request to the communal cooperative, to the dairy, we wrote a request to the local bank, here we got 50 €, there we got 70 €, here we got 20 €, this is not important, how much they gave us, it is good that they did and we could do something, this way or another, certain things. But, if you don't have the courage, if you have nobody to help you or encourage you and you lack the courage to simply go and ask for the money, well, it's difficult … A village fund[14] has been established in our commune, and this year, we wrote a request to the council for next year, concerning the division of funds. [L.R.2_k.l]

It seems that the Polish membership in the EU does not directly affect the rural women's organizations in terms of greater financial independence. Even the members of the only registered association among all the organizations examined made no attempts to obtain funds for activity through a grant competition, relying mainly on their membership fees and money from the local authorities. The interviewed leaders were often skeptical about the programs aimed at applying for EU funds as being too complicated and bureaucratized: "our school, I think it was three years ago, it won the EU project, 'The School of Your Dreams'. But the teachers don't want that, because you have to record every penny and that's a problem ... they also have to deal with various things that are not necessary, formal matters ... if anything is wrong, you have to return the money. You take the money, buy this or that— then the money is gone and how will you return it? It's gone" [P.Ł.4_k.l]. It seems that the rural women's organizations are more eager to undertake tasks in projects implemented by others than as direct applicants. The free floral and regional cooking courses, offered by one of the organizations, men- tioned earlier, were financed from EU funds obtained by the regional organi- zation run by the local government: "In fact, this year, we managed to obtain the funds from the European Union and we offered two courses, here, in the village, but not only for the ladies from the organization, absolutely, for anyone, who wanted to participate ... the applicant was the Association of Communes of Lubelskie Province in Lublin, and they prepared the applica- tion. They devised the project, they helped us with this" [L.R.2_k.l].

It can thus be said that the initial enthusiasm accompanying Poland's ac- cession to the European Union and the hopes for availability of funds for local initiatives is largely gone. Excessive bureaucratization of the programs and procedures for distribution of EU funds leads to a situation where, in order to obtain these funds, one needs knowledge, experience, as well as spe- cific cultural capital resources (e.g., the "skills" of writing grant applications and using the language of bureaucracy).[15] Perhaps this is why relatively few rural women's organizations transform into registered associations. This has been confirmed by the results of quantitative research, conducted in 2014 by "The Shipyard." Among the rural women's organizations examined in 300 communes (N=139), 49 percent act as informal groups, 36 percent are within the structures of the Association of Farmers, Farming Groups and Organizations, and 15 percent as registered associations (Milczewska et al. 2014: 11).

At the same time, it can be assumed that the growing number and popu- larity of local events focused on regional traditions, including cuisine, would increase the financial support for rural women's organizations. However, according to some of the interviewees, the effect may be quite the opposite. The greater popularity of such activities results in more intense competition between the growing number of local entities as the rural women's organi- zations are not the only structures focused on cultivating regional traditions.

Role of Today's Rural Women's Organizations

It seems that the rural women's organization is perceived as a dominant model for female self-organization, strongly accepted by the rural popula- tion: "we are strong enough as an organization ... we have these roots ... this will surely never die ... it has been going on for many years, for generations, it's the way it is" [RK KGW]. This tradition can be used in various ways, depending on the creativity of the members and the needs of the inhabitants of a given area. Still, it is worth asking why women living in the rural areas become members of the rural women's organizations today.

According to the interviewees, for most elderly women, who are widows and/or retired, such engagement provides them with the ability to maintain social contact with other people: "most of the ladies have retired already, this is a certain return to social activity, to seeing people, we don't lock ourselves at home, we come here instead. Even to gossip, even without doing anything, just to meet, exchange thoughts." [M.Z.1] Also, the lack of professional activity of relatively younger women, who are still full of energy, can be compensated for through engagement in the rural women's organizations. One of the interviewed leaders noticed that those particularly eager to get involved in the activity of her organization were women who had decided to retire before reaching the statutory retirement age and needed something to fill the gap that emerged after they stopped working: "It was the period of 1999–2001, there was a possibility of early retirement, if you were fifty something and you had a farm and there were problems [with keeping the job], well, many women retired. They were young, they did not realize that at 50s they would not feel [tired of working] ... they felt free only for a short time, they enjoyed this freedom, because they did not have to work, they were happy to be retired, but they did not realize they were still full of life and energy and that they should be doing something" [P.Ł.1_k.l].

In the case of the younger members, working at home and/or on their family farm and raising children, engagement in the rural women's organization was an opportunity to "get out of the house," to find time for themselves, to talk and cooperate with other women. One of the youngest leaders of the organizations examined pointed out that in her case, involvement in the organization was to compensate her earlier active life as a student: "I needed it ... I was taking university courses on weekends, I had small children, finally I graduated and it turned out I had plenty of time. I don't have to hurry anywhere, I don't have to go to classes, commute, I have plenty of time" [M.K.4_k.l]. For many years the rural women's organizations were almost the only structures through which rural women could undertake collective activities. From this perspective, these organizations can be seen as structures enabling women to take on public roles. For some interviewees, the engagement in the rural women's organization actually worked as a ladder that they climbed to reach other public positions. Some of them became village representatives or won local elections to the communal council, while others were offered membership in another organizations and local structures. In the light of the quantitative research of 2005, as many as 61 percent of the female village representatives (N=100) confirmed their membership in the rural women's organizations at the time or in the past (Matysiak 2005: 148). However, among the leaders of the organizations examined, performance of public functions in the rural or communal self-government was not common, which leads us to the question of perception of activity of the rural women's organizations often associated with traditional female roles.

On the other hand, it is worth asking whether the rural women's organizations could develop any other type of activity. We could also ask whether the potential of the rural women's organizations, as still the most popular and numerous structures associating women living in rural areas, is fully taken advantage of. In the survey of 2005, the female village representatives examined (N=100) were asked whether the rural women's organizations were needed in the modern rural communities—93 percent of them answered positively. The respondents pointed out that apart from addressing needs associated with integration of rural residents, organization of free time, and cultural life, the rural women's organizations were needed for their contributions to solving social problems, such as alcoholism, domestic violence, and poverty (17 percent), it was noted that they also integrate and activate rural women (16 percent) (Matysiak 2005: 148).

In the quantitative research conducted in 2006 for the Ministry of Labor and Social Policy on the representative sample of 1,500 rural women, 64.8 percent of the respondents stated that female organizations in the rural areas should in the future deal with counteracting domestic violence; 38.2 percent stated that they should deal with counteracting discrimination of women in the labor market; 32.4 percent, supporting the professional activity of women; 26.8 percent, supporting the access of rural women to education; 24.4 percent, counteracting sexual abuse of women; and 24.0 percent, supporting entrepreneurship among rural women (Walczak-Duraj 2008: 152). It seems that rural women's organizations could have a much wider range of activities and deal much more with the interests and the needs of women themselves.

Conclusions

First, rural women's organizations seem to be particularly important as the space of female collective actions and as tools of social activation for the elderly, particularly women. The "vitality" of these organizations is clear proof of the needs of rural women, who want to meet and cooperate on behalf of their communities. Such activity is also encouraged by growing interest in local traditions, cuisine, and folk music.

On the other hand, it seems that the potential of rural women's organizations, which are widely accepted in rural communities, is not fully used. Their activities are focused mostly on issues associated with traditional female roles. The growing interest in folklore and regional cuisine feeds demand for rural women's organizations, but, at the same time, might relegate them to providers of free catering services during local events and celebrations. The presented data shows that more feminist women's organizations are also needed in the Polish rural areas—the organizations, which could seriously deal with the problems of domestic violence, discrimination of women in the labor market, and under-representation of women in local politics, not only acting as service providers but also lobbying local authorities to influence political decisions, e.g., concerning budgets. It is worth considering whether the activities of rural women's organizations could be broadened and diversified if more young women and female "newcomers" from the cities engaged, as they may be more eager to combine traditions with new ideas.

This case shows also institutional constraints that some groups of activists face and the ways they overcome them. The present regulations, unchanged since the early 1980s, create a situation in which rural women's organizations are still a part of a structure that cannot provide them with sufficient support and acts mainly on behalf of farmers. Under these circumstances, the rural women's organizations are not independent legal persons. Therefore, depending on the age and experience of the leaders, the period in which they were established, the local traditions and available networks of institutions, rural women's organizations adapt various strategies. Some of them act as informal groups, operating on a small scale mainly to fulfill their own needs or those of selected groups. Others try to look for "institutional umbrellas" among other local organizations and institutions. The third group consists of "young" organizations—reactivated or established in the recent years, led by younger women—registered as associations. However, only the rural women's organizations that adopt the latter strategy can fully and independently participate in the current system of support for third-sector organizations in Poland.

Finally, it should be noted that rural women's organizations are based on long-lasting model that can be traced back to the second half of the nineteenth century. At the same time, they often implement different modes of working depending on the local context. Many of them can be described as located between a formal structure and an informal group or shifting from one category to the other. The analysis presented in this chapter shows that it is necessary to adopt a theoretical and practical perspective depicting Polish civil society as complex and "recombining" new and old organizational forms and types of civic engagement. The dominating "universalist" model of civil society focused on nongovernmental organizations registered after 1989 leads to the marginalization of grassroots groups such as the rural women's organizations. The integration of the variety of their forms and promising potential could open up new perspectives in the study of civil society in Poland. First, the case of rural women's organizations is inspiring in terms of the process of transforming their tradition according to changing (and unfavorable) structural conditions. Second, the studied organizations indicate the significance of the locality dimension. Especially in case of strongly diversified rural communities in Poland, local factors, such as historical traditions, attitudes of local authorities, available human capital, and specific needs expressed by the residents, to a large extent shape the "profiles" of civic organizations and other entities. Therefore, the emphasis in researching civic activism should be put on extensive exploring of "rural civil communities" rather than "adjusting" the reality to the universal model of civil society imported from the Western context. Last but not least, the study presented in this chapter shows that it is necessary to develop more diversified and "sensitive" indicators that would enable analysis of the informal civic engagement in a more efficient and precise way.

Ilona Matysiak holds a Ph.D. in Sociology and is currently Assistant Professor at M. Grzegorzewska University, Poland. She is also a member of the Center of Interdisciplinary Gender Studies at the Robert B. Zajonc Institute for Social Studies, University of Warsaw. Her research interests include social changes in rural areas, civil society, local self-government, and gender. Recent publications include the article "The Feminization of Governance in Rural Communities in Poland: The Case of Village Representatives" (*sołtys*) published in *Gender, Place & Culture: A Journal of Feminist Geography.*

Notes

1. The data on the rural women's organizations come from my doctoral thesis, which has been recently published in the form of a book (Matysiak 2014) and other own research. See also Matysiak (2009).
2. In general, the function of a village representative (sołtys) in Poland is as liaison between the residents of a rural subcommune (*sołectwo*) and the local authorities at the superior levels.
3. Research was conducted within the frame of a project financed by the Ministry of Science and Higher Education (N N116 433 237).
4. For instance, the approach proposed by Putnam, who believed voluntary associations to be of key significance for the process of building social capital in a given community—trust, norms that contribute to cooperation, and horizontal networks of civic engagement (Putnam 1994).
5. According to Eurostat, rural areas are those with population density below 100 inhabitants per 1 km^2, and according to OECD, rural areas are those with population density below 150 inhabitants per 1 km^2.

6. Retrieved 24 October 2014 from http://kolkarolnicze.eu/O-nas/Kola-Gospodyn-Wiejskich.

7. Retrieved 24 October 2014 from http://kolkarolnicze.eu/O-nas/Struktura-KZRK iOR.

8. The available estimates on farmers' organizations indicate that out of thirty thousand in 1989/1990, only slightly above three thousand were left in 2008 (Marczakiewicz et al. 1992: 27; Halamska 2008: 109).

9. Information provided by Mrs. Bernardetta Niemczyk, chairwoman of the National Council of Women's Rural Organizations, during the conference "Conditions of Living and Activity of Women in the Rural Areas in Poland," held on 15 October 2014 at the Institute of Rural and Agricultural Development, Polish Academy of Sciences. It should be underlined that the Association of Farmers has not finished the process of officially verifying the number of rural women's organizations "belonging" to its structures.

10. In 2009, I found in the National Court Register (Krajowy Rejestr Sądowy) 165 nongovernmental organizations with names referring to the tradition of the rural women's organizations (Matysiak 2009: 226).

11. To explain the marking of interviews conducted in 2005: the first letter refers to the province (M—mazowieckie, P—pomorskie, Pd—podkarpackie, Z—zachodniopomorskie), the second letter refers to the first letter of the name of the village, and the number refers to the number of the interview.

12. To explain the marking of interviews conducted in 2008–2010: the first letter refers to the province (Z—zachodniopomorskie, M—mazowieckie, L—lubelskie, W—wielkopolskie, P—podkarpackie), the second letter refers to the first letter(s) of the name of the commune, the letter "f" or "m" refers to the respondent being female or male, and the final letters indicate the category of the respondent—"v" means "village representative," "l" means "local leader," "c" means "commune councilor," and "o" means "public official" or a representative of another local institution.

13. To be more specific, these women's rural organizations receive small donations in exchange for their dishes, cakes, etc. According to the legal regulations, an organization that is not a legal person cannot run any business.

14. Since 2009 the communal councils in Poland can earmark funds from their budgets to financially support the initiatives or projects that are collectively chosen by the residents of villages located within their administrative area.

15. For instance, in Poland, EU funds designated for financing of grassroots local initiatives within the framework of the Human Capital Operational Programme were used to a greater extent by the local authorities and administration than by the local social organizations, which prompts the question of whether they are really funding "grassroots" initiatives.

References

Bartkowski, J. 2003. *Tradycja i polityka. Wpływ tradycji kulturowych polskich regionów na współczesne zachowania społeczne i polityczne* [Tradition and Politics: The Influence of Cultural Traditions of Polish Regions on Contemporary Social and Political Behavior]. Warszawa: Wydawnictwo Akademickie "Żak."

———. 2007. "Kapitał społeczny i jego oddziaływanie na rozwój w ujęciu socjologicznym" [Social Capital and Its Influence on Development from a Sociological Perspective], in *Kapitał ludzki i kapitał społeczny a rozwój regionalny* [Human Capital, Social Capital and Regional Development], ed. M. Herbst. Warszawa: Wydawnictwo Naukowe "Scholar," 54–97.

Bourdieu, P. 1986. "The Forms of Capital," in *Handbook of Theory and Research for the Sociology of Education*, ed. J.G. Richardson. Greenword Press, 46–58.

Bukraba-Rylska, I. 2008. *Socjologia wsi polskiej* [Rural Sociology in Poland]. Warszawa: Wydawnictwo Naukowe PWN.

———. 2011. "O polskiej wsi i tych, co chłopu żywemu nie przepuszczą" [About Polish Countryside and Those Who Hate the Peasantry and Its Legacies] in *Polska po 20 latach wolności* [Poland after 20 Years of Freedom], ed. M. Bucholc, S. Mandes, T. Szawiel, and J. Wawrzyniak. Warszawa: University of Warsaw Publishers, 274–293.

Ekiert, G., and R. Foa. 2011. "Civil Society Weakness in Post-Communist Europe: A Preliminary Assessment." Collegio Carlo Alberto Working Paper, no. 198.

Ekiert, G., and J. Kubik. 2014. "The Legacies of 1989: Myths and Realities of Civil Society." *Journal of Democracy* 25: 46–58.

Fedyszak-Radziejowska, B. 2012. "Społeczności wiejskie: ewolucyjne zmiany, zrównoważony rozwój" [Rural Communities: Evolutionary Changes and Sustainable Development], in *Polska wieś 2012. Raport o stanie wsi*, ed. J. Wilkin and I. Nurzyńska [Rural Poland 2012: Rural Development Report]. Warszawa: FDPA, 101–123.

Grzebisz-Nowicka, Z. 1995. "Działalność organizacji Kół Gospodyń Wiejskich na rzecz kobiet i ich rodzin" [Activities of Rural Women's Organizations for Women and their Families], in *Kobieta wiejska w Polsce: rodzina, praca, gospodarstwo* [Rural Women in Poland: Family, Work, Farm], ed. J. Sawicka. Warszawa: Wydawnictwo SGGW, 145–190.

GUS. 2012. *Raport z wyników. Narodowy Spis Powszechny Ludności i Mieszkań 2011* [Report on the Results: The National Census of Population and Housing 2011]. Warszawa: GUS.

Halamska, M. 2008. "Organizacje rolników: bilans niesentymentalny" [Farmers' Organizations: Numbers Estimated without Nostalgic Sentiments], in *Wiejskie organizacje pozarządowe* [Rural Nongovernmental Organizations], ed. M. Halamska. Warszawa: IRWiR PAN, 103–133.

———. 2013. *Wiejska Polska na początku XXI wieku. Rozważania o gospodarce i społeczeństwie* [Rural Poland at the Beginning of the 21st Century: Reflections on Economy and Society]. Warszawa: Wydawnictwo Naukowe "Scholar."

Herbst, J. 2008. "Inny trzeci sektor. Organizacje pozarządowe na terenach wiejskich" [Different Third Sector: Nongovernmental Organizations in Rural Areas], in *Wiejskie organizacje pozarządowe* [Rural Nongovernmental Organizations], ed. M. Halamska. Warszawa: IRWiR PAN, 33–75.

Kamiński, R. 2008. *Aktywność społeczności wiejskich. Lokalne inicjatywy organizacji pozarządowych* [Rural Communities' Activity: Local Initiatives of Nongovernmental Organizations]. Warszawa: IRWiR PAN.

Klekotko, M. 2005. "Wiejskie społeczeństwo obywatelskie czy wiejskie społeczności obywatelskie? O problemach badania obywatelskości ludności wiejskiej" [Rural Civil Society or Rural Civil Societies? About the Problems Regarding Research on Civicness of Rural Population], in *W obliczu zmiany: wybrane strategie działania mieszkańców polskiej wsi* [Facing the Change: Chosen Strategies of Rural Residents in Poland], ed. K. Gorlach and G. Foryś. Kraków: Wydawnictwo Uniwersytetu Jagiellońskiego, 107–117.

Kornai, J. 1985. *Niedobór w gospodarce* [Economics of Shortage]. Warszawa: Państwowe Wydawnictwo Ekonomiczne.

Kostrzewska, M. 1992. "Koła Gospodyń Wiejskich a oświata w Polsce międzywojennej" [Rural Women's Organizations and Education in Interwar Poland], in *Kobieta i edukacja na ziemiach polskich w XIX i XX w* [Women and Education in Polish Territory in the 19th and 20th Centuries], ed. A. Żarnowska and A. Szwarc.. Warszawa: Instytut Historyczny Uniwersytetu Warszawskiego, 135–144.

Kurczewski, J., and J. Kurczewska. 2001. "A Self-Governing Society Twenty Years After: Democracy and the Third Sector in Poland." *Social Research* 68, no. 4: 937–976.

Lane, D. 2010. "Civil Society in the Old and New Member States." *European Societies* 12, no. 3: 293–315.

Leś, E., S. Nałęcz, and J. Wygnański. 2000. Defining the Nonprofit Sector: Poland. Working Papers of the Johns Hopkins Comparative Nonprofit Sector Project, no. 36. Baltimore: The Johns Hopkins Center for Civil Society Studies.

Lewenstein, B. 1999. *Wspólnota społeczna a uczestnictwo lokalne. Monografia procesów uczestnictwa w samorządzie terytorialnym w pierwszych latach transformacji w Polsce* [Social Community and Local Participation: A Monograph on the Participation in Local Self-government in the Early Years of Transformation in Poland]. Warszawa: ISNS UW.

Marczakiewicz, A., Z. Markowicz, and J. Stępiński. 1992. *130–lecie Kółek Rolniczych. krótki zarys historii Kółek Rolniczych 1862–1992* [130th Anniversary of the Establishment of Farmers' Organizations: A Brief Outline of the History of Farmers' Organizations 1862–1992]. Warszawa: Krajowy Związek Rolników, Kółek i Organizacji Rolniczych.

Matysiak, I. 2005. "'Stare' i 'nowe' formy aktywności społecznej kobiet na obszarach wiejskich w Polsce. Od dożynek do fitness klubu" ["Old" and "New" Forms of Rural Women's Social Activity in Rural Areas in Poland: From Harvest Picnics to Fitness Clubs]. Unpublished Master's thesis, University of Warsaw.

———. 2009. "Koła Gospodyń Wiejskich i ich funkcje w kontekście specyfiki trzeciego sektora w wybranych społecznościach wiejskich" [Rural Women's Organizations and their Functions in the Context of the Specificity of the Third Sector in Chosen Rural Communities], in *Kobiety–Feminizm–Demokracja* [Women—Feminism—Democracy], ed. B. Budrowska. Warszawa: IFiS PAN Publishers, 220–243.

———. 2014. *Rola sołtysów we współczesnych społecznościach wiejskich. Płeć jako czynnik różnicujący kapitał społeczny* [The Role of Village Representatives in Contemporary Rural Communities: Gender as a Factor Influencing Differences in Social Capital]. Warszawa: Wydawnictwo Naukowe "Scholar."

Milczewska, K., J. Mencwel, and J. Wiśniewski. 2014. *Koła gospodyń wiejskich. Nie tylko od kuchni. Raport z badania* [Rural Women's Organizations: Not Only Kitchen-Related Activites. Research Report]. Warszawa: Pracownia Badań i Innowacji Społecznych "Stocznia".

Misztal, W. 2003. "Demokracja lokalna w Polsce" [Local Democracy in Poland]. *Rocznik Lubuski*, 29, part I: 27–42.

Poczta, W. 2012. "Przemiany w rolnictwie ze szczególnym uwzględnieniem przemian strukturalnych" [Changes in Agriculture with Particular Focus on Structural Transformations], in *Polska wieś 2012. Raport o stanie wsi* [Rural Poland 2012: Rural Development Report], ed. J. Wilkin and I. Nurzyńska. Warszawa: FDPA, 65–99.

Przewłocka, J. 2013. *Polskie organizacje pozarządowe 2012* [Polish Nongovernmental Organizations 2012]. Warszawa: Stowarzyszenie Klon/Jawor.

Putnam, R.D. 1994. *Making Democracy Work: Civic Traditions in Modern Italy*. Princeton: Princeton University Press.

Regulska, J. 1998. "Building Local Democracy: The Role of Western Assistance in Poland." *Voluntas: International Journal of Voluntary and Nonprofit Organizations* 9, no. 1: 39–57.

Sawicka, J. 1996. "Koła Gospodyń Wiejskich jako społeczno-zawodowa organizacja kobiet" [Rural Women's Organizations as Female Socioprofessional Organizations], *Wieś i Rolnictwo* 2, no. 91: 75–88.

Siemieńska, R. 2005. "Miejsce i rola organizacji kobiecych w Polsce. Doświadczenia, prognozy, dylematy dotyczące funkcjonowania organizacji kobiecych po wstąpieniu Polski do Unii Europejskiej" [The Position and Role of Women's Organizations in Poland: Experiences, Predictions, Dilemmas Related to the Functioning of Women's Organizations after the Accession of Poland to the European Union], in *Płeć, wybory, władza* [Gender, Elections, Power], ed. R. Siemieńska. Warszawa: Wydawnictwo Naukowe "Scholar," 241–261.

Stanny, M. 2011. "Wieś jako przedmiot badań demograficznych" [Countryside as the Subject of Demographic Research], in *Wieś jako przedmiot badań naukowych na początku XXI wieku* [Countryside as the Subject of Scientific Research at the Beginning of the 21st Century], ed. M. Halamska. Warszawa: Wydawnictwo Naukowe "Scholar," 97–115.

Szacki, J. ed. 1997. *Ani książę, ani kupiec: obywatel* [Neither Prince nor Merchant: Citizen]. Kraków: Społeczny Instytut Wydawniczy Znak Sp. z o.o.

Walczak-Duraj, D. 2008. "Podstawowe sfery potencjalnego uczestnictwa kobiet wiejskich w życiu społeczno-politycznym" [Main Domains of the Potential Participation of Rural Women in the Sociopolitical Life], in *Diagnoza społeczno-zawodowa kobiet wiejskich w Polsce* [Socioprofessional Diagnosis on Rural Women in Poland], ed. J. Krzyszkowski. Warszawa: MPiPS, 125–163.

Wilkin, J. 2011. "Jak zapewnić rozwój wsi w warunkach zmniejszającej się roli rolnictwa" [How to Ensure the Development of Countryside under Conditions of the Decreasing Role of Agriculture], in *Wieś jako przedmiot badań naukowych na początku XXI wieku* [Countryside as the Subject of Scientific Research at the Beginning of 21st Century], ed. M. Halamska. Warszawa: Wydawnictwo Naukowe "Scholar," 117–137.

Chapter 10

ETHNIC BONDING AND HOMING DESIRES
THE POLISH DIASPORA AND CIVIL SOCIETY MAKING

Gabriella Elgenius

This chapter starts from the assumption that the activism of the Polish diaspora needs to be considered as a significant *civil space* of migrant engagement
associated with both civil society of contemporary Poland and the diasporic
structures formed in and by the country of settlement. As such, the Polish
civil space is connected to, formed, and maintained via central ties, links,
norms, and discourses of home, nationhood, and integration. A process-
oriented approach to civil society (see Jacobsson and Korolczuk's introduction to this volume) enables the analysis of Polish civil society development
in the United Kingdom since the Second World War with a focus on significant London-based associations, central in mediating connections with Poland and within the Polish diaspora in the United Kingdom (Lacroix 2012).
The focus of this chapter is the engagement of the Polish diaspora, which
has produced a unique pattern of civil society making, due to dividing homing desires of different generations of Poles arriving after the Second World
War, during the Cold War and Solidarity periods, and post–EU expansion—
stratified also by social status.

The Polish civil space has developed in the United Kingdom with three
main waves of Polish migration and with its precarious position as a space
of migrant activism *in relation* to the British majority space, other spaces
of migrant activism (including cosmopolitan pursuits). As such, it is a civil
space of protective ethnonational ambitions for recognition, political rights
and group elevation against devaluation and discrimination on the basis of
ethnicity and class. This chapter will demonstrate that different "homing

desires" are negotiated within Polish London, and that these, in turn, generate a unique pattern of civil society development according to a four-stage process commencing with the foundation of exile organizations, moving towards the maintenance of these organizations, the rejuvenation and amplification of existing organizations, and the diversification of organizational production including campaigning. These stages are linked to varied expressions and desires for home and renegotiations of status and pride from a minority position of civil engagement. Of particular interest for this analysis are uncompromising, diverging, or even dividing "homing desires" that manifest a "desire for home" rather than the "desire to return home" (Brah 1996: 176). Diversity-and-division within the Polish civil space reveals the uneasy coexistence and separation between what are perceived as three main generations of Polish migrants (many of whom are British citizens) and illuminates civil society development both as a process and as a relationship to other civil spaces and to the contestation of re-created memory spaces abroad. Significantly, internal critique does not undermine the existence of co-ethnic organizations. On the contrary, the creation of a Polish-specific civil space, although stratified, is made possible within a framework of a Polish national community sustained by links within and to Poland, produced by underlying uniting national narrations for minority recognition.

The qualitative data on which this chapter is based, comprised over one hundred in-depth interviews mainly conducted with Polish interviewees within Greater London.[1] More specifically, around eighty interviews were conducted with "affiliated representatives" so that different types of associational attachment were represented via the accounts of chairs, trustees, professionals, volunteers and members, paid and unpaid representatives, and volunteers of a variety of Polish organizations.[2] The sample also includes non-affiliated individuals. For both affiliated and non-affiliated interviewees, sample demography (age, gender, and occupation) has been taken into account. Complementary purposive sampling techniques—snowball, maximum variation and strategic sample—were required in various stages of the interview process to ensure that the affiliated sample of interviewees represented a variety of significant organizations connected to the three generations of Polish migration. It is beyond the scope of this study to assess the proportion of Poles in London involved in associations or the scope or variety of organizational and membership activity. The interview phases also included other diaspora groups (N=200), mainly in Greater London, and stretch over the period 2009 to 2015. I would like to acknowledge the many interviewees who have generously contributed to this research.

Following this brief introduction are sections on the conceptualization of migrant activism and patterns of Polish migration into the United Kingdom. Thereafter, we turn to the analysis of the processual development of the Polish civil space driven by different motivations of migrant generations, relating these to the struggle for recognition. The concluding remarks illuminate processes and relationships associated with the dynamism that characterizes migrant civil society making.

Conceptualizing Migrant Activism

Migrant activism, along with associated civil spaces of voluntary organizations and associations, is key to understanding permanent settlement, maintenance of communities, and changing dimensions of "home" (Castles and Miller 2003; Jordan and Düvell 2003; Portes 1995), contextualized by its development in the "second space"—positioned in between the "first space" of the majority and the "third space" characterized by cosmopolitan intermixtures (Hutnyk 2010; Van Hear, 2015; Vertovec 2010). Polish London has also developed with reference to both known and imagined communities (Anderson 1991; Chojnacki 2012; Van Hear 2015)—in relation to the majority, to other minorities, and alongside struggles for recognition, ethnonational distinction, and evolving notions of home—with voluntary associations on behalf of and as an extension of the Polish diaspora. The focus of this study is the *diaspora* structures visible through and "complete with various associations and more formal organizations" (Brinkerhoff 2009: 38), characterized by the *ethnic bonding of social capital* that encourages particular bonds, relationships, organizations, and networks based on perceptions of similarity, shared history, religion, and language. Diasporic groups are clearly upheld along a continuum of loyalties of those forced to maintain old ties, those escaping the bonds into which they were born, or those never fully integrating or wishing to be part of multiple groups. For this study, the social relationships formed between co-ethnics through formal and voluntary organizations and associations, characterized by the ethnic bonding of social capital,[3] along with the resources generated by these relationships, are of particular interest (Putnam 2000: 134). (See also Heath and Demireva 2014; Elgenius and Heath, 2014; Laurence and Maxwell 2012; Maxwell 2012; Morales and Giugni 2011). Ethnic bonding has been argued to provide a safety net from marginalization (Gittel and Vidal 1998 and others) and, here, arguably a buffer from and platform for protesting discrimination. Interviewees refer to the "Polish community" in terms of "formal organisations, oriented around community centers, clubs and groups" (Burrell 2006: 141; Cohen 1985; Cohen, 2008; Sword 1996). Maintaining Polish traditions, acquiring knowledge about Polish history, and learning Polish is, as expected, important, although much disagreement exists as to what constitutes authentic "Polishness" and the "real Poland"—disagreements develop alongside different migratory experiences and opportunities of returning. The Polish diaspora illuminates therefore the role of ethnic bonds despite diverging homing desires, existing dissimilarities, and continuously re-created civil society processes outside Poland. (Bridging ties between different the Polish diaspora and other ethnic groups and civil initiatives of cosmopolitan intermixtures are undoubtedly also formed as part of the Polish civil space in the United Kingdom.[4])

Polish Migration into the United Kingdom

According to estimates of the Polish Ministry of Foreign Affairs in 2012, 15 to 20 million people of Polish ancestry lived outside Poland, which would make up 39 to 52 percent of the current population of 38 million. As highlighted by Burrell (2006), the history of Polish sociopolitical and socioeconomic emigration is one of border shifts, forced resettlement, and economic crises. Such multifaceted trajectories of mobility had already developed by the Second World War in the aftermath of occupation and warfare. The Polish diaspora settled in a number of European states, such as the United Kingdom, Germany, Ukraine, Russia, Belarus, Lithuania, France, Sweden, and Ireland, but also outside Europe in the United States, Brazil, Canada, Australia, and Argentina.

Around 160,000 Poles had settled in the United Kingdom after the Polish Resettlement Act of 1947, which offered citizenship to displaced Polish troops in the aftermath of the Second World War (Burrell 2006). Their deportation and displacement, their loyalty to Allied forces, the experiences of the postwar generation of not being able to return to Poland and the associated exile narration remain imprinted on contemporary Polish London. The commemoration of the war dead—in Polish parishes, clubs, and supplementary schools—constitutes an essential part of the ceremonial year and stands out as particularly important (see Elgenius 2011a; King 1998). The majority of the postwar generation have passed away, but their children have followed the path of civil engagement of their parents, interestingly (self-)assigned the same position as their parents, as belonging to the Polish postwar migrant cluster of this ranked chain of Polish migrants and British citizens of Polish descent, a matter that will make sense as the arguments in this chapter are developed.

The number of Poles arriving in the United Kingdom varied between a few hundred and a few thousand annually from 1956 to the 1980s, the figure of multiple thousands referring to the 1980s (Sword 1996) when altogether 2 million people left Poland (Iglicka 2001). The emigration from Poland commenced after 1956 with new political opportunities brought about by de-Stalinization and a divided party elite, emanating over Poland's relationship with Soviet Union. Poland also witnessed an upsurge of protests demanding economic improvement, political freedom, and national autonomy with the strike waves of the 1970s and 1980s that highlighted economic grievances and steep price rises. Such realities prepared the way for the Solidarity movement that emerged in August 1980 and that turned into a central node for different core groups or "social/ideological categories" of Polish society. Solidarity coalesced with help from a novel combination of social actors, relying on the strength of the industrial workers within the communist structure, the traditional power of the Catholic Church, and the organizational activity of intellectuals on the secular left (Osa 2003).

Interviewees relate to this period as "having to leave Poland" due to their engagement in Solidarity and not being able to return. Following years of repressive martial laws and banned opposition groups, barriers were lifted after 1989 and Poles were free to leave and free to return to Poland (Iglicka 2001: 38). Polish migration to the U.K. was further facilitated by a relative lack of restrictions on establishing businesses (1993) and minimal visa obligations for short stays (Sword 1996: 69)—which generated undocumented over-stayers (Düvell 2004) as well as short-term and circular migration movements (Wallace 2002).

Polish migration continued with a steady increase into the United Kingdom, and with EU enlargement in 2004 figures increased drastically at a time when unemployment peaked at 21 percent in Poland. (For the impact of emigration on Polish communities in Poland, see White 2011). Polish migration is unique with its recent increase and the Polish language is today the second largest language in the U.K., with Poles being the second largest foreign-born group in the country (after the largest overseas-born group from India). According to the most recent censuses, the numbers of Polish people in the U.K. was estimated to be 579,000 in 2011, reaching 688,000 two years later (Home Office 2013). The Annual Population Survey of 2015 confirms that Poland is the second most common non-U.K. country of birth, with 780,000 residents, and the group in which non-British nationality, with 850,000 residents, is most common (Office for National Statistics 2015a, 2015b).[5]

The Polish diaspora and its creation of memory places, show how nurturing a sense of home is "intrinsically linked to the way in which processes of inclusion or exclusion operate and are subjectively experienced under given circumstances" (Brah 1996: 192). It is therefore critical to say something about the excluding processes and macro-level politics before moving on to related perceptions of exclusion and building of alternative spaces in the civil sphere. With the increase of Polish migration in recent years, the British Prime Minister David Cameron (2010–2016) commented that Britain must avoid a repeat of what he called the "Polish situation" with regard to Bulgarians and Romanians (Economist 2013). Anti-immigrant discourses such as these (driven by party competition and UKIP claim making; see Ford and Goodwin 2014; Koopmans et al. 2005) are significant as exclusive contexts.[6] Paradoxically to Cameron's claim, Poles have been readily absorbed into the British labor market and the Labour Force Survey estimates that 84.6 percent of Polish-born residents (aged 16 to 64) are employed, compared to 70.4 percent for the U.K. population as a whole (Office for National Statistics 2011). However, migrants of Polish descent have mostly ended up in fast-growing parts of the country in low-paid jobs and in particular niches of the labor market (Drinkwater et al. 2009; Eade et al. 2006). The rewards from education are also lower for recent Polish arrivals compared to earlier cohorts (Eade et al. 2006) and demonstrate that an "ethnic penalty" exists for the Poles, too (Heath et al. 2007b). For instance, the Poles in the British labor market have been described as being "Poles apart" (Drinkwater et al. 2009). Burrell aptly notes that in terms of ethnic stratification no amount of "European rebranding could disguise the underlying inequalities among European citizens" (2009: 5). The divide between East and West has remained visible after 1989 with a sustained postcolonial discourse on the "backwardness of Eastern Europe," a theme also reproduced by members of the diaspora of this study.

Coping with stereotypes and prejudice as part of the experience of the Polish diaspora, is especially highlighted by Polish migrants of the 2004 generation in this study, and enforces insider-outsider discourses with competing struggles for recognition.

The Polish Civil Space: A Four-Stage Process of Diaspora Engagement

This study on the civil society in the Polish diaspora is a unique opportunity to apply a process-oriented approach to activism, as suggested by the editors in the introduction. As a processual development it is driven by the different migrant generations and their concerns about integration and Polishness. With reference to civil society in Poland itself, it was described as "weak" and characterized by the absence of "enterprise, civic and discursive cultures" in the 1990s (Sztompka 1993), as well as by activity in the "private sphere" only (Tarkowska and Tarkowski 1991). The "paradoxical combination" of high levels of individual initiative arguably coexisted with a relative lack of collective expression (Gliński 2004)—and such contradictions are addressed and challenged elsewhere in this volume (see chapters by Ekiert and Kubik, Giza-Poleszczuk, and Jacobsson in this volume).[7] In comparison, the London-based Polish space in the U.K. reached well beyond the private sphere long before the 1990s in its first stage of founding exile organizations.

As emphasized at the outset of this book, civil society cannot be reduced to organizational structures but must be understood as "relational and processual" phenomenon (Jacobsson and Korolczuk in this volume). Applied to the Polish civil space, it may be analyzed in broad terms as a four-stage process originating with the founding exile organizations and protecting traditional notions of home to new forms of Polish professional, occupational, or cultural organizations, including also political campaigning for representation. The influence of three generations of Polish migration is integral to this nexus of civil development. A staggering 25 percent of all existing Polish organizations were created after 2004 (Lacroix 2012) with the rejuvenation of original exile organization. As the timeline below (Figure 10.1) illustrates, this development includes the following stages: (1) the *foundation of exile organizations* in the postwar period, (2) the *maintenance* of these by children of the postwar generation and migrants arriving during the Cold War and Solidarity periods, (3) the *rejuvenation and amplification of existing organizations*, and (4) the *diversification of organizations and political campaigning* with the engagement of the post-2004 generation.

Home as Precious and Lost, in Parallel and in Opposition: Stage of Exile Organizations

The aim of the postwar Polish migrants was to create organizations that reflected the traditions and socio-political contexts of Poland before war and communist times. Such efforts were articulated with an overall anti-communist strategy to protect a degree of proper "Polishness" (Lacroix 2012) and political opposition abroad became the blueprint for the early exile organizations for which the postwar generation transferred their efforts when they could not return to Poland. Activities of the emerging Polish diaspora, although originally undertaken within an anti-communist framework, were later reformulated with a clear nationalist ethos (Garapich 2014) that is clearly visible today and for which anti-communist narrations remain integral. Burrell argues that the grand narrative of the postwar generation was built on the mythologization of hardship reaching the United Kingdom, the nation as a "treasured possession," and a sense of community emphasized by the Polish language, its history, and the active participation in the Polish church (2006: 77). The émigré world was constructed in parallel to the national calendar of Poland (Chojnacki 2012). The narratives of martyrdom remained integral to Polish London as it developed along the lines of two

Figure 10.1. Timeline: Polish Diaspora Organizations and Campgaigns.

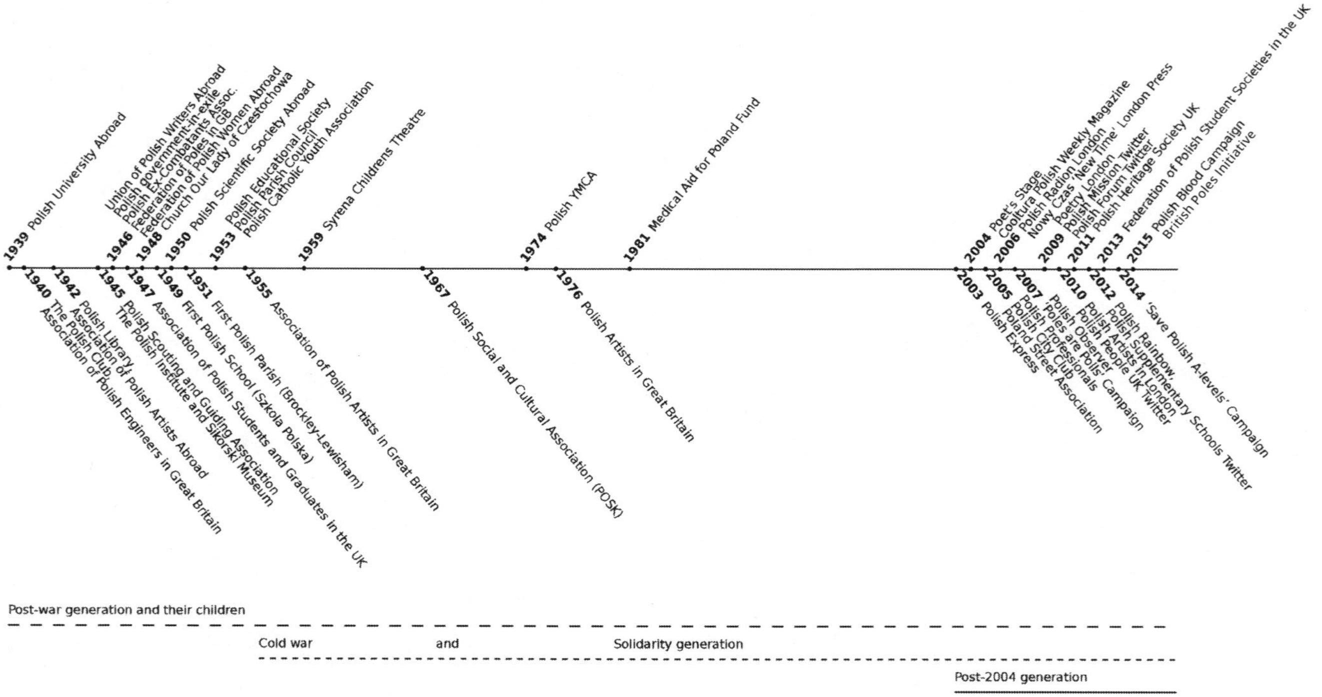

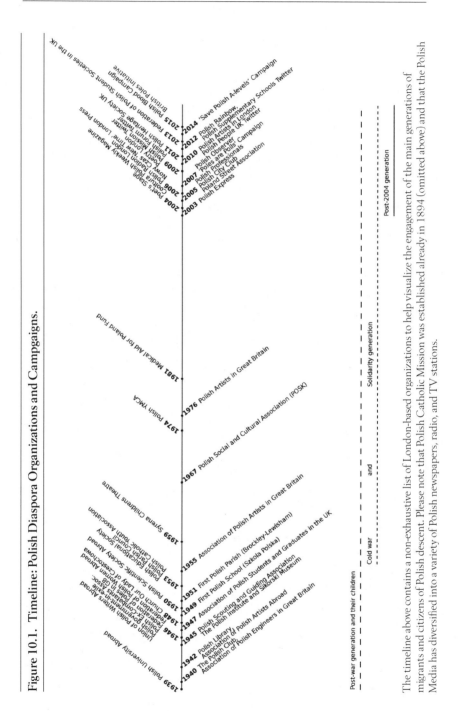

The timeline above contains a non-exhaustive list of London-based organizations to help visualize the engagement of the main generations of migrants and citizens of Polish descent. Please note that Polish Catholic Mission was established already in 1894 (omitted above) and that the Polish Media has diversified into a variety of Polish newspapers, radio, and TV stations.

civil society pillars—a religious one and a secular one. The work by the Polish Catholic Mission (founded in the U.K. in 1894) and the Polish churches (the first founded in 1948) came to play a major role for the Polish diaspora. The Polish churches nurtured close links to existing civil organizations such as the Polish Scouting and Guiding Association (1945). The first Polish Saturday school (opened in 1949) and an increasing number of Polish schools generated an umbrella organization, the Polish Educational Society (1953). A child of the postwar generation reflects on his involvement in Polish youth clubs, schools, and scouts: "In my case everything basically started and was founded around the Parish. So people were involved with the church and within we also had a youth group where I'd say the priests were involved" (former chair of a PSS, Polish Supplementary School).

The secular pillar of founding organizations was based around the government in exile, not officially recognized after 1946 and in principal underground until 1989, after which the Federation of Poles (1946) became the officially recognized representative of Poles in Britain. The Polish Ex-Combatants Association (PECA) was formed by the Polish military (1946). A few years ahead of these initiatives was the first Polish members club—the Polish Heart or *Ognisko*—inaugurated by the Duke and Duchess of Kent in South Kensington in London in 1940. The club constituted a memory space for the higher social strata of the diaspora and tells us something about the significance of social distinction and recognition at a time of loss of status. The first Polish occupational association, the Polish Engineers (1940), was established the same year. Later, the Polish Social and Cultural Association (POSK) was opened (1967) and it remains an official Polish center in London and home to around thirty other organizations.

The foundations were thus laid out to preserve pre-war Poland with the first exile stage as "the postwar generation that did not have a real Poland to go back to tried to recreate the Poland that was before the war, here" (Top Official, the Polish Heart, *Ognisko*). Organizations such as these provided a site for cultivating tradition (the Polish church), and for the children of the postwar generation to learn Polish (Polish school) and culture (Polish Scouts and Guides, Polish youth organizations). For some organizations, prewar social structures remained remarkably intact as the higher strata and traditional Polish hierarchy was re-enacted (Polish club) with particular emphasis on recognition from the majority society for Polish sacrifices during the war (PECA). The formative stage of the founding postwar years was by no means a homogenous effort, and parallel Polish worlds crystallized in London; examples are distinct Polish communities emerging in West and South London (that came to an end by 1976) and in Lewisham (Chojnacki 2012).

Home as Marker of Suspicion and Differentiation Within: Stage of Maintenance

Many Polish organizations would not have survived had it not been for the voluntary engagement of the children of the postwar generation and those who arrived in larger numbers during the Solidarity period. The children of the postwar generation who grew up in England remain a highly visible group in Polish London and explain their connectedness to Poland as nurtured and deep-rooted: "We were all born in England and naturally hold British passports, but our cultural and social allegiances are within a Polish tradition. This generation is currently in the 40's and 50's age group and was brought up on a 'diet' of Polish Saturday Schools, Polish youth organizations and Polish student and graduate groups, all of them established 'na emigracji'" (Ania's Poland Blog). The postwar children and the generation that arrived during the Solidarity years secured the continued success of the Polish Saturday schools, a central institution of the Polish space with a clear agenda of providing a toolkit of "Polishness" of a traditional and pre-communist character to younger generations. It is not surprising that the Polish organizational space was maintained and reformulated with the help of a clear nationalist agenda increasingly absorbing anti-communist strands that followed the successes of the Solidarity movement in Poland. Burrell argues that the Cold War and Solidarity generation (pre–EU enlargement) did not have an "enormous impact on the infrastructure of community" (2009: 3), which is true to the extent that they did not transform existing exile organizational structures or became identified with specific migrant locations. Galasińska notes that the migrants arriving during the Cold War and Solidarity "usually had problems being accepted in centres ruled by the postwar group" (2010: 943). This is a significant finding for this study too and accounts for their relationship to the civil sphere and to its development as a whole. However, the involvement of the second migrant generation, that with the children of the postwar generation maintained Polish London, should not go unnoticed as their engagement contributed to replenishing national narrations of sacrifice with their existence abroad and lack of possibility to return to Poland.

Home as Martyrdom to Combat Devaluation and Regaining Status: Stage of Rejuvenation

By 2004 there was a platform of Polish activity in place and an embryo migrant industry with special concentration to London (Garapich 2008). The decisions of the British authorities in the 1990s not to enforce visa obligations and to facilitate new businesses opened things up for Polish entrepreneurs, lawyers, brokers, consultants, and travel agents and generated Polish enterprises in the United Kingdom. The Polish-specific for-profit sector worked "in parallel to the existing associational framework" and formed a network that "put itself in charge of catering to the needs of newcomers" (Lacroix 2012: 193). The Polish for-profit sector merged to a degree with the civil space as the last obstacles to Polish migration were removed in 2004 (Düvell 2004). The Federation of Poles (formed in 1946) had been the officially recognized representative of Poles in Britain; by 2012 it had been revived and was operating as the umbrella organization for around seventy-five organizations. Interestingly, other original organizations, whose membership had been dwindling, attracted new members from the newly arrived post-2004 migrants. In a puzzling manner, the large wave of Polish migrants arriving after 2004 did not fundamentally challenge or transform the associational Polish arena founded by the exile generation; instead they contributed to the simultaneous rejuvenation and amplification (stage three) and then diversification and campaigning (stage four) of the Polish civil space (changes were brought about by internal contestation between the generations). Membership in the Polish churches in England and Wales had grown steadily until the 1960s, by which time the Polish Mission owned thirty churches, twelve chapels, thirty-nine presbyteries, and fifty-five centers (Lacroix 2012). Today, the assets account for seventy-one local Polish parishes in over two hundred localities in which over one hundred Polish priests exercise spiritual and pastoral leadership.[8] In the London Borough of Ealing, Sunday mass is attended by over ten thousand, and constitutes one of the largest Polish churches in London that celebrates mass six times every Sunday. The myth of the *Catholic nation,* the intertwined nexus of the Catholic Church and the Polish nation through the former's hegemony over Polish history, made possible with 85 percent of the population declaring some form of affiliation to the church (Porter 2001: 289), explains the continued appeal of the church along with the growing strength of nationalist discourses (cf. Płatek and Płucienniczak in this volume). The numbers are striking, but priests of the parishes estimate that they reach around 10 to 15 percent only of the total Polish population in London (Polish Parish Priest, London), and would make secularization a decisively marked trend for the Polish diaspora. Yet, as noted by Lacroix's study of the North of England (2012), the increase of Polish migrants post-2004 "Polish-ified" the churches and led to overcrowding. As a result, the members of the postwar generation, their children, and the Solidarity generation migrated to other Polish or English churches. Leaving the Polish space highlights the diversity within, and is explained by the interviewees as a result of the lack of consideration shown the exile generation who founded the original churches, parishes, and other organizations: "I don't mind saying this because I express my views about this but when the recent waves of immigrants came over, the priests decided that they were only interested in the new Polish immigrant society and all of a sudden they were not interested in people like my mother and like us and the Polish scouts and other organizations based there ... My mother moved to another Polish church that maintains the old émigré, let's say, values. My family, we moved [to an English church] and the majority of people who used to go to the Polish church in Ealing left" (top official, trustee PSS, postwar child).

As a process, this is one of clashing values with regard to deservedness and entitlement but also with regard to home and religion objecting to the "subservience" of newcomers and the hierarchical structures of the Catholic Church transported by the clergy from Poland to the U.K. Significantly, the "émigré values" that materialized with the forming of the first Polish churches, schools, youth clubs, cultural clubs, and political groupings were built upon traditional notions of religion, culture, and politics, too. Yet, interviewee statements disassociated the older generations from the "subservience," linking this to the "backwardness" of "post-communist" Poles. Church mobility in London provides one example of how Polish London is changing—dividing tendencies generated by the uneasy interaction between migrant generations. In her assessment of the church, another interviewee declared the opposite, however: "the Church is the only place where difference [referring to the 'generations of Polish migrants'] does not matter" (official, PES, EU-generation). The statement nevertheless points to dividing structures and is in this case, most likely, a result of the stratification that to a degree characterizes the Polish diaspora churches.

The rejuvenation of another traditional section of the Polish space has also occurred with reference to national narratives of sacrifice and courage in war. A number of scholars have noted that Poland is "constructed in relation to the past, where sacrifice, victimhood and martyrdom" are central virtues (Kania-Lundholm 2012: 159). Raising membership figures in PECA must be seen from this perspective, especially telling in view of prediction that the association was "dying out." PECA's membership quadrupled from 1990 to 2012 (from 7,000 to 27,000; Lacroix 2012). This is a sign of successful unity narration of the migrant space, which highlights Polish sacrifice alongside the Allies against a mutual enemy (Elgenius 2011ab, 2015).

The staggering number of new Polish organizations created after 2004 includes new Polish Supplementary Schools (PSS), new Polish clubs, Polish occupational organizations, Polish media, and Polish cultural interest organizations. With reference to both rejuvenation and amplification of voluntary initiatives, the Polish supplementary schools are of particular relevance for the narration of pride and home with special relation to the younger generation of Poles. The supplementary schools are cofinanced by the Polish government, local authorities, and the parents themselves (Official Representative of PES; Trustees of PSS; Sobków 2014). As White highlights, sending children to Polish schools involve a certain financial investment. Yet the number of supplementary schools doubled during the period from 2004 to 2009, peaking at ninety (White 2011: 169). By 2016, the number of Polish supplementary schools in England and Wales had reached 150; they are run by hundreds of volunteers on weeknights and on Saturdays when two thousand teachers teach over seventeen thousand children (Official representative of PES, PES Official website). More and more, new schools are set up by parents to meet increasing demands. The PSS maintain close links to the PES, the parishes and the Embassy, and they articulate the collective notions of traditional diaspora homeland activism:[9] "to give pupils a grounding in the Polish language, history, geography, culture and tradition. It was set up originally by people like my parents—who left Poland and who wanted their children to know or to have a background in Polish culture, that would make them feel Polish" (Trustee of PSS, postwar child). The curriculum emphasizes Polish language, history, geography, religion, poetry, music, and literature and has been described as "traditional, normative and nostalgic" (Chowaniec 2015). As argued by yet another trustee of a PSS: "if you are out of the country you become more patriotic than you would be when you were living there. That's one of the things we are trying with the children here, it's not only to teach them the language but also culture and tradition" (trustee of a PSS). Statements such as these (by trustees, head teachers, teachers, volunteers, parents, and pupils of the PSS) introduce us to one articulation of "homing desires" and attachment to "home" as "deep-seated" and an "emotional commitment" to "giving the child the Polish language," "the culture of their parents," "an understanding of their heritage" and tradition.

Home as Distinction and Discrimination: Stage of Diversification and Campaigning

A large number of voluntary associations emerged post-2004 (25 percent of all current Polish organizations) and untapped areas were explored and diversified Polish London by adding new concerns and ways of communicating. The diversification of the Polish press and media increased from four weekly papers in 2004 to several dozen papers and websites today: advertising jobs, accommodation, housing, and cultural events. New professional networks formed, most notably the Polish Professionals (established in 2005), which called on membership from various professional groups, and other Polish organizations formed by Poles working in the City of London, such as the Polish City Club (2005). Polish Artists in London (2010) and

Polish Writers are examples of voluntary associations of the cultural sphere. The significance and growth of online portals, websites and blogs reduce the distance between the U.K. and Poland. Over twenty significant online portals with this particular aim had been founded by 2011 (Seredynska-Abou Eid 2011).[10]

Significantly, the Polish diaspora emerged as a political force as per public campaigns such as "Poles are Polls" (2007), "Save-Polish-A-Level" (2014–2015), "British Poles Initiative" (2015), and "Donate Polish Blood" (2015)—and related to empowerment and group recognition in relation to the British majority. First, "Poles are Polls" was initiated by Polish Professionals in 2007 and devised to encourage members of the Polish community to register to vote in local elections. The aim was also to "improve the perception of the group" in an increasingly anti-immigrant climate by distributing key statistics on Poles in the U.K., referring to their high employment rates or conveying messages like "Immigration lowers budget deficit with 7 billion GBP per year." Second, "Save Polish A-level" (#SavePolishALevel) was conducted during 2014–2015 after the Assessment and Qualifications Alliance (AQA) had agreed to terminate the A-level option for Polish-language speakers in 2018. "Save Polish A-level" turned into a unified protest within which petitions were devised and signed at PSS's, the PES, the Embassy, and other centers. It was argued that "the growth over a ten-year period in the number of candidates taking Polish A-Level is remarkable. French decreased by 26%, German by 28%, Spanish increased by 33%, Chinese by 74%, Russian by 90%, and Polish by 1000%" (Polish Educational Society 2015). The Polish ambassador to London (2012 - 2016) Witold Sobków, argued in the *Guardian* that the possibility of taking examinations in Polish at the GCSE or A-level gives pupils a strong motivation to learn the language of their parents. "By attending Saturday schools, Polish children not only learn to speak two languages, but they also learn the history of two countries and two cultures. It is extremely important that over the course of their education they get acquainted with Polish customs" (Sobków 2014). Third, "The British Poles Initiative" (2015), a collaborative volunteer-led project, took campaigning to a new level with the promotion of "Polish matters" in British politics,[11] by making it easier for Poles to ascertain the views of their Members of Parliament on specifically "Polish matters". The Polish diaspora hereby opened another door to Polish identity politics via the construction of a website that facilitated contact with Members of Parliament during pre-election campaigning. Polish residents could hereby easily contact their MPs (identified by postcodes) and send them a set of prewritten questions: "So people were asking the candidates what they thought about Polish immigration and Polish contributions. Forty-five MPs who were asked questions became MPs and since then we continue to ask these MPs. We reached almost a hundred so it is quite, quite a number because and gives you an outlook on the British-Polish relations" (co-organizer of the campaign) (The public elects 650 Members of Parliament to the House of Commons). MPs were asked to help the Polish community with four main concerns: to help lobby for A-level Polish (i.e. for Polish remaining an A-level subject); to challenge British media in instances where Nazi camps were labeled "Polish concentration camps" (in light of the fact that "the Polish army contributed to the defeat of Nazi Germany"); to promote information about the positive contributions of Polish immigration to the British economy; and to support Polish residents' right to the immigration status "indefinite leave to remain" in the event of Brexit. Fourth, the "Donate Polish Blood" campaign (August 2015) encouraged blood donations to the National Health Service in order to demonstrate (continuing) Polish loyalty to Britain and remind the public of Polish sacrifices during World War II. Originally, Polish Blood emerged as a buffer and counter-campaign to a proposed and failed call to a "Polish strike" as protest against the discrimination of Polish workers and to raise awareness of the Polish presence in the labor market (Polish Express). However, the strike faced internal opposition and few attended (co-organizer, Polish Blood Campaign). In sum, 2,500 people committed themselves to donating blood under the banner "I don't strike, I save lives. Polish blood"; this campaign was reported on by the world press (co-organizer, Polish Blood Campaign; Davies and Carrier, 2015).

In conclusion, the development of the civil society of the Polish diaspora and a Polish space in the United Kingdom highlights the significant role of central and close-knit organizations such as the Polish Mission and other London-based associations in the mediation of links within the diaspora and between this and Poland, confirming the findings of an earlier pilot study of Polish organizations in Birmingham and Slough (Lacroix 2012). Many of these central organizations were founded by the exile community and their leadership has remained with the children of the postwar and Solidary generations; furthermore, recent migrants have been disproportionately underrepresented on boards of trustees although a shift toward higher representation has been witnessed in recent years.

Critical Solidarity: Ethnic Bonding vs. Ethnic Solidarity

The processual development of Polish London negotiates different "homing desires" that, in turn, generate a unique pattern of civil society development comprising four distinct stages, simultaneously producing a protective ethnonational space for minority recognition and for regaining lost status, for group elevation in view of devaluation. The generated development is linked to dividing "homing desires" and different cultures of migration, but uniting initiatives for recognition ultimately turns this diaspora space into a Polish one.

Dividing Homing Desires: Home Imagined, Real, or Absolute

The concept of ethnic bonding of social capital is traditionally applied to social ties of long-established groups and tends to hold limited applicability for the newly arrived (Ryan et al. 2008). In the context of the Polish diaspora, ethnic bonding ties are applicable to identify newer forms of activism too, as generated by the post-2004 generation via stages of rejuvenation (of Polish churches, schools, and clubs) and diversification (creation of new forms and types of Polish organizations, clubs, and networks). However, the Polish civil space is, in terms of social ties, characterized by ethnic bonding, which raises questions about the degree to which ethnic bonding may coexist with ethnic hostility or division and a simultaneous lack of ethnic solidarity. Scholars have commented on existing rivalry within and between the various microcosms of Polish civil society previously (Tarkowska and Tarkowski 1991) or argued for the organizational logic of "multiplication by conflict" (Jacobsson 2013), one engine of diversification. The early CRONEM study of Poles by Eade et al. (2006) concluded that "criticism of fellow Poles" was the most "striking feature" of their interviews, combining simultaneously discursive cooperation and hostility. Eade et al. also reported that 60 percent of Poles would not work for a fellow Polish employer, 80 percent felt shame on behalf of other Poles, and 62 percent stated that they were careful about their contact with other co-ethnics (2006: 37).[12] Social tensions and hostility between the generations of Poles are also noted in other significant studies by Burrell (2009) and White (2011), and are described in terms of "Darwinian" life strategies (Garapich 2008) or as mutual evaluation through gossiping (Galasińska 2010). This London-based study reveals discourses of ethnic hostility as a function of "diversity-and-division-within" the Polish civil space and as correlated to different homing desires of the postwar, Cold War–Solidarity, and post-2004 generations. Divided over both associations of and obligations to "home," internal division demonstrates the degree to which ethnic cooperation takes place as a function of migration clusters. Table 10.1 provides summative table of views held.

The challenges associated with the nexus of ethnic bonding and ethnic solidarity yet seem to stand firm in the face of uncompromising notions of each other with regard to nation, identity, home, homing desires, and social status. Brah argues "processes of homing desires include the construction of the local and the creation of habitual and habitable spaces through

Table 10.1. Critical Solidarity within the Polish Diaspora: generations and attitudes

	Post-war generation and their children on	Cold War/Solidarity Generation on	The EU generation on
Post-war generation and their children	(Emotional narration by children of the post-war generation) parents not being able to go back. Hard lives, discrimination in the UK.	They used to ignore me; I had to prove myself. They were clearly distant and worried that we wanted to get married to one of them.	They never paid me any attention to me until I dated one of their sons – then a whole new network opened up to me.
Cold War and Solidarity generation	They were communists but learned to be Poles here We used to be suspicious of them.	Staying on in the UK sometimes illegally. We couldn't go back to Poland, not really.	They integrated very well in the UK The old ones were very suspicious of them – they could be communists.
The EU generation	They did not have to leave Poland but did for material gain. The new generation has no interest in helping out. Poland an "absolute home".	They don't understand what the old generation did for us here. Some give Poles a bad name They expect to be served – we had to work so hard.	I don't always say that I am Polish; Polish people always want something or expect help or money. Many do not want or need to integrate – they settle among other Poles.

collective memory, tradition and ritual" (1996: 176). The collective memory spaces of the Polish diaspora are indeed created with a variety of homing desires that exist in relation to what we may call *homing categories* created along a continuum of *imagined, real, or absolute home*. For the children of the postwar generations Poland constitutes an "imagined home" known through the experiences of their parents whereas the national attachments of the post-EU generations are described as a "real home" or "absolute home," the latter used in derogatory terms for the alleged lack of integration.

The "imagined home" turns home into a nostalgic attachment, as desires remain unrealized: "My home is in London. I'm a Polish person living in London, that's how I would describe myself. I would never describe myself as English. That would just be impossible" (child of postwar generation, Trustee PSS). The "feeling a deep connection with Poland" has materialized through a long-term commitment to various Polish organizations: "Maybe it is a romantic notion because I've never lived in Poland. But I really … those traditions … I love Polish singing, I have done Polish dancing almost whole my life, I am interested in Polish history … maybe feeling home is a bit too strong but you feel you belong to" (vice-chair of PSS, trustee, postwar child). Associations of the "imagined home" in view of the nexus of leaving-arriving-settling-(not)returning is articulated by all generations: "I miss Poland all the time in a sense, you know. You know, it is my home country. I miss Poland, I would love to go there one day" (construction business owner, arrived 1992).

The activities of the Polish diaspora are also intimately connected to the "ideology of return." Sobków (2014) argued for Polish A-levels and the significant role of the supplementary schools teaching language skills opening up new vistas for students' "prosperity" and making it possible for them to return to Poland. However, the Polish schools also constitute memory places of diverse homing desires with reference to imagined and real home. The harsh assessments of the 2004 generation (Table 10.1 above), for instance, lay bare the complexities associated with home and identity as with the critique against those who have left Poland voluntarily, those who wish to return or make Poland an "absolute home" or fail to integrate: "In my generation we had Polish friends in Polish school, Polish scouts and so on, but it wasn't so divided. We mixed more I think. I observe some, not everybody, but some Polish people here do nothing [to integrate]. My family was telling me that in the Polish children theatre … a teenage girl was saying that at home the only language was Polish, she only listened to Polish pop music. As a teenager, who is living in England and goes to school in England: Poland is absolutely home! To me it's quite strange" (top official, trustee POSK, postwar child). The discourses visible in the narrations above bring to the fore processes through which groups become situated and tied both to origin and place of settlement as suggested by Brah (1996: 182–199) or to a time before arrival and the time of arrival. Apparently, the 2004 generation is criticized for leaving and for returning, both actions seemingly indicating disloyalty to Poland as well as Britain. Narrating "loyalty to Poland" is articulated in opposing terms too, as "having to leave" versus "wanting to leave," positioning the political migrants on top of a moral pyramid as they were being forced to leave, whereas the economic migrants left voluntarily or "deserted" their homeland. "The old people would typically say that the new migrants deserted Poland for personal material gain and that they think about themselves instead of thinking of what is best for Poland" (trustee of a PSS, postwar child). Thus, labor migration is portrayed as morally dubious with connotations of "vulgarity" in the distinction-driven sense of the term.

Significantly, debates in Poland also tap into similar discourses of betrayal of those leaving and changing their Polish names, thus failing the main task of migration, which is to "represent Poland and Poles abroad" (Kania-Lundholm 2012: 177). Marciniak and Turowski even conclude that migration is presented as incompatible with loyalty to the homeland and patriotic sentiments "to leave Poland and to establish a niche for oneself in another nation, means to lose one's 'Slavonic soul', to betray the Polish 'core', atrophy the personal 'authenticity'" (2010: 157).

It is through such discourses that the political migrants of the postwar period assume the moral high ground over the EU generation (see Galasińska 2010; Lacroix 2012). The moral superiority that follows these discursive patterns also constructs ideal types for the advancement of "the Polish good" and "acceptable forms of voluntarism" involving "the protection of Polish culture" and the preservation of authentic "Polishness." With regard to variations in levels of voluntarism, the difference between migrants who contribute and "do the actual work" and a lack of commitment among others is explained along the lines of a postcolonial discourse and as the ultimate sign of the "backwardness" of the communist system corrupting authentic forms of "Polishness." Volunteers of the first two generations will typically mention that the EU generation is "not as involved," "does not contribute," and that "the spirit of volunteering is simply not there," whereas the EU migrants explains that they "have to prove themselves" or feel "kept out." In consideration of the 25 percent of Polish organizations that were created after 2004, volunteering obviously takes place within separate clusters of homing desires and within existing organizations or new ones.

Unity Narration, Elevation vs. Devaluation

The Polish civil space has developed as a space for attaining recognition after loss of status. Intergenerational tensions within Polish London are related to perennial forms of "resource-driven" conflicts between old-timers and newcomers (see Ballard 1999); to the loss of socioeconomic status within unequal structures of the economic system but also to the system of "rights" associated with British citizenship, permanent residency, or the lack thereof. The Polish civil space absorbs and negotiates all these forms of resource-generated conflicts, with the rejuvenation or diversification of organizations—within and toward the British majority—supported by the national framework stipulating the need for Polish-specific civil society organizations.

In principle, every wave of Polish migrants seemingly feels undervalued: the postwar migrants by the British, the Solidarity by the postwar, and the post-2004 by the British, the postwar, and the Solidarity generations.

The postwar generation and their children testify to disadvantage and discrimination in the following terms: "Although many of these émigrés were educated professionals, they were obliged to accept menial jobs in England, because their qualifications were not accepted by the British" (postwar child). The engagement of postwar Polish migrants in the creation of exile organizations corresponds to a need for distinction within such "menial realities" and also lays the foundation for the nationalist narratives first united against Nazi Germany, later against communism, and thereafter increasingly in relation to Polish loyalty to Britain during the Second World War. Mythical narratives of courage and sacrifice in the face of adversity, aiding Britain by helping to crush the war enemy, also appeal to the recent Polish migrants, which has led to the rejuvenation of war-related associations (such as PECA). Narratives of pride, loyalty, service, and sacrifice have thus become available to all as ways of renegotiating status in the migrant space.

"Resource-driven criticism" and "criticism-as-defense" is also accounted for by the Solidarity and post-2004 migrants with their experiences of discrimination as a minority, coping with stereotypes, and prejudice: "Maybe we will be more than a nation of waitresses and builders one day" argues a self-employed construction worker who arrived post–EU expansion. "I don't understand," said another interviewee in a lowered voice, "the Poles contribute so much to society by paying taxes—and they helped the Allies during the war and so forth—why is the press writing these things about us?" (self-employed construction worker, 2004 generation). The discourses of group recognition provide an overall uniting narrative for Polish London, but the loss of status also divides the generations of Polish migration. Interviewees from *all* generations speak of *shame* when the "new generation" challenges the reputation of all Poles and they mention that they are careful in contact with other Poles (Table 10.1): "Sometimes I feel ashamed of being Polish. Some of the new ones are really awful. They drink and swear on the street." (volunteer, PSS, Child of Solidarity generation).The post-EU generation is also described as scrounging the system and taking it for granted: "They come here and they know that they can claim benefits; they have the right to have a Council house … We worked so hard and now it's the European Union that has to give me this, has to help me with that. This is why I think they can't appreciate the postwar generation and what they did for us here" (trustee, PSS, Solidarity generation). Similar forms of social stigmatization are fought on behalf of the highly educated migrants within the 2004 generation itself as they oppose stereotypes of the "Polish builder" who want to "make a career and have a higher standard of living" (Fomina and Frelak 2008: 20): "We have so much to offer: Polish people are clever and professional. I don't want them to think that we are all builders or manual workers" (banker, Board of Polish City Club). The diversification of organizations has generated a string of new professional associations providing the younger strata professional platforms from which to act. Previously mentioned are relatively new associations—such as the Polish Professionals, the Polish City Club, City Poles, Polish Writers, Polish Poets, and Polish Artists—that capitalize on occupational belonging as a measure of differentiation within the diverse 2004 generation. Clearly, many of these have experienced devaluation as labels of "Polish" turn "migrant" with derogatory connotations: "I used to get so frustrated because people would be like oh yeah, so you're *Polish,* and like yeah, we've got *Polish* nanny. I'm like I don't care about your *Polish* nanny quite frankly … I don't want to know about your *Polish* family who fought in the Second World War. My family fought in the Second World War too, but so fucking what? That's not the conversation, but suddenly, that became the conversation, because you mentioned *"Polish".* But I used to get really angry, and I think I still do" (director and artist, 2004 generation).

In contexts such as these, identification with voluntary organizations of the postwar and Solidarity generations or with professional groups within the post-EU generation constitute tools for *elevation,* revaluation, self-preservation, and collective retrieval of status loss that despite articulated prejudice in the majority press are facilitated by the "Polish-specific" framework. Ethnonational narrations hereby transcend class divisions and hierarchies, they penetrate the community which becomes united in reference to the majority in the process of status recovery. Overall, the Poles have suffered devaluation as a group—in comparison to the heroic perception of them and their contributions after the Second World War and with increased numbers post–EU expansion. It is in such contexts that the Second World War offers a buffer and platform for unity narration and it still figures as a prominent diaspora narrative in recent political campaigns in the Polish civil space.

Ethnic tension is seemingly enforced by a primordial or perennial stance on national identity and belonging, which is in need of more exploration, as it appears to narrate nationality by linking family to nation via bloodlines: "Being Polish is in my blood" (post-2004 generation). Contexts that turn co-ethnics into extended family are certain to lead to failed expectations, conflicts, or internal critique of fellow co-ethnics, in turn providing fuel for the diversification of the Polish space as a function of the organizational logic and multiplication by conflict mentioned previously. However, internal tension and uneasy coexistence must also be contextualized with reference to home, homing desires, and the loss of social status as a minority in a majority-defined space. Now, division and tension would have extinguished the Polish-specific space had it not been for the voluntary associations sustained by and linked to the ideology of homeland pride, nurtured and aided by the myth of the Catholic nation (Porter 2001: 289). This was concretely translated to "a Catholic elite migration" (Lacroix 2012: 194) as the elite solidified and religious boundaries merged with political ambitions and the foundation of the original exile organizations (Garapich et al. 2010) that have formed a blueprint for Polish London. Moreover, these boundary-making processes shed light on the constant status renegotiation and the unchallenged position of the uniting postwar narratives. The divided London-based Polish civil space has come to rely on the uniting framework that merges Polish identity and nationalism with related identity symbols of Polish martyrdom and Catholicism (e.g., Burrell 2006; Chojnacki 2012; Elgenius 2011a; Graff 2009) in view of devaluation. The vision of the émigrés was to cultivate and transmit Polish identity to younger generations as "heroic, martyrological and Catholic" (Chojnacki 2012: 281) – visions that survived the period of post-enlargement as a buffer against the devaluation faced without and within.

The influence of Catholicism over the Polish civil space has had significant effects with regard to diversity and gender. As a result, Polish groups with other religious affiliations, such as Jews and Orthodox Christians, are seemingly invisible within the Polish community. Other groups, such as the Polish Rainbow, formed for LGBT Polish migrants in the U.K., challenge traditional notions of home and tradition within the Polish civil space (2011–2012, Figure 1) (see also Mole 2017 on "Queer Diaspora"). Arguably, the Polish diasporas formulated alongside a gendered nationalist discourse as a response to the dramatic changes following EU accession (Graff 2009). The propensities of such discourse are beyond the scope of this chapter, yet unity narration and authentication of boundaries in the Polish civil space in London clearly involve the ceremonial forms of the church, enacted around Polish martyrdom and male sacrifice in war, in similar fashion to other cults of this kind (cf. cult of Unknown Soldiers in Britain, Belgium, and France). However, recognition in the present is negotiated with help of sacrifices of the past. In consideration of the historically significant role played by religion and sacrifice in strategies of nation-building, it is not an unusual combination (e.g., Elgenius 2011ab, 2015; Elgenius and Heath 2014). Eade et al. (2006) therefore highlight Polish ethnicity as an ambivalent resource and as a source of vulnerability. However, being Polish also provides social resources via the access to diaspora and civil society structures that help negotiate vulnerabilities through a network that generates information about opportunities and social capital alike. Eade et al. described the Polish network as "well functioning" and "interdependent and interconnected" in 2006 and this study has pointed toward the amplification and diversification of Polish organizations in recent years, with public debates about access to power and lack of representation championed by recent campaigns. Such developments stand in sharp contrast to tangible ethnic divisions and internal mistrust that constitute a crucial driver of civil society and organizational development, aspects in need of further research.

The referendum over EU membership in June 2016, its campaign and the win for "Leave" (Brexit) brought anti-Polish sentiment to the public sphere as Polish organizations were targeted with slogans taking on new meanings of "leave." The aftermath of the referendum generates questions about the degree to which divisions will be reinforced within the already heterogeneous community that is the Polish diaspora, stratified in terms of ethnicity and homing desires, class, and social status but also according to the rights associated with being British citizens of Polish descent born in the U.K. or in Poland or Polish migrants with or without permanent residency.

The findings brought together about civil society in the Polish diaspora illuminate some of the multifaceted dimensions associated with diverging notions of homing desires and show that divisions hold consequences for civil society activity and may produce unique trajectories. As a space of migrant activism, it is appropriately identified as highly stratified along clusters of social status linked to homing desires, where the former is intimately connected to the latter. The imagined horizontal ties of the nation are seemingly contested with the construction of new organizations and associations (occupational niches) that, due to direct competition (about jobs, for recognition and organizational affiliation), generate internal divisions as defense or defiance against devaluation. Interviewees refer to the "Polish community" in terms as a stratified space of uneasy interaction. Significantly, internal critique, diverging or even dividing "homing desires" do not undermine the existence of co-ethnic organizations. On the contrary, (re)building the civil society of the Polish diaspora is made possible by overall arching nationalist narrations of Poland the homeland. The findings presented here thus acknowledge the dynamism of the migrant civil space.

Gabriella Elgenius is Associate Professor in Sociology at University of Gothenburg, Associate Member at the University of Oxford and Member of the Centre for Migration and Diaspora at SOAS, University of London. Her research interests focus on nationalism and nation building, diaspora, and migrant organizations. Publications include *Symbols of Nations and Nationalism: Celebrating Nationhood* (Palgrave, 2011) and *National Museums and Nation-building in Europe: Mobilization and Legitimacy, Continuity and Change* (with Aronsson, Routledge, 2015). She received her Ph.D. at the London School of Economics and Political Science.

Notes

1. This research is related to two projects: "To What Extent Does Homeland Matter? Diaspora in the UK" (funded by the British Academy of Humanities and Social Sciences and the John Fell Foundation, University of Oxford), and "Institutional Constraints and Creative Solutions: Polish Civil Society in Comparative Perspective" (funded by the Swedish Research Council, University of Gothenburg).
2. Organizations include: the Polish Mission, various Polish churches, the Polish Educational Trust (PES) and various Polish Saturday schools, the Polish Heart Club (*Ognisko*) and various Polish clubs, and the Polish Social and Cultural Association (*POSK*), home to several organizations, e.g., the Federation of Poles, the Polish Library, the Polish Jazz Club, the Polish Café, the Polish University Abroad, the Polish theatre (and on occasion the Polish Embassy), the Polish Landowning Association, the Polish Press, Polish Professionals, City Poles, and Polish Artists London, which includes various cultural and recreational organizations. Representative campaigns that were interviewed include "Red Card against Racism," "Hurricane of Hearts" (fundraising for Polish hospitals), "Save Polish A-levels," the "British Poles Initiave" and the "Polish Blood Campaign."
3. Patterns of ethnic bonding and bridging of social capital vary for Britain's minorities. Ethnic bonding may decrease social trust and increase ethnic tensions although high levels of ethnic bonding are also shown to perform important positive functions for members of ethnic communities.
4. A number of bridging associations are noted, e.g., the recreational/youth association "Red Card against Racism," with the specific aim of building links between different ethnic groups.
5. In 2014 the total number of EU Accession 8 (EU8) immigrants was estimated to be 1,242,000 (arriving from Poland, Czech Republic, Estonia, Poland, Hungary, Latvia, Lithuania, Slovakia, and Slovenia, including U.K.-born residents) (Office for National Statistics 2015ab).
6. One of many *Daily Mail* headlines on the subject read: "Polish population in the UK *soars* from 75,000 to more than half a million in eight years" (26 May 2011).
7. Ekiert et al. (2013) argue that in the last two decades civil society in contemporary Poland has transformed into a "robust," dense, and diverse sphere that is less contentious with flourishing voluntarism. The authors find an increase in registered organizations and a "spectacular growth in the NGO sector." The rise of volunteerism counts 20 percent of all adults agreeing to do unpaid work in 2008 and 58 percent admit to volunteering in the past. Simultaneously, the World Value Survey and the European Value Survey rank Poland among the lowest on protest actions and membership in *nonpolitical* organizations and associations (World Value Survey; European Value Survey).
8. See the Polish Catholic Mission, http://www.pcmew.org.
9. The Polish Educational Society (PES) is a registered charity. It was established in 1953 and has been supporting Polish supplementary schools in England and Wales for over sixty years. (Interview, Official Representative of PES 2015). See http://www.polskamacierz.org/en/parents/find-your-nearest-school/.
10. Seredynska-Abou Eid's (2011) study identifies a number of significant online portals such as Poland Street, Ania's Poland, "Wielka Brytania," "Strefa," "Gadatka," "Moja Brytania," "Moja Wyspa," "Polacy."

11. "British Poles: Want to know where your MPs stand on Polish issues?" Retrieved from http://britishpoles.uk/.
12. The in-group relationship (between Poles) is analyzed by Eade et al. (2006) as "opportunistic and individualistic" and as opposing collective forms of ethnic solidarity. Jacobsson picks up on related characteristics within civil society in Poland developed with the concept of "civic privatism" (this volume).

References

Aronsson, P., and G. Elgenius, ed. 2015. *A History of the National Museum in Europe 1750–2010.* London: Routledge,

Anderson, B. 1991. *Imagined Communities.* London, New York: Verso Press.

Ania's Poland Blog. Retrieved 18 December 2015 from http://www.aniaspoland.com/polish_london.php#Social_Clubs.

Ballard, R. 1999. *Britain's Visible Minorities: A Demographic Overview.* Manchester: Centre for Applied South Asian Studies.

Beck, U., and E. Beck-Gernsheim. 2002. *Individualization: Institutionalized Individualism and its Social and Political Consequences.* London: Sage.

Bloemraad, I. 2006. *Becoming a Citizen: Incorporating Immigrants and Refugees in the United States and Canada.* Berkeley: University of California Press.

Brah, A. 1996. *Cartographies of Diaspora: Contesting Identities.* London and New York: Routledge.

Brinkerhoff, J. 2009. *Digital Diasporas: Identity and Transnational Engagement.* Cambridge University Press.

British Poles Initiative. 2015. "Want to know where your MPs stand on Polish issues?" Retrieved 17 December 2016 from http://britishpoles.uk/.

Burrell, K. 2006. *Moving Lives: Narratives of Nation and Migration among Europeans in Postwar Britain.* Aldershot: Ashgate.

———, ed. 2009. *Polish Migration to the UK in the New European Union: After 2004.* Abingdon, Oxon, GBR: Ashgate Publishing Group.

Burrell, K., and K. Hörschelmann, eds. 2014. *Mobilities in Socialist and Post-socialist States: Societies on the Move.* Basingstoke: Palgrave Macmillan.

Castles, S., and Miller, M. 2003. *The Age of Migration: International Population Movements in the Modern World.* Fourth Revised Edition. Basingstoke and New York: Palgrave Macmillan.

Chojnacki, P. 2012. *The Making of Polish London through Everyday Life, 1956–1976.* U.C.L. Ph.D. thesis.

Chowaniec, U. 2015. *Melancholic Migrating Bodies in Contemporary Polish Women's Writing.* Cambridge: Cambridge Scholars Publishing.

Cohen, A. 1985. *The Symbolic Construction of Community.* London: Routledge.

Cohen, R. 2008. *Global Diasporas: An Introduction.* 2nd ed. Seattle, WA: University of Washington Press.

———. 2015. "The Impact of Diaspora," in N. Signoa, A. Gamlen, G. Liberatone, and H. Neveu Kringelbach, eds. *Diasporas Reimagined: Spaces, Practices and Belonging.* Oxford Diaspora Programme and the Leverhulme Trust. Retrieved 17 December 2015 from http://www.migration.ox.ac.uk/odp/essays-oxford-diasporas-programme.shtml.

Davies, C., and D. Carrier. 2015. "Polish Migrants to Strike and Give Blood to Demonstrate Importance to U.K." *The Guardian.* 20 August. Retrieved 17 December 2015 from http://www.theguardian.com/uk-news/2015/aug/20/polish-migrants-strike-blood-donation-protest.

Drinkwater, S., J. Eade, and M. Garapich. 2009. "Poles Apart? EU Enlargement and the Labour Market Outcomes of Immigrants in the United Kingdom." *Journal of International Migration* 47, no. 1: 161–190.

Düvell, F. 2004. "Polish Undocumented Immigrants, Regular High-skilled Workers and Entrepreneurs in the UK: A Comparative Analysis of Migration Patterns, Strategies and Identity Processes." Seria: PRACE MIGRACYJNE, nr 54. Instytut Studiow Społecznych (Institute for Social Studies) Warsaw: University of Warsaw Press.

Eade, J., S. Drinkwater, and M. Garapich. 2006. "Class and Ethnicity: Polish Migrant Workers in London: Full Research Report." ESRC End of Award Report, RES-000-22-1294. Swindon: ESRC.

Ekiert, G., J. Kubik, and M. Wenzel. 2013. "Civil Society in Poland after the Fall of Communism: A Diachronic Perspective." Paper presented at 20th International Conference of Europeanists, Amsterdam, The Netherlands, 25–27 June 2013.

Elgenius, G. 2011a. *Symbols of Nations and Nationalism: Celebrating Nationhood.* Basingstoke: Palgrave Macmillan.

———. 2011b. "The Politics of Recognition: Symbols, Nation-building and Rival Nationalism." *Journal of Nations and Nationalism* 17, no. 2: 296–418.

———. 2015. "National Museums as National Symbols: A Survey of Strategic Nationbuilding: Nations as Symbolic Regimes," in *A History of the National Museum in Europe 1750-2010,* ed. P. Aronsson and G. Elgenius. London: Routledge, 145–166.

Elgenius, G., and A. Heath. 2014. "Does Ethnic Community Organization Promote or Prevent Integration?" Paper for the Home Office UK based on the Ethnic Minority British Election Survey and qualitative research on British Sikhs and Poles. December 2014, Home Office.

European Values Study Longitudinal Data File 1981-2008. Retrieved from GESIS Data Catalogue: https://dbk.gesis.org/dbksearch/SDesc2.asp?ll=10&notabs=&af=&nf=&search=&search2=&db=E&no=4804.

Fennema, M., and J. Tillie. 2005. "Civic Communities and Multicultural Democracy," in *Democracy and the Role of Associations,* ed. S. Roßteutscher. *Political, Organizational and Social Contexts.* Abingdon: Routledge, 219–236.

Fomina, J., and J. Frelak. 2008. *Next Stop London. Public Perceptions of Labour Migration within the EU: The Case of Polish Labour Migrants in the British Press.* Warsaw: Institute of Public Affairs. Retrieved 17 December 2015 from www.isp.org.pl/files/17552 22039044790600120289958 1.pdf.

Ford, R., and M. Goodwin. 2014. *Revolt on the Right: Explaining Support for the Radical Right in Britain.* Abingdon: Routledge.

Galasińska, A. 2010. "Gossiping in the Polish Club: An Emotional Coexistence of 'Old' and 'New' Migrants." *Journal of Ethnic and Migration Studies* 36, no. 6: 939–951.

Garapich, M. 2008. "The Migration Industry and Civil Society: Polish Immigrants in the United Kingdom Before and After EU Enlargement." *Journal of Ethnic and Migration Studies* 34, no. 5: 735–752.

———. 2014. "Homo Sovieticus Revisited—Anti-Institutionalism, Alcohol and Resistance among Polish Homeless Men in London." *International Migration* 52, no. 1: 100–117.

Garapich, M., J. Eade, and S. Drinkwater. 2010. "What's behind the Figures? Polish Migration to the U.K.," in *A Continent Moving West? EU Enlargement and Labour Migration from Central and Eastern Europe,* ed. R. Black, C. Pantiru, G. Engbersen, and M. Okolski. IMISCOE: Amsterdam University Press.

Gianni, M., and Giugni, M. 2014. "Resources, Opportunities, and Discourses: What Explains the Political Mobilization of Muslims in Europe?," in *From Silence to Protest: International Perspectives on Weakly Resourced Groups,* ed. D. Chabanet and F. Royall. Farnham: Ashgate, 103–118.

Gittel, R., and Vidal, A. 1998. *Community Organizing: Building Social Capital as a Development Strategy.* Thousand Oaks, CA: Sage Publications.

Gliński, P. 2004. "How Active Are the Social Actors?" *Polish Sociological Review* 4, no. 148: 429–450.

Graff, A. 2009. "Gender, Sexuality, and Nation: Here and Now: Reflections on the Gendered and Sexualized Aspects of Contemporary Polish Nationalism," in *Intimate Citizenship: Gender, Sexualities, Politics,* ed. E. Oleksy. London: Routledge, 133–147.

Heath, A., J. Martin, and G. Elgenius, 2007a. "Who Do We Think We Are? The Decline of Traditional Social Identities," in *British Social Attitudes: the 23rd Report–Perspectives on a Changing Society,* ed. A. Park and J. Curtice et al. London: Sage for the National Centre for Social Research, 17–34.

Heath, A., and S.Y. Cheung, eds. 2007b. *Unequal Chances: Ethnic Minorities in Western Labour Markets.* Oxford: Oxford University Press for the British Academy.

Heath, A., S. Fisher, G. Rosenblatt, D. Saunders, and M. Sobolewska. 2013. *The Political Integration of Ethnic Minorities in Britain: Ethnic Minority British Election Survey Data.* ESRC. Oxford: Oxford University Press.

Heath, A., and N. Demireva. 2014. "Has Multiculturalism Failed in Britain?" *Journal of Ethnic and Racial Studies* 37, no. 1: 161–180.

Home Office. 2013. "Table 1.3: Overseas-Born Population in the United Kingdom, Excluding Some Residents in Communal Establishments, by Sex, by Country of Birth, January 2013 to December 2013." Retrieved 10 December 2015 from www.ons.gov .uk.

Hutnyk, J. 2010. "Hybridity," in *Diasporas: Concepts, Intersections, Identities,* ed. Knott and McLoughlin. New York: Zed Books, 59–62.

Iglicka, K. 2001. *Poland's Post-war Dynamic of Migration.* Aldershot: Ashgate.

Jacobs, D., and J. Tillie. 2004. "Introduction: Social Capital and Political Integration of Migrants." *Journal of Ethnic and Migration Studies* 30, no. 3: 497–427.

Jacobsson, K. 2013. "Channeling and Enrollment: The Institutional Shaping of Animal Rights Activism in Poland," in *Beyond NGO-ization: The Development of Social Movements in Central and Eastern Europe,* ed. K. Jacobsson and S. Saxonberg. Farnham: Ashgate, 27–47.

Jordan, B., and Düvell, F. 2003. *Migration: The Boundaries of Equality and Justice.* Cambridge: Polity Press.

Kania-Lundholm, M. 2012. *Re-Branding a Nation Online: Discourses on Polish Nationalism and Patriotism.* Uppsala University. Ph.D. dissertation.

Kawalerowicz, J., and M. Biggs. 2015. "Anarchy in the UK: Economic Deprivation, Social Disorganization, and Political Grievances in the London Riot of 2011." *Social Forces.* Retrieved 17 December 2015 from http://sf.oxfordjournals.org/content/ early/2015/03/05/sf.sov052.full.pdf+html.

King, A. 1998. *Memorials of the Great War in Britain: The Symbolism of Politics of Remembrance.* Oxford: Berg.

Knott, K., and S. McLoughlin, eds. 2010. *Diasporas: Concepts, Intersections, Identities.* New York: Zed Books.

Koopmans, R., P. Statham, M. Guigni, and F. Passy. 2005. *Contested Citizenship: Immigration and Cultural Diversity in Europe.* Minnesota: University of Minnesota Press.

Lacroix, T. 2012. "Indian and Polish Migrant Organizations in the UK," in *Cross Border Migrant Organizations in Comparative Perspective,* ed. L. Pries and Z. Sezgin. Basingstoke: Palgrave Macmillan, 152–209.

Laurence and Maxwell. 2012. "Political Parties and Diversity in Western Europe," in *Immigrant Politics: Race and Representation in Western Europe,* ed. T. Givens and R. Maxwell. Boulder, CO: Lynne Rienner Publishers, 13–31.

Marciniak, K., and K. Turowski. 2010. *The Streets of Crocodiles: Photography, Media, and Postsocialist Landscapes in Poland.* Bristol and Chicago: Intellect Ltd.

Maxwell, R. 2012. *Ethnic Minority Migrants in Britain and France: Integration Trade-Offs.* Cambridge: Cambridge University Press.

Ministry of Foreign Affairs of the Republic of Poland. The Polish Diaspora. Retrieved 10 December 2015 from http://www.msz.gov.pl/en/foreign_policy/polish_diaspora/?printMode=true.

Mole, R.C.M. 2017. "Identity, Belonging and Solidarity among Russian-Speaking Queer Migrants in Berlin." *Slavic Review* (forthcoming).

Morales, L., and M. Giugni, eds. 2011. *Social Capital, Political Participation and Migration in Europe: Making Multicultural Democracy Work?* Basingstoke: Palgrave Macmillan.

Office for National Statistics. 2011. Labour Force Survey 2011. Retrieved 10 December 2015 from http://www.ons.gov.uk/ons/rel/lms/labour-market-statistics/november-2011/index.html.

———. 2015a. Annual Population Survey 2015. Retrieved 10 December 2015 from http://www.ons.gov.uk/ons/search/index.html?content-type=Publication&pubdateRangeType=allDates&newquery=%27Annual+Population+Survey%27&pageSize=50&applyFilters=true.

———. 2015b. "Population by Country of Birth and National Estimates, Frequently Asked Questions." *Annual Population Survey.* August.

Osa, M.J. 2003. *Solidarity and Contention: Networks of Polish Opposition.* Minnesota: University of Minnesota Press.

Polish Educational Society. 2015. Petition Change.org "AQA, keep the A-Level Polish Exam after 2018." Retrieved 10 December 2015 from Change.org, https://www.change.org/p/andrew-hall-chief-executive-officer-aqa-aqa-keep-the-a-level-polish-exam-after-2018.

Porter, B. 2001. "The Catholic Nation: Religion, Identity, and the Narratives of Polish History." *The Slavic and East European Journal* 45, no. 2: 289–299.

Portes, A. 1995. *The Economic Sociology of Immigration.* New York: Russell Sage Foundation

Pries, L., and Z. Sezgin, eds. 2012. *Cross Border Migrant Organizations in Comparative Perspective.* Basingstoke: Palgrave Macmillan.

Putnam, R.D. 2000. *Bowling Alone: The Collapse and Revival of American Community.* New York: Simon and Schuster.

Ryan, L., R. Sales, M. Tilki and B. Siara. 2008. "Social networks, social support and social capital: The experiences of recent Polish migrants in London". *Sociology* 42, no. 4: 672–690.

Seredynska-Abou Eid, R. 2011. "The Role of Online Communities for Polish Migrants in the United Kingdom," in *Selling One's Favourite Piano to Emigrate: Mobility Patterns in Central Europe at the Beginning of the 21st Century*, ed. J. Isański and P. Luczys. Newcastle upon Tyne: Cambridge Scholars Publishing, 31–44.

Sobków, W. 2014. "Learning Polish, the UK's second most spoken language, is a plus." Retrieved 10 December 2015 from http://www.theguardian.com/education/2014/jun/05/learning-polish-a-plus-ambassador.

Sword, K. 1996. *Identity in Flux: The Polish Community in Britain.* London: School of Slavonic and Eastern European Studies, University College London.

Sztompka, P. 1993. "Civilizational Incompetence." *Zeitscrift für Soziologie* 22, no. 2: 85–95.

Tarkowska, E., and J. Tarkowski. 1991. "Social Disintegration in Poland: Civil Society or Amoral Familism?" *Telos* 21: 103–109.

Tillie, J. 2004. "Social Capital of Organisations and their Members: Explaining Political Integration in Amsterdam." *Journal of Ethnic and Migration Studies* 30, no. 3: 529–541.

The Economist. 2013. "The Polish Paradox", December 14. Retrieved 20 December 2016: http://www.economist.com/news/britain/21591588-britons-loathe-immigration-principle-quite-immigrants-practice-bulgarians.

Van Hear, N. 2015. "Spheres of Diaspora Engagement," in *Diaspora Reimagined: Spaces, Practices and Belonging.* Oxford: Oxford University Press.

Vertovec, S. 2007. "Super-diversity and its Implications." *Ethnic and Racial Studies* 30, no 6: 1024–1054.

Vertovec, S. 2010. "Cosmopolitanism," in 2010. *Diasporas: Concepts, Intersections, Identities*, ed. K. Knott and S. McLoughlin. New York: Zed Books, 63–68.

Wallace, C. 2002. "Opening and Closing Borders: Migration and Mobility in East-Central Europe." *Journal of Ethnic and Migration Studies* 28, no. 4: 603–625.

White, A. 2011. *Polish Families and Migration since EU Accession.* Bristol: The Policy Press.

World Values Study Longitudinal Data File 1981-2014. Retrieved from World Values Survey Website: http://www.worldvaluessurvey.org/WVSDocumentationWVL.jsp. Aggregate File Producer: Asep/JDS, Madrid Spain.

Chapter 11

MOBILIZING ON THE EXTREME RIGHT IN POLAND
MARGINALIZATION, INSTITUTIONALIZATION, AND RADICALIZATION

Daniel Płatek and Piotr Płucienniczak

Introduction: The Extreme Right in Postcommunist (Un)civil Society

The first March for Tolerance in Poland, a legal demonstration organized in Krakow in 2004 in defense of sexual minorities' rights, was affected by attacks on participants. Eggs, stones, and bottles were thrown toward protesters, several of whom were beaten by extreme-right activists. In the riot that followed, several police officers were also injured. A few weeks earlier, the LGBT festival of which the March for Tolerance was part had attracted enormous media attention. Right-wing and conservative organizations tried to put pressure on the rector of the Jagiellonian University, as well as on the Krakow authorities, to stop the event from occurring. The case came to the fore not only throughout Poland, but also abroad. The incident sparked a debate on the situation of sexual minorities and their place in Polish society. Some public figures, including high-ranking politicians and Catholic priests, openly instigated hatred and condemned LGBT individuals. This was only the beginning of a long right-wing campaign for xenophobic "normality" (Graff 2009), which even today has not ended. One year later, several hundred skinheads and hooligans again tried to disrupt the march, but the confrontation was thwarted by police. The situation repeated itself year after year, with increasing numbers of people being injured. However, these incidents were only the visible tip of the iceberg; the real activity of the extreme-right movement in Poland goes far beyond that.

Since the beginning of the twenty-first century, aggressive homophobic rhetoric has escalated and the number of attacks on the LGBT communities has increased greatly. In 2011 alone, the Never Again (Nigdy Więcej) association, the biggest NGO engaged in the eradication of racism and xenophobia, registered more than three hundred cases of hate speech, attacks on members of ethnic and sexual minorities, acts of vandalism against religious minorities, and similar incidents aimed at leftist or liberal activists. Nevertheless, only a few such incidents aroused interest and action at the highest political level. For many commentators, scholars, and state agencies the extreme right as a political actor and perpetrator of violence was an entirely new phenomenon. Pankowski and Kornak (2005) argue that the state and its elites were blind to the fact that the extreme-right movement had existed and been active since the 1990s, and not even when an extreme-right party came to power (in 2001) and then left it (in 2007) did this attitude change.

The landscape of social mobilizations in Poland has changed radically since 1989. Civil society understood as the third sector (nongovernmental, nonprofit organizations and associations) is today recognized as an important part of the democratic order filling the gap between the state, the market, and the private sphere, but social movements, sometimes disruptive ones, also claim this space. Normative definitions of civil society reflect the assumption that civic activism should build social capital, trust, and shared values, which are transferred into the political sphere and help to hold society together (Putnam et al. 1994, see also Jezierska in this volume). However, there are types of social movements that deviate from the vision of civil society as a sphere populated by civic-minded organizations that support democracy and its sustainability. The main feature of such kinds of movements is the use of violence and anti-state, undemocratic ideology. The extreme-right movement, with its anti-democratic attitudes, seems to be particularly relevant.

Many sociologists categorize anti-systemic movements as part of "uncivil society." Laurence Whitehead (1997) defines "uncivil society" by (1) the lack of commitment to act within the constraints of legal or pre-established rules, and (2) the lack of a spirit of civility, "civic responsibilities," or "civic mindedness." However, the case of the extreme right in Poland seems to confirm the doubts voiced by Cas Mudde over the notion of "uncivil society." According to Mudde, "uncivil movements and contentious politics should be included in the study of civil society (in post-communist Europe)" (Mudde 2003: 164). This is particularly important in the case of Poland because at the beginning of the twenty-first century, the extreme right moved from the margins it had occupied after the postcommunist transformation and claimed its place in the very center of the public sphere: its representatives were present in the parliament, government, and various state agendas, while its activists, skinheads, and hooligans were considered by a large part of Polish society to be defenders of the "proper" society. Of course, the extreme right still adheres to the definitional traits of the "uncivil society," such as an anti-systemic attitude, lack of spirit of civility, enmity toward minority groups, and honest will to use violence against their opponents (Piotrowski 2009: 179), yet its repertoire of actions changes and—as shown in this chapter—under favorable conditions the movement can blend into the broader civil and political society.

This trend emphasizes the need to pay careful attention to the political and cultural contexts in which collective actions take place. The extreme right should not be dismissed as an actor occupying the dangerous margins or mean streets only. The extreme-right movement is a mosaic composed of divergent ideological trends mobilizing around different targets and using varied repertoires of actions. Moreover, there are many connections between political actors at different levels: be it parliamentary, extraparliamentary, or clandestine. To disentangle this network, a close empirical study is required. There is, however, a serious gap in sociological research on the Polish extreme right. This chapter offers an analysis that, in contrast to existing models (Pankowski and Kornak 2005; Pankowski 2010; Lipiński 2013; Ost 2006) includes not only cultural factors, but also the structure of political opportunities available to the extreme right.

Drawing on social movement theory and the methodology of protest event analysis, which uses information gleaned from national newspapers to measure occurrences of protest events, we propose a way to conceptualize the specific field of mobilization of the Polish extreme right as a combination of political and discursive opportunities. Our central task here is to explain variations in the mobilization by the extreme right across time and to analyze the three distinct phases of this phenomenon: marginalization (1989–1999), institutionalization (2000–2005) and radicalization (2006–2013). Our general thesis is that the extreme-right movement is stable in its anti-systemic and anti-minority aims, while its action repertoire and targets change accordingly to the shifts in the abovementioned opportunity structures. In some contexts, extreme-right groups can use democratic institutions to attain power or to become a part of the ruling institutions. In this way, the movement is able to transcend the boundaries between civil and uncivil society as it adapts to political and social trends.

This claim is supplemented by two detailed hypotheses. First, the extreme-right political movement that operates in the presence of a strong extreme-right political party is more likely to reduce the share of extraparliamentary mobilization and choose moderate types of action. Under such conditions the repertoire of action tends to be much more conventional and the overall level of violent (confrontational) events is relatively low. Second, when the political and discursive opportunity structure is unfavorable to the emergence of a strong extreme-right political party, the level of extra-parliamentary mobilization is relatively high, and the presence of violent (confrontational) acts is more likely.

Defining the Extreme Right

Definition of the extreme right is not an easy task, as the ideology of the movement depends on local historical and cultural variables to a greater degree than is the case, for example, left-wing movements. There is also the question of the distinction between the extreme right, the radical right and the far right. In many cases the terms are used interchangeably, yet we have decided to use the term "extreme right" to delineate our research interests for reasons presented below.

Probably the simplest difference between the extreme and far right is the movement's attitude toward democracy: while the former despises and rejects the notion, using democratic institutions only in rare cases and clearly instrumentally, other factions of the right tend to accept it, at least nominally, and follow the rules of an electoral game distancing themselves from open authoritarianism. For Rafał Pankowski (2010: 4), the extreme right cherishes a "radically anti-pluralist, homogeneous vision of the national community and rejects the basic democratic values." It positions itself close to fascism and Nazism, sometimes attempting to re-invent or re-invigorate these ideological trends in the forms of, respectively, neofascism and neo-Nazism. According to Roger Eatwell (1996: 7), "the radical [right] category is mainly seen as a half-way house towards extremism." In other words, while for the radical and far right it is mainstream politics where the stakes are, thus, they embrace conventional means of struggle; for the extreme right the streets are the main space of activity and physical violence is a viable instrument to achieve political goals. What is certain is that the borders between these two categories are fuzzy and not always obvious.

Many typologies of the extreme right are based on ideologies of particular extreme-right organizations, but such an approach is severely limited, and more universal descriptions are pursued (Griffin 1991; Kitschelt 1995). The definition of the extreme right usually includes such traits as xenophobia, nationalism, and anti-democratic authoritarianism (Carter 2005). Andreas Wimmer's (2002) comparative study shows that extreme-right ideology always includes an ethnic and a political aspect—ethnic exclusiveness and devotion to the nation-state. Koopmans and Statham (1999) also stress the ethnic element in the discourse of the extreme right. According to them, the movement conveys an ethnocultural conception of national identity. The idea of cultural supremacy in many cases supersedes traditional racism, which was attached to the idea of differences between separate "biological" races. Aurélien Mondon (2013) calls this ideology "neo-racism."

Other authors stress the movement's "all or nothing" radical stance (Caiani and Parenti 2013). Perhaps the common denominator of all actors belonging to the category of extreme-right groups is their commitment to an ideology of intrinsic inequality among humans on the one hand, and the acceptance of violence as a mean of political expression on the other (Eatwell 1996). Manuela Caiani et al. (2012: 6) states: "Beyond ideology, the extreme right has also been defined by a preference for disruptive or even violent forms of action. Anti-democratic and anti-egalitarian frames have normally been accompanied by aggressive behavior towards political opponents as well as ethnic, religious, or gender minorities." We find this general definition especially accurate and apt for our aims, yet it should be complemented with a note on the specificity of Polish society.

Most of the theories of the extreme right created in the West presuppose a cultural heterogeneity of society and tensions between major and minor cultural groups (Klandermans et al. 2006: 181). In contemporary Poland, however, the society is virtually homogeneous ethnically and culturally: in the Polish census of 2011, 97 percent of respondents declared Polish nationality (GUS 2013). Instead of focusing on foreign-origin minorities, the extreme right is forced to construct its enemy in a different way. Its attitude toward other nationalities is based on historical sentiments rather than current affairs, as in the case of traditional anti-Semitism or Germanophobia. Contemporary political claims refer to the notion of traditional national identity defined by Catholicism, the Polish language, and Polish ethnicity. Consequently, one of the central elements of Polish extreme-right ideology is anti-Semitism (Pankowski 2010: 3) and an important point of reference is the interwar period with its nationalist programs and organizations (Lipiński 2013: 5).

As we will show, references to traditional values, such as the traditional family and Catholicism, constitute a more prominent part of the activities of the Polish extreme right (particularly in the second and third phase of mobilization) than is the case with its Western counterparts. The Polish movement also emphasizes its attachment to so-called traditional gender roles and openly despises not only sexual minorities but also the notion of social construction of sexual roles itself in its pursuit of "normality" (Graff 2009). What movements in the West and the East have in common, of course, is a desire for a culturally or ethnically homogeneous society.

Consequently, in our chapter we will use the term "extreme right" to refer to those political groups that adopt nationalist ideology as well as extremist forms of action. In terms of social movement theory, by the extreme right we mean interventions, confrontational or nonconfrontational, conventional or nonconventional in the public domain by groups who mobilize around the task of preserving the "national identity" (defined by Catholicism, Polish language, ethnicity, and heteronormativity), demanding that the state enforce measures that support this particular vision and oppose competing visions, especially the idea of the nation as a political and civic community (cf. Koopmans et al. 2005: 180).

Theoretical Explanations of the Mobilization of the Extreme Right

Ruud Koopmans et al. (2005: 181) argue that there are two competing explanations for the rise of the extreme right within sociological theory. The first is *grievance theory*, and the second *opportunity structure theory.* According to the former, the extreme right should be considered a byproduct of an increasing tension associated with unemployment and the presence of immigrants (Lipset and Raab 1970), social resistance to crises of the capitalist system (Polanyi 2001) or a reaction to modernization (Norris 2005). In another version, grievance theory refers to atomization and longing for community as a breeding ground for the extreme right (Kornhauser 1959). In short, grievance theorists claim that the scale of extreme-right activity is correlated with objective conditions. As for Poland, David Ost (2006) argues that the re-emergence of the extreme right is a direct consequence of an acceptance of neoliberal policies by trade unions and social democratic parties. The anger that was stirred by unjust economic transformation was channeled into hatred toward minorities instead of into mobilization based on shared working-class interests. Stating this, Ost rephrases Thomas Frank's (2004) Augustinian thesis on the right being in an absence of the left.

Grievance theory, however, faces heavy criticism for its oversimplification of the processes taking place during the mobilization. For example, Ost's account does not explain why extreme-right parties succeeded only more than ten years after the transformation and, even more importantly, why the extreme right voiced almost no socioeconomic grievances during the first phase of its mobilization (1989–1999), focusing on political ones instead. This lack of resonance between popular contention and the extreme right's actions was especially visible during the first wave of protests after the transformation as described by Ekiert and Kubik (1999). Especially during the

1989–1993 period, collective protest in Poland was intense. Waves of strike swept through entire sectors of the economy, but the extreme right was not a part of these campaigns.

The second group of explanations, opportunity structure theory, emphasizes the importance of the political and discursive opportunities that shape the activities of the extreme right. Within this paradigm, the extreme right is not only a byproduct of an anomic situation, but rather an agent seeking favorable opportunities and actively adjusting to its social environment. There is relatively little systematic research on the Polish extreme right employing this perspective. Rafał Pankowski's *The Populist Radical Right in Poland* (2010) is the only volume to date dedicated in its entirety to the study of the extreme right in Poland. Yet, although Pankowski refers to social movement theory, his book is mainly a sociohistorical and narrative account of populist radical-right incursions into mainstream politics, and is not really concerned with the extremist faction of the right. He has a strong argument, however, that the mobilization of the right in Poland is a product of its exploitation of the available cultural opportunities rather than grievances connected with neoliberal policies and economic crises. For him, the re-invigoration of the national democracy tradition, anti-Semitism, and fundamentalist Catholicism at the turn of the century served as a vehicle for the right-wingers to enter the mainstream political discourse. Similarly, Artur Lipiński (2012) argues that the critical failures of the left and liberals created a political space for the radical right-wing critique of the status quo. He focuses on the rampant corruption of the nominally social democratic government that was exposed by subsequent parliamentary investigation commissions and the media: "The product of that was a dramatic picture of the state as a structure overrun by postcommunists and secret agents" (Lipiński 2012: 83). This coincided with the rebirth of Catholic and patriotic tradition and created an explosive mixture of resentment toward the state and its elites, connected with a desire to reintroduce proven, traditional values into social life. Both Pankowski's and Lipiński's accounts are supplemented by what Agnieszka Graff (2009) calls "a well-planned and funded public relations effort to build a solid link between anti-choice politics and Polish national identity" (Graff 2009: 135). For her, the extreme right not only exploited existing cultural frames, but also managed to bridge and expand on them, constructing a master frame connecting nationalism, the ideology of Polish martyrdom, homophobia, and Catholicism.

We consider this approach, which focuses on opportunities rather than on presupposed objective grievances, to be adequate for the explanation of the mobilization of the extreme right. Furthermore, political factors should be included in the analysis. For Koopmans et al. (2005: 188) "the extent and forms of claims making by extreme right actors stem more from the competition between parties in the institutional arenas than from the competition between ethnic groups." Such an approach seems especially viable in the case of virtually culturally homogeneous societies such as the Polish one. The mobilization of the extreme right is conditioned not by the number of immigrants or unemployment rate, but above all by the configuration of opportunities available to the movement and identified by its members or leaders. Two specific variables seem to determine the extent of the extreme-right protest the most: (1) competition from electoral political parties and the composition of the government; and (2) the issues in "the public discourse that determine a message's chance of diffusion in the public sphere" (Olzak and Koopmans 2004: 201–202).[1] The former constitutes political opportunity structure, meaning "signals to social or political actors which either encourage or discourage them to use their internal resources to form social movements" (Tarrow 1996: 54). The political space defined by the opportunity structure can be either *narrow,* when the entrance to the parliamentary arena is blocked for the movement, or *wide,* when there is a possibility of entering it. A wide political opportunity for the extreme right exists when the political space is left uncovered by a strong right-wing political party, thus allowing this space to be exploited by the extreme right in conventional electoral competition. A narrow political opportunity structure exists when the political space is closed for the extreme right because of the presence of a strong right-wing party in the parliament (Koopmans et al. 2005: 188). Second, discursive opportunities can be either *strong* (when extreme-right claims are highly visible, resonant, and legitimate in the society in which the movement operates) or *weak* (when radical-right actors have a low degree of visibility, resonance, and legitimacy in the society) (ibid.: 188).

The first situation, when discursive opportunities are weak and the political space narrow, is called *marginalization.* Here, Koopmans et al. (2005: 190) expect "a low level of mobilization, but at the same time a radical action repertoire; it is also unlikely that a strong party will emerge in such a situation." The level of confrontational events in this situation is expected to be relatively high, as radical extraparliamentary political movements tend to focus on easily reachable targets. The organizational structures of such actors are weak and exposed to disintegration.

The second situation, *institutionalization,* results from the combination of a wide-open political space and strong discursive opportunities. This situation favors the presence of the extreme-right party in the parliamentary arena, which then draws attention to radical claims. The overall level of mobilization is expected to be higher than in the situation of marginalization, but the repertoire to be much more conventional. In this situation, violence can be counterproductive for the movement's mainstream-targeted campaigns, so it is expected to be shunned by the movement's leaders.

The third situation (*radicalization*) emerges from the combination of narrow political opportunities and strong discursive opportunities. In this situation, we expect the extreme-right actors to express themselves through mobilization mainly in the extraparliamentary arena because channels of political expression are closed. A narrow political space prevents the formation of a strong political party. However, due to the rich opportunities on the discursive side, the degree of visibility and legitimacy of the extreme-right claims in the public sphere is expected to be high, compared to in marginalization. Consequently, the presence of extreme-right activists on the streets during episodes of demonstrative and confrontational actions is predominantly high. Again, an increase in the number of violent acts is expected.

The last situation, called *populism,* is a combination of favorable opportunities for the extreme-right party and low legitimacy of its claims. This should lead to a moderate level and moderate forms of activism. The level of violence should also be relatively moderate, on par with the level of conventional actions.

As stated in the theoretical section above, we aim to place our distinctive intervals of the Polish extreme right's mobilizations within this typology and explain cross-time variations in the form of political and discursive opportunities, organizational structures, action repertoires, and movement targets. However, before we turn to empirical analysis, we present the methodological aspects of our study.

Data and Research Method

In order to create a dataset on the whole range of the extreme right's activities in the last twenty-five years, we build on the concept and techniques of protest event analysis (PEA). The main unit of analysis in PEA is a single protest event. For defining a protest event we take as a basis the concept of "political claim" (Koopmans et al. 2005: 180). This means that we consider as a "protest event" every intervention in the public domain, verbal or nonverbal, that includes a political claim. In order to be coded, events must be political in the sense that they relate to collective social problems and solutions. What is more, a political claim must be backed by an identifiable political act. We do not analyze the individual statements of politicians as in text analysis, but a concrete act, for example a demonstration, march, strike, letter, lawsuit, etc. The characteristics of such acts (events) are derived from mentions in the daily newspapers. One such article can describe several events, and the opposite is also true—one event can be described in a number of press articles.

PEA is a method that allows for the quantification of many detailed properties of protests (McCarty et al. 1996). It informs a researcher about changes in the forms of action, targets, and scale of violence, and helps to identify periods of intensification or decrease in frequency of protests and other similar phenomena. With precautions and many weaknesses, the newspaper-based analysis allows us to present, if not the real number of protests, at least the associations among specific variables of forms of protest events, as well as much more general trends (Franzosi 1987; McCarthy et al. 1996). At present, the dominant position on the press market belongs to one national "prestige" newspaper, *Gazeta Wyborcza*. For all the analyzed phases we used articles published in *Gazeta Wyborcza* and the Polish Press Agency—the largest and most reliable press agency in Poland.

Our research project is based on a small-N comparative analysis of three phases of the extreme-right mobilization in Poland. We used a standardized codebook and coded all protest events that fit our operational definition of an extreme-right action. As a result, we created a database consisting of a total of 962 (293 for the first phase of mobilization, 336 for the second phase of mobilization, and 333 for the third phase) protest events that we divided into three temporal groups ("phases") identified on the basis of similarities and differences between the characteristics of the events.

Regarding the operational criteria used for the dataset, three aspects of protest event (our unit of analysis) are important. All of these aspects are variables for coding. The first aspect concerns the repertoire of the extreme-right actions. Since we are interested in all forms of Polish radical-right actions, the spectrum of codes ranged from (1) **confrontational actions** (usually illegal) against people considered enemies, whose aim is to disrupt official meetings or opponents' demonstrations, to (2) **demonstrative actions** (mostly legal or illegal but nonviolent demonstrations, pickets, marches, occupations of buildings, etc.), and, finally, (3) **conventional actions** (such as press conferences, lawsuits, letters, and campaigns including those in the parliamentary arena). The last type of action is (4) **expressive actions**. This type is beyond the scale of confrontational–conventional action. It contains legal actions directed at extreme-right activists themselves, in order to reinvigorate in-group cohesion and identity; activists usually come together during national holidays, anniversaries, or conventions.

The second aspect applies to the thematic focus of the covered events. Our codes encompass acts performed by extreme-right-wingers directed at any targets and any issue field. Thus, the codes corresponding to them were grouped into eight categories: (1) **politics** is a code concerning political actors (persons and organizations) appearing in the parliamentary arena; (2) the **socioeconomic** code includes all issues concerning the living conditions of the Polish people: privatization, loss of job, taxation, sale of national assets to foreigners, etc.; (3) **leftist organizations and individuals** includes all the extraparliamentary leftist organizations targeted by the extreme right (anarchists, socialists, punk subculture) and also public figures (e.g., public intellectuals); (4) the **ethnic minorities; foreigners** code refers to all people considered by the extreme right as foreign or racially inferior (Roma, black people, and also those from other countries, like Germans and Jews); (5) the **sexual minorities** code refers to homosexuals (gays and lesbians) as well as the political and cultural organizations that defend LGBT rights or support same-sex relationships (feminist movements, human rights activists, etc.); (6) the **international politics** code means international organizations, foreign institutions (e.g., the European Union), embassies of foreign countries targeted by extreme right; (7) in the category **traditional values; Us** we included all the targets and issues dedicated to celebration of national holidays, various national anniversaries, conventions dedicated to celebration of the extreme-right organizations' historical moments, etc.; part of this category also includes acting in defense of the values considered purely Polish (e.g., protecting the lives of the "unborn" against the pro-choice movement, etc.).

The third aspect concerns types of political actors. In order to control the coherence between different characteristics of extreme-right political actors, we classified them into broader categories: (1) under the **political parties** category, we encoded groups that openly partake in political activities in the parliamentary arena; (2) in the **political movements** category we included those less institutionalized organizations and groups that openly partake in political activities, but do not act in the parliamentary arena;[2] (3) in the category of **subcultural groups** we included those protest events in which the members of extreme-right subcultures, such as skinheads, soccer hooligans, and nationalists take part. Now, we turn to the empirical findings.

Phase of Marginalization (1989–1999)

Political and discursive opportunity structure. The first phase of the extreme-right mobilization took place in the context of the beginning of the economic and social transformation. In 1989 the general aim of the political elites was the rejection of the communist system and privatization of state enterprises. The sociological analysis focused on the social consequences of transition. A dominant metaphor was that of "revolutionary moment" (Pakulski and Higley 1992): the end of the old world (Pakulski 1991: 4), and also "the state of social anomie" (Szafraniec 1986). Reforms of the political system and the accompanying harsh economic conditions of the privatization process, connected with the desire to develop closer economic links with Western countries, all also came under some criticism from the extreme right wing of the political forces.

The parliamentary elections of 1991 brought to power the Democratic Union (Unia Demokratyczna), a political party of liberal elites that supervised the process of transformation. The second place was taken by the postcommunist Democratic Left Alliance (Sojusz Lewicy Demokratycznej—hereafter SLD), the party that gathered the votes of public sector workers worried about their fate in the destabilized economy. Catholic Election Action (Katolicka Akcja Wyborcza), a committee formed mostly by the representatives of the biggest conservative party of the time—Christian National Union (Zjednoczenie Chrześcijańsko Narodowe), won forty-nine seats. The presence of a strong right-wing party in the parliament made it more difficult for the extreme right to establish a foothold in politics. What is more, sixth place in the election went to the Confederation of Independent Poland (Konfederacja Polski Niepodległej—hereafter KPN), a party that was very visible in the public sphere because of its demonstrations involving occupations of buildings. The extreme right was then left without many opportunities to expand its structures and make resonant claims. It had to turn toward historical ethnic enemies, "Jews" and "Germans," and other groups that it could attack directly: the Roma and leftist movements and subcultures (anarchists, socialists, punks, etc.).

Popular sentiments toward Germans were far from enmity, yet the extreme-right movement tried to mobilize supporters on the basis of historical animosities between the two nations. In a public opinion survey from 1995, 38 percent of Poles declared an aversion toward Germans (CBOS VI 1995). Under this period other European nations and Americans were treated with open sympathy but 39 percent of Poles agreed with the opinion that "the Jews have too much influence on Polish politics and economy" (CBOS I 1997). This is evidence of the enduring vitality of anti-Semitic stereotypes at the time. Yet only the Roma were treated with a firm aversion. As many as 73 percent of respondents declared their aversion toward the Roma in 1995, and the percentage of those sympathetic toward them was negligible (CBOS VI 1995). In contrast, international institutions were generally trusted, e.g., accession to NATO, which was concluded in 1999, was seen not as a threat to Poland's sovereignty but rather as a warranty of the state's safety.

In this first phase of mobilization, the extreme-right movement found relatively strong discursive opportunities in relation to the alleged Jewish and Roma "menace" whereas American imperialism, German revisionism, and other similar issues did not resonate strongly in Polish society. Thus, the general structure of discursive opportunities for the movement was rather weak, not providing a chance to build a strong framework for mobilization.

Organizational structures. Between 1989 and 1999, the extreme right was represented by one major political movement—the Polish National Community (Polska Wspólnota Narodowa—hereafter PWN). PWN was registered as an official political party, yet its activities and organizational structures resembled a youth gang consisting of skinheads. This is why we do not treat it as a political party proper, but rather as a political movement. PWN neither kept a record of its members nor ran regular enlistment. People appearing or speaking during its demonstrations were often not officially affiliated with PWN and a great number of press reports claimed culprits of beatings or murders were merely "sympathizers" of the movement. The movement was composed mainly of skinhead subculture, loosely related to the core of the PWN activists.

Skinheads were also the main extreme-right political actors at that time. Their fanzines were full of pictures and symbols highlighting violence, as was the whole "Oi!" culture. For skinheads, fighting physically against an enemy was not only a political action but also an act of bravery. However, there was one important feature that distinguished Polish skinheads from their Western counterparts. For ideological reasons, Polish skinheads were not in favor of contacts with their German neo-Nazi colleagues. Ideologically, Germans were considered the enemies of the nation, even though the set of subcultural features (the skinhead's dress code: flags, clothes, music, etc.), remained the same.

Characteristically, the dominant political movement of the early transformation period was inspired by doctrines hostile to the Catholic tradition. PWN worked on the development of Pan-Slavism, which is mostly viewed as pagan and racist ideology. This is the likely cause for their failure in struggles to win an important place in the political discourse, as the general society was Catholic and Western-oriented (as opposed to the post-Soviet East).

The analysis shows that the PWN political movement organized 43.7 percent (128) of protest events in the period between 1989 and 1999. Some 36.5 percent (107) of events were classified as independent skinheads' actions while events that involved both the political movement and the skinhead subculture make up 15 percent (44) of all events. This means that more than 90 percent of all events in that period were organized either by the political movement or the subculture named above, or by both of them.

Repertoire of action. The repertoire of action consisted mostly of street demonstrations (36.9 percent, 108 events) and confrontational actions (38.6 percent, 113 events). Less than one-fifth of events were conventional (18.4 percent, 54 events). Even fewer were directed at strengthening the identity of the movement (6.1 percent, 18 events). The political movement and the subculture never cooperated during conventional actions, yet skinheads joined the ranks of the political movement during demonstrations, confrontational actions, and expressive actions. It was the skinhead subculture (82.3 percent of confrontational actions, 93 events) and the political movement together with subculture (9 events) that were the most frequent perpetrators of violence in the analyzed period. This fact is also confirmed by Cramér's V, a measure of association between two nominal variables.[3] V=0.49 (with high significance). This means that different actors tend to choose distinct methods of action. Skinheads and confrontational actions are the most strongly correlated pair.

Our analysis shows that the marginalization of the movement led to the eruption of violence, similar to what we will see in the case of the radicalization, yet the pattern is different. The violence became a way for the extreme right to communicate with an external world: *violence is a message.* This confirms what Koopmans et al. (2005) observed in the Western context, proving false the old myth that the extreme right uses violence as an answer to the rising number of immigrants or similar phenomena. Rather, the scale of violence is directly related to the political and discursive opportunities available to the extreme-right movement (ibid. 196). For example, in Germany, where the law forbids the existence of Nazi organizations (ECRI 1998, 2001) and the neo-Nazi NPD never passed the election threshold and never managed to become a full-fledged party, the scale of violence incited by German neo-Nazis was the biggest among the Western European countries analyzed by Koopmans (2005: 197). At the same time in France, where a big nationalist party, the Front National, acts in compliance with the law, only 6.7 percent events of a total of 683 involved violence (ibid.). Poland is not an exception to this rule but the frequency of confrontational events does not tell the whole story. In the years 1989–1999, skinheads killed 20 people and 153 were injured. The fact that such events occur only rarely in other phases of mobilization confirms the thesis that the level of extreme-right violence is connected to the process of the movement's institutionalization, rather than the factors stressed by the adherents of grievance theory.

Targets and issues of protest. As Table 11.1 shows, the majority of events coded in this period targeted ethnic minorities (28.7 percent, 74 events).[4] Cramér's V is high (0.60) and highly significant, which shows that the targets and issues of protest are strongly correlated with the repertoire of action.

This means that every type of action has its distinct counterpart in target and issue. The majority of the conventional actions organized by the political movement were concentrated on politics—political enemies in the government. Such actions were never aimed at ethnic minorities though. Demonstrative actions were mostly directed at said ethnic minorities and international institutions (such as the EU and NATO). Left-wing organizations and ethnic minorities were targeted mostly during confrontational actions, usually organized by the political movement with the support of skinheads, whereas expressive actions were concentrated on traditional values and political identities.

Table 11.1. Type of action per type of target and issue

Target & Issue

Type of action	Politics	Socio-economic	Leftist organi-zations	Ethnic minorities, foreign	Inter-national politics	Tradi-tional values, Us	Total
CONVENTIONAL	66.7%	5.9%	3.9%	0.0%	9.8%	13.7%	100% (51)
DEMONSTRATIVE	13.7%	9.8%	5.9%	31.4%	28.4%	10.8%	100% (102)
CONFRONTATIONAL	6.9%	0.0%	43.7%	48.3%	0.0%	1.1%	100% (87)
EXPRESSIVE ACTION	0.0%	0.0%	0.0%	0.0%	5.6%	94.4%	100% (18)
Total	20.9%	5.0%	17.8%	28.7%	13.6%	14.0%	100% (258)

Row percentages; Cramér's V= 0.60***

As Kenneth Andrews and Bob Edwards (2005) stress, the newly emerged or rebuilt movements are often characterized by an inability to form long-lasting alliances, weak identification of proper political targets and a narrow repertoire. The Polish case confirms this view as the extreme-right political movement only rarely raised socioeconomic issues, which were predominant issues in the public sphere in the first years of the systemic transformation.

Institutionalization Phase (2000–2005)

Political and discursive opportunities. The breakthrough came with the parliamentary elections in 2001. The elections opened a new phase in the career of several extreme-right organizations. One of these organizations was the League of Polish Families (Liga Polskich Rodzin—hereafter LPR) political party. The LPR was founded that year as a coalition of various conservative and nationalist organizations. The party managed to win thirty-eight seats in the Polish parliament.[5] It was formally supported by the All-Polish Youth (Młodzież Wszechpolska—hereafter MW), a political movement grouping youth and aspiring nationalist politicians.

The position of the extreme right was strengthened in the face of Poland's integration with the European Union, as all parliamentary parties strongly supported the integration. Even the biggest conservative party, *Law and Jus-*

tice (Prawo i Sprawiedliwość—hereafter PiS), which held forty-four seats in the parliament, was pro-European. As no politician wanted to discuss the uncertainties of the integration, the LPR and MW became the sole representatives of people afraid of integration or uncertain of its outcomes.

Surveys conducted during the period in question prove the existence of a relatively stable group of opponents of integration. In 2000, the number of opponents of the EU was almost equal to the number of its enthusiasts (29 percent to 30 percent) (CBOS VII 2000). At the beginning of 2003, one year before the said integration, 25 percent of people opposed it and 60 percent were declared supporters (CBOS II 2003). The number of opponents dropped suddenly to 18 percent on the eve of the integration referendum, due to the massive pro-EU campaign, but in 2004 the number of "eurosceptics" again rose to 31 percent (CBOS III 2004). The relatively high and stable number of opponents was in great part a consequence of the campaigning of the extreme right. Its influence is evident in the opinion polls showing that one of the most frequent reasons for the opposition to the EU was "negative, emotional judgments expressing fears of the loss of sovereignty, of Poland's submission to foreign capital, threat of the enslavement of the Poles and turning them into a cheap labor force" (CBOS II 2002: 7).

Organizational structures. The origins of MW date back to 1922, when the organization adopted the Ideological Declaration[6]—a national political program built on Catholic values, which were considered an integral component of Polish identity and the ethnic unity of the Polish national community.[7] From the beginning, MW portrayed itself as a national organization in the spirit of the politics of patriotism. The organization actively took part in educational activities aimed at popularizing its ideology.[8] After the outbreak of the Second World War, members of MW engaged in the fight against Nazi Germany. In postwar communist Poland, the organization was banned and many former activists were imprisoned. A revival came, as for other nationalistic groups, in postcommunist Poland. One of the main tasks of the newly reformed organizations was the building of central and regional structures, but in the first period of the activity, MW, National Radical Camp (ONR) and other minor groups invested their political sympathies without success.

With the advent of the twenty-first century, the Polish extreme right became a network of well-structured organizations. The movement managed to change its image by distancing itself from negative connotations, such as open ties with the skinhead subculture or the word *nacjonalista* (nationalist) itself, which was replaced with *narodowiec,* a word meaning essentially the same thing, but that does not evoke negative connotations, and that is rooted in the tradition of the organizations of the interwar period (Pankowski 2010: 9).

MW and the LPR accounted for almost all the events organized in this period: the party focused on conventional actions, while the political movement organized demonstrative and conventional actions. There were 336 protest events in this phase: 43.5 percent (146) of them were organized by the political movement (MW) and 28 percent (94) by the party (LPR). The movement cooperated with the party during 44 events. There were 23 episodes when coalitions spanned three different actors: MW and the LPR were supported by a third, weaker companion. In sum, then, 84.5 percent of all events were organized by the League of Polish Families and the All-Polish Youth movement or the coalition formed by them. The skinhead subculture, prominent in the previous phase with 107 events, was slowly fading away, with only 35 events organized in this phase. Both organizations clearly wanted to avoid any associations with violent and unpredictable skinheads.

Repertoire of action. In comparison to the first phase of mobilization, in this phase conventional actions were predominant, as the parliamentary party employed mainly legal means of political struggle and discouraged confrontational (violent) interventions. Having a parliamentary party on its side allowed the extreme right to employ conventional instruments of protest: appeals, conferences, open letters, legislative initiatives, and lawsuits. Some 43.9 percent (147) of all events in this period were conventional. They were organized by the party, and to a lesser extent by the political movement. Demonstrative actions were the domain of the political movement (71 events, 48.6 percent of all political movement actions). The party alone only rarely appeared during such events (9 events), but in cooperation with the political movement the party appeared during the demonstrations in 61.4 percent (27 events) of all joint actions. This means that the LPR party and MW political movement preferred to take actions separately (conventional vs. demonstrative) and to a lesser extent to act together.

Cramér's V suggests that the correlation between types of action and political actors during institutionalization is the same as in the first phase of mobilization (0.49 with high significance). This is a consequence of the concentration of almost one-third of all events in the category "political party—conventional action" and almost all episodes involving confrontation in the category "subculture." This is proof of the process of institutionalization taking place: the movement is organized around certain formal institutions (political party) and adopts an appropriate repertoire. Actions associated with the previous phase of marginalization are actively discouraged by dedicated activists, as they could do more harm to the institutionalized movement.

Manifestations of confrontational behaviors in this period are consistent with our theoretical predictions. A reduction in the number of violent incidents is evident. In 2000 and 2001, violence stayed at levels comparable to the previous period, yet after the LPR entered parliament violence disappeared from the picture almost entirely (see Figure 11.1). The extreme-right organizations focused instead on claim making intermediated by legal institutions, and had, at least formally, cut its ties with the skinheads responsible for the majority of violent acts.

The situation in Poland between 1999 and 2005 was similar to that in Switzerland, as described by Peter Gentile (1999). Before the biggest Swiss extreme-right party—the Swiss People's Party/Democratic Union of the Centre (Schweizerische Volkspartei/Union Démocratique du Centre)—entered the parliament in 1999, the level of violence in the country was high (circa 100 violent episodes every year), but it fell quickly afterward.

Targets and issues of actions. In this period the association between types of action and targets (Cramér's V) equals 0.50 (with high significance, p < 0.01). This is evidence of the division of targets and issues between the party and its political movement. The party focused its conventional actions mainly on parliamentary politicians, while the movement employed demonstrative actions focused mainly on international politics, especially regarding the European Union. An efficient division of labor allowed these two interconnected organizations to virtually dominate the extreme-right movement.

The European Union was, after opposing politicians, the second most important receiver of claims—it was a target of 27 percent (87 events) of all actions. The conventional repertoire was used against the EU during 23 events, while during 63 events the demonstrative repertoire was used. Sexual minorities were attacked during only 18 confrontational events, mainly

Table 11.2. Type of action per type of target and issue

	Target & Issue							
Type of action	Politics	Socio-eco-nomic	Leftist organi-zations	Ethnic minor-ities, foreign	Sexual minor-ities	Inter-national politics	Tradi-tional values, Us	Total
CONVENTIONAL	53.7%	11.6%	3.4%	0.7%	0.7%	15.6%	14.3%	100% (147)
DEMONSTRATIVE	17.8%	4.2%	2.5%	2.5%	4.3%	53.4%	15.3%	100% (118)
CONFRONTATIONAL	13.2%	0.0%	11.3%	32.1%	34.0%	1.9%	7.5%	100% (53)
EXPRESSIVE ACTION	0.0%	0.0%	0.0%	0.0%	0.0%	0.0%	100.0%	100% (4)
Total	33.2%	6.8%	4.3%	6.5%	7.6%	27.0%	14.6%	100% (322)

Row percentages; Cramér's V = 0.50***

by skinheads and the members of the political movement, but, as we emphasized earlier, the members of MW distanced themselves from such actions. The second target of confrontational actions was ethnic minorities (17 events), and the perpetrators were the same as in the case of attacks on sexual minorities. Except for one event, the LPR party also clearly distanced itself from such actions.

In this phase of mobilization, the extreme right distanced itself not only from violence, but also from issues and targets that could be regarded as most controversial. The LPR seldom, if ever, openly confronted or demonstrated against sexual and ethnic minorities (not counting the verbal attacks frequently presented in the party propaganda). The party made an effort to break any associations with neo-Nazism, fascism, or skinhead subculture. Its aims were as legitimate as possible, and did not involve breaking the law. More controversial issues or actions were left for the political movement (MW) to tackle. "Jews" left the group of targeted enemies of the extreme right in this period, but it was clear that sexual minorities had taken their place.

Phase of Radicalization (2006–2013)

Political and discursive opportunities. After the parliamentary elections in 2005, the political scene became dominated by two parties: the conservative-liberal Civic Platform (Platforma Obywatelska—hereafter PO) and the conservative right-wing Law and Justice (PiS). The political opportunity structure narrowed for the extreme right after the re-elections to parliament two years later when President Lech Kaczyński decided to shorten the terms of parliament. As a result of the repeated elections, the LPR lost all its 34 seats and PiS obtained a virtual hegemony on the right wing of the political scene (Pankowski 2010: 194). At the same time, opponents of the extreme right mobilized: a number civil society groups began monitoring the extreme right organizations and started to publicize their findings (see Grell et al. 2009). What is more, the movement faced the first serious repressive measures by the police and security agencies. In 2013 a special team to combat neo-Nazism was formed at the Polish Internal Security Agency. Extreme-right organizations were deemed a threat to the public and legal order and persecutions of groups promoting fascism began. Altogether between 1999 and 2008 there were 234 crimes related to promotion of totalitarian ideologies, but according to police sources there were as many as 267 in 2013 alone.[9]

Despite the repression, the movement found new, strong discursive opportunities. Ousted from mainstream politics, it launched a negative campaign against its newfound enemies: the feminist, pro-choice, and LGBT movements. At the same time, it managed to construct a positive program focused on the necessity not only to defend, but also to promote "traditional" values. The negative and positive programs supplemented and strengthened each other, as, for example, attacks on homosexual pride parades were justified as means of protecting Polish families from Western decadence. These extreme-right actions against the LGBT communities were, in fact, largely supported by public opinion. In 2008 66 percent of Poles were against demonstrations of LGBT groups, and 76 percent were against formalization of same-sex marriages (CBOS VI 2008). In 2013 83 percent of those surveyed considered homosexuality a deviation and 26 percent of them stated that it should not be accepted in Poland at all (CBOS II 2013).

As Agnieszka Graff (2009: 138) notes, "... nationalism depends on the clarity of boundaries, a neat demarcation between "us" and "them." These boundaries are often gendered and/or sexualized." This is especially true in the third phase of the extreme-right mobilization we have identified. The politicians of the LPR connected Western culture, homosexuality, and European Union in one ideological frame, yet the LPR's career outlasted that of its creators and has become a part of conservative "common sense" (Graff 2009: 138). The second important trend was the politics of history: activists spend their time commemorating "cursed soldiers" of anti-communist guerrillas after World War II, heroes of Warsaw Uprising, and so on.

Organizational structures. In the third phase, a few organizations dominated the picture. The LPR party dissolved amid political scandals and left the movement broken into several factions but two formerly dormant neofascist organizations, the ONR and National Rebirth of Poland (Narodowe Odrodzenie Polski—hereafter NOP), were reactivated. The NOP is the only organization in Poland openly expressing racist ideology. It is a member of several neofascist international organizations, such as International Third Position and European National Front. The MW and ONR political movements distance themselves from such ideologies and instead manifest their ties with traditional interwar nationalist organizations. In 2012 the nationalist part of the movement tried to unite and attempted a return to parliamentary politics. The National Movement (Ruch Narodowy—hereafter RN)—an umbrella organization—was formed by the coalition of the All-Polish Youth, ONR, and the conservative-libertarian Real Politics Union (Unia Polityki Realnej—UPR), but so far the coalition has not achieved electoral success.

The last phase of the extreme-right mobilization is dominated by the political movements, as they organized 68.2 percent (227) of all coded events. The activity of political parties was significantly lower than in the previous phase. Political parties participated in just 7.5 percent of all events (25 events). Most of the events had a singular character (52.9 percent, 176 events), whereas coalitions of two or more organizations took place in 30.9 percent (103) of protest events. With 48 events it was not possible to identify the name of the organization.

Repertoire of action. Cramér's V shows a decreasing correlation between actors and their actions. In this phase it attains 0.39 (with very high significance). Actors are therefore assigned to more diverse types of action than in the previous phase. This mainly applies to the political movement. Political movement organizations employed conventional instruments of protest in 13.7 percent (31 events) of their actions, a demonstrative repertoire in 35.7 percent (81 events), and a confrontational one in 39.6 percent (90 events). A total of 84 percent (21 events) of the political parties' actions were conventional. At the same time, the overall frequency of conventional actions decreased from 43.9 percent (147 events) in the second phase to only 16.2 percent (54 events) in this one, and the number of expressive events rose from 4 to 28. This is a consequence of the project of the extreme right's political movements (especially organizations involved with the RN) to reconstruct its ideology and "traditional" identity.

Acts of confrontation in this period make up the majority of all events, as in the phase of marginalization: 38.6 percent in the first phase to 42 percent in this phase (113 to 140) of all events. In contrast to the model of mobilization in the first phase, they are performed not by independent skinheads, but mainly by the members of the political movements. What is new in this phase is the increasing number of confrontational actions appearing during the street demonstrations. The number of such acts rose with a peak between 2008 and 2010, when they comprised one-fifth of all events (see: Figure 11.1).

Targets and issues of protest. The indicator of ordering of targets and repertoire decreased slightly in this period (Cramér's V = 0.48 with high significance). Most of the demonstrative actions were targeted at organizational identity and an attachment to tradition (53.2 percent, 58 events). Most actions targeted at traditional values occurred during cycles of protest connected to the celebration of several national holidays, but traditional values were also defended during conventional and expressive actions. This was the most frequent category of targets in this phase of mobilization (32.5 percent (105) of all events). Some 19.4 percent (63 events) of all episodes were targeted at sexual minorities and feminist groups. Most of them were confrontational in nature (57 events). These targets, together with the promotion of traditional values, are the most characteristic for the third phase of mobilization of the extreme right.

It must be emphasized that the percentage of confrontational actions in the first and the last phase was quite similar (38.6 percent and 42 percent of all events, respectively) but the targets were different, except for the "leftist

Table 11.3. Type of action per type of target and issue

Type of action	Politics	Socio-eco-nomic	Leftist organi-zations	Ethnic minor-ities, foreign	Sexual minor-ities	Inter-national politics	Tradi-tional values, Us	Total
				Target & Issue				
CONVENTIONAL	31.5%	9.3%	11.1%	1.9%	7.4%	7.4%	31.4%	100% (54)
DEMONSTRATIVE	25.7%	1.8%	3.7%	3.7%	1.8%	10.1%	53.2%	100% (109)
CONFRONTATIONAL	11.2%	0.0%	28.4%	14.2%	42.5%	0.0%	3.7%	100% (134)
EXPRESSIVE ACTION	3.7%	0.0%	0.0%	3.7%	0.0%	0.0%	92.6%	100% (27)
Total	18.8%	2.2%	14.8%	7.7%	19.4%	4.6%	32.5%	100% (324)

Row percentages; Cramér's V = 0.48***

organizations," which was targeted in the two compared phases by exactly 38 confrontational events.

Conclusions

The extreme right in postcommunist Poland went through three distinct phases of mobilization. At the same time the movement has changed and remained the same: it never relinquished its fundamental aims, while its action repertoire and targets change according to shifts in the opportunity structures.

The extreme-right movement is stable in its anti-systemic attitude toward politicians from the ruling parties and its actions are always directed against various kinds of minorities. In this way, the movement belongs to the "un-civil" part of the society. When we look at the analyzed period as a whole, without division into phases, we can see that most of the extreme-right actions were targeted at the politicians and international institutions (37.3 percent, 359 events). As many as 21.5 percent (228 events) of all actions were directed against minorities (ethnic and sexual). What is more, the percentage of such events in each phase was stable and accounted for an average of 21.7 percent.

However, the fact that the movement remains faithful to its general convictions, which is expressed in terms of the choice of targets and types of actions, does not tell the whole story. The difference lies in the scale of specific actions against specific targets. As we demonstrated, radical rightists can and do employ both "civil" and "uncivil" repertoire of actions, including violent, clandestine interventions, depending on the current public debates and political configurations. This does not happen, of course, automatically. In the marginalization phase (1989–2000) the movement was testing the ground and searching for suitable repertoires and discursive framework. Only on the brink of the centuries had it managed to find its foundations in reborn ideology of Catholic nationalism. With extreme right party in the government, the movement became more "civil" and the level of physical violence felt sharply, which confirms our first detailed hypothesis.

After the fall of the LPR party, the movement again was forced to occupy margins of the political sphere; however, discursive opportunities related to homophobia and so-called traditional values became wider. This confirms our second detailed hypothesis that when the political and discursive opportunity structure are unfavorable to the emergence of a strong extreme-right political party, the level of extraparliamentary mobilization is relatively high. Inability to turn this popular support into political influence makes the movement violent and again puts it in search of new repertoires of contention.

Our empirical analysis also confirms the theoretical assumptions concerning the way in which the extreme right mobilization depends on favorable or unfavorable political and discursive opportunities. Consequently, opportunity structure determines the position of the extreme right on the parliamentary or extraparliamentary level. The changes in the movement's strategy are clearly visible in the changing scale of confrontational actions during the studied periods. In the first and third phases there are many confrontational actions against the movement's enemies. Its "uncivil" and antisystemic character is evident in the first years after the transformation, when

Figure 11.1. Confrontational actions as a percentage of all actions.

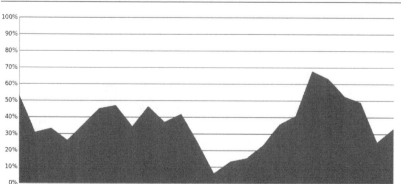

skinheads repeatedly attack and kill minorities and left-wing activists. The second phase, which we have called institutionalization, stands in contrast with relatively low intensity of confrontational incidents in the streets. It can be argued that in this phase violence changed from physical into verbal or symbolic (Graff 2009). Nevertheless, in the times of the LPR the extreme right shifts away from uncivil society into the political mainstream.

In this chapter we have been looking at how specific repertoires of actions and targets of the extreme-right movement resonate in the public discourse and on the political scene, while others are delegitimized. In other words, we critically approach the ways in which the extreme-right is seen as a byproduct of the objective social conditions. The re-emergence of the extreme right in Poland is not a direct consequence of the implementation of neoliberal policies, but instead it is much more relational. Recalling David Ost (2009), it should be noted that the anger was not automatically stirred toward minorities rather than those responsible for unjust economic transformations, but instead it was a complex process of movements' adaptation to the prevailing political, cultural, social, and economic conditions that requires further in-depth research.

Daniel Płatek works as a visiting researcher in the Institute for Analytical Sociology, Linköping University, Sweden. He is currently investigating the social network determinants of the radical right repertoires of collective violence in Poland. He has also conducted research in historical sociology, including the articles "Between the Ottoman Empire and the Turkish Republic: Historical Sociology of Armenian Genocide" (2011) and "Traditional Protest, Modern Social Movement: Tobacco Rebellion in Iran, 1905-1908" (2015).

Piotr P. Płucienniczak holds a Ph.D. in Sociology and is an independent researcher. He is currently working on dynamics of mobilization of the extreme right in Poland together with Daniel Płatek; practices of institutional critique in visual arts in Poland; and social unionism and economic contention in Poland after the EU integration. His most recent project is an edited volume on the politics of enmity in Central and Eastern Europe.

Notes

*The research project was financed by the National Science Centre Poland, decision number DEC-2012/05 / N / HS6 / 03892.

 1. For Olzak and Koopmans (2004: 202) this "argument starts from the assumption that the public sphere is a bounded space for political communication characterized by a high level of competition."

2. In the Polish context, most extreme-right groups participate in local or parliamentary elections, but their organizational structures differ significantly from the classical political party composition; for example, formal membership is not required.
3. Cramér's V varies from 0 (corresponding to no association between the variables) to 1 (complete association) and can reach 1 only when the two variables are equal to each other. In the social sciences, it is assumed that Cramér's V is strong when it exceeds 0.40.
4. The total number of confrontational events (113) is underestimated in Table 11.1 due to the missing data concerning targets and issues of actions.
5. Their overall support amounted to 7.87 percent of the Polish population. See http://www.pkw.gov.pl, http://www.sejm.gov.pl, and http://www.senat.gov.pl, last accessed 23 January 2015.
6. The leader of this most influential nationalist interwar organization was Roman Dmowski. Born in 1864 in Warsaw, under Russian occupation, he was one of the most popular politicians in Poland's interwar period. In 1903 he published his nationalist manifesto entitled *Thoughts of the Modern Pole*. This book is still very significant in the canon of Polish political thought, dedicated to issues such as national sovereignty and anti-Semitism.
7. The adjective "All-" expressed the desire to unite all the Polish lands lost as a result of the third partition of Poland in 1795, and emphasized national solidarity and the equal status of all citizens of Polish nationality, regardless of their social condition and wealth.
8. In 1937, under the influence of nationalist youth organizations (including the All-Polish Youth and the National Radical Camp—Obóz Narodowo Radykalny, hereafter ONR), rectors of several Polish universities created *numerus clausus*—reductions of the permitted percentage of students of Jewish origin to 10 percent. This was a part of a comprehensive discriminatory campaign that also aimed to bring about segregation of Jewish students from Polish students.
9. See http://statystyka.policja.pl/.

References

Andrews, K., and B. Edwards. 2005. "The Organizational Structure of Local Environmentalism." *Mobilization* 10: 213–234.

Caiani, M., D. della Porta, and C. Wagemann. *Mobilizing on the Extreme Right: Germany, Italy, and the United States.* Oxford: Oxford University Press.

Caiani, M., and L. Parenti. 2013. *European and American Extreme Right Groups and the Internet.* London: Ashgate.

Carter, E. 2005. *The Extreme Right in Western Europe.* Manchester and New York: Manchester University Press.

Eatwell, R. 1996. "In Defining the 'Fascist Minimum': The Centrality of Ideology." *Journal of Political Ideologies* 3: 303–319.

Ekiert, G., and J. Kubik. 1999. *Rebellious Civil Society: Popular Protest and Democratic Consolidation in Poland.* Ann Arbor: University of Michigan Press.

Frank, T. 2004. *What's The Matter With Kansas? How Conservatives Won the Heart of America.* New York: Metropolitan Books.

Franzosi, R. 1987. "The Press as a Source of Socio-Historical Data: Issues in the Methodology of Data Collection from the Newspapers." *Historical Methods* 20: 5–16.

Gentile, P. 1999. "Radical Right Protest in Switzerland," in *Acts of Dissent: New Developments in the Study of Protest,* ed. D. Rucht, R. Koopmans, and F. Niedhardt. Oxford: Rowman & Littlefield Publishers, 227–252.

Graff, A. 2009. "Gender, Sexuality, and Nation—Here and Now: Reflections on the Gendered and Sexualized Aspects of Contemporary Polish Nationalism," in *Intimate Citizenship: Gender, Sexualities, Politics,* ed. E.H. Oleksy. London: Routledge, 133–147.

Grell, B., T. Kohler, R. Pankowski, N. Sineava, and M. Starnawski. 2009. *Hate Crime Monitoring and Victim Assistance in Poland and Germany.* Warszawa: Nigdy Więcej.

Griffin, R. 1991. *The Nature of Fascism.* London: Palgrave McMillan.

Kitschelt, H. 1995. *The Extreme Right in Western Europe: A Comparative Analysis.* Ann Arbor: University of Michigan Press.

Klandermans, B., and N. Mayer. 2006. *Extreme Right Activists in Europe: Through the Magnifying Glass.* New York: Routledge.

Koopmans, R. 1994. "The Dynamics of Protest Waves: West Germany, 1965 to 1989." *American Sociological Review* 58: 637–658.

Koopmans, R., and S. Olzak. "Discursive Opportunities and the Evolution of Right-Wing Violence in Germany." *American Journal of Sociology* 110: 198–230.

Koopmans, R., and P. Statham. 1999. "Challenging the Liberal Nation-State? Postnationalism, Multiculturalism, and the Collective Claims Making of Migrants and Ethnic Minorities in Britain and Germany." *American Journal of Sociology* 105: 652–696.

Koopmans, R., P. Statham, M. Guigni, and F. Passy. 2005. *Contested Citizenship: Immigration and Cultural Diversity in Europe.* Minnesota: University of Minnesota Press.

Kornhauser, W. 1959. *The Politics of Mass Society.* Glencoe, IL: Free Press.

Lipiński, A. 2012. "Deligitymizacja III Rzeczpospolitej, budowanie partyjnej tożsamości i dyskursywne struktury możliwości." *Środkowoeuropejskie Studia Polityczne* 4: 75–92.

———. 2013. *Radykalizacja czy "patologiczna normalność"? Ugrupowania i ruchy radykalne a partie polityczne w Polsce i Europie Zachodniej.* Warszawa: Otwarta Rzeczpospolita.

Lipset, S.M., and E. Raab. 1970. *The Politics of Unreason: Right-Wing Extremism in America 1790-1970.* New York: Harper and Row.

McCarty, J., C. McPhail, and J. Smith. 1996. "Images of Protest: Dimensions of Selection Bias in Media Coverage of Washington Demonstrations, 1982 and 1991." *American Sociological Review* 61: 478–499.

Mondon, A. 2013. *The Mainstreaming of the Extreme Right in France and Australia.* Farnham: Ashgate.

Mudde, C. 2003. "Civil Society in Post-Communist Europe: Lessons From The 'Dark Side,'" in *Uncivil Society? Contentious Politics in Post-Communist Europe,* ed. P. Kopecký and C. Mudde. London, New York: Routledge, 1–18.

Norris, P. 2005. *Radical Right: Voters and Parties in the Electoral Market.* Cambridge: Cambridge University Press.

Olzak, S., and R. Koopmans. 2004. "Discursive Opportunities and the Evolution of Right-Wing Violence in Germany." *American Journal of Sociology* 110: 198–230.

Ost, D. 2006. *The Defeat of Solidarity: Anger and Politics in Postcommunist Europe.* New York: Cornell University Press.

Pakulski, J. 1991. "Rewolucje wschodnioeuropejskie." *Kultura i Społeczeństwo* 3: 4–16.

———, and J. Higley. 1992. "Rewolucje i transformacje elit władzy w Europie Wschodniej." *Kultura i Społeczeństwo* 2: 19–35.

Pankowski, R. 2010. *The Populist Radical Right in Poland.* London: Routledge.

Pankowski, R., and M. Kornak. 2005. "Poland," in *Racist Extremism in Central and Eastern Europe,* ed. C. Mudde. London, New York: Routledge.

Piotrowski, G. 2009. "Civil Society, Un-Civil Society and the Social Movements." *Interface: Journal for and about Social Movements* 1: 166–189.

Polanyi, K. 2001. *The Great Transformation: The Political and Economic Origins of Our Times.* Boston: Beacon Press Books.

Putnam, R.D., R. Leonardi, and R.Y. Nanetti. 1994. *Making Democracy Work: Civic Traditions in Modern Italy.* Princeton: Princeton University Press.

Szafraniec, K. 1986. *Anomia–przesilenie tożsamości. Jednostka i społeczeństwo wobec zmiany.* Toruń: Wydawnictwo UMK.

Tarrow, S. 1996. "States and Opportunities: The Political Structuring of Social Movements," in *Comparative Perspectives on Social Movements: Political Opportunities, Mobilizing Structures, and Cultural Framings,* ed. D. McAdam, J.D. McCarthy, and M.N. Zald. New York: Cambridge University Press, 41–61.

Whitehead, L. 1997. "Bowling in the Bronx: The Uncivil Interstices between Civil and Political Society." *Democratization* 4: 94–114.

Wimmer, A. 2002. *Nationalist Exclusion and Ethnic Conflict.* Shadows of Modernity. Cambridge: Cambridge University Press.

Reports

Central Statistical Office (GUS) 2013. "Ludność. Stan i struktura demograficzno-społeczna. Narodowy spis powszechny ludności i mieszkań 2011 Retrived July 2014 from http://stat.gov.pl/cps/rde/xbcr/gus/LUD_ludnosc_stan_str_dem_spo_NSP2011.pdf.

European Commission Against Racism and Intolerance (ECRI) 1998. First Report on Germany, CRI (98) 22, Strasbourg. Retrieved July 2014 from http://www.refworld.org/pdfid/51bee2714.pdf.

European Commission Against Racism and Intolerance (ECRI) 2001. Second Report on Germany, CRI (2001) 36, Strasbourg. Retrieved July 2014 from http://www.coe.int/t/dghl/monitoring/ecri/Country-by-country/Germany/DEU-CbC-II-2001-036-EN.pdf.

Public Opinion Research Center (CBOS) VI 1995. "Inne narody, nasze sympatie i antypatie." Retrieved July 2014 from http://www.cbos.pl/SPISKOM.POL/1995/K_105_95.PDF.

Public Opinion Research Center (CBOS) I 1997. "Żydzi i Polacy w opiniach społeczeństwa." Retrieved July 2014 from http://www.cbos.pl/SPISKOM.POL/1997/K_003_97.PDF.

Public Opinion Research Center (CBOS) VII 2000. "Opinie o skutkach integracji z Unią Europejską i przebiegu negocjacji akcesyjnych." Retrieved August 2014 from http://www.cbos.pl/SPISKOM.POL/2000/K_105_00.PDF.

Public Opinion Research Center (CBOS) II 2002. "Argumenty zwolenników i przeciwników integracji Polski z Unią Europejską." Retrieved August 2014 from http://www.cbos.pl/SPISKOM.POL/2002/K_023_02.PDF.

Public Opinion Research Center (CBOS) II 2003. "Społeczne poparcie dla integracji z Unią Europejską." Retrieved August 2014 from http://www.cbos.pl/SPISKOM.POL/2003/K_063_03. PDF.

Public Opinion Research Center (CBOS) III 2004. "Załamanie się optymizmu w myśle-niu o efektach integracji z Unią Europejską." Retrieved August 2014 from http://www.cbos.pl/SPISKOM.POL/2004/K_044_04.PDF.

Public Opinion Research Center (CBOS) VI 2008. "Prawa gejów i lesbijek." Retrieved August 2014 from http://www.cbos.pl/SPISKOM.POL/2008/K_088_08.PDF.

Public Opinion Research Center (CBOS) II 2013. "Stosunek do praw gejów i lesbijek oraz związków partnerskich." Retrieved August 2014 from http://www.cbos.pl/SP ISKOM.POL/2013/K_024_13.PDF.

CONCLUSION
EMPIRICAL AND THEORETICAL LESSONS
FROM THE VOLUME

Kerstin Jacobsson and Elżbieta Korolczuk

This volume provides an updated view on contemporary Polish civil society, one that puts focus on both its diversity and its complexity. Investigating a wide range of forms of social engagement in the country, including low-key, ephemeral, and local forms of civil engagement, as well as those embedded in the family structures and the private sphere, the contributors point out the exclusionary implications of the usual definitions and measurements of Polish civil society. In challenging the dominant view in the literature that presents postsocialist civil societies as uniformly weak, they at the same time provide theoretical insights of more general relevance for the study of civil society. In this concluding chapter, we distill some key empirical and theoretical lessons to be drawn from the case studies presented in this book.

The main message emerging from this book is that, viewed against the Polish context in particular, the understandings of civil society as diffused by academics and policy makers and in public discourse have been rather narrow, and frequently aspirational in nature rather than analytically derived. As a result, ideals of social organization have spread that reflect particular sociocultural and political conditions difficult to replicate outside of their birth context; ideals, moreover, that do not correspond to reality even in most places in the West where they first developed (Dunn and Hann 1996; Ekiert and Kubik in this volume). Indeed, some have argued, the whole concept of civil society is too vague and blurred, and empirically and ideologically either too broad or too narrow, to be retained for research (e.g., Ahrne 1998; Ahrne and Papakostas 2002: 42). We, however, do not share such a pessimistic view, nor do we wish to abandon the concept of civil society altogether:

we believe that it continues to help us to see the broader picture, allowing for analyses that go beyond specific cases of social activism, nongovernmental organizations, and social movements (see also Howell and Pearce 2002). Where we agree, however, is that the concept should be "handled with care": proceeding from a narrow understanding of civil society, and the implicit ideals carried with it, means engaging in boundary drawing in which certain forms of collective action and social engagement are excluded from "legitimate" civil society. The risk here is that civil society in contexts other than the idealized "West" will then always appear as deficient and lacking, in need of constant development and support (cf. Fábián and Korolczuk 2017).

Accordingly, the first lesson to be drawn from the studies in this book concerns the limitations of the concept of civil society as applied, in particular, in the Polish context in the past decades. Relying on the dominant conceptualizations within civil society studies has narrowed our view on civic engagement and social activism in a number of ways. It has led to a focus on formal organizations (often NGOs/public benefit organizations) at the expense of informal and grassroots forms of civic engagement; to the privileging of the post-1989 organizational development at the expense of older associations; to the privileging of middle-class action and organizing at the expense of mobilizations and collective action by socioeconomically weaker groups; and, finally, to a focus on actors representing liberal ideals at the expense of more conservative or radical groups and claims.

As several of the chapters in this volume illustrate, such bias in favor of formalized, "NGO-ized", donor-responsive, "new" civil society actors in the dominant model is reflected also in official registers and statistics, which fail to cover all existing forms of engagement or even organizations (see, e.g., Giza-Poleszczuk in this volume). Taking into account all the forms of grassroots activism, collective problem solving and low-key, local, small-scale activism actually encountered on the ground, including also those forms inherited from state-socialist times and those mobilizing underprivileged groups, a picture is presented to us of civil society that shows it to be considerably more robust and active than what the official figures would lead us to believe (for the situation in this regard in postsocialist Europe more broadly, see, e.g., Jacobsson 2015a). The same is true about the tendency to exclude conservative or right-wing groups from the analysis. Even when they do not subscribe to liberal values, they certainly warrant scholarly attention and should not be excluded on normative grounds. Civil society understood as collective action undertaken by citizens in the public sphere is usually heterogeneous as regards its goals and normative orientations. In Poland, for instance, the dissenting opposition had ceased to be homogenous already in the 1980s, with populist, republican and even openly illiberal social actors also making their presence felt alongside more liberal groups (Cohen and Arato

1992). Even though acutely aware of the dangers of conceptual stretching when dealing with a complex phenomenon of this type, one ought not sacrifice the multifarious nature of one's subject matter for categorical clarity by accepting narrow and static interpretations of civil society for use.

The second lesson, then, is that postsocialist civil societies, such as the Polish one, are best understood as "recombined" (see Ekiert and Kubik 2014; Ekiert and Kubik in this volume). That is, they are characterized by a combination not just of old and new organizations/associations, but also of old and new imaginaries and vocabularies regarding activism as well as old and new forms of activism and voluntary work (Giza-Poleszczuk in this volume). What this means, among other things, is that, over time, the same unchanging organizational forms, whether pertaining to rural women's groups or co-operatives, can become filled with highly different content. For this reason, looking at them as all representing a homogeneous phenomenon makes little sense. Conceptualizing Polish civil society as recombined also, however, has relevance for the way we approach and study civil societies in general. The nature and actors of civil society are not unchanging, but vary across contexts and over time, responding to social, political, and cultural changes but also (ideally) inducing these. Static definitions of civil society, which focus on organizational forms, quantitative measures, and normative expectations, can hardly capture the fluid and heterogeneous nature of people's social engagement. Consequently, we propose thinking of civil society as more of a process than structure, which in turn requires a more nuanced conceptual and methodological apparatus to study this phenomenon.

A third lesson thus concerns the hybridity of organizational forms and the combination of formality and informality in Polish civil society organizing. In the country, both legal regulations and economic opportunities have provided incentives for informal groups to formalize, in order to become eligible for tax donations or meet consultation requirements. Thus, as scholars often stress, the channeling of civic engagement into the third sector in the postsocialist region has been facilitated by both external donors and incentives—among them European Union support—and domestic legal regulations and incentives, such as Poland's percentage law (e.g., Graff 2009; Narozhna 2004; Mendelson and Glenn 2002). Nevertheless, the formalization into public benefit organizations that this has meant has not always been accompanied by a concomitant development of top-down and professionalized forms of activism, and did not apply to all groups and grassroots mobilizations. With formalization into legally constituted entities thus not necessarily implying a higher degree of institutionalization, dichotomous views counterposing formalization/NGOs and grassroots organizing are of little help in understanding the nature of organizational life in postsocialist countries (see also Fábián and Korolczuk 2017). Many activists engage in both formal and informal initiatives, and since many formal associations have very limited organizational resources, they retain a certain grassroots dimension for themselves that they then can draw on. The same is true about informality, which they maintain a high degree of as part of their everyday way of operating. It represents for them a problem-solving strategy, a way to "get things done" in an environment characterized by low social trust, lack of trust in formal institutions, and limited organizational resources (e.g., Hayoz 2013: 1). Informality is enabling, as it allows building collective action capacity despite organizational constraints. Recognizing as much is, however, not to turn a blind eye to the many side effects noted for high degrees of informality, such as the emergence of informal power hierarchies, issues of unequal voice, and lack of transparency in civil society organizing (e.g., Jacobsson in this volume and 2015b). Yet, as stressed in the introductory chapter, informal activism usually takes place on the basis of existing social relations between neighbors, parents whose children go to the same school, or people who live on the same street, which makes it considerably easier to overcome any lack-of-trust problems otherwise impeding collective action capacity.

A related lesson here is that the hybridity of action forms forces us to call into question dichotomous views that present civil society collectives as either depoliticized service providers and self-help collectives or actors openly pursuing political claim-making functions. Examples of the latter include lobbying and contentious action. In practice, many groups and organizations engage in both, although not always simultaneously (Jacobsson and Saxonberg 2013). Moreover, while the tendency toward depoliticization of civil society actors is an alarming trend present in various sociopolitical contexts, the question of what is defined as political requires a closer look. The case of parental mobilizations in contemporary Poland shows that even actors who stress their distance from political life engage in actions that are deeply political (Hryciuk and Korolczuk in this volume). This trend can be interpreted as a different way of negotiating the social meaning of political activism, which accompanied the development of civil society from its very beginnings. As shown by Lang (2014), already in eighteenth- and nineteenth-century Europe different social groups made very strong claims to publicity and to voice their—highly political—concerns in the public sphere, but the structure of gender order and construction of the public/private divide allowed only some groups to act politically, while others, such as women, had to disguise their engagement as providing help to the needy or enhancing the physical fitness of the population. Today, mobilizations that focus on tangible, immediate outcomes, concerning mostly the good of one's family and immediate social circle, offer people a possibility to engage in collective action while remaining highly skeptical of institutionalized political life, which is associated with corruption, unproductive conflict, and privileged access for special interest groups (cf. Eliasoph 1997; Bennett et al. 2013). In doing so, one could also argue that they contest and renegotiate the meaning of the political.

A fourth lesson then is that hybridity of more explicitly politically oriented and practically oriented activism can be understood in terms of the interdependence of social spheres and of the spillover of different action logics that tend to overlap in the everyday practices of civic action. Several studies included in this volume help challenge the dichotomous views of personal versus common interest and the presupposition that private/domestic and public/political spheres exist in separation from each other (see also, e.g., Howell 2005; Mulinari 2015; Okin 1998). The cases of Polish mothers', tenants' or rural women's engagement show that social activism is deeply embedded in nonpolitical everyday practices and can take place in, or evolve from, the domestic sphere, and that the difference between common good and particularistic interests of individuals or families remains typically negotiable and blurry (Hryciuk, Korolczuk, Matysiak, and Polanska in this volume).

These cases also demonstrate that social activism is a gendered process, because gender (as well as class, ethnicity, disability, etc.) can enable or restrict people's access to the public sphere, to the types of collective identities that can be constructed, and to the types of claims that can be made and gain social resonance (cf. Hagemann et al. 2008; Howell 2005). Moreover, action logics from the domestic sphere can often color civil society organizations, resulting in a combination of informality and formality and in a tendency toward a personalization of organizational structures. When action logics from the market sphere do the same, entrepreneurial virtues, efficiency norms, and status competition among organizational representatives come to mark the organizational culture and practices of these organizations (Jacobsson in this volume).

As research has shown, the private sphere's importance for civil society organizing was heightened under state socialism when the state controlled the public sphere, making it inaccessible for most citizens (e.g., Howard 2003; Nautz et al. 2013). In conditions of liberal democracy, the expectation is usually very different. Yet, the cases presented in this volume suggest that also in our time the public sphere remains inaccessible to certain groups (or is accessible to them in a limited fashion only). This, to be sure, is no longer because of the actions of an authoritarian state, but an effect of the neoliberal logic of exclusion according to which the public is managed today.

A fifth and more general lesson to be drawn thus concerns the logic of inclusion and exclusion as linked not only to local trends and legacies, but also to transnational or even global processes, such as migration, the renewal of nationalist ideologies and discourses that clash with liberal ideals of citizenship, and neoliberalization entailed by precarization of living and working conditions, retrenchment of welfare provisions, privatization, and rising economic inequalities. Of particular importance here is the last-mentioned process, which creates new inequalities, promotes exploitative relations, and limits the responsibilities of the state, profoundly changing the practices of citizenship and the parameters within which civil society actors operate. As shown by Howell and Pearce (2002: 2), under conditions of late capitalism, donor discourses and practices reify civil society as "a natural and histori- cally inevitable component of a developed capitalist economy" standing in a triadic relationship with the state and the market. Yet, in this setup the task of civil society actors in redefining the way the state operates and problema- tizing the role of the market is neither recognized nor defined. Furthermore, neoliberalization of citizenship, rather than recognizing citizens' rights as universal, entails making them contingent on their productivity and eco- nomic position, which strengthens trends toward marginalization and exclu- sion of specific groups, such as single mothers, the homeless, poor tenants, and people from rural communities in the Polish context.

In postsocialist societies these trends are, arguably, even more visible than in long-standing liberal democracies. Indeed, these societies proved critical for neoliberalism's advance, with the people there even more readily embrac- ing the new paradigm and the practices seen as representing "the West" (see, e.g., Hirt 2012; Kennedy 2013). This applies not least to Poland, which after 1989 quickly became a testing ground for neoliberal policies and practices and where the elitist discourses blaming the "losers" of the transformation for their own misfortune legitimized the exclusionary logic of the new ide- ology (Buchowski 2006; Hryciuk in this volume; Polanska in this volume).

Although neoliberalization undoubtedly poses a challenge to civil society organizing, especially among economically underprivileged groups, it can also be viewed as a syncretic process in which possibilities for some groups are closed while simultaneously being opened up for others. In this fashion, civil society can still constitute "an arena where the possibilities for hope and change reside" and where "power relations are not only reproduced but challenged" (Howell and Pearce 2002: 3). Despite neoliberalization, which privatizes the social and the cultural, effectively reducing the space for free debate and cooperation, and the model of a donor-dependent, profes- sionalized, and NGO sector–based civil society that often appears as but a handmaiden to it, new ways of organizing and new sets of shared practices continue to be invented and implemented, with new aims and new means being articulated. Evidence of this is visible not only in Poland, but also in other postsocialist and post-Soviet countries (Jacobsson 2015a), includ- ing Armenia, Bosnia and Herzegovina, Bulgaria, and others where "self- determined citizens" (Ishkanian 2015) mobilize to address a wide range of issues, be they about cultural preservation, the environment, employment or, more broadly, the deficiencies of the existing institutions of democracy and the bankruptcy of political and economic elites. The final outcomes of this new wave of social activism are undecided as yet, but what seems clear is that it may mark the end of an era of civil-society-made-from-above. This shift, however, if it is to be completed, requires new approaches and paradigms in conceptualizing, studying, and supporting civil society activism.

What is more still, as also illustrated in this volume, neoliberalization with its rampant individualism and socioeconomic insecurity also provokes counter-mobilization in the form of a renewal of conservative and/or nationalist ideologies and discourses (e.g., Płatek and Płucienniczak in this volume). As one outcome of this trend, the notion of civil society becomes a contested territory once again, in different ways. Recent studies on conservative parental movements and mobilizations against gender equality show that a new type of civil society group has emerged, not least in Central Eastern Europe and Russia, that links nationalist rhetoric with an illiberal ideological stance (Fábián and Korolczuk 2017; Graff and Korolczuk 2015, 2017; Kováts and Põim 2015). As shown by Höjdestrand's (2017) study of parental movements in Russia, for instance, while the notion of civil society may appeal to nationalist and conservative groups, these tend to associate it with anti-liberalism, patriotism, and a religious worldview rather than with liberal values, positioning themselves as the true representatives of the grassroots against external, top-down influence. In contemporary urban movements, too, a wide range of claims and ideological orientations can be observed that permit, and even foster, "unholy alliances" between populist, nationalist, and new-left activists (Florea 2015; Jacobsson 2015b). Phenomena like these call for new, less normative ways of conceptualizing civil society if we are to understand the dynamics of "real" or "vernacular" civil societies and the full range of existing forms of social activism as practiced in both Western Europe and Central and Eastern Europe (cf. Kopecký and Mudde 2003).

Our sixth and final set of lessons is more theoretical in nature and concerns the benefits of using a practice-based and process-oriented concept of civil society. A practice-based conceptualization will sensitize us to the ways in which resources and experiences from different spheres are involved in the actual making of civil societies. The pragmatist turn in social theory has brought with it a greater focus on practices (and their action logics), as a way of bridging the structure–agency divide (see, e.g., Schatzki et al. 2001). Our practice-based approach also resonates with Isin and Nielsen's (2008) suggestion to focus on "acts of citizenship" and the role they play in processes of becoming political. Moreover, a practice-based understanding of civil society/civic action entails focusing not just on tactical, but also everyday activities. As Melucci has argued in the case of social movements, these cannot be understood just by looking at protest events without taking into account the networks emerging and sustained in everyday life, because "the molecular change brought about by the hidden structure should not be seen as a 'private' and residual fact, but as a condition for possible mobilization" (Melucci 1996: 116; cf. Yates 2015). A focus on practices, moreover, enables us to capture processes within civil society, such as deliberative processes and processes of network and relationship building. Some of these will be more organized and structured than others, but all should be paid due attention and be included in the study of civil society.

Another theoretical lesson is that if we conceive of the borders between the civil sphere, family, state, and market as blurred and changing, as argued in this volume, we also need concepts that allow us to analyze these intersections as well as concepts enabling the analysis of diversity, change, and causal relations *within* the civil sphere. The various chapters in this volume have given some suggestions in this respect, offering an emerging toolkit for the analysis of civil society conceived as practice, to be explored and developed further in future research. Examples of such theoretical concepts and classifications are Ekiert and Kubik's distinction between contentious and accommodating civil society (chapter 1), Jacobsson's notion of "civic privatism" (chapter 3), the triad of actors-actions-functions as axes of "defining in" and "defining out" in the construction of civil society as analyzed by Jezierska (chapter 4), the division of "practical" and "strategic interests" enabling us to distinguish between common good and individual good, as in Korolczuk's analysis of parental activism (chapter 5), or the concept of "civic spaces" employed by Elgenius (chapter 10) in her analysis of civil society making by the Polish diaspora. These conceptual understandings, and in some cases innovations, have enabled a more fine-grained picture of Polish civil society and the various multilayered and vibrant forms of social activism that coexist in contemporary Poland. Their relevance goes beyond the Polish context.

Nevertheless, the different types of social activism in contemporary Poland as featured in this volume do not, to be sure, reflect all the facets of existing Polish civil society. Examples of collective participation that are not covered in this volume include feminist and LGBTQ activism; trade unionism; mobilizations of Polish peasants or miners; forms of engagement among football fans or sports clubs organizers; radical right-wing organizing and religious activism, particularly the networks formed by the supporters of Radio Maryja and the TV station Trwam. Further research is needed to investigate these cases along with various types of informal or semiorganized activities to have emerged in the country in recent years, including those characterizing deliberative processes in civil society, as well as the cases of mass protests against the rule of Law and Justice after the party won the elections in October 2015, especially the emergence and role of Komitet Obrony Demokracji (Committee for the Defence of Democracy) and mobilizations against the plan to further restrict abortion law. Likewise, the growing and changing role of the Internet and social media in facilitating collective action needs to be clarified further—Komitet Obrony Demokracji started as a Facebook page and developed mostly due to the wide availability of information and communication technologies. Similarly, opposition toward the plans to change the abortion law resulted in over 100,000 people (mostly women) joining the Facebook group Dziewuchy Dziewuchom (Gals to Gals) in order to take action, discuss ways to stop the introduction of the new law, and voice their dissent. Finally, the consequences of the major political and social changes on both the local and the transnational levels need to be examined as they unfold, including the long-term consequences of the economic crisis, European Union integration and possible disintegration, the rise of conservative nationalism, and the onset and escalation of the current refugee crisis. Developments like these require us to adopt new ways of thinking of and studying civil societies, positioned as these are at the intersection of public and private, local and transnational, "civil" and "uncivil," as well as liberal and "illiberal."

References

Ahrne, G. 1998. "Civil Society and Uncivil Organizations,'" in *Real Civil Societies,* ed. J. Alexander. London: Sage, 85–95.

Ahrne, G., and A. Papakostas. 2002. *Organisationer, samhälle och globalisering.* [Organizations, Society, and Globalization]. Lund: Studentlitteratur.

Bennett, E.A., A. Cordner, P.T. Klein, S. Savell, and G. Baiocchi. 2013. "Disavowing Politics: Civic Engagement in an Era of Political Scepticism." *American Journal of Sociology* 119, no. 2: 518–548.

Buchowski, M. 2006. "The Specter of Orientalism in Europe: From Exotic Other to Stigmatized Brother." *Anthropology Quarterly* 79, no. 3: 463–482.

Cohen, J., and A. Arato. 1992. *Civil Society and Political Theory.* Cambridge and London: MIT Press.

Ekiert, G., and J. Kubik. 2014. "Myths and Realities of Civil Society." *Journal of Democracy* 25, no. 1: 46–58.

Eliasoph, N. 1997. "'Close to Home': The Work of Avoiding Politics." *Theory and Society* 26, no. 5: 605–647.

Fábián, K., and E. Korolczuk, eds. 2017. *Rebellious Parents: Parental Movements in Central-Eastern Europe and Russia.* Indiana University Press.

Graff, A. 2009. "What Ails Civil Society?" *Trust for Civil Society in Central and Eastern Europe (CEE Trust) Civil Society Forum.* Retrieved 14 October 2015 from http://csf.ceetrust.org/paper/3/.

Graff, A., and E. Korolczuk. 2015. "Facing an Illiberal Future: Conceptualising the Polish Gender Crusade in a Transnational Context," paper presented at 22nd International Conference of Europeanists organized by Council for European Studies, 8–10 July, in Paris, France.

Graff, A., and E. Korolczuk. 2017. "'Worse than Communism and Nazism Put Together': War on Gender in Poland," in *Anti-gender Campaigns in Europe: Religious and Political Mobilizations against Equality,* ed. R. Kuhar and D. Paternotte. Lanham: Rowman and Littlefield (forthcoming).

Florea, I. 2015. "The Ups and Downs of a Symbolic City: The Architectural Protection Movement in Bucharest," in *Urban Grassroots Movements in Central and Eastern Europe,* ed. K. Jacobsson. Farnham: Ashgate, 55–78.

Hagemann, K., Michel S., and G. Budde, eds. 2008. *Civil Society and Gender Justice: Historical and Comparative Perspectives.* New York, Oxford: Berghahn Books.

Hann, C., and E. Dunn, eds. 1996. *Civil Society: Challenging Western Models.* London: Routledge.

Hayoz, N. 2013. "Observations on the Changing Meaning of Informality," in *Informality in Eastern Europe: Structures, Political Cultures and Social Practices,* ed. C. Giordano and N. Hayoz. Bern: Peter Lang, 47–65.

Hirt, S. 2012. *Iron Curtains: Gates, Suburbs and Privatization of Space in the Post-socialist City.* Chichester: Wiley-Blackwell.

Höjdestrand, T. 2017. "Nationalism and Civicness in Contemporary Russia: Grassroots Mobilization in Defense of Traditional Family Values," in *Rebellious Parents: Parental Movements in Central-Eastern Europe and Russia,* ed. K. Fábián and E. Korolczuk. Bloomington: Indiana University Press.

Howard, M.M. 2003. *The Weakness of Civil Society in Post-Communist Europe.* Cambridge: Cambridge University Press.

Howell, J. 2005. "Gender and Civil Society," in *Global Civil Society 2005/06. Global Civil Society–Year Books,* ed. H. Anheier, M. Kaldor, and M. Glasius. London: SAGE, 38–63.

Howell, J., and J. Pearce. 2002. *Civil Society and Development: A Critical Exploration.* Boulder, London: Lynne Rienner Publishers.

Ishkanian, A. 2015. "Self-determined Citizens? A New Wave of Civic Activism in Armenia." *Open Democracy / ISA RC-47: Open Movements,* 16 June. Retrieved 12 October 2015 from https://opendemocracy.net/armine-ishkanian/selfdetermined-citizens-new-wave-of-civic-activism-in-armenia.

Isin, E., and G. Nielsen, eds. 2008. *Acts of Citizenship.* London and New York: Zed Books.

Jacobsson, K., ed. 2015a. *Urban Grassroots Movements in Central and Eastern Europe.* Farnham: Ashgate.

———. 2015b. "Conclusion: Towards a New Research Agenda," in *Urban Grassroots Movements in Central and Eastern Europe,* ed. K. Jacobsson. Farnham: Ashgate, 273–287.

Jacobsson, K., and S. Saxonberg, eds. 2013. *Beyond NGO-ization: The Development of Social Movements in Central and Eastern Europe.* Farnham: Ashgate.

Kennedy, M.D. 2013. "Afterword. Mobilizing Justice Across Hegemonies in Place: Critical Postcommunist Vernaculars," in *Post-Communism from Within: Social Justice, Mobilization, and Hegemony,* ed. J. Kubik and A. Linch. New York: New York University Press, 385–408.

Kopecký, P., and C. Mudde. 2003. "Rethinking Civil Society." *Democratization* 10, no. 3: 1–14.

Kováts, E., and M. Põim, eds. 2015. *Gender as Symbolic Glue: The Position and Role of Conservative and Far Right Parties in the Anti-Gender Mobilizations in Europe.* http://www.feps-europe.eu/assets/cae464d2-f4ca-468c-a93e-5d0dad365a83/feps-gender-as-symbolic-glue-wwwpdf.pdf.

Lang, S. 2014. *Civil Society and the Public Sphere.* Cambridge: Cambridge University Press.

Lomax, B. 1997. "The Strange Death of 'Civil Society' in Post-communist Hungary." *Journal of Communist Studies and Transition Politics* 13, no. 1: 41–63.

Melucci, A. 1996. *Challenging Codes: Collective Action in the Information Age.* New York: Cambridge University Press.

Mendelson, S.E., and J.K. Glenn, eds. 2002. *The Power and Limits of NGOs: A Critical Look at Building Democracy in Eastern Europe and Eurasia.* New York: Columbia University Press.

Mulinari, D. 2015. "Human Rights in Argentina: Between Family Memories and Political Identities." *Journal of Civil Society* 11, no. 2: 123–136.

Narozhna, T. 2004. "Foreign Aid for a Post-Euphoric Eastern Europe: The Limitations of Western Assistance in Developing Civil Society." *Journal of International Relations and Development* 7: 243–266.

Nautz, J., P. Ginsborg, and T. Nijhuis, eds. 2013. *The Golden Chain: Family, Civil Society and the State.* New York: Berghahn.

Okin, M.S. 1998. "Gender, The Public and the Private," in *Feminism and Politics,* ed. A. Phillips. Oxford, New York: Oxford University Press, 116–141.

Schatzki, T., K. Knorr-Cetina, and E. von Savigny. 2001. *The Practice Turn in Contemporary Theory.* London: Routledge.

Yates, L. 2015. "Everyday Politics, Social Practices and Movement Networks: Daily Life in Barcelona's Social Centres." *The British Journal of Sociology* 66, no. 2: 236–258.

INDEX